Learning Word Programming

Learning Word Programming

Steven Roman

O'REILLY®

Beijing · Cambridge · Köln · Paris · Sebastopol · Taipei · Tokyo

Learning Word Programming
by Steven Roman

Copyright © 1998 Steven Roman. All rights reserved.
Printed in the United States of America.

Published by O'Reilly & Associates, Inc., 101 Morris Street, Sebastopol, CA 95472.

Editor: Ron Petrusha

Production Editor: Nancy Wolfe Kotary

Printing History:

        October 1998:   First Edition.

This book is printed on acid-free paper with 85% recycled content, 15% post-consumer waste. O'Reilly & Associates is committed to using paper with the highest recycled content available consistent with high quality.

ISBN: 1-56592-524-6   [2/99]

To Donna

Table of Contents

Preface

As the title suggests, this book is intended for those who want to learn how to program Microsoft Word 97 or later.

I guess that I cannot avoid the question, "Why would anyone want to program Microsoft Word?" The answer is simple: to get more power out of this formidable application. As you will see, there are many things that you can do at the programming level that you cannot do at the user-interface level, that is, with the menus and dialog boxes of Word. Chapter 1, *Introduction*, provides some concrete examples of this.

This book provides an introduction to programming the Word object model using Visual Basic for Applications (VBA). However, it is not intended to be an encyclopedia of Word programming. The goal here is to acquaint you with the main points of Word programming—enough so that you can continue your education (as we all do) on your own. The point is that after reading this book, you should not need to rely on any other source except the Word VBA help file or a good Word VBA reference book (such as O'Reilly's forthcoming *Programming the Word Object Model* by Julianne Sharer and Arthur Einhorn) and a nice object browser (such as the Enhanced Object Browser, a coupon for which is included in the back of this book).

It has been my experience that introductory programming books (and, sadly, most trade computer books) tend to do a great deal of handholding (to put the matter euphemistically). They cover concepts at a very slow pace, primarily by padding them heavily with overblown examples and irrelevant anecdotes that only the author could conceivably find amusing, especially the second or third time that we are forced to read them while looking for a few facts. Frankly, I find such unprofessionalism incredibly infuriating. In my opinion, it does the reader a great disservice to take perhaps 400 pages of information and pad it with another 600 pages of irrelevant junk.

There is no doubt in my mind that we need much more professionalism from our authors, but it is not easy to find writers who have both the knowledge to write about a subject and the training (or talent) to do so in a pedagogical manner. (I should hasten to add that there are a number of excellent authors in this area; it's just that there are not nearly enough of them.) Moreover, publishers tend to encourage the creation of 1000-plus-page tomes because of the general feeling among the publishers that a book must be physically wide enough to stand out on the bookshelf! I shudder to think that this might, in fact, be true. (I am happy to say that O'Reilly does not seem to have succumbed to this opinion.)

On the other hand, *Learning Word Programming* is not a book in which you will find much handholding. (Nor will you find much handholding in any of my books.) The book proceeds at a relatively rapid pace from a general introduction to programming, through an examination of the Visual Basic for Applications programming language to an overview of the Word object model. Given the enormity of the subject, not everything is covered, nor should it be. Nevertheless, the essentials of both the VBA language and the Word object model are covered, so when you have finished the book, you will know enough about Word VBA to begin creating effective working programs.

I have tried to put my experience as a professor (about 20 years) and my experience writing books (about 30 of them) to work here to create a true learning tool. I hope that this book can be read (perhaps more than once) and also serve as a useful reference.

The Book's Audience

As an introduction to programming in Word VBA, the book is primarily addressed to two groups of readers:

- Word users who are not programmers but would like to be. If you fall into this category, it is probably because you have begun to appreciate the power of Word and want to take advantage of its more advanced features or just simply to accomplish certain tasks more easily.

- Word users who are programmers (in virtually any language—Visual Basic, Visual Basic for Applications, BASIC, C, C++, and so on) but are not familiar with the Word object model. In this case, you can use *Learning Word Programming* to brush up on some of the details of the VBA language (if necessary) and learn about the Word object model and how to program it.

Organization of This Book

Learning Word Programming consists of 21 chapters divided into three parts. In addition, there are four appendixes.

Chapter 1, *Introduction*, examines why you might want to learn programming, and provides a few examples of the sorts of problems that can best be solved through programming.

Chapter 2, *Preliminaries*, introduces the Visual Basic for Applications language. Chapters 3 and 4, *The Visual Basic Editor, Part I* and *The Visual Basic Editor, Part II*, examine the Visual Basic integrated development environment (IDE), which is the programming environment used to develop Word VBA applications.

The second part of the book consists of Chapters 5 through 8, which provide an introduction to the VBA language, the language component common to Microsoft Visual Basic and to many of Microsoft's major applications, including Word, Excel, PowerPoint, and Project, as well as to software from some other publishers. Individual chapters survey VBA's data types, constants, and variables (Chapter 5, *Variables, Data Types, and Constants*), functions and subroutines (Chapter 6, *Functions and Subroutines*), intrinsic functions and statements (Chapter 7, *Built-in Functions and Statements*), and control statements (Chapter 8, *Control Statements*).

The last part of the book is devoted to the Word object model itself. This model determines which elements of Word (documents, paragraphs, fonts, and so on) are accessible through code and how they can be controlled programmatically. This portion of the book begins with a discussion of object models in general (Chapter 9, *Object Models*) and the Word object model in particular (Chapter 10, *The Word Object Model*). Subsequent chapters are devoted to taking a closer look at some of the main objects in the Word object model, such as the Application object, which represents the Word application itself, the Document object, which represents an individual Word document, and the Range and Selection objects, which represent contiguous blocks of text in a document. In addition, the final three chapters discuss methods to control the Word user interface programmatically through Word's built-in dialog boxes (Chapter 19, *Built-in Dialog Objects*); UserForms, also called custom dialog boxes (Chapter 20, *Custom Dialog Boxes*); and Word's menus and toolbars (Chapter 21, *Menus and Toolbars*). These three chapters can be read in any order, so if there is something in particular that you are interested in, you can skip ahead. I have included useful examples at the end of most of these chapters.

The appendixes provide a diverse collection of supplementary material. In particular, Appendix A, *Programming Word from Another Application*, provides a discussion of how to control Word programmatically from certain other VBA-hosted applications, including Microsoft Access, Excel, and PowerPoint. Appendix B, *The Shape Object*, is devoted to the Shape object, which can be used to add some interesting artwork to Word documents. Appendix C, *Getting the Installed Printers*, covers an important technique for determining what printers are available on a user's system. (This is not quite as easy as you might think.) Finally, Appendix D, *High-Level and Low-Level Languages*, contains a brief overview of programming languages, which is designed to give you a perspective on where VBA fits into the great scheme of things.

The Book's Sample Code

When reading this book, you will encounter many small programming examples to illustrate the concepts. I use small coding examples, if possible, to illustrate a point.

Personally, I seem to learn much more quickly and easily by tinkering with and tracing through short program segments than by studying a long, detailed example that has a lot of irrelevant stuff in it, as many do. Also, the difficulty in tinkering with a long program is that changing a few lines can affect other portions of the code to the point where the program will no longer run. Then you have to waste time trying to figure out why it won't run.

On the other hand, if, for example, I want to figure out exactly what Word VBA thinks is a word (you might be surprised), I write a short program of perhaps a half-dozen lines with which to experiment. This is a great way to learn, is often much quicker than hunting through online documentation (which may very well not have the answer anyway), and also shows off the advantages of an interpreted language (a language that is easily traced one line at a time).*

I encourage you to follow along with the code examples by typing them yourself. (Nevertheless, if you'd rather save yourself the typing, sample programs are available online; see "Obtaining the Sample Programs" later in this preface.) Also, I encourage you to experiment; it is definitely the best way to learn.

However, I must add a small caveat. Word programming is very powerful. To protect yourself, I strongly suggest that you do two things:

- Make a new Word template and store all sample programs in this template, or in documents based on this template. (I discuss how to store programs in templates or documents in Chapters 3 and 4, which cover the Visual Basic Editor.) The point is that you do not want to use your Normal template or any other templates that you cannot afford to delete if necessary. (Once you are

---

* Incidentally, in case you are curious: for Word VBA, a word includes any trailing spaces (even more than one space), if present. Also, a punctuation mark is considered a word.

happy with a program and think you might want to use it for real work, you can copy it to your Normal template.)

- Back up all of your templates, especially your Normal template (*normal.dot*), before beginning your Word programming career.

Incidentally, you do not need to worry about doing any damage to your computer. The only damage that you can do in experimenting with Word programming (under normal circumstances) is to a Word template or document. If you have backed up your templates, you should be safe.

One final comment about the sample code is worth making, particularly because this book and its coding examples are intended to teach you how to write VBA programs for Microsoft Word. Generally speaking, there is somewhat of a horse-before-the-cart problem in trying to write about a complicated object model, because it is almost impossible to give examples of one object and its properties and methods without referring to other objects that may not yet have been discussed.

As an example, when I discuss the Bookmark object in Chapter 11, I also must discuss the Add method, used to create new bookmarks. This method has the following syntax:

```
BookmarksObject.Add(Name, Range)
```

where *Range* represents a Range object, which we will have not yet discussed officially.

Frankly, I don't see any way to avoid this problem completely, so rather than try to rearrange the material in an unnatural way, it seems better to simply proceed in an orderly fashion. Occasionally, we will need to refer to objects that we have not yet discussed, but this should not cause any serious problems, because most of these forward references are fairly obvious.

Obtaining the Sample Programs

The sample programs presented in the book are available online and can be freely downloaded from our web site at *http://www.oreilly.com/catalog/lrnwdpr/*.

Conventions in This Book

Throughout this book, I have used the following typographic conventions:

`Constant width`
indicates a language construct such as a language statement, a constant, or an expression. Lines of code also appear in constant width, as do function and method prototypes and variable and parameter names.

Italic

> represents intrinsic and application-defined functions, method names, the names of system elements such as directories and files, and Internet resources such as web documents and email addresses. New terms are also italicized when they are first introduced.

`Constant width italic`

> in prototypes or command syntax indicates replaceable parameter names.

How to Contact Us

We have tested and verified all the information in this book to the best of our ability, but you may find that features have changed (or even that we have made mistakes!). Please let us know about any errors you find, as well as your suggestions for future editions, by writing to:

> O'Reilly & Associates, Inc.
> 101 Morris Street
> Sebastopol, CA 95472
> 800-998-9938 (in the U.S. or Canada)
> 707-829-0515 (international/local)
> 707-829-0104 (fax)

You can also send messages electronically. To be put on our mailing list or to request a catalog, send email to:

> *nuts@oreilly.com*

To ask technical questions or comment on the book, send email to:

> *bookquestions@oreilly.com*

Acknowledgments

I would like to express my sincerest thanks to Ron Petrusha, my editor at O'Reilly. Frankly, I don't know what I would have done without his help. He is one of the best editors that I have worked with over the last 17 years of book writing.

Also thanks to the production staff at O'Reilly & Associates, including Nancy Kotary, production editor and copyeditor; Kristine Simmons, proofreader; Edie Freedman, for designing another memorable cover; Nancy Priest, for interior design; Mike Sierra, for tools support; Robert Romano, for illustrations; Mary Anne Mayo, Jane Ellin, and Sheryl Avruch, for quality control; and Ruth Rautenberg, for the index.

1

Introduction

Microsoft Word is a word processor of enormous power and flexibility. But despite its powerful feature set, there is a great deal that Word either does not allow you to do or does not allow you to do easily through its user interface. In these cases, we must turn to Word programming.

Let me give you two examples. I can assure you that these are real-life examples, because they happened to me.

In writing this book, I was faced with the problem of turning long columns of words into tables. Word's built-in *ConvertToTable* command was not flexible enough for my needs for three reasons.

First, I wanted the items to be placed in the table in column-major order (the first column is filled first) rather than in row-major order (the first row is filled first). Second, I wanted to choose the number of columns based on the number of words (cells), so I needed to know the word count before I made the choice of the number of columns. Finally, I wanted a row at the top of the table for a title.

To illustrate, I wanted to be able to select the following column of words:

Border
Cell
Column
Document
Font
Options
PageSetup
Paragraph
ParagraphFormat
Range

Row
Selection
Style
Table
Template
Window

and be presented with a dialog box similar to the one shown in Figure 1-1. Then, if I entered 3 for the number of columns and hit the OK button, I wanted Word to automatically construct Table 1-1 for me.

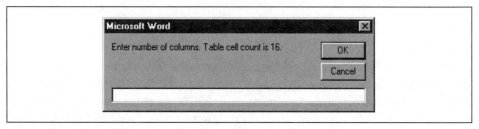

Figure 1-1. Table-making dialog box

Table 1-1. Table in Column-Major Order

Table

Border	PageSetup	Style
Cell	Paragraph	Table
Column	ParagraphFormat	Template
Document	Range	Window
Font	Row	
Options	Selection	

I show you how to write the code to perform this little bit of table prestidigitation in Chapter 16, *The Table Object.* I cannot tell you how many hours of tedious keyboarding this little gem has saved me.

The second example has to do with shortcut keys. I am very fond of shortcut keys, because using the mouse gives me a pain in the shoulder (for which I have spent many hours in physical therapy, by the way). In any case, while experimenting with shortcut keys, I created a shortcut for the *FileOpenFile* command and assigned it the hotkey combination Alt-O,1, forgetting that Alt-O is used to open the Format menu.

My work on the book (and on the computer in general) was interrupted for several days. When I returned to work, at some point I hit Alt-O, expecting to get the Format menu. But nothing happened. Now I had to figure out why.

The first thing that occurred to me is that I might have reassigned the Alt-O key, but I couldn't remember how. This left me with three choices. First, I could painstakingly search through each of the hundreds of commands and macros using the Customize Keyboard dialog box, trying to find a keystroke assignment that began with Alt-O. This was my least favorite choice. Second, I could invoke the FindKey method (discussed in Chapter 18, *Shortcut Key Bindings*) that searches for a command that corresponds to a given hotkey combination. The problem with this choice is that I would need to know the exact keystroke combination. I did try searching for Alt-O, but this returned nothing.

The final (and best) choice was to write a short program that makes a list of all of the current key bindings. This made it easy to spot the offending key assignment. I show you this program in Chapter 18. My advice: Keep this program handy!

Word programming shines when there is a need for user interaction. For instance, in Chapter 20, *Custom Dialog Boxes*, I construct a simple program that helps create a fax cover sheet by presenting the user with the custom dialog box shown in Figure 1-2. After you fill in this dialog box and click the OK button, the program automatically creates a fax cover sheet with this information. (Incidentally, I made $500 creating this little program for a company because no one at the company knew how to program in Word!)

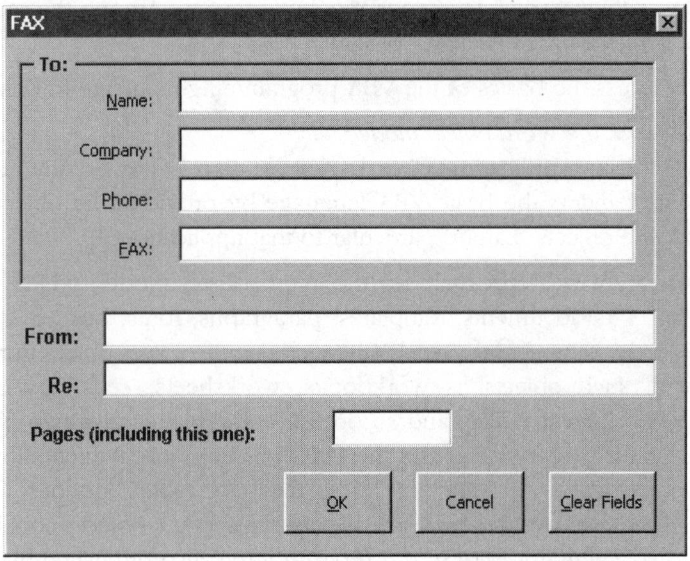

Figure 1-2. The fax dialog box

I hope that these three illustrations have convinced you that Word programming can be very useful. Of course, you can do much more mundane things with Word programs. For instance, you can automate repetitive tasks, such as searching through a document, finding all the headings and placing them in a new document, or printing the statistics on a given document.

In general, the education of a Word programmer breaks down into a few main categories:

The Visual Basic Editor

First, you need to learn a bit about the environment in which Word programming is done. This is the so-called Visual Basic Editor or Word VBA Integrated Development Environment (IDE for short). We take care of this in Chapters 3 and 4.

The basics of programming in VBA

Next, you need to learn a bit about the basics of the programming language that Word uses. This language is called Visual Basic for Applications or VBA. Actually, VBA is used not only by Microsoft Word, but also by the other major components of the Microsoft Office application suite: Access, Excel, and PowerPoint. It is also used by the standalone programming environment called Visual Basic (or VB). Any application that uses VBA in this way is called a *host application for VBA*. (There are also a number of non-Microsoft products that use VBA as their underlying programming language. Among the most notable is Visio, a vector-based drawing program.)

We will discuss the basics of the VBA programming language in Chapters 5–8.

Object models and the Word object model

Each VBA host application (Word, Access, Excel, PowerPoint, and Visual Basic) supplements the basic VBA language by providing an object model to deal with the objects that are particular to that application.

For instance, Word VBA includes the Word object model, which deals with such objects as documents, templates, paragraphs, fonts, headers, tables, and so on. On the other hand, Excel VBA includes the Excel object model, which deals with such objects as workbooks, worksheets, cells, rows, columns, ranges, charts, pivot tables, and so on. Access VBA includes two object models: the Access object model and the DAO object model, which allow the programmer to deal with such objects as database tables, queries, forms, and reports. (To learn more about the Access and DAO object models, see my book *Access Database Design and Programming*, also published by O'Reilly & Associates.)

Thus, a Word programmer must be familiar with the general notion of an object model and with the Word object model in particular. We discuss object models in general in Chapter 9, *Object Models*, after which we begin our discussion of the Word object model, which occupies most of the remainder of the book.

Incidentally, the Word object model is quite extensive—the largest among the Office applications, with almost 200 different objects. (The Excel object model is a close second, but 52 of the Excel objects are included only for compatibility with earlier versions of Excel and are on their way out.)

Lest you be too discouraged by the size of the Word object model, I should point out that you need to be familiar with only a handful of objects in order to program meaningfully in Word VBA. Many of the Word objects relate to rather esoteric areas of Word, such as spelling dictionaries, autocorrect entries, captions, endnotes, footnotes, and so on. In fact, as we will see, the vast majority of the "action" is related to just four objects: the Application object, the Document object, the Range object, and the Selection object.

To help you get an overall two-dimensional picture of the Word object model, as well as detailed local views, I have written special object browser software. (The object browser comes with over a dozen other object models as well.) There is a coupon at the back of the book that you can use to obtain this object browser.

Whether you are interested in Word programming in order to be more efficient in your own work, or whether you intend to make money writing Word programs for others to use, I think you will enjoy the increased sense of power that you get by knowing how to manipulate Word at the programming level. Indeed, once you have read this book, you will be halfway to being an Excel, Access, and Power-Point programmer as well!

2

Preliminaries

We begin with some general facts related to programming and programming languages to give the main subject matter of this book some perspective. After all, VBA is just one of many programming languages and anyone who wants to be a VBA programmer should have some perspective on where VBA fits into the greater scheme of things. Rest assured, however, that we will not dwell on side issues. The purpose of this chapter is to give a brief overview of programming and programming languages that will be of interest to readers who have not had any programming experience, as well as to those who have.

What Is a Programming Language?

Simply put, a programming language is a very special and very restricted language that is understood by the computer at some level. We can roughly divide programming languages into three groups, based on the purpose of the language:

- Languages designed to manipulate the computer at a low level—that is, to manipulate the operating system (Windows or DOS) or even the hardware itself—are called low-level languages. An example is assembly language.

- Languages designed to create standalone applications, such as Microsoft Word itself, are high-level languages. Examples are BASIC, COBOL, FORTRAN, C, C++, and Visual Basic.

- Languages that are designed to manipulate an application program, such as Microsoft Word, are application-level languages. Examples are Word VBA, Excel VBA, and PowerPoint VBA, each of which is a different form of VBA, designed to manipulate a different application.

These terms are not set in concrete and may be used differently by others. However, no one would disagree with the fact that some languages are intended to be used at a lower level than others.

The computer world is full of programming languages—hundreds of them. In some cases, languages are developed for specific computers. In other cases, languages are developed for specific types of applications. Table 2-1 gives some examples of programming languages and their general purposes.

Table 2-1. Some Programming Languages

Language	General Purpose
BASIC	A simple, easy-to-learn language designed for beginners
Visual Basic	A version of BASIC designed for creating Windows applications
C, C++	Very powerful languages with excellent speed and control over the computer
Visual C++	A version of C++ designed for creating Windows applications
Pascal	To teach students how to program "correctly"
COBOL	For business programming
FORTRAN	For scientific programming: excels in number crunching
Lisp	List processing (used in artificial intelligence)
ALGOL	An attempt to design a universal language
SIMULA	For simulating (or modeling) physical phenomena
Smalltalk	For object-oriented programming

Programming languages vary quite a bit in their syntax. Indeed, some languages are much easier to read than others (as with spoken languages). As a very simple example, Table 2-2 shows some ways in which different programming languages assign a value (in this case, 5) to a variable named X. Notice the variation even in this simple task.

Table 2-2. Assignment in Various Languages

Language	Assignment Statement
APL	X <- 5
BASIC	LET X = 5 or X = 5
BETA	5 -> X
C, C++	X = 5;
COBOL	MOVE 5 TO X
FORTRAN	X = 5
J	X =. 5
Lisp	(SETQ X 5)
Pascal	X := 5
Visual Basic	X = 5

If you're interested in how Visual Basic compares with some of the other major languages used in programming, see Appendix D, *High-Level and Low-Level Languages.*

Programming Style

The issue of what constitutes good programming style is, of course, subjective, just as is the issue of what constitutes good writing style. Probably the best way to learn good programming style is to learn by example and to keep the issue somewhere in your consciousness while programming.

This is not the place to enter into a detailed discussion of programming style. However, in my opinion, the two most important maxims for good programming are:

- Fill your programs with a lot of meaningful comments.
- When in doubt, favor readability over cleverness or elegance.

Comments

It is impossible to overstate the importance of adding meaningful comments to your programs—at least any program with more than a few lines.

The problem is this: good programs are generally used many times during a reasonably long lifetime, which may be measured in months or even years. Inevitably, a programmer will want to return to his or her code to make changes (such as adding additional features) or to fix bugs (errors). However, despite all efforts, programming languages are not as easy to read as spoken languages. It is just as inevitable that a programmer will not understand (or perhaps even recognize!) code that was written several months or years earlier and must rely on carefully written comments to help reacquaint himself with his own code. (This has happened to me more times that I care to recall.)

Let me emphasize that commenting code is almost as much of an art as writing the code itself. I have often seen comments similar to the following:

```
' Set x equal to 5
x = 5
```

This comment is pretty useless, because the actual code is self-explanatory. It simply wastes time and space. (In a teaching tool, such as this book, you may find some comments that would otherwise be left out of a professionally written program.)

An interesting test of the quality of your comments is to read just the comments (not the code) to see if you get a good sense not only of what the program is designed to do, but also of the steps that are used to accomplish the program's goal. For example, here are the comments from the BASIC program shown in Appendix D:

```
' BASIC program to compute the average
' of a set of at most 100 numbers

' Ask for the number of numbers

' If Num is between 1 and 100 then proceed
    ' Loop to collect the numbers to average
      ' Ask for next number
       ' Add the number to the running sum
    ' Compute the average
    ' Display the average
```

Readability

Readability is also a subjective matter. What is readable to one person may not be readable to another. In fact, it is probably fair to say that what is readable to the author of a program is likely to be less readable to everyone else, at least to some degree. It is wise to keep this in mind when you start programming (that is, assuming you want others to be able to read your programs).

One of the greatest offenders to code readability is the infamous GOTO statement, of which many languages (including VBA) have some variety or other. It is not my intention to dwell upon the GOTO statement, but it will help illustrate the issue of good programming style.

The GOTO statement is very simple—it just redirects program execution to another location. For instance, the following BASIC code asks the user for a positive number. If the user enters a nonpositive number, the GOTO portion of the code redirects execution to the first line of the program (the label **TryAgain**). This causes the entire program to be executed again. In short, the program will repeat until the user enters a positive number:

```
TryAgain:
INPUT "Enter a positive number: ", x
IF x <= 0 THEN GOTO TryAgain
```

Although the previous example may not be good programming style, it is at least readable. However, the following code is much more difficult to read:

```
TryAgain:
INPUT "Enter a number between 1 and 100: ", x
IF x > 100 THEN GOTO TooLarge
IF x <= 0 THEN GOTO TooSmall
PRINT "Your number is: ", x
GOTO Done
TooLarge:
```

```
PRINT "Your number is too large"
GOTO TryAgain
TooSmall:
PRINT "Your number is too small"
GOTO TryAgain
Done:
END
```

Because we need to jump around in the program in order to follow the possible flows of execution, this type of programming is sometimes referred to as spaghetti code. Imagine this style of programming in a program that is thousands of lines long! The following version is much more readable, although it is still not the best possible style:

```
TryAgain:
INPUT "Enter a number between 1 and 100: ", x
IF x > 100 THEN
  PRINT "Your number is too large"
  GOTO TryAgain
ELSEIF x <= 0 THEN
  PRINT "Your number is too small"
  GOTO TryAgain
END IF
PRINT "Your number is: ", x
END
```

The following code does the same job but avoids the use of the GOTO statement altogether and would no doubt be considered better programming style by most programmers:

```
DO
  INPUT "Enter a number between 1 and 100: ", x
  IF x > 100 THEN
    PRINT "Your number is too large"
  ELSEIF x <= 0 THEN
    PRINT "Your number is too small"
  END IF
LOOP UNTIL x >= 1 AND x <= 100
PRINT "Your number is: ", x
END
```

Another place where readability can suffer is at the hands of programmers who like to think that their code is especially "clever" or "elegant" but in reality just turns out to be hard to read and more error-prone. This is especially easy to do when programming in the C language. For instance, as a very simple example, consider the following three lines in C:

```
x = x + 1;
x = x + i;
i = i - 1;
```

The first line adds 1 to **x**, the second line adds **i** to **x**, and the third line subtracts 1 from **i**. This is certainly readable (if not terribly meaningful). However, it can also be written as:

```
x = ++x+i--;
```

This may be some programmers' idea of clever programming, but to me it is just obnoxious. This is why a sagacious programmer always favors readability over "cleverness" or "elegance."

Modularity

Another major issue that relates to readability is modular programming. In the early days of PC programming (in BASIC), most programs were written as a single code unit, sometimes with many hundreds or even thousands of lines of code. It is not easy to follow such a program, especially six months after it is written. Also, these programs tended to use the same code segments repeatedly, which is a waste of time and space.

The following BASIC example illustrates the point. Line numbers have been added for reference. (Don't worry too much about following each line of code. You can still follow the discussion in any case.)

```
10   ' Program to reverse the letters in your name

20   ' Do first name
30   INPUT "Enter your first name: ", name$
40   reverse$ = ""
50   FOR i = LEN(name$) TO 1 STEP -1
60      reverse$ = reverse$ + MID$(name$, i, 1)
70   NEXT i
80   PRINT "First name reversed: " + reverse$

90   ' Do middle name
100  INPUT "Enter your middle name: ", name$
110  reverse$ = ""
120  FOR i = LEN(name$) TO 1 STEP -1
130     reverse$ = reverse$ + MID$(name$, i, 1)
140  NEXT i
150  PRINT "Middle name reversed: " + reverse$

160  ' Do last name
170  INPUT "Enter your last name: ", name$
180  reverse$ = ""
190  FOR i = LEN(name$) TO 1 STEP -1
200     reverse$ = reverse$ + MID$(name$, i, 1)
210  NEXT i
220  PRINT "Last name reversed: " + reverse$
```

Now, observe that lines 40–70, 110–140, and 180–210 (in bold) are identical. This is a waste of space. A better approach would be to separate the code that does the reversing of a string (name) into a separate code module and call upon that module thrice, as in the following example:

```
' Program to reverse your name

DECLARE FUNCTION Reverse$ (name$)

' Do first name
INPUT "Enter your first name: ", name$
PRINT "First name reversed: " + Reverse$(name$)

' Do middle name
INPUT "Enter your middle name: ", name$
PRINT "Middle name reversed: " + Reverse$(name$)

' Do last name
INPUT "Enter your last name: ", name$
PRINT "Last name reversed: " + Reverse$(name$)
```

The separate code module to reverse a string is:

```
' Reverses a string
FUNCTION Reverse$ (aname$)
   Temp$ = ""
   FOR i = LEN(aname$) TO 1 STEP -1
      Temp$ = Temp$ + MID$(aname$, i, 1)
   NEXT i
   Reverse$ = Temp$
END FUNCTION
```

Of course, the saved space is not great in this example, but you can imagine what would happen if we replace the reversing procedure with one that requires several hundred lines of code and we perform this procedure a few hundred times in the main program. This modularization could save literally thousands of lines of code.

There is another important advantage to modular programming. If we decide to write another program that requires reversing some strings, we can simply add our string-reversing code module to the new program, without having to write any new code. Indeed, professional programmers often compile custom code libraries containing useful code modules that can be slipped into new applications when necessary.

It is hard to overestimate the extreme importance of modular programming. Fortunately, as we will see, VBA makes it easy to create modular programs.

Generally speaking, there are two main groups of code modules: *functions* and *subroutines*. The difference between them is that functions return a value, whereas subroutines do not. (Of course, we may choose not to use the value returned from a function.) For instance, the **Reverse** function described earlier returns the reversed string. On the other hand, the following code module performs a service but does not return a value—it simply pauses a certain number of seconds (given by sec):

```
SUB delay (sec)
    ' Get the current time
    StartTime = TIMER
    ' Enter a do-nothing loop for sec seconds
    DO
    LOOP UNTIL TIMER - StartTime > sec
END SUB
```

Functions and subroutines are extremely common in modern coding. Together, they are referred to as *procedures*.

I

The VBA Environment

3

The Visual Basic Editor, Part I

The first step in becoming a Word VBA programmer is to become familiar with the environment in which Word VBA programming is done. Each of the main Office applications has a programming environment referred to as its Integrated Development Environment or IDE. Microsoft also refers to this programming environment as the Visual Basic Editor.

My plan in this chapter and the next is to describe the major components of the Word IDE. I realize that you are probably anxious to get to some actual programming, but it is necessary to gain some familiarity with the IDE before you can use it. Nevertheless, you may want to read quickly through this chapter and the next and then refer to them as needed.

The Word, Excel, and PowerPoint IDEs have the same appearance, shown in Figure 3-1. (The Microsoft Access IDE has a different appearance.) To start the Word IDE, simply choose Visual Basic Editor from the Macros submenu of the Tools menu or press Alt-F11.

The Project Window

The window in the upper-left corner of the client area (below the toolbar) is called the Project Explorer. Figure 3-2 shows a close-up of this window.

Note that the Project Explorer has a treelike structure, similar to the Windows Explorer's folders pane (the lefthand pane). Each entry in the Project Explorer is called a *node*. The top nodes, of which there are three in Figure 3-2, represent the currently open Word VBA projects (hence the name Project Explorer). The view of each project can be expanded or contracted by clicking on the small boxes (just as with Windows Explorer). In particular, there is one project for each open document and each attached template. There is also a project for the Normal template and for any other attached global templates.

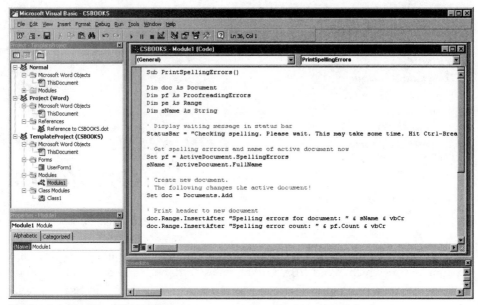

Figure 3-1. The Word VBA IDE

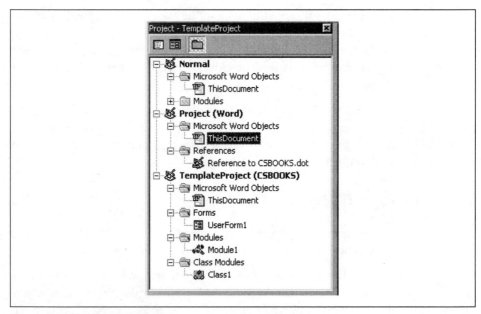

Figure 3-2. The Project Explorer

Project Names

Each project has a name, which the programmer can choose. The default name for a project related to a document is Project. The default name for a project related to a template is TemplateProject. The top node for each project is labeled:

```
ProjectName (DocumentName)
```

where *ProjectName* is the name of the project and *DocumentName* is the name of the document or template.

For instance, the active document at the time that Figure 3-2 was created is the manuscript for this book and is named *Word.doc*. Since I never changed the default project name, there is a node in Figure 3-2 labeled:

```
Project (Word)
```

Since *Word.doc* is based on the template *CSBOOKS.DOT* (which I use for writing computer science books), there is also a node labeled:

```
TemplateProject (CSBOOKS)
```

Project Contents

In general, each project may contain one of several different types of objects: Document objects, standard modules, class modules, UserForm objects, and references. I discuss each of these types of objects later in this section.

First, note that two of the objects that can make up a project—the Document object and the UserForm object—can themselves have two components: a code component, consisting of any code that is associated with the object, and a visual interface (also called a user interface), which is the component that is visible to the user and with which the user interacts. On the other hand, standard modules and class modules have only a code component, with no visual interface.

More specifically, the visual interface of a Document object is the Word document itself, whereas the code component is any event code that is associated with the document's Open, Close, and New events (discussed in the "Document Events" section of this chapter), as well as any additional supporting code. A UserForm object represents a custom form or dialog box, which is its visual interface, along with the code that underlies the form and its controls.

Now let us take a closer look at each of these objects.

Document objects

Under each node in the Project Explorer labeled Microsoft Word Objects is a node labeled ThisDocument. This node represents a document or template, along with the code module that stores event code for the document or template. Word recognizes three events related to a document or template:

- The Close event occurs when the document or template closes.

- The Open event occurs when the document is opened.

- The New event applies only to templates and occurs when a new document is created based on that template.

The purpose of these events is to allow the VBA programmer to write code that will execute whenever one of these events fires (occurs). I discuss these events in more detail later in the chapter.

Standard modules

A standard module is a code module that contains general procedures (functions and subroutines). These procedures may be macros designed to be run by the user or to support programs that are used by other programs. (Remember the discussion of modular programming.)

Class modules

Class modules are code modules that contain code related to custom objects. As you will see, the Word object model has a great many built-in objects (almost 200), such as document objects, template objects, paragraph objects, font objects, and so on. However, it is also possible to create custom objects and endow them with various properties. To do so, you would place the appropriate code within a class module.

However, since creating custom objects is beyond the scope of this book, we will not be using class modules. (For an introduction to object-oriented programming using VB, allow me to suggest my book *Concepts of Object-Oriented Programming with Visual Basic*, published by Springer-Verlag, New York.)

UserForm objects

As you no doubt know, Word contains a great many built-in dialog boxes (over 200). It is also possible to create custom dialog boxes, also called forms or User-Forms. This is done by creating UserForm objects. Figure 3-3 shows the design environment when a UserForm object is selected in the Project window.

The large window on the upper right in Figure 3-3 contains the custom dialog box (entitled My Dialog Box) in its design mode. There is also a floating Toolbox window that contains icons for various Windows controls.

To place a control on the dialog box, simply click on the icon in the Toolbox and then drag a rectangle on the dialog box. This rectangle is replaced by the control

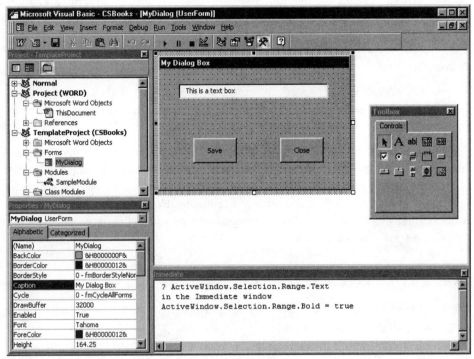

Figure 3-3. A UserForm dialog box

of the same size as the rectangle. The properties of the UserForm object or of any controls on the form can be changed by selecting the object and making the changes in the Properties window, which I discuss later in the chapter in "The Properties Window."

In addition to the form itself and its controls, a UserForm object contains code that the VBA programmer writes in support of these objects. For instance, a command button has a Click event that fires when the user clicks on the button. If I place such a button on the form, then I must write the code that is run when the Click event fires; otherwise, clicking the button does nothing. For instance, here is the code for the Close button's Click event in Figure 3-3. Note that the button is named cmdClose; that is, the Name property of the command button has been set to cmdClose:

```
Private Sub cmdClose_Click()
    Unload Me
End Sub
```

All this code does is unload the form.

Along with event code for a form and its controls, we can also include support procedures within the UserForm object.

Don't worry if all this seems rather vague now. I devote an entire chapter (Chapter 20, *Custom Dialog Boxes*) to creating custom dialog boxes (that is, User-Form objects).

References

As you will see, to call a procedure written in one project from another project, the calling project must have a reference to the project that contains the procedure—that is, to the called project.

Generally, a project that is associated with a document is interested only in procedures that lie within that project or in the template project that is attached to the document (or perhaps in the normal template). For this reason, Word automatically provides a reference to the attached template. However, if necessary, additional references can be added to a project. I will revisit this issue when I discuss public and private procedures in Chapter 5, *Variables, Data Types, and Constants.*

The Properties Window

The Properties window (see Figure 3-4) displays the properties of an object and allows us to change these properties.

When a standard module is selected in the Project window, the only property that appears in the Properties window is the module's name. However, when a document is selected in the Projects window, many of the document's properties appear in the Properties window, as shown in Figure 3-4.

The Properties window can be used to change some of the properties of the object while no code is running—that is, at design time. Note, however, that some properties are read-only and cannot be changed. Other properties can be changed only by code, that is, at run time. Such properties generally do not appear in the Properties window.

The Code Window

The Code window displays the code that is associated with the selected item in the Project window. To view this code, select the item in the Projects window and either choose Code from the View menu or hit the F7 function key. Alternatively, just double-click on the item in the Projects window.

Procedure and Full-Module Views

Generally, a code module (standard, class, or UserForm) contains more than one procedure. The IDE offers the choice between viewing one procedure at a time (called *procedure view*) or all procedures at one time (called *full-module view*),

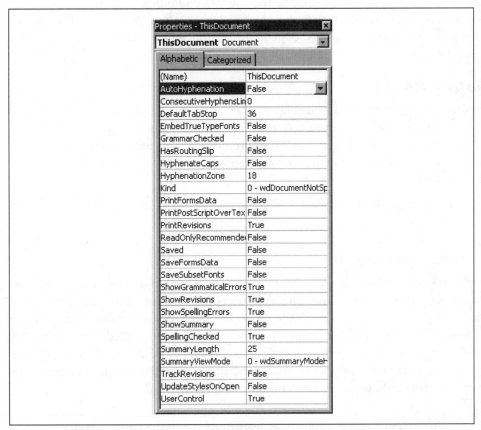

Figure 3-4. The Properties window

with a horizontal line separating the procedures. Each view has its advantages and disadvantages, and you will probably want to use both views at different times. Unfortunately, Microsoft does not seem to have supplied a menu choice for selecting the view. To change views, click on the small buttons in the lower-left corner of the Code window. (The default view can be set using the Editor tab of the Options dialog box.)

Incidentally, the default font for the module window is Courier, which has a rather thin-looking appearance and may be somewhat difficult to read. You may want to change the font to FixedSys (on the Editor Format tab of the Options dialog box, under the Tools menu), which is very readable.

The Object and Procedure List Boxes

At the top of the Code window are two drop-down list boxes (see Figure 3-1). The Object box contains a list of the objects (such as forms and controls) that are associated with the current project, and the Procedure box contains a list of all of the procedures associated with the object selected in the Object box. The precise contents of these boxes vary depending on the type of object selected in the Project Explorer.

A Document object

When a document (ThisDocument) is selected in the Project window, the Object box contains only two entries: General, for general procedures, and Document. When Document is selected, the Procedure box contains empty code shells for the three events mentioned earlier (Open, Close, and New). For example, the Open code shell is:

```
Private Sub Document_Open()

End Sub
```

A standard module

When a standard module is selected in the Project window, the Object box contains only the entry General, and the Procedure box lists all of the procedures written for that module. Figure 3-5 shows the open Procedure box, with a list of the current procedures for a particular module. The section called (Declarations) is where to place variable declarations for module-level variables—that is, variables that you want to be available in every procedure within the module. (I discuss this in more detail in Chapter 4, *The Visual Basic Editor, Part II*.)

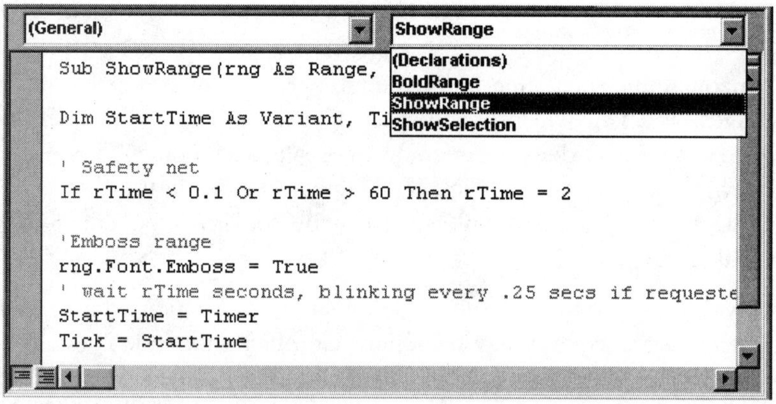

Figure 3-5. The Procedure box

A UserForm object

When a UserForm object is selected in the Project Explorer, the Object box contains a list of all of the objects in the module. For instance, Figure 3-6 shows the contents of the Object box for the UserForm object in Figure 3-3. Note that there are entries for the Close button (named `cmdClose`), the Save button (named `cmdSave`), the text box (named `txtName`), and the UserForm itself.

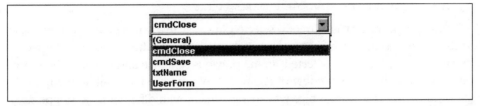

Figure 3-6. The Object box

Figure 3-7 shows the contents of the Procedure box when the `cmdClose` object is selected in the Object box. This list contains the names of the 13 different events that are associated with a command button.

Figure 3-7. The Procedure box

For example, if you select Click, you will be placed within the Code window between the following two lines:

```
Private Sub cmdClose_Click()

End Sub
```

where you can write event code for the Click event of the `cmdClose` command button.

The Immediate Window

The Immediate window (see Figure 3-8) has two main functions. First, we can send output to this window using the command:

```
Debug.Print
```

For instance, the code:

```
Debug.Print ActiveWindow.Selection.Range.Text
```

will print whatever text is currently selected in the active window to the Immediate window. For instance, Figure 3-8 shows what happened when I selected the words "whatever text is currently selected" in the previous sentence and then ran the procedure shown in the Code window of Figure 3-8. We can see the result in the Immediate window. This provides a nice way to experiment with different code snippets.

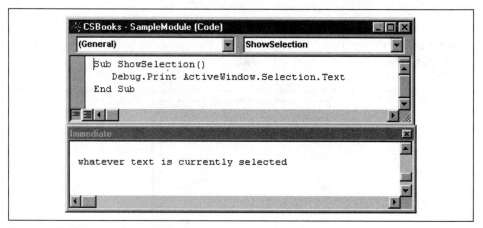

Figure 3-8. The Immediate window

The other main function of the Immediate window is to execute commands. For instance, by selecting some text in the active document, switching to the Immediate window, and entering the line shown in Figure 3-9, the selected text will be boldfaced (after pressing the Enter key to execute the code).

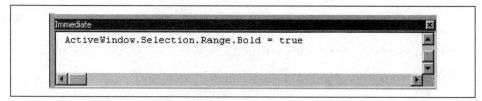

Figure 3-9. The Immediate window: command execution

The Immediate window is an extremely valuable tool for debugging (finding errors in) a program, and you will probably use it often (as I do).

Arranging Windows

If you need more space for writing code, you can close the Properties window, the Project window, and the Immediate window. On the other hand, if you are fortunate to have a large monitor, then you can split your screen as shown in Figure 3-10 in order to see the Word VBA IDE and a Word document at the same time. Then you can trace through each line of your code and watch the results in the document! (You can toggle between Word and the IDE using the Alt-F11 function key combination.)

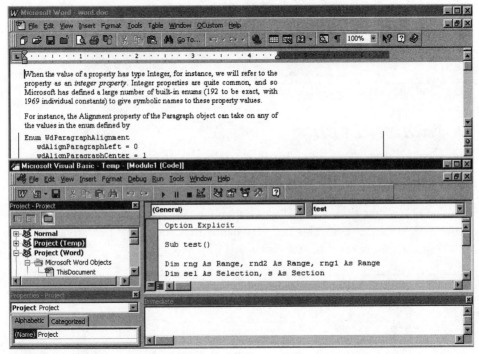

Figure 3-10. A split-screen approach

Docking

Many of the windows in the IDE (including the Project, Properties, and Immediate windows) can be in one of two states: docked or floating. This state can be set using the Docking tab on the Options dialog box shown in Figure 3-11.

A docked window is one that is attached, or anchored, to an edge of another window or to one edge of the client area of the main VBA window. When a dockable window is moved, it snaps to an anchored position. On the other hand, a floating window can be placed anywhere on the screen.

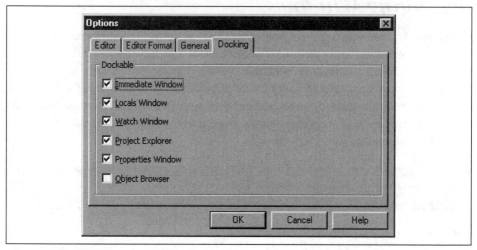

Figure 3-11. The docking options

Document Events

As we have discussed, each Word document has three events associated with it: Open, Close, and New. Any code that we place in the event procedure for one of these events will execute when the event occurs (or fires, as programmers say). To experiment with these events and when they fire, we can add the code shown in Figure 3-12 to each event. (This is a very handy trick for events that are associated with controls on a user form, as well.)

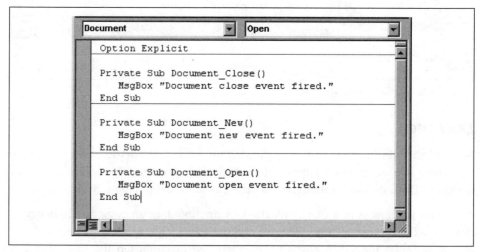

Figure 3-12. Illustrating the document events

As you will see in the next chapter, the *MsgBox* command displays a simple dialog box containing some text on the screen.

To follow along, you should first select the ThisDocument node for a Word document in the Project window (don't forget to double-click on the node to open the corresponding code window, or use the F7 key). Then select Document in the Object box and each of Close, New, and Open in turn in the Procedure box. For each event, type in the single line of code that you see in Figure 3-12. Then repeat the process with the TemplateProject that the document is based upon. However, change the code slightly by replacing the word "Document" with "Template", as in:

```
MsgBox "Template close event fired."
```

Now close the active document. You should see two message boxes in succession. The first dialog box (see Figure 3-13) indicates that the template's Close event has fired, and the second one (see Figure 3-14) indicates that the document's Close event has fired. (Thus, the template event fires before the document event.)

Figure 3-13. Message box opened by the template's Document_Close event procedure

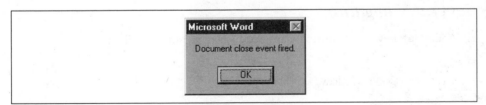

Figure 3-14. Message box opened by the document's Document_Close event procedure

If you now reopen the document, two message boxes will be displayed indicating that the template Open event is fired, followed by the document Open event. Note that the New event fires only when it is part of a template project (not a document project) and a new document based on that template is opened.

4

The Visual Basic Editor, Part II

In this chapter:
- *Navigating the IDE*
- *Getting Help*
- *Creating a Procedure*
- *Run Mode, Design Mode, and Break Mode*
- *Errors*
- *Debugging*
- *Macros*

In this chapter, I conclude discussion of the Visual Basic Editor by moving from its basic organization to a discussion of how you use the Editor when programming. Again, you may want to read quickly through this chapter and refer to it later as needed.

Navigating the IDE

If you prefer the keyboard to the mouse (as I do), then you might want to use keyboard navigating shortcuts. Here are some tips.

General Navigation

The following keyboard shortcuts are used for navigating the IDE:

F7
> Go to the Code window

F4
> Go to the Properties window

Ctrl-R
> Go to the Project window

Ctrl-G
> Go to the Immediate window

Alt-F11
> Toggle between Word and VB IDE

Navigating the Code Window at Design Time

Within the code window, the following keystrokes are very useful:

F1 Help on the item under the cursor.

Shift-F2
> Go to the definition of the item under the cursor. (If the cursor is over a call to a function or subroutine, pressing Shift-F2 sends you to the definition of that procedure.)

Ctrl-Shift-F2
> Return to the last position where editing took place.

Tracing Code

The following keystrokes are useful when tracing through code (discussed later):

F8 Step Into

Shift-F8
> Step Over

Ctrl-Shift-F8
> Step Out

Ctrl-F8
> Run To Cursor

F5 Run

Ctrl-Break
> Break

Shift-F9
> Quick Watch

F9 Toggle Breakpoint

Ctrl-Shift-F9
> Clear All Breakpoints

Bookmarks

It is also possible to insert bookmarks within code. A bookmark marks a location to which you can return easily. To insert a bookmark, or to move to the next or previous bookmark, use the Bookmarks submenu on the Edit menu. The presence of a bookmark is indicated by a small blue square in the left margin of the code.

Getting Help

If you are like me, you will probably make extensive use of Microsoft's Word VBA help files while programming. The simplest way to get help on an item is to place the cursor on that item and press the F1 key. This works not only for VBA language keywords but also for portions of the VBA IDE.

Note that Microsoft provides multiple help files for Word, the VBA language, and the Word object model. While this is quite reasonable, occasionally the help system gets a bit confused and refuses to display the correct help file when you hit the F1 key. (I have not found a simple resolution to this problem, other than shutting down Word and the Visual Basic Editor along with it!)

Note also that a standard installation of Microsoft Office does not install the VBA help files for the various applications. Thus, you may need to run the Office setup program and install Word VBA help by selecting that option in the appropriate setup dialog box. (Do not confuse Word help with Word VBA help.)

Creating a Procedure

There are two ways to create a new procedure (subroutine or function) within a code module. First, after selecting the correct project in the Project Explorer, we can select the Procedure option from the Insert menu. This will produce the dialog box shown in Figure 4-1. Just type the name of the procedure and select Sub or Function. (The Property choice is used with custom objects in a class module.) I discuss the issue of public versus private procedures and static variables later in this chapter.

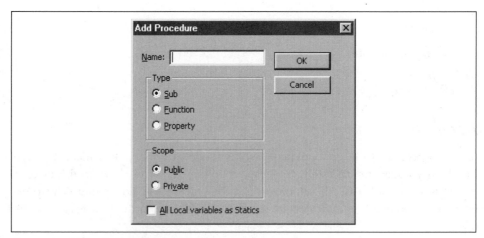

Figure 4-1. The Add Procedure dialog box

A simpler alternative is to simply begin typing:

```
Sub SubName
```

or:

```
Function FunctionName
```

in any code window (following the current **End Sub** or **End Function** statement) or in the General window. As soon as you press the Enter key, Word will move the line of code to a new location and thereby create a new subroutine. (It will even add the appropriate ending—**End Sub** or **End Function**.)

Run Mode, Design Mode, and Break Mode

The VBA IDE can be in any one of three modes: run mode, break mode, or design mode. The IDE is in design mode when you are writing code or designing a form.

Run mode occurs when a procedure is running. To run (or execute) a procedure, just place the cursor anywhere within the procedure code and hit the F5 key (or select Run from the Run menu). If a running procedure seems to be hanging, you can usually stop the procedure by hitting Ctrl-Break (hold down the Control key and hit the Break key).

Break mode is entered when a running procedure stops because of either an error in the code or a deliberate act on your part (described later in this chapter). In particular, if an error occurs, Word will stop execution and display an error dialog box with an error message, an example of which is shown in Figure 4-2.

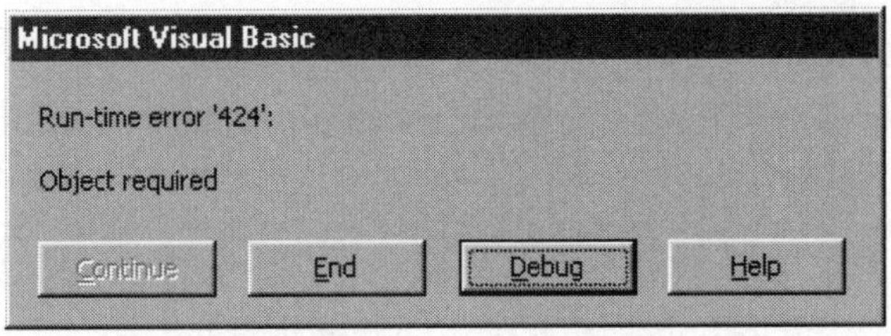

Figure 4-2. An error message

Error dialog boxes offer a few options: end the procedure, get help (such as it may be) with the problem, or enter break mode to debug the code. In the latter case, Word will stop execution of the procedure at the offending code and high-light that code in yellow. (I discuss the process of debugging code in the "Debugging" section later in this chapter.)

Aside from encountering an error, there are several ways we can deliberately enter break mode for debugging purposes:

- Hit Ctrl-Break and choose Debug from the resulting dialog box.

- Include a `Stop` statement in the code, which causes Word to enter break mode.

- Insert a breakpoint on an existing line of executable code. This is done by placing the cursor on that line and hitting the F9 key (or using the Debug menu). Word will place a red dot in the left margin in front of that line and will stop execution when it reaches the line. You may enter more than one breakpoint in a procedure. This is generally preferred to using the `Stop` statement, because breakpoints are automatically removed when you close down the Visual Basic Editor, so you don't need to remember to remove them, as you do with `Stop` statements.

- Set a watch statement that causes Word to enter break mode if a certain condition becomes true. (I discuss watch expressions later in this chapter.)

To exit from break mode, choose Reset from the Run menu.

Note that the caption in the titlebar of the VBA IDE indicates which mode is currently active. In particular, the caption contains the word "[running]" when in run mode and "[break]" when in break mode.

Errors

In computer jargon, an error is referred to as a bug.[*] Errors can be grouped into three types based on when they occur—design time, compile time, or run time.

Design-Time Errors

As the name implies, a design-time error occurs during the writing of code. Perhaps the nicest feature of the Visual Basic Editor is that it can be instructed to watch as we type code and stop us when we make a syntax error. This automatic syntax checking can be enabled or disabled in the Options dialog box shown in Figure 4-3, but I strongly suggest that you keep it enabled.

Notice also that there are other settings related to the design-time environment, such as how far to indent code in response to the Tab key.

---

[*] In case you are interested in the origin of this word, the story goes that when operating the first large-scale digital computer, called the Mark I, an error was traced to a moth that had found its way into the hardware. Incidentally, the Mark I (circa 1944) had 750,000 parts, was 51 feet long, and weighed over 5 tons. How about putting that on your desktop? It also executed about one instruction every 6 seconds, as compared to over 200 million instructions per second for a Pentium!

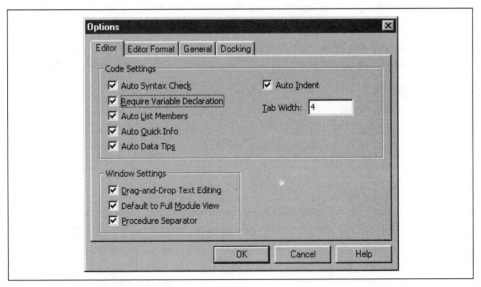

Figure 4-3. The Options dialog box

To illustrate automatic syntax checking, Figure 4-4 shows what happens when we deliberately enter the syntactically incorrect statement **x == 5** and then attempt to move to another line. Note that Microsoft refers to this type of error as a compile error in the dialog box, and perhaps we should as well. However, it seems more descriptive to call it a design-time error or just a syntax error.

Figure 4-4. A syntax error message

Compile-Time Errors

Before a program can be executed, it must be compiled, or translated into a language that the computer can understand. (This is not the place to go into a detailed discussion of compilation.) The compilation process occurs automatically when we request that a program be executed. We can also specifically request compilation by choosing the Compile Project item under the Debug menu.

If Word encounters an error while compiling code, it displays a compile error message. For example, the code in Figure 4-5 contains a compile-time error. In particular, the first line:

```
Dim doc As Document
```

defines a variable of type Document to represent a Word document. (I will discuss all of this at the appropriate time, so don't worry about the details now.) However, the second line:

```
Set doc = ActiveDocument.Name
```

attempts to assign the variable **doc** not to the active document (which would be legal), but to the name of the active document. This error is not caught during design time because it is not a syntax error. It is only at compile time, when Word considers the statement in the context of the first statement, that the error becomes evident.

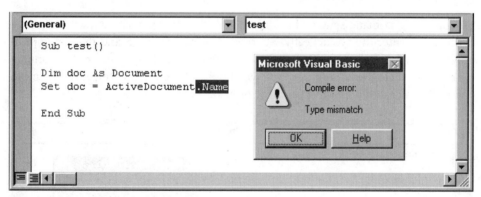

Figure 4-5. A compilation error message

Run-Time Errors

An error that occurs while a program is running is called a run-time error. Figure 4-6 illustrates a run-time error and its corresponding error message.

In this example, the code:

```
Documents.Open "d:\temp\ipx.doc"
```

attempts to open a Word document that does not exist. Notice that this error message is actually quite friendly—not only does it describe the error in clear terms (the file could not be found), but it also offers some (albeit obvious) suggestions for eliminating the problem. (I find the second suggestion a bit amusing—you could not open the file you need because it could not be found; try opening a file

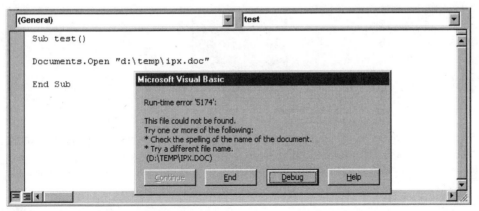

Figure 4-6. A run-time error message

that you don't need! A more useful suggestion would have been to double-check the path for the requested file, but I certainly don't want to complain, since this error message is far better than most.)

Logical Errors

There is one more type of error that we should examine, since it is the most insidious kind of all. A logical error can be defined as the production of an unexpected and incorrect result. As far as Word is concerned, there is no error, because Word has no way of knowing what we intend. (Thus, a logical error is not a run-time error, in the traditional sense, even though it does occur at run time.)

To illustrate, the following code purports to compute the average of some numbers:

```
Dim x(3) As Integer
Dim Ave As Single
x(0) = 1
x(1) = 3
x(2) = 8
x(3) = 5
Ave = (x(0) + x(1) + x(2) + x(3)) / 3
MsgBox "Average is: " & Ave
```

The result is the message box shown in Figure 4-7. Unfortunately, it is incorrect. The penultimate line in the preceding program should be:

```
Ave = (x(0) + x(1) + x(2) + x(3)) / 4
```

(note the 4 in the denominator), since there are 4 numbers to average. The correct average is 4.25. Of course, Word will not complain because it has no way of knowing whether we really want to divide by 3.

Figure 4-7. The result of a logical error

Precisely because Word cannot warn us about logical errors, they are the most dangerous, because we think that everything is correct. Another problem is that logical errors can be very subtle, as illustrated by the following example from the Word object model.

Word VBA provides a very simple way to count the number of words in the currently selected text in a document. For instance, if I select the paragraph shown in Figure 4-8 and execute the code:

```
MsgBox Selection.Words.Count
```

I will get a message box containing the number 57.

> Precisely because VBA cannot warn you about logical errors, they are the most dangerous, because you *think* that everything is copacetic. Another problem is that logical errors can be very subtle. To illustrate, Word VBA provides a very simple way to count the number of words in a selection of text.

Figure 4-8. How many words are in this paragraph?

However, my count of the words in this paragraph is 51. The Word VBA help file neglects to mention that each punctuation mark is also considered a word! Thus, 3 periods plus 3 commas plus 51 words equals 57. The point here is that we need to be very circumspect in order to avoid logical errors.

Here is another example. How many words are selected in Figure 4-9? Answer: 2. Reason: Word counts each partially selected word as a whole word and considers the trailing spaces following a word as part of that word! Enjoy.

> Precisely because VBA cannot warn you about logical errors, they are the most dangerous, because you *think* that everything is copacetic. Another problem is that logical errors can be very subtle. To illustrate, Word VBA provides a very simple way to count the number of words in a selection of text.

Figure 4-9. How many words are selected?

Debugging

Invariably, you will encounter errors in your code. Design-time and compile-time errors are relatively easy to deal with because Word helps us out with error messages and by indicating the offending code. Logical errors are much more difficult to detect and to fix. This is where debugging plays a major role. The Word IDE provides some very powerful ways to find bugs.

Debugging can be quite involved, and I could include a whole chapter on the subject. There are even special software applications designed to assist in complex debugging tasks. However, for most purposes, a few simple techniques are sufficient. In particular, Word makes it easy to trace through programs, executing one line at a time, watching the effect of each line as it is executed.

Try a very simple example, with which you should follow along on your PC. If possible, you should arrange your screen as in Figure 4-10. This will make it easier to follow the effects of the code, since you won't need to switch back and forth between the Word window and the Word VBA window. The code that we will trace is shown in Example 4-1. (Note that lines beginning with an apostrophe are comments that are ignored by Word.)

Example 4-1. A Simple Program to Trace

```
Sub test()

Dim sent As Range
' Get the third sentence
Set sent = ActiveDocument.Range.Sentences(3)
' Select it
sent.Select
' Boldface it
sent.Bold = True
' Select the first character in the sentence
sent.Characters(1).Select
' Change the font
Selection.Font.Size = 24

End Sub
```

Begin by entering a paragraph containing at least three sentences into a Word document and leave the cursor anywhere in the document. When you finish, switch to the VBA IDE. Make sure that the code window is active and the insertion point is somewhere in the code. Then hit the F8 key once, which starts the tracing process. (You can also choose Step Into from the Debug menu.)

Continue striking the F8 key, pausing between keystrokes to view the effect of each instruction in the Word window. (You can toggle between Word and the IDE using Alt-F11.) As you trace through this code, you will see the third sentence

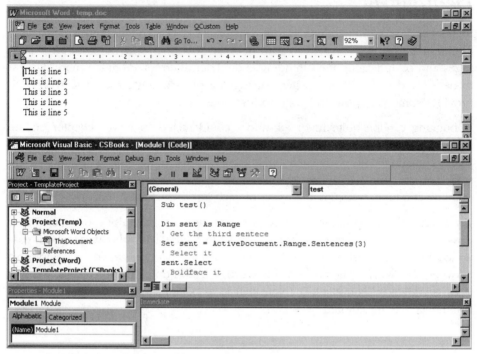

Figure 4-10. Side-by-side windows for easy debugging

selected, made bold, the first character selected, and finally its font size increased. Now you can begin to see what Word VBA programming is all about!

I will now examine some of the tools that Word provides for debugging code.

Tracing

The process of executing code one line at a time, as I did in the previous example, is referred to as tracing or code stepping. Word provides three options related to tracing: stepping into, stepping over, and stepping out of. The differences between these methods refers to handling calls to other procedures.

To illustrate the difference, consider the code shown in Example 4-2. In *ProcedureA*, the first line of code sets the contents of the active Word document to the line "To be or not to be." The second line calls *ProcedureB* and the third line boldfaces the contents of the active document. *ProcedureB* simply formats the first paragraph of the active Word document with the Heading 1 style. Don't worry about the exact syntax of this code. The important thing to notice is that the second line of *ProcedureA* calls *ProcedureB*.

Example 4-2. Sample Code for Tracing Methods

```
Sub ProcedureA()
    ActiveDocument.Content.Text = "To be or not to be"
    Call ProcedureB
    ActiveDocument.Content.Bold = True
End Sub

Sub ProcedureB()
    Set para = ActiveDocument.Paragraphs(1)
    para.Style = "Heading 1"
End Sub
```

Step Into (F8)

Step Into executes code one statement (or instruction) at a time. If the statement being executed calls another procedure, stepping into that statement simply transfers control to the first line in the called procedure. For instance, with reference to the previous code, stepping into the line:

```
Call ProcedureB
```

in *ProcedureA* transfers control to the first line of *ProcedureB*:

```
Set para = ActiveDocument.Paragraphs(1)
```

Further tracing proceeds in *ProcedureB*. Once all of the lines of *ProcedureB* have been traced, control returns to *ProcedureA* at the line immediately following the call to *ProcedureB*, that is, at the line:

```
ActiveDocument.Content.Bold = True
```

Step Into has another important use. Namely, if we choose Step Into while still in design mode—that is, before any code is running—execution begins but break mode is entered before the first line of code is actually executed. This is the proper way to begin tracing a program.

Step Over (Shift-F8)

Step Over is similar to Step Into, except that if the current statement is a call to another procedure, the entire called procedure is executed without stopping (rather than tracing through the called procedure). Thus, for instance, stepping over the line:

```
Call ProcedureB
```

in the previous procedure executes *ProcedureB* and stops at the next line:

```
ActiveDocument.Content.Bold = True
```

in *ProcedureA*. This is useful if we are certain that *ProcedureB* is not the cause of our problem and we don't want to trace through that procedure line by line.

Step Out (Ctrl-Shift-F8)

Step Out is intended to be used within a called procedure (such as *ProcedureB*). Step Out executes the remaining lines of the called procedure and returns to the calling procedure (such as *ProcedureA*). This is useful if we are in the middle of a called procedure and decide that we don't need to trace any more of that procedure, but want to return to the calling procedure. (If you trace into a called procedure by mistake, just do a Step Out to return to the calling procedure.)

Run To Cursor

If the Visual Basic Editor is in break mode, we may want to execute several lines of code at one time. This can be done using the Run To Cursor feature. Simply place the cursor on the statement immediately following the last line you want to execute and then press Ctrl-F8 (or choose Run To Cursor from the Debug menu).

Changing the next statement to execute

We can also change the flow of execution while in break mode by placing the cursor on the statement that we want to execute next and hitting Ctrl-F9 or choosing Set Next Statement from the Debug menu. This will set the selected statement as the next statement to execute (but will not execute it until we continue tracing). What power!

Breaking out of debug mode

When we no longer need to trace our code, we have two choices. To return to design mode, we can choose Reset from the Run menu (no hotkey for this). To have Word finish executing the current program, we can hit F5 or choose Run from the Run menu.

Watching Expressions

It is often useful to watch the values of certain expressions or variables as we trace through a program. Word provides several ways to do this.

Quick Watch (Shift-F9)

The Quick Watch feature is used to check the value of a variable or expression quickly while in break mode. Just place the insertion point over the variable name and hit Shift-F9 (or choose Quick Watch from the Debug menu). For instance, Figure 4-11 shows the Quick Watch dialog box when the expression $x + 2$ is selected in the code in Figure 4-12. According to Figure 4-11, at the time that Quick Watch was invoked, the expression $x + 2$ had the value 8. Note that if I had just placed the insertion point in front of the letter **x**, then Quick Watch would have reported the value of this variable alone.

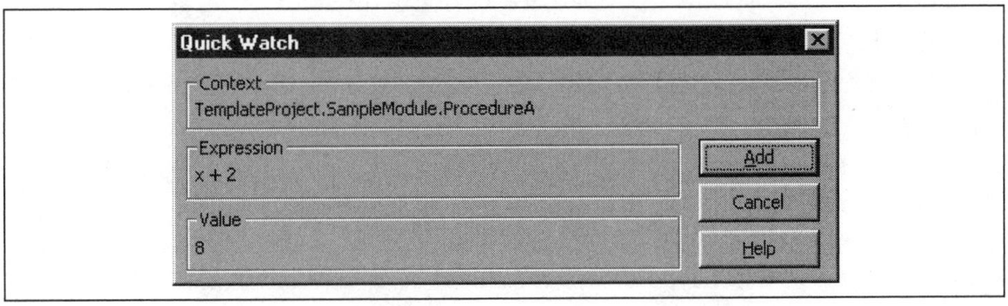

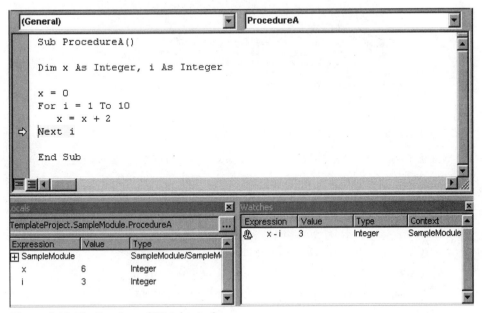

Figure 4-11. The Quick Watch window

Another way to get values for expressions or variables quickly is to enable Auto Data Tips on the Editor tab of in Word VBA's Options dialog box. With this feature enabled, when we place the mouse pointer over a variable or select an expression and place the mouse pointer over the selection, after a slight delay, a small yellow window will appear containing the value of the variable or expression. This is very useful!

The Locals and Watch Window

Two special windows aid in watching expressions: the Locals window and the Watch window. These are shown in Figure 4-12.

Figure 4-12. The Locals and Watch windows

The Locals window shows the values of all local variables. A local variable is a variable defined within the current procedure and is therefore not valid in any other procedure. (I discuss local variables in Chapter 5, *Variables, Data Types, and Constants*.)

The Watch window shows all of the watches that have been set. A watch is a variable or expression that is placed in the Watch window. Word automatically updates the expressions in the Watch window after each line of code is executed and acts according to the type of watch defined, as described next.

To add a watch, choose Add Watch from the Debug menu. This will produce the dialog box shown in Figure 4-13.

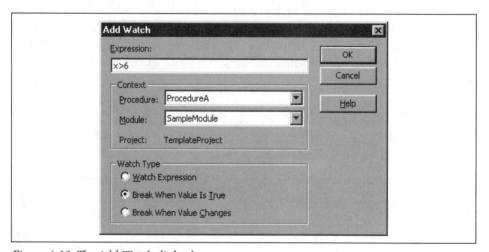

Figure 4-13. The Add Watch dialog box

You can then enter a variable or expression, such as **x** > 6, in the Expression text box. Note that there are three types of watches:

- Watch Expression simply adds the expression to the Watches window so you can watch its value as code is executed. In this example, the value of the expression will be either True or False, depending upon whether **x** > 6 or not.

- Break When Value Is True asks Word to stop execution and enter break mode whenever the expression is true. In this example, VBA will break execution when **x** > 6 is true, that is, when **x** becomes greater than 6.

- Break When Value Changes asks Word to enter break mode when the value of the expression changes in any way (in this case, from True to False or vice-versa).

Altogether, the various tracing modes and watch types provide a very powerful set of tools for debugging code. I use them often!

Macros

In earlier days, a macro consisted of a series of keystrokes that was recorded and assigned to a hotkey. When a user invoked the hotkey, the recording would play and the recorded keystrokes would be executed.

These days, macros (at least for Microsoft Office) are much more sophisticated. In fact, a Word macro is just a special type of subroutine—one that does not have any parameters. (I discuss subroutines and parameters in Chapter 6, *Functions and Subroutines.*)

Recording Macros

Word has the capability of recording very simple macros. When we ask Word to record a macro, it takes note of our keystrokes and converts them into a VBA subroutine (with no parameters).

For example, suppose you record a macro that does a find and replace, replacing the word "macro" with the word "subroutine." When you look in the Projects window under the project in which the macro was recorded (usually the attached template), you will find a new standard module called NewMacros containing the following subroutine:

```
Sub AMacro()
'
AMacro Macro
Macro recorded 04/27/98 by sr
'
    Selection.Find.ClearFormatting
    Selection.Find.Replacement.ClearFormatting
    With Selection.Find
        .Text = "macro"
        .Replacement.Text = "subroutine"
        .Forward = True
        .Wrap = wdFindContinue
        .Format = False
        .MatchCase = False
        .MatchWholeWord = False
        .MatchWildcards = False
        .MatchSoundsLike = False
        .MatchAllWordForms = False
    End With
    Selection.Find.Execute
    Selection.Find.Execute Replace:=wdReplaceAll
End Sub
```

This is the same code that someone might have written in order to perform this find and replace operation.

Word does a very thorough job of translating keystrokes into VBA code, essentially matching in code every item in the Find and Replace dialog box shown in Figure 4-14—even the ones that we have not changed—because it has no way of knowing what we have and have not changed!

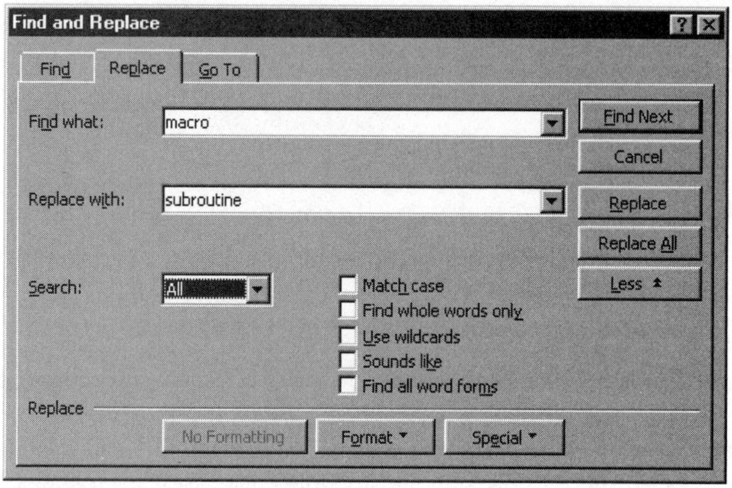

Figure 4-14. The Find and Replace dialog box

In certain situations, the macro recorder can serve as a useful learning tool. If we can't figure out how to code a certain action, we can record it in a macro and cut and paste the resulting code into our own program.

However, before you get too excited about this cut-and-paste approach to programming, we should point out that it is not anywhere near the panacea one might hope. First (and least serious), since the macro recorder does such a thorough job of translating our actions into code, it tends to produce very bloated code, which can run very slowly. For instance, the previous search and replace can also be done using the following code, which is considerably more compact:

```
Sub AMacro()
    Selection.Find.ClearFormatting
    Selection.Find.Replacement.ClearFormatting
    With Selection.Find
        .Text = "macro"
        .Replacement.Text = "subroutine"
        .Wrap = wdFindContinue
    End With
    Selection.Find.Execute
    Selection.Find.Execute Replace:=wdReplaceAll
End Sub
```

Second (and more serious), the macro recorder is capable of recording only very simple procedures. Most useful Word programs are far too complicated to be recorded automatically by the macro recorder.

Running Macros

As you may know, to run a macro from the user interface, you just choose Macros from the Macro submenu of the Tools menu (or hit Alt-F8). This displays the Macro dialog box shown in Figure 4-15. This dialog box lists all macros in the current document or in any attached templates (including *normal.dot* and any other attached global templates). From here, we can do several things, including running, editing, creating, or deleting macros. (Choosing Edit or Create places you in the VB Editor.)

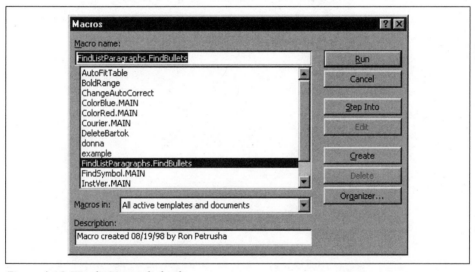

Figure 4-15. Word's Macro dialog box

We should also comment on what appears and does not appear in the Macro list box. All written macros will appear in the Macros dialog box (as will all recorded macros). However, there are a few variations. If you give the macro a unique name (within the context given in the Macros In list box), then only the name of the macro will appear in the list box. If the name is not unique, then it must be qualified by the name of the module in which the macro appears, as in:

```
FindListParagraphs.FindBullets
```

in Figure 4-15. (It happens that I have another *FindBullets* macro, in another module, that is not visible in Figure 4-15.) Finally, note that if the macro is one that has been converted by Word from WordBasic (which is used by Word 95), then Word calls the procedure *Main.* Hence, if there are several such macros, their names must be qualified (as in *ColorBlue.Main, ColorGreen.Main,* and so on).

Note that we can prevent a macro procedure from appearing in the Macros list box by making the procedure private, using the **Private** keyword, as in:

```
Private Sub HideThisMacro()
```

I discuss private and public procedures in Chapter 6.

Finally, if you are like me, you will collect a great many macros over the years. As time goes by, you may forget the names of some of these macros and thus have trouble finding a macro when you need it. I strongly advise you to give some careful thought to creating a consistent naming convention for macros. I begin the names of all macros with a word that categorizes the macro. For instance, all of my macros that deal with tables begin with the word Table, as in:

```
Table_AutoFit
Table_MakeMultiColumn
Table_DeleteCellandCloseUp
```

II

The VBA Programming Language

5

Variables, Data Types, and Constants

In the next few chapters, I discuss the basics of the VBA programming language, which underlies all of the Microsoft Office programming environments. During the discussion, I provide many short coding examples. I hope that you will take the time to enter some of these examples and experiment with them.

Comments

We have already examined the importance of comments. Any text that follows an apostrophe is considered a comment and is ignored by Word. For example, the first following line is a comment, as is everything following the apostrophe on the third line:

```
' Declare a string variable
Dim DocName as String
DocName = ActiveDocument.Name    ' Get name of active doc
```

One of the more useful tools when debugging code is to temporarily comment out lines of code so that they will not execute. The lines can subsequently be uncommented to restore them to active duty. The CommentBlock and UncommentBlock buttons, which can be found on the Edit toolbar, will place or remove comment marks from each currently selected line of code and are very useful for commenting out several lines of code in one step. (There are no keyboard shortcuts for these commands, but they can be added to a menu and given menu accelerator keys.)

Line Continuation

The very nature of Word VBA syntax often leads to long lines of code, which can be difficult to read, especially if we need to scroll horizontally to see the entire line. For this reason, Microsoft recently introduced a line-continuation character into VBA. This character is the underscore (_), which must be preceded by a space and cannot be followed by any other characters (including comments). For example, the following code:

```
ActiveDocument.Paragraphs(1).Alignment =_
wdAlignParagraphCenter
```

is treated as one line by Word.

A line-continuation character cannot be inserted in the middle of a literal string constant, which is enclosed in quotation marks.

Constants

The VBA language has two types of constants. A *literal constant* (also called a *constant* or *literal*) is a specific value, such as a number, date, or text string, that does not change and that is used exactly as written. Note that string constants are enclosed in double quotation marks, as in:

```
"Donna Smith"
```

and date constants are enclosed between number signs, as in:

```
#1/1/96#
```

For instance, the following code stores a date in the variable called dt:

```
Dim dt As Date
dt = #1/2/97#
```

The second type of constant, a *symbolic constant* (also sometimes referred to simply as a constant), is another name for a literal constant.

To define or declare a symbolic constant in a program, use the Const keyword:

```
Const InvoicePath = "d:\Invoices\"
```

In this case, Word will replace every instance of InvoicePath in our code with the string "d:\Invoices\". Thus, InvoicePath is a constant, since it never changes value, but it is not a literal constant, since it is not used as written.

The virtue of using symbolic constants is that, if we decide later to change "d:\Invoices\" to "d:\OldInvoices\", you need to change only the definition of InvoicePath:

```
Const InvoicePath = "d:\OldInvoices\"
```

rather than search through the entire program for every occurrence of the phrase "d:\Invoices\"!

Note that it is generally good programming practice to declare any symbolic constants at the beginning of the procedure in which they are used (or in the Declarations section of a code module). This improves readability and simplifies housekeeping.

In addition to the symbolic constants that you can define using the `Const` statement, VBA has a large number of built-in symbolic constants (about 700), whose names begin with the lowercase letters **vb**. Word VBA adds additional symbolic constants (about 2,000!) that begin with the letters **wd**. You will encounter many of these constants throughout the book.

Among the most commonly used VBA constants are **vbCrLf**, which is equivalent to a carriage return followed by a line feed, and **vbTab**, which is equivalent to the tab character. Also, Word uses **vbCr** for its paragraph mark.

Enums

Microsoft has recently introduced a structure into VBA to categorize the plethora of symbolic constants. This structure is called an *enum*, which is short for enumeration. For instance, among Word's 192 enums, there is one for paragraph alignment settings, defined as follows:

```
Enum WdParagraphAlignment
    wdAlignParagraphLeft = 0
    wdAlignParagraphCenter = 1
    wdAlignParagraphRight = 2
    wdAlignParagraphJustify = 3
End Enum
```

Thus, the following line of code will center align the first paragraph in the active document:

```
ActiveDocument.Paragraphs(1).Alignment = wdAlignParagraphCenter
```

Note that this enum is built-in, so we do not need to add it to our programs in order to use these symbolic constants. (We can create our own enums, but this is generally not necessary in Word VBA programming, since Word has done such a good job of this for us.)

As another example, the built-in enum for the constant values that can be returned when the user dismisses a message box (by clicking on a button) is:

```
Enum VbMsgBoxResult
    vbOK = 1
    vbCancel = 2
    vbAbort = 3
```

```
        vbRetry = 4
        vbIgnore = 5
        vbYes = 6
        vbNo = 7
    End Enum
```

For instance, when the user hits the OK button on a dialog box (assuming it has one), VBA returns the value **vbOK**. Certainly, it is a lot easier to remember that VBA will return the symbolic constant **vbOK** than to remember that it will return the constant 1. (I discuss how to get and use this return value later in this chapter.)

VBA also defines some symbolic constants that are used to set the types of buttons that will appear on a message box. These are contained in the following enum (which includes some additional constants not shown):

```
    Enum VbMsgBoxStyle
        vbOKOnly = 0
        vbOKCancel = 1
        vbAbortRetryIgnore = 2
        vbYesNoCancel = 3
        vbYesNo = 4
        vbRetryCancel = 5
    End Enum
```

To illustrate, consider the following code:

```
    If MsgBox("Proceed?", vbOKCancel) = vbOK Then

        ' place code to execute when user hits OK button

    Else

        ' place code to execute when user hits any other button

    End If
```

In the first line, the code:

```
    MsgBox("Proceed?", vbOKCancel)
```

causes Word to display a message box with an OK button and a Cancel button and the message "Proceed?", as shown in Figure 5-1.

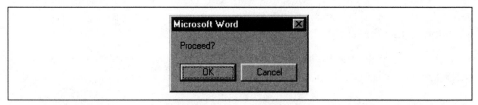

Figure 5-1. Sample message box

If the user clicks the OK button, Word will return the constant value **vbOK**; otherwise, it will return the value **vbCancel**. Thus, the If statement in the first line will distinguish between the two responses. (I discuss the If statement in detail in Chapter 8, *Control Statements*. Here we are interested in the role of symbolic constants.)

Clearly, the first line in the earlier example is much more readable than:

```
If MsgBox("Proceed?", 1) = 1 Then
```

In case you are not yet convinced of the value of symbolic constants, consider the following enum for color constants:

```
Enum ColorConstants
    vbBlack = 0
    vbBlue = 16711680
    vbMagenta = 16711935
    vbCyan = 16776960
    vbWhite = 16777215
    vbRed = 255
    vbGreen = 65280
    vbYellow = 65535
End Enum
```

Which would you rather type:

```
ATextBox.ForeColor = vbBlue
```

or:

```
ATextBox.ForeColor = 16711680
```

Need I say more?

Variables and Data Types

A *variable* can be thought of as a memory location that can hold values of a specific type. The value in a variable may change during the life of the program—hence the name "variable."

In VBA, each variable has a specific data type, which indicates which type of data it may hold. For instance, a variable that holds text strings has the data type String and is called a *string variable*. A variable that holds integers (whole numbers) has the data type Integer and is called an *integer variable*. For reference, Table 5-1 shows the complete set of VBA data types, along with the amount of memory that they consume and their range of values. (I will discuss a few of the more commonly used data types in a moment.)

Table 5-1. VBA Data Types

Type	Size in Memory	Range of Values
Byte	1 byte	0 to 255
Boolean	2 bytes	True or False
Integer	2 bytes	−32,768 to 32,767
Long (long integer)	4 bytes	−2,147,483,648 to 2,147,483,647
Single (single-precision real)	4 bytes	Approximately −3.4E38 to 3.4E38
Double (double-precision real)	8 bytes	Approximately −1.8E308 to 4.9E324
Currency (scaled integer)	8 bytes	Approximately −922,337,203,685,477.5808 to 922,337,203,685,477.5807
Date	8 bytes	1/1/100 to 12/31/9999
Object	4 bytes	Any Object reference
String	Variable length: 10 bytes + string length; fixed length: string length	Variable length: <= about 2 billion (65,400 for Win 3.1); fixed length: up to 65,400
Variant	16 bytes for numbers 22 bytes + string length	Number: same as Double; String: same as String
User-defined	Varies	

Variable Declaration

To *declare* a variable means to define its data type. Variables are declared with the Dim keyword (or with the keywords **Private** and **Public**, which I discuss later in this chapter). Here are some examples:

```
Dim Name As String
Dim Holiday As Date
Dim Age As Integer
Dim Height As Single
Dim Money As Currency
Dim doc as Document
Dim para as Paragraph
```

The general syntax of a variable declaration is:

```
Dim VariableName As DataType
```

If a particular variable is used without first declaring it, or if it is declared without mentioning a data type, as in:

```
Dim Age
```

then VBA will treat the variable as having type Variant. As we can see from Table 5-1, this is generally a waste of memory, since variants require more memory than most other types of variables.

For instance, an integer variable requires 2 bytes, whereas a variant that holds the same integer requires 16 bytes, which is a waste of 12 bytes. It is not uncommon to have hundreds or even thousands of variables in a complex program, so the memory waste could be significant. For this reason, it is a good idea to declare all variables.

You can place more than one declaration on a line to save space. For instance, the line:

```
Dim Age As Integer, Name As String, Money As Currency
```

declares three variables. Note, however, that a declaration such as:

```
Dim Age, Height, Weight As Integer
```

is legal, but **Age** and **Height** are declared as Variants, not Integers. In other words, you must specify the type for each variable explicitly.

It is also possible to tell VBA the type of the variable by appending a special character to the variable name. In particular, VBA allows the type-declaration suffixes shown in Table 5-2. (I dislike these suffixes, but they do save space.)

Table 5-2. Type-Declaration Suffixes

Suffix	Type
%	integer
&	long
!	single
#	double
@	currency
$	string

For instance, the line:

```
Dim Name$
```

declares a variable called **Name$** of type String. We can then write:

```
Name$ = "Donna"
```

Finally, note that although Word allows variable and constant declarations to be placed anywhere within a procedure (before the item is used, that is), it is generally good programming practice to place all such declarations at the beginning of the procedure. This improves code readability and simplifies housekeeping.

The Importance of Explicit Variable Declaration

I have said that using the Variant data type generally wastes memory. There is an additional, even more important reason to declare all variables explicitly. This has to do with making typing errors, which we all do from time to time. In particular, if you accidentally misspell a variable name, VBA will think you meant to create a new variable!

To illustrate how dangerous this can be, consider the *NewLetter* procedure in Example 5-1, whose purpose is to take the first open document, change its contents, ask the user for a name under which to save the changed document, and then save the document under the new name.

Example 5-1. A Procedure with a Typo

```
Sub NewLetter()

Dim LetterDoc As Document
Dim LetterDocName As String

' Get first open document
Set LetterDoc = Documents(1)

' Get the document name
LetterDocName = LetterDoc.Name

' Change the contents of the document
LetterDoc.Content = "How do I love thee..."

' Ask user for new name for document
LettrDocName = InputBox("Enter new name for document " & LetterDocName)

' Save the document
LetterDoc.SaveAs LetterDocName

End Sub
```

Observe that there is a typographical error in the line:

```
LettrDocName = InputBox("Enter new name for document " & _
    LetterDocName)
```

Since the variable **LettrDocName** is not declared, Word will treat it as a new variable and give it the Variant data type. Moreover, VBA will assume that we want the new filename to be assigned to the variable **LettrDocName** and will save the changed document under its original name, which is stored in **LetterDocName**. Thus, we will lose the original document when it is inadvertently overwritten without warning!

Option Explicit

To avoid the problem described in the previous example, we need a way to make Word refuse to run a program if it contains any variables that we have not explicitly declared. This is done simply by placing the line:

```
Option Explicit
```

in the Declarations section of each code module. Since it is easy to forget to do this, VBA provides an option called Require Variable Declaration in its Options dialog box. When this option is selected, VBA automatically inserts the `Option Explicit` line for us. Therefore, I strongly recommend that you enable this option.

Next, I briefly discuss some of the data types in Table 5-1.

Numeric Data Types

The numeric data types include Integer, Long, Single, Double, and Currency. As a Word VBA programmer, you will probably have most use for Integer and Long. For instance, the number of characters in a Word document is a Long integer.

Incidentally, the Word VBA help documentation occasionally says that a value is an Integer when it is actually a Long. This is probably due to the fact that in the old days of Windows 3.1 (which is a 16-bit operating system), many of these values were Integers. However, in the 32-bit world of Windows 95 and later, these values were upgraded to Longs. (A Long is also sometimes referred to as a *long integer*. And you thought computer language was confusing.)

Boolean Data Type

A Boolean variable is a variable that takes on one of two values: True or False. This very useful data type was only recently introduced into VBA. Prior to its introduction, VBA recognized 0 as False and any nonzero value as True, and you may still see this usage in older code.

String Data Type

A string is a sequence of characters. (The empty string has no characters, however.) A string may contain ordinary text characters (letters, digits, and punctuation), as well as special control characters such as **vbCrLf** (carriage return/line feed characters) or **vbTab** (tab character). As we have seen, a string constant is enclosed within quotation marks. The empty string is denoted by a pair of adjacent quotation marks, as in:

```
EmptyString = ""
```

There are two types of string variables in VBA: fixed-length and variable-length. A fixed-length string variable is declared as follows:

```
Dim FixedStringVarName As String * StringLen
```

For instance, the following statement declares a fixed-length string of length 10 characters:

```
Dim sName As String * 10
```

Observe that the following code:

```
Dim s As String * 10
s = "test"
Debug.Print s & "/"
```

produces the output

```
test      /
```

This shows that the content of a fixed-length string is padded with spaces in order to reach the correct length.

A variable-length string variable is a variable that can hold strings of varying lengths (at different times, of course). Variable-length string variables are declared simply as:

```
Dim VariableStringVarName as String
```

As an example, the code:

```
Dim s As String
s = "test"
Debug.Print s & "/"
s = "another test"
Debug.Print s & "/"
```

produces the output:

```
test/
another test/
```

Variable-length string variables are used much more often than fixed-length strings, although the latter have some very specific and important uses (which I will not discuss in this book).

Date Data Type

Variables of the Date data type require 8 bytes of storage and are actually stored as decimal (floating-point) numbers that represent dates ranging from January 1, 100 to December 31, 9999 (no year 2000 problem here) and times from 0:00:00 to 23:59:59.

As discussed earlier, literal dates are enclosed within number signs, but when assigning a date to a Date variable, we can also use valid dates in string format. For example, the following are all valid date/time assignments:

```
Dim dt As Date
dt = #1/2/98#
dt = "January 12, 2001"
dt = #1/1/95#
dt = #12:50:00 PM#
dt = #1/13/76 12:50:00 PM#
```

VBA has a large number of functions that can manipulate dates and times. If you need to manipulate dates or times in your programs, you should probably spend some time with the Word VBA help file (start by looking under "Date Data Type").

Variant Data Type

The Variant data type provides a catch-all data type that is capable of holding data of any other type except fixed-length string data and user-defined types. (I have already noted the virtues and vices of the Variant data type and discussed why variants should generally be avoided.)

Word Object Data Types

Word VBA has a large number of additional data types that fall under the general category of Object data type. (I provide a complete list in Chapter 10, *The Word Object Model*.) To get the feel for the types of objects in the Word object model, here is a partial list:

Border
Document
Font
Options
PageSetup
Paragraph
ParagraphFormat
Selection
Style
Table, Cell, Row, and Column
Template
Window

Thus, we can declare variables such as:

```
Dim doc As Document
Dim fnt As Font
```

```
Dim opt As Options
Dim para As Paragraph
Dim sel As Selection
Dim tbl As Table
Dim tmp As Template
```

I devote much of this book to studying the objects in the Word object model, for it is through these objects that we can manipulate Word documents.

The generic As Object declaration

It is also possible to declare any Word object using the generic object data type `Object`, as in the following example:

```
Dim para As Object
```

While you may see this declaration from time to time, it is much less efficient than a specific object declaration, such as:

```
Dim para As Paragraph
```

because Word cannot tell what type of object the variable **para** refers to until the program is running, so it must use some execution time to make this determination. This is referred to as *late binding* and can make programs run significantly more slowly. (For more on late versus early binding, see Appendix A, *Programming Word from Another Application.*) Thus, generic object declarations should be avoided.

I discuss object variables in some detail in Chapter 10. However, I will briefly discuss the `Set` statement here, since it will appear from time to time in upcoming code examples.

The Set statement

Declaring object variables is done in the same way as declaring nonobject variables. For instance, here are two variable declarations:

```
Dim int As Integer   ' nonobject variable declaration
Dim doc As Document  ' object variable declaration
```

On the other hand, when it comes to assigning a value to variables, the syntax differs for object and nonobject variables. In particular, we must use the `Set` keyword when assigning a value to an object variable. For example, the following line assigns the currently active Word document to the variable **doc**:

```
Set doc = ActiveDocument
```

Arrays

An array variable is a collection of variables that use the same name, but are distinguished by an index value. For instance, to store the first 100 paragraphs of a document, we could declare an array variable as follows:

```
Dim Para(1 To 100) As Paragraph
```

The array variable is **Para**. It has size 100. The lower bound of the array is 1 and the upper bound is 100. Each of the variables:

```
Para(1), Para(2),..., Para(100)
```

are Paragraph variables (that is, variables of the object type Paragraph). Note that if we omit the first index in the declaration, as in:

```
Dim Para(100) As Paragraph
```

then VBA will automatically set the first index to 0, so the size of the array will be 101.

The virtue of declaring array variables is clear, since it would be very unpleasant to have to declare 100 separate variables! In addition, as we will see, there are ways to work collectively with all of the elements in an array, using a few simple programming constructs. For instance, the following code boldfaces each of the 100 paragraphs in the array:

```
For i = 1 To 100
    Para(i).Range.Bold = True
Next i
```

The dimension of an array

The Para array defined in the preceding section has one dimension. We can also define arrays of more than one dimension. For instance, the array:

```
Dim sCells(1 To 10, 1 To 100) As String
```

is a two-dimensional array whose first index ranges from 1 to 10 and whose second index ranges from 1 to 100. Thus, the array has size 10×100 = 1000.

Dynamic arrays

When an array is declared, as in:

```
Dim sFiles(1 To 10) As String
```

the upper and lower bounds are both specified, so the size of the array is fixed. However, there are many situations in which we do not know at declaration time how large an array we may need. For this reason, VBA provides dynamic arrays and the **ReDim** statement.

A dynamic array is declared with empty parentheses, as in:

```
Dim sFiles() as String
```

Dynamic arrays can be sized (or resized) using the **ReDim** statement, as in:

```
ReDim sFiles(1 to 10)
```

This same array can later be resized again, as in:

```
ReDim sFiles(1 to 100)
```

Note that resizing an array will destroy its contents unless you use the **Preserve** keyword, as in:

```
ReDim Preserve sFiles(1 to 200)
```

However, when **Preserve** is used, we can change only the upper bound of the array (and only the last dimension in a multidimensional array).

The UBound function

The *UBound* function is used to return the current upper bound of an array. This is very useful in determining when an array needs redimensioning. To illustrate, suppose we want to collect an unknown number of filenames in an array named **sFiles**. If the next file number is **iNextFile**, the following code checks to see if the upper bound is less than **iNextFile**, and if so, it increases the upper bound of the array by 10, preserving its current contents, to make room for the next file-name:

```
If UBound(sFiles) < iNextFile Then
    ReDim Preserve sFiles(UBound(sFiles) + 10)
End If
```

Note that redimensioning takes time, so it is wise to add some "working room" at the top to cut down on the number of times the array must be redimensioned. This is why we added 10 to the upper bound in the example, rather than just 1. (There is a tradeoff here between the extra time it takes to redimension and the extra space that may be wasted if we do not use the entire redimensioned array.)

Variable Naming Conventions

VBA programs can get very complicated, and we can use all the help we can get in trying to make them as readable as possible. In addition, as time goes on, the ideas behind the program begin to fade, and we must rely on the code itself to refresh our memory. This is why adding copious comments to a program is so important.

Another way to make programs more readable is to use a consistent naming convention for constants, variables, procedure names, and other items. In general, a name should have two properties. First, it should remind the reader of the purpose or function of the item. For instance, suppose I want to assign Document variables to several Word invoice documents. The code:

```
Dim doc1 As Document, doc2 as Document
Set doc1 = Documents.Open("d:\Word\InvoiceToIBM.doc")
Set doc2 = Documents.Open("d:\Word\InvoiceToDEC.doc")
```

is perfectly legal, but 1000 lines of code and 6 months later, will I remember which invoice is `doc1` and which is `doc2`? Since we went to the trouble of naming the invoice files in a descriptive manner, we should do the same with the Document variables, as in:

```
Dim docIBM As Document, docDEC as Document
Set docIBM = Documents.Open("d:\Word\InvoiceToIBM.doc")
Set docDEC = Documents.Open("d:\Word\InvoiceToDEC.doc")
```

Of course, there are exceptions to all rules, but in general, it is better to choose descriptive names for variables (as well as other items that require naming, such as constants, procedures, controls, forms, and code modules).

Second, a variable name should reflect something about the properties of the variable, such as its data type. Many programmers use a convention in which the first few characters of a variable's name indicate the data type of the variable. This is sometimes referred to as a Hungarian naming convention, after the Hungarian programmer Charles Simonyi, who is credited with its invention.

Tables 5-3 and 5-4 describe the naming convention that I will generally use for standard and object variables, respectively. Of course, you are free to make changes for your own personal use, but you should at least try to be reasonably consistent. These prefixes are intended to remind us of the data type, but it is not easy to do this perfectly using only a couple of characters, and the longer the prefix, the less likely it is that we will use it! (Note the `c` prefix for integers or longs. This is a commonly used prefix when the variable is intended to count something.)

Table 5-3. Naming Convention for Standard Variables

Variable	Prefix
Boolean	b or f
Byte	b or bt
Currency	cur
Date	dt
Double	d or dbl
Integer	i, c, or int
Long	l, c, or lng

Table 5-3. Naming Convention for Standard Variables (continued)

Variable	Prefix
Single	s or sng
String	s or str
User-defined type	u or ut
Variant	v or var

Table 5-4. Naming Convention for Some Object Variables

Variable	Prefix
Bookmark	bmk
Dialog	dial
Document	doc
Field	fld
Font	fnt
Frame	fra
Paragraph	para
Range	rng
Selection	sel
Table	tbl
Word	wrd

In addition to a data type, every variable has a scope and a lifetime. Some programmers advocate including a hint as to the scope of a variable in the prefix, using g for global and m for module level. For example, the variable giSize is a global variable of type Integer. I discuss the scope and lifetime of a variable next (but I do not include scope prefixes in variable names).

Variable Scope

Variables and constants have a scope, which indicates where in the program the variable or constant is recognized (or visible to the code). The scope of a variable or constant can be either *procedure-level* (also called local), *module-level private*, or *module-level public*. The rules may seem a bit involved at first, but they do make sense.

Procedure-level (local) variables

A local or procedure-level variable or constant is a variable or constant that is declared within a procedure, as is the case with the variable LocalVar and the constant LocalConstant in Figure 5-2. A local variable or constant is not visible outside of the procedure. Thus, for instance, if we try to run *ProcedureB* in Figure 5-2, we will get the error message "Variable not defined," and the name LocalVar will be highlighted.

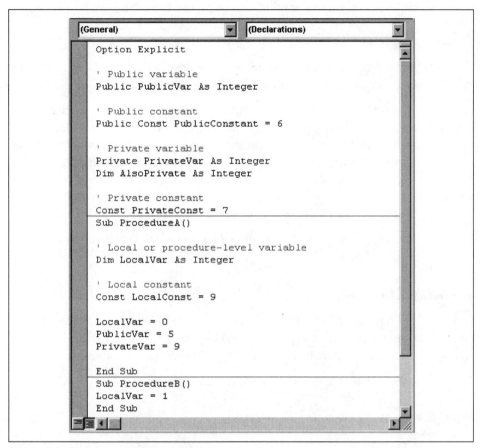

Figure 5-2. Examples of variable scope

One of the advantages of local variables is that you can use the same name in different procedures without conflict, since each variable is visible only to its own procedure.

Module-level variables

A module-level variable (or constant) is one that is declared in the declarations section of a code module (standard, class, or UserForm). Module-level variables and constants come in two flavors: private and public. Simply put, a module-level public variable (or constant) is available to all procedures in all of the modules in the project, not just the module in which it is declared, whereas a module-level private variable (or constant) is available only to the procedures in the module in which it was declared.

Public variables and constants are declared using the **Public** keyword, as in:

```
Public APubInt As Integer
Public Const APubConst = 7
```

Private variables and constants are declared using the `Private` keyword, as in:

```
Private APrivateInt As Integer
Private Const APrivateConst = 7
```

The `Dim` keyword, when used at the module level, has the same scope as `Private` but is not as clear, so it should be avoided.

There is one more catch to scoping. A `Public` variable or constant declared in a standard module or class module (but not a UserForm module) is also visible within any project that references the project in which the variable is declared. For instance, since a document project always references its attached template's project, any public variables or constants declared in the template's project are also visible in the document's project. In addition, any public variables or constants declared in the Normal project are visible in all projects.

Public variables are also referred to as *global variables*, but this descriptive term is not de rigueur.

Variable Lifetime

Variables also have a *lifetime*. The difference between lifetime and scope is quite simple: lifetime refers to how long (or when) the variable is valid (that is, retains a value), whereas scope refers to where the variable is accessible or visible.

To illustrate the difference, consider the following procedure:

```
Sub ProcedureA()
    Dim LocalVar As Integer
    LocalVar = 0
    Call ProcedureB
    LocalVar = 1
End Sub
```

Note that `LocalVar` is a local variable. When the line:

```
Call ProcedureB
```

is executed, execution switches to *ProcedureB*. While the lines of *ProcedureB* are being executed, the variable `LocalVar` is out of scope, since it is local to *ProcedureA*. But it is still valid. In other words, the variable still exists and has a value, but it is simply not accessible to the code in *ProcedureB*. In fact, *ProcedureB* could also have a local variable named `LocalVar`, which would have nothing to do with the variable of the same name in *ProcedureA*.

Once *ProcedureB* has completed, execution continues in *ProcedureA* with the line:

```
LocalVar = 1
```

which is a valid instruction, since the variable `LocalVar` is back in scope.

Thus, the lifetime of the local variable `LocalVar` extends from the moment that *ProcedureA* is entered to the moment that it is terminated, including the period during which *ProcedureB* is being executed as a result of the call to this procedure, even though during that period, `LocalVar` is out of scope.

Incidentally, you may notice that the Microsoft help files occasionally mix up the notions of scope and visibility. The creators of the files seem to understand the difference, but they don't always use the terms correctly.

Static variables

To repeat, a variable may go in and out of scope and yet remain valid during that time, that is, retain a value during that time. However, once the lifetime of a variable expires, the variable is destroyed and its value is lost. It is the lifetime that determines the existence of a variable; its scope determines its visibility.

Thus, consider the following procedures:

```
Sub ProcedureA()
    Call ProcedureB
    Call ProcedureB
    Call ProcedureB
    Call ProcedureB
    Call ProcedureB
End Sub
Sub ProcedureB()
    Dim x As Integer
    x = 5
    . . .
End Sub
```

When *ProcedureA* is executed, it simply calls *ProcedureB* five times. Each time *ProcedureB* is called, the local variable **x** is created anew and destroyed at the end of that call. Thus, **x** is created and destroyed five times.

Normally, this is just want we want. However, there are times when we would like the lifetime of a local variable to persist longer than the lifetime of the procedure in which it is declared. As an example, we may want a procedure to do something special the first time it is called, but not subsequent times. For instance, the following one-line macro changes the font of the selected text to Comic Sans:

```
Sub ToComic()
    Selection.Font.Name = "Comic Sans"
End Sub
```

Suppose, however, that we want to warn the user that Comic Sans is a bit informal and ask whether he or she really wants to make this change. We don't want to make a pest of ourselves by asking every time the user invokes this macro. What we need is a local variable with a "memory" that will allow it to keep track of whether a particular call to *ToComic* is the first call or not. This is done with a static variable.

A *static variable* is a local variable whose lifetime is the lifetime of the entire module, not just the procedure in which it was declared. In fact, a static variable retains its value as long as the document or template containing the code module is active (even if no code is running).

Thus, a static variable has the scope of a local variable, but the lifetime of a module-level variable. *C'est tout dire!*

Consider now the modification of the preceding macro, which is shown in Example 5-2. The code first declares a static Boolean variable called `NotFirst-Time`. It may seem simpler to use a variable called `FirstTime`, but there is a problem: namely, Boolean variables are automatically initialized as False, so the first time that the *ToComic* macro is run, `FirstTime` would be False, which is not want we want. (I discuss variable initialization a bit later.)

Example 5-2. ToComic() Modified to Use a Static Variable

```
Sub ToComic()

' Declare static Boolean variable
Static NotFirstTime As Boolean

' If first time, then ask for permission
If NotFirstTime = False Then

   If MsgBox("Comic Sans is a bit informal. Proceed?", _
             vbYesNo) = vbYes Then

       ' Make the change
     Selection.Font.Name = "Comic Sans MS"

   End If

   ' No longer the first time
   NotFirstTime = True

Else

    ' If not the first time, just make the change
   Selection.Font.Name = "Comic Sans MS"

End If

End Sub
```

The `If` statement checks to see whether the value of `NotFirstTime` is False, as it will be the first time the procedure is called. In this case, a message box is displayed, as shown in Figure 5-3. If the user chooses the Yes button, the font is changed. In either case, the static Boolean variable `NotFirstTime` is set to True. Precisely because `NotFirstTime` is static, this value will be retained even after the macro ends (but not if the document is closed).

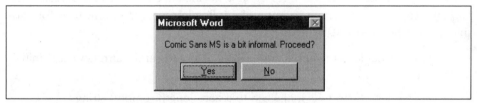

Figure 5-3. Dialog that appears if the static NotFirstTime is false

The next time the macro is executed, the variable `NotFirstTime` will be True, so the `If` condition:

```
If NotFirstTime = False Then
```

will be False and the *MsgBox* function will not be executed. Instead, the **Else** code will execute. This code just changes the font, without bothering the user with a message box. Static variables are not used very often, but they can be quite useful at times.

It may have occurred to you that you could accomplish the same effect by using a module-level private variable to keep a record of whether the macro has been called, instead of a static local variable. However, it is considered better programming style to use the most restrictive scope possible, which, in this case, is a local variable with an "extended" lifetime. This helps prevent accidental alteration of the variable in other portions of the code. (Remember that this code may be part of a much larger code module with a lot of things going on. It is better to hide the `NotFirstTime` variable from this other code.)

Variable Initialization

When a procedure begins execution, all of its local variables are automatically initialized, that is, given initial values. In general, however, it is not good programming practice to rely on this initialization, since it makes the program less readable and somewhat more prone to logical errors. Thus, it is a good idea to initialize all local variables explicitly, as in the following example:

```
Sub Example()

Dim x As Integer
Dim s As String

x = 0        ' Initialize x to 0
s = ""       ' Initialize s to empty string

' more code here . . .

End Sub
```

Note, however, that static variables cannot be initialized, since that defeats their purpose! Thus, it is important to know the following rules that VBA uses for variable initialization (note also that they are intuitive):

- Numeric variables (Integer, Long, Single, Double, and Currency) are initialized to zero.

- A variable-length string is initialized to a zero-length (empty) string.

- A fixed-length string is filled with the character represented by the ASCII character code 0, or *Chr*(0).

- Variant variables are initialized to **Empty**.

- Object variables are initialized to **Nothing**.

The **Nothing** keyword actually has several related uses in Word VBA. As you will see in Chapter 8, it is used to release an object variable. Also, it is used as a return value for some functions, generally to indicate that some operation has failed. Finally, it is used to initialize object variables.

VBA Operators

VBA uses a handful of simple operators and relations, the most common of which are shown in Table 5-5.

Table 5-5. VBA Operators and Relations

Type	Name	Symbol
Arithmetic Operators	Addition	+
	Subtraction	–
	Multiplication	*
	Division	/
	Division with Integer result	\
	Exponentiation	^
	Modulo	Mod
String Operator	Concatenation	&
Logical Operators	AND	And
	OR	Or
	NOT	Not
Comparison Relations	Equal	=
	Less than	<
	Greater than	>
	Less than or equal to	<=
	Greater than or equal to	>=
	Not equal to	<>

The **Mod** operator returns the remainder after division. For example:

```
8 Mod 3
```

returns 2, since the remainder after dividing 8 by 3 is 2.

To illustrate string concatenation, the expression:

```
"To be or " & "not to be"
```

is equivalent to:

```
"To be or not to be"
```

6

In this chapter:
- *Calling Functions*
- *Calling Subroutines*
- *Parameters and Arguments*
- *Exiting a Procedure*
- *Public and Private Procedures*
- *Referencing a Project*

Functions and Subroutines

As we have seen, VBA allows two kinds of procedures: *functions* and *subroutines*. As a reminder, the only difference between a function and a subroutine is that a function returns a value.

Calling Functions

A function declaration has the form:

```
[Public or Private] Function FunctionName(Param1 As DataType1, _
        ,Param2 As DataType2,...) As ReturnType
```

Note that you must declare the data types not only of each parameter to the function, but also of the return type. Otherwise, VBA declares these items as variants.

I discuss the optional keywords **Public** and **Private** later, but you can probably guess that they are used here to indicate the scope of the function, just as they are used in variable declarations. For example, the *AddOne* function in Example 6-1 adds 1 to the original value.

Example 6-1. The AddOne Function

```
Public Function AddOne(Value As Integer) As Integer
   AddOne = Value + 1
End Function
```

To use the return value of a function, just place the call to the function within the expression in the location where you want the value. For instance, the code:

```
    MsgBox "Adding 1 to 5 gives: " & AddOne(5)
```

produces the message box in Figure 6-1, where the expression *AddOne*(5) is replaced by the return value of *AddOne*, which in this case is 6.

Figure 6-1. The message dialog displayed by Example 6-1

Note that in general, any parameters to a function must be enclosed in parentheses within the function call.

To return a value from a function, we must assign the function's name to the return value somewhere within the body of the function. Example 6-2 shows a more complicated example of a function.

Example 6-2. Assigning a Function's Return Value

```
Function ReturnCount(OfWhat As String) As Long

' Return count of characters or words
' in the active document. Return -1 if
' OfWhat is not "Characters" or "Words"

If OfWhat = "Characters" Then
    ' Return count of characters
    ReturnCount = ActiveDocument.Characters.Count
ElseIf OfWhat = "Words" Then
    ' Return count of words
    ReturnCount = ActiveDocument.Words.Count
Else
    ' Return -1
    ReturnCount = -1
End If

End Function
```

This function returns a count of the number of characters or the number of words in the active document, depending on the value of the parameter to the function. (I will discuss parameters in more detail later in this chapter.) Note that **Return-Count** is assigned several times within the body of the function. Its value, and hence the value of the function, is set differently depending upon the value of the parameter. (Since these assignments are mutually exclusive, only one of them will occur each time the function is called.)

Ignoring Return Values

Since functions can do more than just return a value, there are situations where we want to call a function but we don't care about its return value. To illustrate, suppose that **rng** is a variable that represents a range of text within a Word document. Then we can adjust the end of this range using Word's MoveEnd method. This method is just a function that moves the end of the range a specified number of units and returns the actual number of units moved, which may be less than the specified number if the range "bumps up" to the beginning or end of the document before completion.

For instance, the code:

```
Dim dist as Long
dist = rng.MoveEnd(wdCharacter, 5)
```

attempts to move the end of **rng** five characters to the right. If it is successful, it returns the number 5. However, if there are fewer than five characters to the right of the current end position, then the range is moved as many characters as possible and this value is returned.

The return value of the *MoveEnd* method can often be useful, but there are times when it is not. For instance, the following code selects the first paragraph in the active document, including the ending paragraph mark:

```
Dim rng As Range
Set rng = ActiveDocument.Paragraphs(1).Range
rng.Select
```

If we do not want to include the ending paragraph, we can use the *MoveEnd* method to move the end of the range one character to the left before selecting it, as follows:

```
Dim dist as Long
Dim rng As Range
Set rng = ActiveDocument.Paragraphs(1).Range
dist = rng.MoveEnd(wdCharacter, -1)
rng.Select
```

Since there is at least one character to the left of the current end point (the paragraph mark is always present, so the range includes at least this character), we know that the return value **dist** of the *MoveEnd* function will be −1. (It is negative since the move is to the left.) Hence, we don't really care about **dist**.

In previous versions of VBA, we would have had no choice but to declare the variable **dist** and then just ignore its value, as in the previous code. However, the current version of VBA lets us streamline this code to:

```
Dim rng As Range
Set rng = ActiveDocument.Paragraphs(1).Range
rng.MoveEnd wdCharacter, -1
rng.Select
```

Note that the function is called without specifying a return value and without the parentheses surrounding the parameters. This tells VBA to simply discard the return value.

Calling Subroutines

A subroutine declaration has the form:

```
[Public or Private] Sub SubroutineName(Param1 As DataType1, _
        Param2 As DataType2,...)
```

This is similar to the function declaration, with the notable absence of the `As ReturnType` portion. (Note also the word `Sub` in place of `Function`.)

Since subroutines do not return a value, they cannot be used within an expression. To call a subroutine named *SubroutineA*, we can write either:

```
Call SubroutineA(parameters, . . .)
```

or simply:

```
SubroutineA parameters, . . .
```

Note that any parameters must be enclosed in parentheses when using the `Call` keyword, but not otherwise.

Parameters and Arguments

Consider the following very simple subroutine, which does nothing more than display a message box declaring a person's name:

```
Sub DisplayName(sName As String)
    MsgBox "My name is " & sName
End Sub
```

To call this subroutine, we would write, for example:

```
DisplayName "Wolfgang"
```

or:

```
Call DisplayName("Wolfgang")
```

The variable `sName` in the procedure declaration:

```
Sub DisplayName(sName As String)
```

is called a *parameter* of the procedure. In general, it must be filled in when we call the procedure (see the discussion of optional parameters coming soon). The value used in place of the parameter when we make the procedure call is called an *argument*. Thus, in the previous example, the argument is the string "Wolfgang".

Note that many programmers fail to make a distinction between a parameter and an argument, using the names interchangeably. However, since a parameter is like a variable and an argument is like a value of that variable, failing to make this distinction is like failing to distinguish between a variable and its value!

Optional Arguments

In VBA, the arguments to a procedure may be specified as optional, using the **Optional** keyword. (It makes no sense to say that a parameter is optional; it is assigning its value that is optional.) To illustrate, consider the procedure in Example 6-3, which simply changes the font name and font size of the current selection.

Example 6-3. Using an Optional Argument

```
Sub ChangeFormatting(FontName As String, Optional FontSize As Variant)

' Change font name
Selection.Font.Name = FontName

' Change font size if argument is supplied
If Not IsMissing(FontSize) Then
    Selection.Font.Size = CInt(FontSize)
End If

End Sub
```

The second parameter is declared with the **Optional** keyword. Because of this, we may call the procedure with or without an argument for this parameter, as in:

```
    ChangeFormatting("Arial Narrow", 24)
```

and:

```
    ChangeFormatting("Arial Narrow")
```

Note that the *IsMissing* function is used in the body of the procedure to test whether the argument is present. If the argument is not missing, then the font size is changed. Note also that we declared the FontSize parameter as type Variant because *IsMissing* works only with parameters of type Variant (unfortunately). Thus, we converted the Variant to type Integer using the *CInt* function.

A procedure may have any number of optional arguments, but they must all come at the end of the parameter list. Thus, for instance, the following declaration is not legal:

```
    Sub ChangeFormatting(Optional FontName As String, FontSize As Single)
```

If we omit an optional argument in the middle of a list, we must include an empty space when calling that procedure. For instance, if a procedure is declared as follows:

```
Sub ChangeFormatting(Optional FontName As String, _
                     Optional FontSize As Single, _
                     Optional FontBold as Boolean)
```

then a call to this procedure to set the font name to Arial and the boldfacing to True would look like:

```
ChangeFormatting "Arial", , True
```

To avoid confusion, we should point out that some built-in Word procedures have optional arguments and others do not. Of course, we cannot leave out an argument unless the documentation or declaration for the procedure specifically states that it is optional.

Named Arguments

Some VBA procedures can contain a large number of parameters. For example, the Word *ConvertToTable* function formats selected text as a table. The declaration is:

```
ConvertToTable(Separator, NumRows, NumColumns, _
    InitialColumnWidth, Format, ApplyBorders, ApplyShading, _
    ApplyFont, ApplyColor, ApplyHeadingRows, ApplyLastRow, _
    ApplyFirstColumn, ApplyLastColumn, AutoFit)
```

where all of the parameters are optional and of type Variant. Here is an example of a call to this procedure:

```
ConvertToTable wdSeparateByTabs, 5, 7, , , True, True, True, _
               , , True, , , True
```

Not very readable, is it?

The arguments shown in the previous call are said to be *positional arguments* because it is their position that tells VBA which parameters they are intended to replace. This is why we need to include space for missing arguments.

However, VBA can also use named arguments, in which case the previous call would be written:

```
ConvertToTable _
    Separator:=wdSeparateByTabs, NumRows:=5, _
    NumColumns:=7, ApplyBorders:=True, _
    ApplyShading:=True, ApplyFont:=True, _
    ApplyLastRow:=True, AutoFit:=True
```

Note the special syntax for named arguments—in particular, the colon before the equal sign.

This function call is a great improvement over the positional argument version. Besides being considerably more readable, named arguments provide two other major benefits: you do not need to include space for missing arguments, and you can place the arguments in any order in the procedure call!

Named arguments can improve readability quite a bit and are highly recommended. However, they can require considerably more space, so for the short examples in this book, I generally do not use them.

ByRef Versus ByVal Parameters

Parameters come in two flavors: **ByRef** and **ByVal**. Many programmers do not have a clear understanding of these concepts, but they are very important and not that difficult to understand.

To understand the difference, consider the two procedures in Example 6-4. *ProcedureA* simply sets the value of the module-level variable x to 5, displays that value, calls the procedure *AddOne* with the argument x, and then displays the value of x again.

Example 6-4. Testing the ByVal and ByRef Keywords

```
Sub ProcedureA()
    x = 5              ' Set x to 5
    MsgBox x           ' Display x
    Call AddOne(x)      ' Call AddOne
    MsgBox x           ' Display x again
End Sub

Sub AddOne(ByRef i As Integer)
    i = i + 1
End Sub
```

Note the presence of the **ByRef** keyword in the *AddOne* procedure declaration. This keywords tells VBA to pass a reference to the variable x to the *AddOne* procedure. Therefore, the *AddOne* procedure in effect replaces its parameter i by the variable x. As a result, the line:

```
    i = i + 1
```

effectively becomes:

```
    x = x + 1
```

and so, after *AddOne* is called, the variable x has the value 6.

On the other hand, suppose we change the *AddOne* procedure, replacing the keyword **ByRef** with the keyword **ByVal**:

```
    Sub AddOne(ByVal i As Integer)
        i = i + 1
    End Sub
```

In this case, VBA does not pass a reference to the variable **x**, but rather passes its value. Hence, the variable **i** in *AddOne* simply takes on the value 5. Adding 1 to that value gives 6. Thus, **i** equals 6, but the value of the argument **x** is not affected! Hence, both message boxes will display the value 5 for **x**.

ByRef and **ByVal** both have their uses. When you want to change the value of an argument, you must declare the corresponding parameter as **ByRef**, so that the called procedure has access to the actual argument itself. This is the case in the previous example. For otherwise, the *AddOne* procedure does absolutely nothing, since the local variable **i** is incremented, but it is destroyed immediately afterwards, when the procedure ends.

On the other hand, when you pass an argument for informational purposes only, and you do not want the argument to be altered, then it should be passed by value, using the **ByVal** keyword. In this way, the called procedure gets only the value of the argument.

To illustrate further, *ProcedureA* in Example 6-5 gets the text of the active document and "feeds" it to the *CountCharacters* function. The returned value (the number of characters in the active document) is then displayed in a message box.

Example 6-5. Passing an Argument by Value

```
Sub ProcedureA()
   Dim sText As String
   sText = ActiveDocument.Content.Text
   MsgBox CountCharacters(sText)
End Sub

Function CountCharacters(ByVal sTxt As String)
   CountCharacters = Len(sTxt)
End Function
```

Now, *CountCharacters* does not need to—and indeed should not—change the text. It only counts the number of characters in the text. This is why we pass the argument by value. In this way, the variable **sTxt** gets the value of the text in **sText**; that is, it gets a copy of the text.

To appreciate the importance of this, imagine for a moment that *CountCharacters* is replaced by a procedure that contains hundreds or thousands of lines of code, written by someone else, perhaps not as reliable as we are. Naturally, we are concerned that this procedure should not change our text. Rather than having to check the code for errors, all we need to do is notice that the **sTxt** parameter is called by value, which tells us that the procedure does not even have access to our text! Instead, it gets only a copy of the text.

There is one downside to passing arguments by value. For instance, in the previous example, VBA needs to make a copy of the text to pass to the parameter

sTxt. This can take a lot of memory (and time), especially since in this case we are passing the contents of the entire document. If the document is several hundred thousand characters long, the procedure might be just too slow.

Thus, to summarize, if you want the procedure to modify an argument, it must be passed by reference. If not, the argument should be passed by value, unless this will produce an unacceptable decrease in performance, or unless you are very sure that it will not get changed by accident.

It is important to note that VBA defaults to **ByRef** if you do not specify otherwise. This means that the values of arguments are subject to change by the called procedure, unless you explicitly include the keyword **ByVal**. Caveat scriptor!

Exiting a Procedure

VBA provides the **Exit Sub** and **Exit Function** statements, should you want to exit from a procedure before the procedure would terminate naturally. For instance, if the value of a parameter is not suitable, you might want to issue a warning to the user and exit, as Example 6-6 shows.

Example 6-6. Using the Exit Sub Statement

```
Sub DisplayName(sName As String)
   If sName = "" then
      Msgbox "Please enter a name."
      Exit Sub
   End If
   MsgBox "Name entered is " & sName

End Sub
```

Public and Private Procedures

Just as variables and constants have a scope, so do procedures. We can declare a procedure using the **Public** or **Private** keyword, as in:

```
    Public Function AddOne(i As Integer) As Integer
```

or:

```
    Private Function AddOne(i As Integer) As Integer
```

The difference is simple: a **Private** procedure can be called only from within the module in which it is defined, whereas a **Public** procedure can be called from within any module in the project.

Note that if the **Public** or **Private** keyword is omitted from a procedure declaration, then the procedure is considered to be **Public**.

Referencing a Project

For code in one project to call a public procedure in another project, the calling project must have a reference to the called project.

Generally, a project that is associated with a document is interested only in procedures that lie in that project, in the template that is attached to the document, or in the Normal template. (It would probably be bad programming practice to require a procedure in one document project to call a procedure in another document project.)

In the first case, no references need be set. The second case is taken care of by Word, since it automatically provides a reference to the attached template.

On the other hand, if the attached template is not the Normal template and you want to call a procedure in the Normal template, or if you want to call a procedure in another nonreferenced project, then you need to add a reference to the calling project. This is done using the References dialog box (under the Tools menu) shown in Figure 6-2.

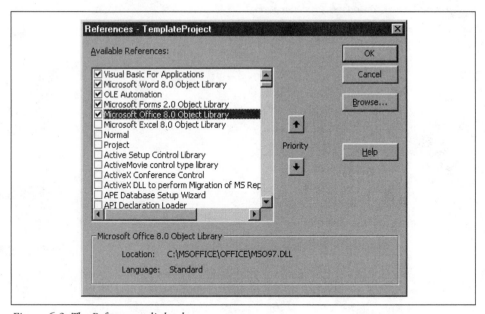

Figure 6-2. The References dialog box

It is important to note that if the template that is attached to a document is not the Normal template, then Word does not automatically provide a reference to the Normal project in the document project. This may seem a bit surprising, for although we can execute any macros that reside in the Normal template from within the document itself (using the Macros menu item, for instance), we cannot call such macros from code within the document project without first adding a reference to the Normal project.

Fully Qualified Procedure Names

When you call a public procedure that lies in another module, there is a potential problem with ambiguity, for there may be more than one public procedure with the same name in different modules. VBA will execute the first one it finds, and this may not be the one you had in mind!

The solution is to use a qualified procedure name, which has the form:

```
ModuleName.ProcedureName
```

For instance, if a public procedure named *AddOne* lies in a module named Utilities, then you can call this procedure using the syntax:

```
Utilities.AddOne
```

If necessary, you can also specify the project name, using the syntax:

```
ProjectName.ModuleName.ProcedureName
```

7

Built-in Functions and Statements

VBA has a large number of built-in functions and subroutines. We will take a look at a few of the more commonly used ones (at least for programming Word VBA) in this chapter and the next. The VBA functions are:

Abs	DateSerial	Int	Oct
Array	DateValue	Ipmt	Partition
Asc	Day	IRR	Pmt
AscB	DDB	IsArray	PPmt
AscW	Dir	IsDate	PV
Atn	DoEvents	IsEmpty	QBColor
Cbool	Environ	IsError	Rate
Cbyte	EOF	IsMissing	RGB
Ccur	Error	IsNull	Right
Cdate	Exp	IsNumeric	RightB
CDbl	FileAttr	IsObject	Rnd
Cdec	FileDateTime	Lbound	RTrim
Choose	FileLen	Lcase	Second
Chr	Fix	Left	Seek
ChrB	Format	LeftB	Sgn
ChrW	FreeFile	Len	Shell
Cint	FV	LenB	Sin
CLng	GetAllSettings	LoadPicture	SLN
Command	GetAttr	Loc	Space
Cos	GetAutoServerSettings	LOF	Spc
CreateObject	GetObject	Log	Sqr
CSng	GetSetting	Ltrim	Str
CStr	Hex	Mid	StrComp
CurDir	Hour	MidB	StrConv
Cvar	Iif	Minute	String
CVDate	IMEStatus	MIRR	Switch
CVErr	Input	Month	SYD
Date	InputB	MsgBox	Tab
DateAdd	InputBox	Now	Tan
DateDiff	InStr	Nper	Time
DatePart	InStrB	NPV	Timer

TimeSerial	TypeName	Val	Year
TimeValue	UBound	VarType	
Trim	UCase	Weekday	

The VBA statements are:

AppActivate	Do...Loop	Mid	Reset
Beep	End	MidB	Resume
Call	Enum	MkDir	Return
ChDir	Erase	Name	RmDir
ChDrive	Error	On Error	RSet
Close	Event	On...GoSub	SavePicture
Const	Exit	On...GoTo	SaveSetting
Date	FileCopy	Open	Seek
Declare	For Each...Next	Option Base	Select Case
DefBool	For...Next	Option Compare	SendKeys
DefByte	Function	Option Explicit	Set
DefCur	Get	Option Private	SetAttr
DefDate	GoSub...Return	Print #	Static
DefDbl	GoTo	Private	Stop
DefDec	If...Then...Else	Property Get	Sub
DefInt	Implements	Property Let	Time
DefLng	Input #	Property Set	Type
DefObj	Kill	Public	Unload
DefSng	Let	Put	Unlock
DefStr	Line Input #	RaiseEvent	While...Wend
DefVar	Load	Randomize	Width #
DeleteSetting	Lock	ReDim	With
Dim	LSet	Rem	Write #

To help simplify the exposition, I follow Microsoft's lead and use square brackets to indicate optional parameters. Thus, for instance, the second parameter in the following procedure is optional:

```
Sub ChangeFormat(FontName [, FontSize])
```

Note that I have also omitted the data type declarations, which will be discussed separately.

The MsgBox Function

I have been using the *MsgBox* function unofficially for some time now. Let me introduce it officially. The *MsgBox* function is used to display a message and wait for the user to respond by pushing a button. The most commonly used syntax is:

```
MsgBox(prompt [, buttons] [, title])
```

(This is not the most general syntax possible. There are some additional optional parameters related to help contexts that you can look up in the help documentation.)

In this example, ***prompt*** is a String parameter containing the message to be displayed in the dialog box. Note that a multiline message can be created by interspersing the **vbCrLf** constant within the message.

Next, ***buttons*** is a Long parameter giving the sum of values that specify various properties of the message box. These properties include the number and type of buttons to display, the icon style to use, the identity of the default button, and the modality of the message box. (A *system modal* dialog box remains on top of all currently open windows and captures the input focus systemwide, whereas an *application modal* dialog box remains on top of the application's windows only and captures the application's focus.) The various values of ***buttons*** that can be summed are shown in Table 7-1. (They are officially defined in the **VbMsgBox-Style** enum.)

Table 7-1. The MsgBox buttons Argument Values

Purpose	Constant	Value	Description
Button Types	vbOKOnly	0	Display OK button only
	vbOKCancel	1	Display OK and Cancel buttons
	vbAbortRetryIgnore	2	Display Abort, Retry, and Ignore buttons
	vbYesNoCancel	3	Display Yes, No, and Cancel buttons
	vbYesNo	4	Display Yes and No buttons
	vbRetryCancel	5	Display Retry and Cancel buttons
Icon Types	vbCritical	16	Display Critical Message icon
	vbQuestion	32	Display Warning Query icon
	vbExclamation	48	Display Warning Message icon
	vbInformation	64	Display Information Message icon
Default Button	vbDefaultButton1	0	First button is default
	vbDefaultButton2	256	Second button is default
	vbDefaultButton3	512	Third button is default
	vbDefaultButton4	768	Fourth button is default
Modality	vbApplicationModal	0	Application modal message box
	vbSystemModal	4096	System modal message box

For instance, the code:

```
MsgBox "Proceed?", vbQuestion + vbYesNo
```

displays the message box shown in Figure 7-1, which includes a question mark icon and two command buttons, labeled Yes and No.

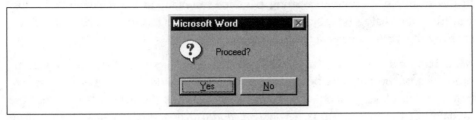

Figure 7-1. A MsgBox dialog box

The `title` parameter is a string expression that is displayed in the titlebar of the dialog box. If we omit this argument, then "Microsoft Word" will be displayed, as in Figure 7-1.

The *MsgBox* function returns a number indicating which button was selected. These return values are given in Table 7-2. (They are officially defined in the VbMsgBoxResult enum.)

Table 7-2. MsgBox Return Values

Constant	Value	Description
vbOK	1	OK button pressed
vbCancel	2	Cancel button pressed
vbAbort	3	Abort button pressed
vbRetry	4	Retry button pressed
vbIgnore	5	Ignore button pressed
vbYes	6	Yes button pressed
vbNo	7	No button pressed

The InputBox Function

The *InputBox* function is designed to get input from the user. The most commonly used (but not the complete) syntax is:

```
InputBox(prompt [, title] [, default])
```

where **prompt** is the message in the input box, `title` is the title for the input box, and `default` is the default value that is displayed in the text box. For instance, the code:

```
sName = InputBox("Enter your name.", "Name", "Albert")
```

produces the dialog box in Figure 7-2.

The *InputBox* function returns the string that the user enters into the text box. Thus, in our example, the string variable sName will contain this string.

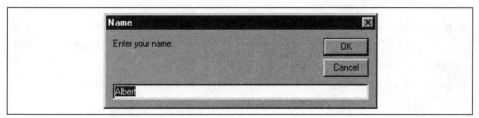

Figure 7-2. An InputBox dialog box

Note that if we want a number from the user, we can still use the *InputBox* function and simply convert the returned string (such as "12.55") to a number (12.55) using the *Val* function, discussed later in this chapter.

VBA String Functions

Here are a handful of useful functions that apply to strings (both constants and variables):

The Len function

The *Len* function returns the length of a string; that is, the number of characters in the string. Thus, the code:

```
Len("January Invoice")
```

returns the number 15.

The UCase and LCase functions

These functions return an all uppercase or all lowercase version of the string argument. The syntax is:

```
UCase(string)
LCase(string)
```

For instance:

```
MsgBox UCase("Donna")
```

will display the string "DONNA".

The Left, Right, and Mid functions

These functions return a portion of a string. In particular:

```
Left(string, number)
```

returns the leftmost *number* characters in *string* and:

```
Right(string, number)
```

returns the rightmost *number* characters in *string*. For instance:

```
MsgBox Right("Donna Smith", 5)
```

displays the string "Smith".

The syntax for *Mid* is:

```
Mid(string, start, length)
```

This function returns the first **length** number of characters of **string**, starting at character number **start**. For instance:

```
Mid("Library.doc",9,3)
```

returns the string "doc". If the **length** parameter is missing, as in:

```
Mid("Library.doc",9)
```

the function will return the rest of the string, starting at **start**.

The Instr function

The syntax for this very useful function is:

```
Instr(Start, StringToSearch, StringToFind)
```

The return value is the position, starting at **Start**, of the first occurrence of **StringToFind** within **StringToSearch**. If **Start** is missing, then the function starts searching at the beginning of **StringToSearch**. For instance:

```
MsgBox Instr( , "Donna Smith", "Smith")
```

displays the number 7, because "Smith" begins at the seventh position in the string "Donna Smith".

The Str and Val functions

The *Str* function converts a number to a string. For instance:

```
Str(123)
```

returns the string "123". Conversely, the *Val* function converts a string that represents a number into a number (so that we can do arithmetic with it, for instance). For example:

```
Val("4.5")
```

returns the number 4.5 and:

```
Val("1234 Main Street")
```

returns the number 1234. Note, however, that *Val* does not recognize dollar signs or commas. Thus:

```
Val($12.00)
```

returns 0, not 12.00.

The Trim, LTrim, and RTrim functions

The *LTrim* function removes leading spaces from a string. Similarly, *RTrim* removes trailing spaces and *Trim* removes both leading and trailing spaces. Thus:

```
Trim("  extra   ")
```

returns the string "extra".

The String and Space functions

The *String* function provides a way to create a string quickly that consists of a single character repeated a number of times. For instance:

```
sText = String(25, "A")
```

sets **sText** to a string consisting of 25 As. Also, the *Space* function returns a string consisting of a given number of spaces. For instance:

```
sText = Space(25)
```

sets **sText** to a string consisting of 25 spaces.

The Like operator and StrCmp function

The **Like** operator is very useful for comparing two strings. Of course, we can use the equal sign:

```
string1 = string2
```

which is True when the two strings are identical. However, **Like** will also make a case-insensitive comparison or allow the use of pattern matching.

The expression:

```
string Like pattern
```

returns True if *string* fits *pattern* and False otherwise. (Actually, the expression can return **Null**, but I won't go into that here, since it is much more likely to happen in Access VBA than Word VBA.) I will describe *pattern* in a moment.

The type of string comparison that the **Like** operator uses depends upon the setting of the **Option Compare** statement. There are two possibilities:

```
Option Compare Binary
Option Compare Text
```

one of which should be placed in the Declarations section of a module (in the same place as **Option Explicit**). Note that the default is **Option Compare Binary**.

Under **Option Compare Binary**, string comparison is in the order given by the ANSI character code:

A < B < . . . < Z < a < b < . . . < z < À < . . . < Ø < à < . . . < ø

Under **Option Compare Text**, string comparison is based on a case-insensitive sort order (determined by your PC's locale setting). This gives a sort order as follows:

A = a < À = à < B = b < . . . < Z = z < Ø = ø

By the way, the last item in the **Text** sort order is the [character, with ANSI value 91. This is useful to know if you want to place an item last in alphabetical order—just surround it by square brackets.

The pattern-matching features of the `Like` operator allow the use of wildcard characters, character lists, or character ranges. For example:

?   matches any single character

*   matches zero or more characters

matches any single digit (0–9)

[charlist]

> matches any single character in `charlist`

[!charlist]

> matches any single character not in `charlist`

For more details, check the VBA help file.

The *StrCmp* function also compares two strings. Its syntax is:

```
StrCmp(string1, string2 [, compare])
```

and it returns a value indicating whether **string1** is equal to, greater than, or less than **string2**. For more details, check the VBA help file.

Miscellaneous Functions and Statements

The Immediate If function

The *Immediate If* function has the syntax:

```
IIf(Expression, TruePart, FalsePart)
```

If **Expression** is True, then the function returns **TruePart**. If **Expression** is False, the function returns **FalsePart**. For instance, the following code displays a dialog box indicating whether the first paragraph in the active document is too long (that is, if it contains over 100 words):

```
Dim cWords As Long
cWords = ActiveDocument.Paragraphs(1).Range.Words.count

MsgBox "First paragraph is " & _
       IIf(cWords > 100, "too long", "not too long")
```

It is very important to note that the *Immediate If* function (*IIf*) always evaluates *both* **TruePart** and **FalsePart**, even though it returns only one of them. Hence, we must be careful about undesirable side effects. For example, the following code will produce a division-by-zero error because even though the *IIf* function returns $1/x$ only when x is not equal to 0, the expression $1/x$ is evaluated in all cases, including when $x = 0$:

```
x = 0
y = IIf(x = 0, x ^ 2, 1 / x)
```

The Switch function

The syntax of the *Switch* function is:

```
Switch(expr1, value1, expr2, value2, ... , exprn, valuen)
```

where **exprx** and **valuex** are expressions. Note that there need be only one expression-value pair, but the function is more meaningful if there are at least two such pairs.

The *Switch* function evaluates each expression **exprx**. When it encounters the first True expression, it returns the corresponding value. As with the *IIf* function, *Switch* always evaluates all of the expressions. If none of the expressions is True, the function returns **Null**. This can be tested with the *IsNull* function.

For example, the procedure in Example 7-1 displays the type of Word document based on its extension: Document or Template.

Example 7-1. The Switch Function

```
Sub ShowDocType(DocExt As String)

Dim DocType As Variant

DocType = Switch(DocExt = "dot", "Template", _
                 DocExt = "doc", "Document")

' Display result
If Not IsNull(DocType) Then
    MsgBox DocType
Else
    MsgBox "Unrecognized type"
End If

End Sub
```

There is one subtlety in this code. Since the *Switch* function can return a **Null** value, you cannot assign the return value to a String variable, as you might first try to do:

```
Dim DocType As String

DocType = Switch(DocExt = "dot", "Template", _
                 DocExt = "doc", "Document")
```

This will not produce an error *unless* **DocExt** is not "dot" or "doc," in which case you will get the very annoying error message "Invalid use of Null." The solution is to declare **DocType** as a Variant, which can hold any data type, including *no* data type, which is indicated by the **Null** keyword. (This issue can be avoided by using a **Select Case** statement, discussed in the next chapter.)

The Units conversions

The *InchesToPoints* function converts a measurement given in inches to one given in points (a printer's measurement; there are 72 points in an inch). The reason that this is important is that many Word values must be given in points, but most of us prefer to think in inches.

For example, the LeftIndent property is used to set the left indent value of a paragraph and requires a value in points. Thus, to set the left indent of the first paragraph in the active Word document to .25 inches, we would write:

```
ActiveDocument.Paragraphs(1).LeftIndent = _
        InchesToPoints(.25)
```

There is also a *PointsToInches* function that is useful for displaying the return value of a function in inches when the function returns the value in points.

Similarly, Word supports the following conversion functions:

- *CentimetersToPoints* and *PointsToCentimeters*

- *MillimetersToPoints* and *PointsToMillimeters*

- *LinesToPoints* and *PointsToLines* (1 line = 12 points = $1/6$ inch)

- *PicasToPoints* and *PointsToPicas* (1 pica = 12 points = $1/6$ inch)

The Beep statement

This simple statement, whose syntax is:

```
Beep
```

sounds a single tone through the computer's speakers. It can be useful (when used with restraint) to get the user's attention. However, there is a caveat: the results are dependent upon the computer's hardware, so the statement may not produce a sound at all. Thus, if you use this statement in your code, be sure to warn the user. (It is possible to use the Word status bar to display messages to the user that do not interfere with execution of a program. You will see some examples of this in later chapters.)

8

Control Statements

I conclude our discussion of the VBA language with a discussion of the main VBA *control statements*, which are statements that affect the flow of control (or flow of execution) in a program.

The If ... Then Statement

The `If...Then` statement is used for conditional control. The syntax is:

```
If Condition Then
    ' statements go here . . .
ElseIf AnotherCondition Then
    ' more statements go here . . .
Else
    ' more statements go here . . .
End If
```

Note that you may include more than one **ElseIf** part and that both the **ElseIf** part(s) and the **Else** part are optional. We can also squeeze all parts of this statement onto a single line, which is generally only a good idea when the **ElseIf** and **Else** parts are missing.

As an example, the following code deletes the current selection in the active Word document if it contains the word "Bartok":

```
Dim sText As String
sText = Selection.Text
If InStr(sText, "Bartok") Then Selection.Delete
```

The following example changes the font size of the selected text based upon its style. If the style is not Heading 1, Heading 2, or Heading 3, then the point size is set to 11 points:

```
If Selection.Style = "Heading 1" Then
    Selection.Font.Size = 24
```

```
ElseIf Selection.Style = "Heading 2" Then
    Selection.Font.Size = 18
ElseIf Selection.Style = "Heading 3" Then
    Selection.Font.Size = 14
Else
    Selection.Font.Size = 11
End If
```

The For Loop

The `For...Next` statement provides a method for repeatedly looping through a block of code (that is, one or more lines of code). This loop is naturally referred to as a `For` loop. The basic syntax is:

```
For counter = start To end
    ' block of code goes here . . .
Next counter
```

The first time that the block of code is executed, the variable *counter* (called the loop variable for the `For` loop) is given the value *start*. Each subsequent time that the block of code is executed, the loop variable *counter* is incremented by 1. When *counter* exceeds the value *end*, the block of code is no longer executed. Thus, the code block is executed a total of *end – start* + 1 times, each time with a different value of *counter*.

Note that we can omit the word *counter* in the last line of a `For` loop (replacing `Next` *counter* with just `Next`). This may cause the `For` loop to execute a bit more quickly, but it also detracts a bit from readability.

For example, the following code loops through the collection of all paragraphs in the active Word document. (I discuss collections at length in Chapter 9, *Object Models*.) If the paragraph has style Heading 1, the style is changed to Heading 2:

```
Dim i As Integer
Dim para As Paragraph

For i = 1 To ActiveDocument.Paragraphs.Count
    ' Get the next paragraph
    Set para = ActiveDocument.Paragraphs(i)
    ' Change style from Heading 1 to Heading 2
    If para.Style = "Heading 1" Then
        para.Style = "Heading 2"
    End If

Next i
```

`For` loops are often used to initialize an array. For instance, the code:

```
For i = 0 To 10
    iArray(i) = 0
Next i
```

assigns a value of 0 to each of the 11 variables `iArray(0)` through `iArray(10)`.

Note that the loop variable *counter* will usually appear within the block of code, as it does in this array initialization example, but this is not a requirement. However, if it does appear, you need to be very careful not to change its value, since that will certainly mess up the `For` loop. (VBA automatically increments the loop variable each time through the loop, so you should leave it alone.)

You can also control the step size and direction for the counter in a `For` loop using the `Step` keyword. For instance, in the following code, the counter i is incremented by 2 each time the block of code is executed:

```
For i = 1 to 10 Step 2
    ' code block goes here
Next i
```

The following loop counts down from 10 to 1 in increments of –1. This can be useful when we want to examine a collection (such as the paragraphs in a document) from the bottom up:

```
For i = 10 to 1 Step -1
    ' code block goes here
Next i
```

Exit For

VBA provides the `Exit For` statement to exit a `For` loop prematurely. For instance, the following code finds the first paragraph in the active document whose first word is "Thanks." When this word is found, the `For` loop is exited and the paragraph is boldfaced:

```
Dim i As Integer
Dim para As Paragraph

For i = 1 To ActiveDocument.Paragraphs.Count

    ' Get the next paragraph
    Set para = ActiveDocument.Paragraphs(i)

    ' If first word is "Thanks" then exit For loop
    If Trim(para.Range.Words(1)) =    "Thanks" Then Exit For

Next i

para.Range.Bold = True
```

Observe the use of the *Trim* function, because for Microsoft Word, a word includes any trailing spaces, if present.

The For Each Loop

The `For Each` loop is a variation on the `For` loop that was designed to iterate through a collection of objects (as well as through elements in an array) and is generally much more efficient than using the traditional `For` loop. The general syntax is:

```
For Each ObjectVar In CollectionName
    ' block of code goes here . . .
Next ObjectVar
```

where *ObjectVar* is a variable of the same object type as the objects within the collection. The code block will execute once for each object in the collection.

To illustrate, here is how the earlier example that changes Heading 1 style to Heading 2 style would appear using a `For Each` loop:

```
Dim para As Paragraph

For each para in ActiveDocument.Paragraphs

    ' Change style from Heading 1 to Heading 2
    If para.Style = "Heading 1" Then
        para.Style = "Heading 2"
    End If

Next para
```

As you can see, this code is much more concise.

Thus, when iterating through a collection of objects, we have two choices:

```
For Each object in Collection
    ' code block here
Next object
```

or:

```
For i = 1 to Collection.Count
    ' code block here
Next i
```

However, I must emphasize the point that the `For Each` loop can be *much* faster than the `For` loop when dealing with collections of Word objects. Thus, except for small collections, it is the preferred method. I will provide a rather dramatic example of this when I discuss an example related to the Style object.

The `For Each` statement can also be used to iterate through collections of non-object items. For instance, the FontNames collection contains the names of all of the currently available fonts. Thus, this is a collection of strings. To iterate through this collection, write:

```
Dim FontName As Variant
For Each FontName In Application.FontNames
```

```
     ' do something here
   Next FontName
```

Note that we must declare **FontName** as a Variant, since VBA allows only variants and object variables as the loop variable in a **For Each** loop. (A String variable would have been the most efficient choice, but it is not allowed.)

The Do Loop

The **Do** loop has several variations. To describe these variations, I use the notation:

```
{While | Until}
```

to represent either the word **While** or the word **Until**, but not both. With this in mind, here are the possible syntaxes for the **Do** loop:

```
Do {While | Until} condition
   ' code block here
Loop
```

or:

```
Do
   ' code block here
Loop {While | Until} condition
```

Actually, there is a fifth possibility, because you can dispense with *condition* completely and write:

```
Do
   ' code block here
Loop
```

Some of these variations are actually quite subtle. For instance, the following code cycles through the paragraphs in the active document as long as the paragraphs have some characters in them (other than the end of paragraph mark):

```
' Set para to first paragraph
Set para = ActiveDocument.Paragraphs(1)
Do While para.Range.Characters.Count
   ' Code here
   ' Set para to next paragraph
Loop
```

Consider also the following code, whose purpose is similar:

```
' Set para to first paragraph
Set para = ActiveDocument.Paragraphs(1)
Do
   ' Code here
   ' Set para to next paragraph
Loop While para.Range.Characters.Count > 1
```

The difference between these two versions is that in the first case, the condition is checked immediately, before any code within the Do loop is executed. Thus, if the first paragraph has no text (so it has only an ending paragraph mark), its character count will be 1 and the condition will fail. Thus, no code will be executed within the Do loop.

On the other hand, in the second case, the condition is checked at the end of each loop, so the loop will execute the first time, even if the first paragraph has no text.

The following example uses a Do loop to italicize each word in a paragraph until it reaches a word that is bold (this could also be done with a For loop, by the way):

```
Dim para As Paragraph
Dim wrd As Range
Dim iWord As Long
Dim iWordCount As Long

' Initialize
iWord = 1

' Get first paragraph
Set para = ActiveDocument.Paragraphs(1)

' Get word count for paragraph
iWordCount = para.Range.Words.Count

' Loop while there are more words
Do While iWord <= iWordCount

    ' Get ith word
    Set wrd = para.Range.Words(iWord)

    ' Exit Do loop if word is bold
    If wrd.Bold = True Then Exit Do

    ' Italicize word
    wrd.Italic = True

    iWord = iWord + 1    ' next word

Loop
```

Note the use of the **Exit Do** statement, which is the analog of the **Exit For** statement.

Infinite Loops

You need to be very careful when coding Do loops, because a flawed Do loop can run forever! This condition, called an *infinite loop,* can occur if there is a flaw in the condition that is supposed to terminate the loop.

Note that an infinite loop can also occur with a **For** loop, but this does not happen as often, since it requires the deliberate act of changing the loop counter or one of the loop bounds. On the other hand, it is relatively easy to make a subtle error in a **Do** loop that causes an infinite loop.

As a simple example, suppose you decide that each paragraph in the active document should have a heading that indicates the number of the paragraph. For instance, the following four-line document:

> The party of the first part shall be named Dr. Steven Roman.
> The party of the second part shall be named O'Reilly & Associates.
> The parties hereby enter into the following agreement.
> The agreement shall be governed by the laws of the State of California.

should become:

> Paragraph 1:
> The party of the first part shall be named Dr. Steven Roman.
> Paragraph 2:
> The party of the second part shall be named O'Reilly & Associates.
> Paragraph 3:
> The parties hereby enter into the following agreement.
> Paragraph 4:
> The agreement shall be governed by the laws of the State of California.

Consider the following code to do the job. Can you spot the reason that this code will never terminate?

```
iPara = 1
' Do while there are more paragraphs
Do While iPara <= ActiveDocument.Paragraphs.Count

    ' Get ith para
    Set para = ActiveDocument.Paragraphs(iPara)

    ' Add heading with paragraph count
    para.Range.InsertBefore "Paragraph" _
        & Format(iPara) & ":" & vbCr

    ' Next paragraph
    iPara = iPara + 1

Loop
```

The problem is that adding a heading adds a new paragraph to the document, which increases the value of **ActiveDocument.Paragraphs.Count**, so the condition:

```
iPara <= ActiveDocument.Paragraphs.Count
```

is always true, since the left side increases along with the right side!

This example illustrates the point that it is very dangerous to place a value that may change in the *condition* portion of a Do loop (or any loop for that matter). If we look again at the previous example, which italicizes each word until it encounters one that is bold, we see the following code:

```
' Get word count for paragraph
iWordCount = para.Range.Words.Count

' Loop while there are more words
Do While iWord <= iWordCount
```

The first line gets the word count and puts it in a variable. This variable, whose value is under our control (and not VBA's), does not change (since we do not change it), so it can be used safely in the *condition* portion of the Do loop.

The Select Case Statement

As we have seen, the If...Then construct is used to perform different tasks based on different possibilities. An alternative construct that is often more readable is the Select Case statement, whose syntax is:

```
Select Case testexpression
   Case value1
       ' statements to execute if testexpression = value1
   Case value2
       ' statements to execute if testexpression = value2
   . . .

   Case Else
       ' statements to execute otherwise
End Select
```

Note that the Case Else part is optional. To illustrate: the following code is the Select Case version of the earlier example (see the previous discussion of the If...Then statement) that changes the font size of different headings. I think you will agree that this is a bit more readable than the previous version:

```
Select Case Selection.Style
   Case "Heading 1"
      Selection.Font.Size = 24
   Case "Heading 2"
      Selection.Font.Size = 18
   Case "Heading 3"
      Selection.Font.Size = 14
   Case Else
      Selection.Font.Size = 11
End Select
```

A Final Note on VBA

There is a lot more to the VBA language than I have covered here. (In fact, the VBA reference manual is about 300 pages long.) However, I have covered the main points needed to begin Word VBA programming.

Actually, many Word VBA programming tasks require only a small portion of VBA's features; you will probably find yourself wrestling much more with Word's object model than with the VBA language itself.

I conclude our discussion of the VBA language per se with a brief outline of topics for further study, which you can do using the VBA help files.

File-Related Functions

VBA has a large number of functions related to file and directory housekeeping. Some of these are:

Dir
> Find a file with a certain name

FileLen
> Get the length of a file

FileTimeDate
> Get the date stamp of a file

FileCopy
> Copy a file

Kill
> Delete a file

Name
> Rename a file or directory

RmDir
> Delete a directory

MkDir
> Make a new directory

In addition to these file-related functions, there may be times when it is useful to create new text files (as opposed to Word files) to store data. VBA provides a number of functions for this purpose, headed by the **Open** statement, whose (simplified) syntax is:

```
Open pathname For mode As [#]filenumber
```

Once a file has been opened, you can read or write to the file. I want to emphasize that opening files in this way creates text files, *not* Word documents.

Date- and Time-Related Functions

VBA has a large number of functions related to manipulating dates and times. Some of these are:

Date, Now, Time
> Get the current date or time

DateAdd, DateDiff, DatePart
> Perform date calculations

DateSerial, DateValue
> Return a date

TimeSerial, TimeValue
> Return a time

Date, Time
> Set the date or time

Timer
> Time a process

The Format Function

The *Format* function is used to format strings, numbers, and dates. Table 8-1 gives a few examples.

Table 8-1. Format Function Examples

Expression	Return Value
Format(Date, "Long Date")	Thursday, April 30, 1998
Format(Time, "Long Time")	5:03:47 PM
Format(Date, "mm/dd/yy hh:mm:ss AMPM")	04/30/98 12:00:00 AM
Format(1234.5, "$##,##0.00")	$1,234.50
Format("HELLO", "<")	"hello"

Errors!

I discussed the various types of errors in Chapter 3, *The Visual Basic Editor, Part I*, but I have scrupulously avoided the question of how to handle run-time errors in code. Indeed, VBA provides several tools for handling errors (`On Error`, `Resume`, the Err object, and so on) and I could have included an entire chapter on the subject in this book.

Proper error handling is *extremely* important. Indeed, if you are or intend to become a professional application developer, then you should familiarize yourself with error-handling procedures. (I suggest my book *Concepts of Object-Oriented*

Programming in Visual Basic, published by Springer-Verlag. It has a complete chapter on error handling.)

On the other hand, if your intention is to produce Word VBA code for your own personal use, then the reasons for adding error-handling routines are somewhat mitigated. When an error occurs within one of your own programs, VBA will stop execution, display an error message, and highlight the offending code. This should enable you to debug the application and fix the problem. (It would be unreasonable to expect another user of your program to debug your code, however.)

III

Objects and Object Models

9

Object Models

In this chapter, I present a general overview of object models and the syntax used to manipulate them in code. After this, we can turn specifically to the Word object model.

As I have discussed, VBA is the programming language that underlies several important Windows applications, including Microsoft Word, Excel, Access, Power-Point, and Visual Basic. Any application that uses VBA in this way is called a *host application*. I also discussed how each host application enhances VBA by providing an *object model* (perhaps more than one) to deal with the objects that are particular to that application.

Microsoft provides over a dozen different object models for its Office application suite and related products. These include object models for Word, Excel, Access, DAO (Data Access Objects), Outlook, PowerPoint, Binder, Graph, Forms, VBA, VB, ASP (Active Server Pages), and more. Of course, our interest in this book is with the Word object model, and I will devote the rest of the book to describing the major portions of this model. (I also discuss a portion of the Office object model in Chapter 21, *Menus and Toolbars.*)

Objects, Properties, and Methods

In the parlance of VBA programming, an *object* is something that is identified by its properties and its methods. For example, documents, templates, paragraphs, fonts, and borders are all examples of objects in the Word object model. Actually, the Word object model contains 188 different objects (including a few normally hidden ones).

Properties

The term *property* is used in the present context in pretty much the same way that it is used in everyday English—it is a trait, attribute, or characteristic of an object. For instance, a Paragraph object has 34 properties, among which are Alignment, LineSpacing, LeftIndent, and RightIndent. A property's value can be any valid data type, such as Integer, Single, String, or even another object type.

When the value of a property has type Integer, for instance, I refer to the property as an *integer property*. Integer properties are quite common, so Microsoft has defined a large number of built-in enums (192 to be exact, with 1,969 individual constants) to give symbolic names to these property values.

For instance, the Alignment property of the Paragraph object can take on any of the values in the enum defined by:

```
Enum WdParagraphAlignment
    wdAlignParagraphLeft = 0
    wdAlignParagraphCenter = 1
    wdAlignParagraphRight = 2
    wdAlignParagraphJustify = 3
End Enum
```

As I said, a property can also have a value that is an object, in which case it is referred to as an *object property*. For instance, a Paragraph object has a Format property that returns another object called a ParagraphFormat object. The ParagraphFormat object has its own set of properties and methods.

Because a ParagraphFormat object can be obtained from a Paragraph object, we refer to ParagraphFormat as a *child object* of Paragraph, and Paragraph is a *parent* of ParagraphFormat. I will have more to say about this parent-child relationship a bit later.

Methods

A *method* of an object is an action that can be performed on (or on behalf of) the object. For instance, a Paragraph object has an Indent method that causes the paragraph to be indented. It also has a Next method that returns the next paragraph in the document. Thus, in some cases, the return value of a method or property can be another object, as is the case with the Next method.

In programming terms, the properties and methods of an object are just built-in functions or subroutines. It is important to emphasize that the distinction between property and method is one of intent and is often made somewhat arbitrarily. (In fact, the Item member is sometimes classified as a property and sometimes as a method, depending upon the object in question, so it appears that even Microsoft has trouble making up its collective mind from time to time.) For instance, as I just remarked, a Paragraph object has an Alignment property that can be set to one of the constants in the `WdParagraphAlignment` enum. This causes the paragraph to assume the corresponding alignment. Microsoft could have equally well defined an Align method to set the alignment, reasoning that aligning a paragraph is an action.

The properties and methods of an object are collectively referred to as the object's *members*. This should not be confused with an object's children.

Reading the help files

I should comment on the way that methods are described in the Microsoft help files (to which you will probably refer often). To illustrate, consider the *MoveEnd* method, which Microsoft denotes in its help files by:

```
expression.MoveEnd(Unit, Count)
```

The help file states that **expression** returns a Range or Selection object, to which the *MoveEnd* method applies. It further defines the parameters *Unit* as an optional variant indicating the type of unit (character, word, sentence, and so on) by which to move the ending position of the range or selection and *Count* as an optional variant indicating the number of units to move. Finally, the help file states that the *MoveEnd* method returns an integer that indicates the number of units the range or selection was actually moved. (Don't worry about the purpose of this method now; we are interested only in the syntax.)

However, since the *MoveEnd* method is a function, you might have expected the help file to contain a more traditional function declaration, such as:

```
Public Function MoveEnd (Optional Unit As Variant, _
                    Optional Count As Variant) As Integer
```

Indeed, in the actual Word object library, from which VBA gets its information about the Word object model, the declaration for the *MoveEnd* method is:

```
[method] MoveEnd ([Unit] As VARIANT, [Count] As VARIANT) _
            As Long
```

(square brackets indicate optional parameters), which is closer to a traditional function declaration. (It also points out that *MoveEnd* returns a Long rather than an Integer!)

In any case, Microsoft probably figured that there was no need to use a formal function declaration in its help files, so they opted for a more concise and probably more readable form of declaration, which resembles an actual call to this method (as we will see).

Collection Objects

In programming with the Word object model (or indeed any object model), it is common to have a great many objects "alive" at the same time. For instance, each character within an open Word document is an object, as is each word, sentence, paragraph, and so on. Hence, at any given time, there may be thousands of objects in existence. To manage these objects, the designers of an object model generally include a special type of object called a *collection object*.

As the name implies, collection objects represent collections of objects—generally objects of a single type. For instance, the Word object model has a collection object called Characters that represents the set of all characters in the document in question. It is customary to say that the Characters collection object *contains* the characters in the document, so we will use this terminology as well. There is one Characters collection for each open document. Also, every time we select text within a document, Word creates another Characters collection object that contains the selected characters.

Collection objects are generally just called *collections*, but it is very important to remember that a collection is just a special type of object. As we will see, the properties and methods of a collection object are specifically designed to manage the collection.

We can generally spot a collection object because its name is the plural of the name of the objects contained within the collection (as with the Characters collection or the Paragraphs collection). However, in some cases, this naming convention is not followed. For instance, the FontNames collection, which represents a list of the names of all the currently available fonts, is a collection of names—that is, of strings. (There is no FontName object.)

Another important exception to this naming convention occurs because the Word object model does not have a Character, Word, or Sentence object. Instead, each character, word, or sentence is actually a Range object. Hence, the Characters, Words, and Sentences collections each contain Range objects. (I have a great deal to say about Range objects in Chapter 14, *The Range and Selection Objects*.)

Collections are extremely common in the Office object models. In fact, of the 188 objects in the Word object mode, 76 are collection objects! The following list shows some of the more commonly used collections in the Word object model:

Bookmarks	Fields	PageNumbers
Borders	FontNames	Paragraphs
Cells	Footnotes	RecentFiles
Characters	Frames	Rows
Columns	HeadersFooters	Sections
Documents	HeadingStyles	Sentences

Styles	Templates	Words
Tables	Windows	Zooms
TabStops		

I should emphasize that a collection is just a special type of object. Indeed, the properties and methods of a collection object are specifically designed to manage the collection. Accordingly, the basic requirements for a collection object are:

- A property called Count that returns the number of objects in the collection. This is a read-only property; that is, it cannot be set by the programmer. It is automatically updated by VBA itself.

- A method called *Add* (or something similar, such as *AddNew*) that allows the programmer to add a new object to the collection.

- A method called *Remove* or *Close* (or something similar) that allows the programmer to remove an object from the collection.

- A method called *Item* that permits the programmer to access any particular object in the collection. The item is usually identified either by name or by an index number.

Note that these basic requirements are not hard and fast. Some collection objects may not implement all of these members, and many implement additional members.

For instance, the Characters, Words, Sentences, Paragraphs, and Templates collections (and others) do not have an *Add* method, since you are not allowed to add objects to these collections directly. You can create new characters, for instance, simply by inserting text into the document and Word will automatically add them to the Characters collection and adjust the value of the Count property. On the other hand, the Documents collection does have an *Add* method.

Some Word collections are considerably more complicated than others, since they have several properties and methods that relate specifically to the type of object they contain. For instance, the Paragraphs collection has 36 properties and 18 methods, which is rather unusual for a collection object. Many of these members, such as the Alignment property, are included specifically so that they can operate on all of the paragraphs in the collection at the same time.

The Documents Collection: An Example of a Collection

To get a feel for a collection object, let's take a look at some of the members of the Documents collection. (I discuss the specifics of object syntax later in this chapter, and I discuss the Documents collection more formally in Chapter 12, *The Document Object.*)

The Count property

The Count property of the Documents collection returns the number of currently open Word documents. Thus, the code:

```
MsgBox "Open documents: " & Application.Documents.Count
```

displays a message box with the number of open documents. I want to comment on the syntax in:

```
Application.Documents.Count
```

First, the Application object is at the top of the Word object hierarchy. One of its properties is the Documents property, which is an object property that returns the Documents collection, consisting of all open documents. Thus:

```
Application.Documents
```

refers to this Documents collection. The Documents collection in turn has a Count property. Hence:

```
Application.Documents.Count
```

returns the value of this property.

The Add method

The *Add* method of the Documents collection has the following syntax:

```
DocumentsCollection.Add(Template, NewTemplate)
```

where *DocumentsCollection* refers to a Documents collection object (I elaborate on the meaning of "refers to" later in the chapter).

The *Add* method has two parameters. *Template* is the name of the template to be used for the new document. If this argument is omitted, the Normal template is used. If the *NewTemplate* parameter is set to True, then the document is opened as a template. For instance, the code:

```
Application.Documents.Add "CSBOOKS", False
```

opens a new Word document based on the CSBOOKS template (*CSBOOKS.DOT*). However, to manipulate this document further in code, I should assign a variable of type Document to this document as follows:

```
Dim Doc As Document
Set Doc = Application.Documents.Add("CSBOOKS", False)
```

This works because the *Add* method is a function that actually returns the new Document object that it creates. This is typical of *Add* methods.

The Item method

The Item method has syntax:

```
DocumentsCollection.Item(Index)
```

where *DocumentsCollection* refers to a Documents collection. The *Index* parameter is a variant that can be either the name of a document or the index number of a member of the collection. For instance, the code:

```
Application.Documents.Item(2)
```

refers to the second document in the Documents collection. If there is no second document, this code will return the following friendly error message: "The requested member of the collection does not exist." As another example, if there is an open document named *Temp.doc*, it can be referred to as:

```
Application.Documents.Item("Temp.doc")
```

If this document is not open, Word will issue the error message "Bad file name."

Since the *Item* method is the default method for most collection objects, we can shorten the preceding examples to:

```
Application.Documents(2)
```

and:

```
Application.Documents("Temp.doc")
```

Default methods are discussed a bit later in the chapter.

The Base of a Collection

Note that collections can be either 0-based or 1-based. In a *0-based collection*, the first member has index 0, and in a *1-based collection*, the first member has index 1. Most, *but not all*, collections in the Word object model and in VBA itself are 1-based. However, some older collections tend to be 0-based. (I guess that Microsoft got a lot of complaints about 0-based collections, so they decided to switch.)

It is important to determine the base of any collection before trying to access members by index. This can be done by checking the help system (sometimes) or trying some sample code. For instance, the code:

```
For i = 1 To Word.Documents.Count
    Debug.Print Application.Documents(i).Name
Next i
```

is correct, since the Documents collection is 1-based. However, the UserForms collection, which represents all currently loaded user forms in Word, is 0-based, so:

```
For i = 1 To UserForms.Count
    Debug.Print UserForms(i).Name
Next i
```

will produce an error. The correct code is:

```
For i = 0 To UserForms.Count - 1
    Debug.Print UserForms(i).Name
Next i
```

Object Model Hierarchies

The fact that one object's properties and methods can return another object, thus creating the concept of *child objects*, is of paramount importance, for it adds a very useful structure to the object model.

It seems by looking at the literature that there is not total agreement on when one object is considered a child of another object. For our purposes, if object A has a property or method that returns object B, then we will consider object B a child of object A and object A a parent of object B.

For example, the Range object, which represents a contiguous area within a document, has a Font property, which returns a Font object. Hence Font is a child of Range and Range is a parent of Font. The Font object is also a child of the Selection object, which represents the current selection in a document window. In fact, an object can have many parents and many children.

It is worth elaborating on my choice of definition for child objects. I could take a more restrictive view by requiring that the object property or method actually have the same name as the child object. For instance, the Application object has a Documents property that returns the Documents collection. Hence Documents is a child of Application. However, this definition is too restrictive. For instance, the only property or method of the Application object that returns a Dictionaries collection object is the CustomDictionary property. Hence the Dictionaries object would not be considered a child of Application under this restrictive definition, although it should be.

On the other hand, my definition of child object is quite liberal in some ways. For instance, the Application object has a property called ActiveDocument that returns a Document object, and so both Document and Documents are children of Application. This is not a problem in any way, but might offend some programmers who are not used to it.

It is important not to take the parent-child analogy too literally. For instance, the object hierarchy is full of circular parent-child relationships. As an example, Document is a parent of Window, which is a parent of Pane, which is a parent of Document. Indeed, in most object models, most objects have a property that returns the top object of the model. (In the Word object model, almost every object has an Application property that returns the Application object, which is the top object in the Word object model.) This provides a quick way to return to the top of the object hierarchy. Hence almost every object in the object model is a parent of the top object.

I'll now illustrate one important use of object properties with the Font object. The basic idea is that once you have defined a Font object and set its properties, you can apply these properties en masse to any object that has a Font object as a child.

The following code creates a Font object and assigns some of its properties:

```
Dim fnt As Font
Set fnt = New Font

fnt.Name = "Arial"
fnt.Bold = True
fnt.Italic = True
fnt.Size = 12
fnt.Shadow = True
fnt.AllCaps = True
```

Now, you can apply the character formatting of this Font object to as many objects as you like with only a single statement (provided that these objects have a child Font object). For example, to apply the formatting to the first paragraph of the active document, you just write:

```
ActiveDocument.Paragraphs(1).Range.Font = fnt
```

To apply the same font formatting to the third paragraph, you simply write:

```
ActiveDocument.Paragraphs(3).Range.Font = fnt
```

To apply the formatting to the current selection, you write:

```
ActiveWindow.Selection.Font = fnt
```

The object hierarchy of an object model is often pictured in a tree-like structure. A small portion of the Word object model is shown in Figure 9-1.

Object Model Syntax

It is time to discuss formally the basic syntax used when programming with an object model. The general syntax for referring to an object's properties and methods is very simple. If **objVar** is an object variable that refers to a particular object and AProperty is a property of this object, then you can access this property (for reading or for changing) using the syntax:

```
objVar.AProperty(any required parameters)
```

For instance, the following code sets the LeftAlign property of the first paragraph in the active document:

```
' Declare object variable
Dim para As Paragraph

' Set para to refer to first paragraph
Set para = ActiveDocument.Paragraphs(1)

' Set left align property to 36 points
para.LeftAlign = 36
```

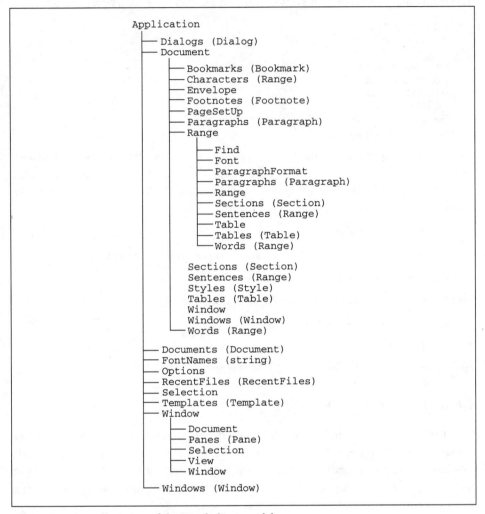

Figure 9-1. A small portion of the Word object model

If *AMethod* is a method for this object, then that method can be invoked with the syntax:

```
objVar.AMethod(any required parameters)
```

Note that this syntax is quite similar to the syntax used to call an ordinary VBA subroutine or function, except that here it requires qualification with the name of the variable that points to the object whose property or method is being called.

For instance, continuing the previous code, we can apply the *OpenUp* method to the paragraph referred to by **para** as follows:

```
para.OpenUp
```

(This method sets the spacing before the paragraph to 12 points.)

Object Variables

To access a property of an object, or to invoke a method, you can generally take two approaches: *direct* or *indirect*. The indirect approach uses an object variable—that is, a variable that has an object data type, whereas the direct approach does not.

For instance, to set the Bold property of the Font object for the first paragraph in the active document, you can take a direct approach, as in:

```
ActiveDocument.Paragraphs(1).Range.Font.Bold = True
```

Alternatively, you can assign an object variable. Here are two possibilities:

```
Dim rng as Range
Set rng = ActiveDocument.Paragraphs(1).Range
rng.Font.Bold = True

Dim fnt as Font
Set fnt = ActiveDocument.Paragraphs(1).Range.Font
fnt.Bold = True
```

Object variables are actually more important than they might seem at first. The most obvious reason for their use is that they can improve code readability when you need to refer to the same object more than once. For instance, instead of writing:

```
ActiveDocument.Paragraphs(1).Range.Font.Bold = True
ActiveDocument.Paragraphs(1).Range.Font.Italic = True
ActiveDocument.Paragraphs(1).Range.Font.Underline = False
ActiveDocument.Paragraphs(1).Range.Font.Size = 12
ActiveDocument.Paragraphs(1).Range.Font.Name = "Arial"
```

you can use a Font variable to improve readability as follows:

```
Dim fnt As Font
Set fnt = ActiveDocument.Paragraphs(1).Range.Font
fnt.Bold = True
fnt.Italic = True
fnt.Underline = False
fnt.Size = 12
fnt.Name = "Arial"
```

The With Statement

In fact, VBA provides a With statement to handle just this situation in this example, which could be written as follows:

```
Dim fnt As Font
Set fnt = ActiveDocument.Paragraphs(1).Range.Font
With fnt
    .Bold = True
```

```
      .Italic = True
      .Underline = False
      .Size = 12
      .Name = "Arial"
   End With
```

The general syntax of the `With` statement is:

```
With object
    ' statements go here
End With
```

where the statements generally refer to the object, but do not require qualification using the object's name (as in the previous example).

Object Variables Save Execution Time

The main purpose of object variables is not to improve readability, but to save execution time. In particular, to execute each of the five lines in the first version of the previous code, VBA must resolve the references to the various Word objects ActiveDocument, Paragraphs(1), Range, and Font. That is, VBA must "climb down" the Word object model. This takes time.

However, in the code that uses an object variable of type Font, VBA must resolve these references only once. Hence the second version runs much more quickly. This difference can be very noticeable when there are hundreds or thousands of references to resolve!

An Object Variable Is a Pointer

There are some very important differences between object variables and non-object variables, such as those of type Integer, Single, or String. As I have mentioned, a non-object variable can be thought of as a name for a location in the computer's memory that holds some data. For instance, in the code:

```
Dim iVar As Integer
iVar = 123
```

the variable `iVar` is a 4-byte memory location that holds the integer value 123. This can be pictured as in Figure 9-2. (Actually, the 4-byte memory location holds the value 123 in binary format, but that is not relevant to our discussion.)

Now, if I were to write:

```
Dim iVar2 As Integer
iVar2 = iVar
iVar2 = 567
```

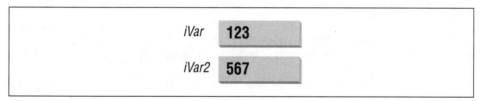

Figure 9-2. Integer variables in memory

I would not expect the last line of code to have any effect upon the value of the variable iVar, which should still be 123. This is because iVar and iVar2 represent different areas of memory, as pictured in Figure 9-2.

However, an object variable is *not* the name of a memory location that holds the object. Rather, an object variable is the name of a memory location that holds the *address* of the memory location that holds the object, as shown in Figure 9-3. Put another way, the object variable holds a *reference to* or *points to* the object. For this reason, it is an example of a *pointer variable*, or simply a *pointer*. In Figure 9-3, the object variable **para** points to an object of type Paragraph, namely, the first paragraph in the active document.

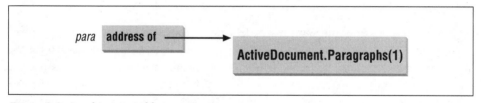

Figure 9-3. An object variable in memory

The code that goes with Figure 9-3 is:

```
Dim para as Paragraph
Set para = ActiveDocument.Paragraphs(1)
```

One of the consequences of the fact that object variables are pointers is that more than one object variable can point to (or refer to) the same object, as in:

```
Dim para as Paragraph
Dim para2 as Paragraph
Set para = ActiveDocument.Paragraphs(1)
Set para2 = para
```

This code creates the situation pictured in Figure 9-4.

I want to emphasize that while **para** and **para2** are different object variables, they hold the same value and so point to the same object. Thus, I can change the first paragraph using either of these object variables.

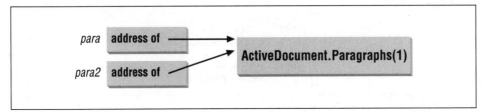

Figure 9-4. Two object variables referencing the same object

It is important when programming with objects to keep careful track of all object variables and what they are referencing. Furthermore, it is generally not a good idea to have more than one object variable pointing to the same object (as in Figure 9-4) unless there is a compelling reason to do so, for it is very easy to change the object using one object variable (say, **para**) and then later use the other variable (**para2**), thinking it refers to the unchanged object.

This is a good time to mention a point of potential confusion in terminology. To illustrate, consider the code:

```
Dim para As Paragraph
Set para = ActiveDocument.Paragraphs(1)
para.Range.Font.Size = 24
```

You will often hear people say "this code sets the font size for the paragraph **para** to 24 points." However, the correct statement is "this code sets the font size for the paragraph *referred to* by **para** to 24 points." After all, the variable **para** is not the same as the Paragraph object itself—it only *refers* to that object. (This is the same distinction between a variable and its value that occurs with parameters and arguments to procedures; namely, **para** is a variable and ActiveDocument.Paragraphs(1) is its value.) Nevertheless, it is quite common and convenient to abuse the terminology in this way, and I will do it as well.

Freeing an Object Variable: The Nothing Keyword

To free an object variable so that it no longer points to anything, use the Nothing keyword, as in:

```
Set para2 = Nothing
```

It is good programming practice to free object variables (by setting them to Nothing) when they are no longer needed, since this can save resources. (An object variable is set to Nothing automatically when its lifetime expires.)

Note that once an object no longer has any references to it, the object will be automatically destroyed by VBA, thus freeing up resources (memory). However, *all* references to the object must be freed before the object is destroyed. This is another reason not to point more than one object variable at the same object if possible.

The Is Operator

To compare the values of two ordinary variables `Var1` and `Var2`, just write:

```
If Var1 = Var2 Then . . .
```

However, the syntax for comparing two object variables to see whether they refer to the same object is special (as is the syntax for setting the value of an object variable—using the `Set` statement). In particular, it is done using the `Is` operator:

```
If para Is para2 Then . . .
```

Similarly, to test whether an object variable has been set to `Nothing`, write:

```
If para Is Nothing Then . . .
```

Be advised that there is a problem with the `Is` operator in the current version of VBA. Microsoft has acknowledged a problem with respect to Excel VBA, but it seems also to exist in Word VBA. For example, the code:

```
Dim doc As Document
Dim doc2 As Document

Set doc = ActiveDocument
Set doc2 = ActiveDocument

MsgBox doc Is doc2
```

will correctly display the value True. However, the analogous code:

```
Dim para As Paragraph
Dim para2 As Paragraph

Set para = ActiveDocument.Paragraphs(1)
Set para2 = ActiveDocument.Paragraphs(1)

MsgBox para Is para2
```

incorrectly displays the value False (at least on my system)! If we change the penultimate line to:

```
Set para2 = para
```

then the message box correctly displays True.

Default Members

Most (but not all) Word objects have a *default member* (property or method) that is invoked when a property or method is expected but you do not specify one. For instance, the default member for the Range object is the Text property. Hence the code:

```
Dim rng As Range
Set rng = ActiveDocument.Words(1)
rng = "Donna"
```

sets the first word in the active document to Donna, since Word applies the default property in the last line, effectively replacing it with:

```
rng.Text = "Donna"
```

Similarly, the following code:

```
Dim rng1 As Range, rng2 as Range
Set rng1 = ActiveDocument.Words(1)
Set rng2 = ActiveDocument.Words(2)
rng2 = rng1
```

replaces the second word in the active document by the first word, since Word interprets the final line as:

```
rng2.Text = rng1.Text
```

Note the difference between:

```
rng2 = rng1
```

and:

```
Set rng2 = rng1
```

In the latter case, the variable **rng2** is set to refer to the range pointed to by **rng1**. (This is similar to the situation pictured in Figure 9-4.) In the former case, **rng2** and **rng1** still point to their original ranges. Only the text in the range pointed to by **rng2** is changed.

Of course, you are free to use default members whenever you wish, and Microsoft uses them often in the help documentation. However, default members tend to make code less readable, and for this reason I generally avoid them in this book. One notable exception is for a collection object. It is generally the case that the default member of a collection object is the *Item* method. Hence, for instance, the fourth word in the active document can be referred to by:

```
ActiveDocument.Words(4)
```

rather than the more clumsy:

```
ActiveDocument.Words.Item(4)
```

Since this use of the default member is not likely to cause any confusion, I will use it.

Named Arguments

I discussed named arguments in Chapter 5, *Variables, Data Types, and Constants*, but I'll revisit the subject briefly here. Many of the properties and methods of objects in the Word object model are rather complex. For instance, the *SaveAs* method of the Document object is:

```
DocObject.SaveAs(FileName, FileFormat, LockComments, _
                Password, AddToRecentFiles, WritePassword, _
                ReadOnlyRecommended, EmbedTrueTypeFonts, _
                SaveNativePictureFormat, SaveFormsData, _
                SaveAsAOCELetter)
```

The following call to this method:

```
doc.SaveAs "test", , , "guest", True, , False, False, _
          False, True, False
```

is not easy to read, since it is very hard to tell to what the arguments refer. For this reason, many (but not all) of the methods in VBA allow named arguments. For instance, I could write the previous declaration as:

```
doc.SaveAs    FileName:="test", Password:="guest", _
             AddToRecentFiles:=True, ReadOnlyRecommended:=False, _
             EmbedTrueTypeFonts:=False, SaveNativePictureFormat:=False, _
             SaveFormsData:=True, SaveAsAOCELetter:=False
```

which makes the meaning of this call to *SaveAs* very clear.

The advantages of named arguments over positional arguments are threefold:

- Named arguments can improve readability and clarity.

- Blank spaces (separated by commas) are required for missing optional arguments when using a positional declaration, but not when using named arguments. It's extremely easy to accidentally omit a blank space or insert an extra one, causing an error that can be difficult to detect.

- The order in which named arguments are listed is immaterial, which of course is not the case for positional arguments.

Named arguments can improve readability quite a bit, and are highly recommended. However, they can require considerably more space, so for the short examples in this book, I will generally not use them.

The New Keyword

As I have explained, the **Set** statement assigns an object reference to an object variable. There are several variations on the use of the **Set** statement:

```
Set ObjectVar = ObjectExpression
Set ObjectVar = New ObjectExpression
Set ObjectVar = Nothing
```

where *ObjectVar* is an object variable (already declared with a **Dim** statement) and *ObjectExpression* is an expression that returns an object of the same type as *ObjectVar*. In particular, *ObjectExpression* can be any of the following:

- The name of an object of the same object type as *ObjectVar*.

- A declared object variable of the same object type as *ObjectVar*.

- A function or method that returns an object of the same object type as *ObjectVar*.

I have already provided examples of the first and third syntaxes.

The **New** keyword can be used, under certain limited circumstances, to create a new Word object. In particular, the **New** keyword applies only to the following six objects:

Application	Font	OLEControl
Document	LetterContent	ParagraphFormat

To illustrate, the following code creates a new Font object and applies its character formatting to every even numbered paragraph:

```
' Declare variables
Dim i as Integer
Dim fnt As Font

' Create new Font object
Set fnt = New Font

' Set the properties of fnt
With fnt
    .Bold = True
    .Size = 12
    .AllCaps = True
End With

' Apply the formatting
For i = 1 to ActiveDocument.Paragraphs.Count
    If (i Mod 2) = 0 then
        ActiveDocument.Paragraphs(i).Range.Font = fnt
    End If
Next i
```

The use of the **New** keyword with the ParagraphFormat object is similar to its use with the Font object. (I will provide an example later in the book.)

The **New** keyword can be used with the Document object to create a new Word document:

```
Dim doc As Document
Set doc = New Document
```

This code automatically adds the document to the Documents collection. Note, however, that if the **doc** variable is declared within a procedure, as soon as the procedure exits, the variable will be destroyed and the document will be destroyed along with it, without warning (unless you save it first). Therefore, you may want to declare the variable at a higher (module) level.

When applied to the Application object, the **New** keyword creates a new session of Microsoft Word, as in the following example:

```
Dim newWord As Application
Set newWord = New Application
newWord.Visible = True
```

I will have more to say about this in Appendix A, *Programming Word from Another Application*.

Global Objects

Many of the properties and methods of the Application object can be used without qualifying them with the word Application. These are called *global members*. For instance, the Documents property is global, so you can write:

```
Documents.Count
```

instead of:

```
Application.Documents.Count
```

To identify the global members, the Word object model has a special object called the Global object. This object is not used directly—its purpose is simply to identify the global members of the object model. Note that the members of the Global object form a proper subset of the members of the Application object (which means that not all of the members of the Application object are global). The 68 global members of the Word object model are:

ActiveDocument	DDETerminateAll	Options
ActivePrinter	Dialogs	Parent
ActiveWindow	Documents	PicasToPoints
AddIns	FileConverters	PointsToCentimeters
Application	FindKey	PointsToInches
Assistant	FontNames	PointsToLines
AutoCaptions	GetSpellingSuggestions	PointsToMillimeters
AutoCorrect	HangulHanjaDictionaries	PointsToPicas
BuildKeyCode	Help	PortraitFontNames
CaptionLabels	InchesToPoints	PrintPreview
CentimetersToPoints	IsObjectValid	RecentFiles
ChangeFileOpenDirectory	KeyBindings	Repeat
CheckSpelling	KeysBoundTo	Selection
CleanString	KeyString	ShowVisualBasicEditor
CommandBars	LandscapeFontNames	StatusBar
Creator	Languages	SynonymInfo
CustomDictionaries	LinesToPoints	System
CustomizationContext	ListGalleries	Tasks
DDEExecute	MacroContainer	Templates
DDEInitiate	MillimetersToPoints	VBE
DDEPoke	Name	Windows
DDERequest	NewWindow	WordBasic
DDETerminate	NormalTemplate	

10

In this chapter:
- *The Word Object
  Model: A Perspective*
- *Word Enums*
- *The VBA Object
  Browser*

The Word
Object Model

The Word object model is the most extensive in Microsoft's Office arsenal, with 188 objects and more than 3,000 properties and methods in total. It is certainly not my intention in this book to cover all, or even most, of these objects and their members. My goal is to acquaint you with the major portions of this model so that you can easily learn more as needed.

It seems appropriate to begin by presenting an overall view of the Word object model, using pictures of the model taken from various viewpoints, along with some tables. I suggest that you stare at these pictures and tables for a little while and then read on, returning to them as needed.

The Word Object Model: A Perspective

To put the Word object model in some perspective, Table 10-1 gives some statistics on various Microsoft object models. As you can see from this table, the Word object model has more objects than any other model. (Excel is a close second, but 52 of the Excel objects are included only for compatibility with earlier versions of Excel and are on their way out. Also, when you consider only those members of the Excel objects that are not obsolete, the count drops to 1,974 properties and 985 methods. Thus, Word is truly the largest object model in this group!)

Table 10-1. Some Object Model Statistics

Application	Objects	Properties	Methods	Enums	Constants
Access 8	51	1,596	532	31	485
Binder 8	4	37	15	4	11
DAO 35	37	235	174	26	185
Excel 8	184	5,956	3,119	152	1,266
Forms 2	64	588	352	42	191

Table 10-1. Some Object Model Statistics (continued)

Application	Objects	Properties	Methods	Enums	Constants
Graph 8	44	1,120	234	58	447
Office 97	40	615	209	78	801
Outlook 8	42	1,568	534	34	154
PowerPoint 8	110	1,197	322	53	370
Word 8	188	2,300	837	192	1,969

For reference, the following list shows all objects in the Word object model, along with the number of children for each object:

AddIn(0)
AddIns(1)
Adjustments(0)
Application(37)
ApplicationEvents(0)
AutoCaption(0)
AutoCaptions(1)
AutoCorrect(4)
AutoCorrectEntries(1)
AutoCorrectEntry(0)
AutoTextEntries(1)
AutoTextEntry(1)
Bookmark(2)
Bookmarks(1)
Border(0)
Borders(1)
Browser(0)
CalloutFormat(0)
CaptionLabel(0)
CaptionLabels(1)
Cell(6)
Cells(3)
Characters(1)
CheckBox(0)
ColorFormat(0)
Column(4)
Columns(3)
Comment(1)
Comments(1)
ConnectorFormat(1)
CustomLabel(0)
CustomLabels(1)
Dialog(0)
Dialogs(1)
Dictionaries(1)
Dictionary(0)
Document(45)
DocumentEvents(0)
Documents(1)
DropCap(0)
DropDown(1)

Endnote(1)
Endnotes(2)
Envelope(2)
Field(5)
Fields(1)
FileConverter(0)
FileConverters(1)
FillFormat(1)
Find(4)
FirstLetterException(0)
FirstLetterExceptions(1)
Font(3)
FontNames(0)
Footnote(1)
Footnotes(2)
FormField(5)
FormFields(1)
Frame(3)
Frames(1)
FreeformBuilder(1)
GroupShapes(1)
HangulAndAlphabetException(0)
HangulAndAlphabetExceptions(1)
HangulHanjaConversionDictionaries(1)
HeaderFooter(3)
HeadersFooters(1)
HeadingStyle(0)
HeadingStyles(1)
Hyperlink(2)
Hyperlinks(1)
Index(1)
Indexes(2)
InlineShape(10)
InlineShapes(1)
KeyBinding(0)
KeyBindings(1)
KeysBoundTo(1)
Language(1)
Languages(1)
LetterContent(1)
LineFormat(1)

LineNumbering(0)
LinkFormat(0)
List(2)
ListEntries(1)
ListEntry(0)
ListFormat(2)
ListGalleries(1)
ListGallery(1)
ListLevel(1)
ListLevels(1)
ListParagraphs(1)
Lists(1)
ListTemplate(2)
ListTemplates(1)
Mailer(0)
MailingLabel(2)
MailMerge(2)
MailMergeDataField(0)
MailMergeDataFields(1)
MailMergeDataSource(2)
MailMergeField(2)
MailMergeFieldName(0)
MailMergeFieldNames(1)
MailMergeFields(1)
MailMessage(0)
OCXEvents(0)
OLEControl(0)
OLEFormat(0)
Options(0)
PageNumber(0)
PageNumbers(1)
PageSetup(2)
Pane(5)
Panes(1)
Paragraph(7)
ParagraphFormat(4)
Paragraphs(5)
PictureFormat(0)
ProofreadingErrors(1)
Range(36)
ReadabilityStatistic(0)

ReadabilityStatistics(1)   StoryRanges(1)   Templates(1)
RecentFile(1)   Style(6)   TextColumn(0)
RecentFiles(1)   Styles(1)   TextColumns(1)
Replacement(3)   Subdocument(2)   TextEffectFormat(0)
Revision(1)   Subdocuments(1)   TextFrame(3)
Revisions(1)   SynonymInfo(0)   TextInput(0)
RoutingSlip(0)   System(0)   TextRetrievalMode(1)
Row(5)   Table(7)   ThreeDFormat(1)
Rows(4)   TableOfAuthorities(1)   TwoInitialCapsException(0)
Section(4)   TableOfAuthoritiesCategory(0)   TwoInitialCapsExceptions(1)
Sections(2)   TableOfContents(2)   Variable(0)
Selection(31)   TableOfFigures(2)   Variables(1)
Sentences(1)   Tables(1)   Version(0)
Shading(0)   TablesOfAuthorities(2)   Versions(1)
ShadowFormat(1)   TablesOfAuthoritiesCategories(1) View(1)
Shape(21)   TablesOfContents(2)   Window(6)
ShapeNode(0)   TablesOfFigures(2)   Windows(1)
ShapeNodes(1)   TabStop(1)   Words(1)
ShapeRange(19)   TabStops(1)   WrapFormat(0)
Shapes(3)   Task(0)   Zoom(0)
SpellingSuggestion(0)   Tasks(1)   Zooms(1)
SpellingSuggestions(1)   Template(4)

The following list shows the Word objects that have at least four children. As we can see by comparing the previous and following lists, the majority of objects have fewer than four children. In fact, 52 of the 188 objects (almost one-third) have no children at all:

Document (45)   Paragraph (7)   FormField (5)
Application (37)   Style (6)   AutoCorrect (4)
Range (36)   Cell (6)   ParagraphFormat (4)
Selection (31)   Window (6)   Find (4)
Shape (21)   Row (5)   Rows (4)
ShapeRange (19)   Paragraphs (5)   Column (4)
InlineShape (10)   Pane (5)   Section (4)
Table (7)   Field (5)   Template (4)

The following list contains the objects that have 25 or more members (properties and methods) and shows that the member count drops off rather dramatically:

Document (169)   Shape (57)   Font (37)
Options (145)   Paragraphs (54)   LetterContent (35)
Application (139)   Paragraph (52)   PageSetup (31)
Selection (133)   ParagraphFormat (43) Find (29)
Range (126)   Window (40)   Borders (28)
ShapeRange (62)   View (40)   FillFormat (26)

By looking at the previous lists, you should get the feeling that much of the power of the Word object hierarchy is concentrated in the four objects:

Application   Range
Document   Selection

Indeed, I will devote much of the remainder of the book to these four objects.

Word Enums

It is also interesting to glance over the list of 192 Word enums. Note that there are some rather large enums in the object model, to wit:

WdWordDialog: 171 constants
WdPageBorderArt: 164 constants
WdKey: 98 constants
WdBuiltinStyle: 91 constants
WdFieldType: 88 constants
WdLanguageID: 64 constants
WdWordDialogTab: 55 constants
WdTextureIndex: 53 constants
WdPaperSize: 42 constants
WdTableFormat: 40 constants

The following list shows these enums, along with a count of the number of constants per enum:

WdAlertLevel (3)	WdDeletedTextMark (4)	WdIndexType (2)
WdAnimation (7)	WdDictionaryType (8)	WdInformation (35)
WdArrangeStyle (2)	WdDictionaryTypeHID (2)	WdInlineShapeType (5)
WdAutoMacros (5)	WdDocumentKind (3)	WdInsertCells (4)
WdAutoVersions (2)	WdDocumentType (2)	WdInsertedTextMark (5)
WdBaselineAlignment (5)	WdDropPosition (3)	WdInternationalIndex (10)
WdBookmarkSortBy (2)	WdEditionOption (8)	WdJustificationMode (3)
WdBorderDistanceFrom (2)	WdEditionType (2)	WdKey (98)
WdBorderType (6)	WdEmphasisMark (5)	WdKeyCategory (9)
WdBorderTypeHID (2)	WdEnableCancelKey (2)	WdLanguageID (64)
WdBreakType (7)	WdEndnoteLocation (2)	WdLetterheadLocation (4)
WdBrowseTarget (12)	WdEnvelopeOrientation (9)	WdLetterStyle (3)
WdBuiltInProperty (30)	WdFarEastLineBreakLevel (3)	WdLineSpacing (6)
WdBuiltinStyle (91)	WdFieldKind (4)	WdLineStyle (23)
WdCaptionLabelID (3)	WdFieldShading (3)	WdLineWidth (9)
WdCaptionNumberStyle (5)	WdFieldType (88)	WdLinkType (8)
WdCaptionNumberStyleHID (15)	WdFindMatch (21)	WdListApplyTo (3)
WdCaptionPosition (2)	WdFindWrap (3)	WdListGalleryType (3)
WdCellVerticalAlignment (3)	WdFontBias (3)	WdListLevelAlignment (3)
WdCharacterCase (6)	WdFootnoteLocation (2)	WdListNumberStyle (13)
WdCharacterCaseHID (4)	WdFramePosition (7)	WdListNumberStyleHID (31)
WdChevronConvertRule (4)	WdFrameSizeRule (3)	WdListType (6)
WdCollapseDirection (2)	WdGoToDirection (6)	WdMailMergeActiveRecord (5)
WdColorIndex (19)	WdGoToItem (17)	WdMailMergeComparison (8)
WdCompatibility (32)	WdHeaderFooterIndex (3)	WdMailMergeDataSource (6)
WdConstants (7)	WdHeadingSeparator (5)	WdMailMergeDefaultRecord (2)
WdContinue (3)	WdHelpType (11)	WdMailMergeDestination (4)
WdCountry (24)	WdHelpTypeHID (2)	WdMailMergeMainDocType (5)
WdCursorType (4)	WdIMEMode (10)	WdMailMergeState (6)
WdCustomLabelPageSize (9)	WdIndexFilter (7)	WdMailSystem (4)
WdDefaultFilePath (17)	WdIndexFormat (7)	WdMeasurementUnits (4)
WdDeleteCells (4)	WdIndexSortBy (2)	WdMeasurementUnitsHID (1)

WdMovementType (2)
WdMultipleWordConversionsMode (2)
WdNoteNumberStyle (6)
WdNoteNumberStyleHID (11)
WdNumberingRule (3)
WdNumberType (3)
WdOLEPlacement (2)
WdOLEType (3)
WdOLEVerb (7)
WdOpenFormat (6)
WdOrganizerObject (4)
WdOrientation (2)
WdOriginalFormat (3)
WdOutlineLevel (10)
WdPageBorderArt (164)
WdPageFit (3)
WdPageNumberAlignment (5)
WdPageNumberStyle (5)
WdPageNumberStyleHID (11)
WdPaperSize (42)
WdPaperTray (15)
WdParagraphAlignment (4)
WdParagraphAlignmentHID (1)
WdPartOfSpeech (4)
WdPasteDataType (9)
WdPictureLinkType (3)
WdPrintOutItem (7)
WdPrintOutPages (3)
WdPrintOutRange (5)
WdProofreadingErrorType (2)
WdProtectionType (4)
WdReferenceKind (13)

WdReferenceType (5)
WdRelativeHorizontalPosition (3)
WdRelativeVerticalPosition (3)
WdRelocate (2)
WdReplace (3)
WdRevisedLinesMark (4)
WdRevisedPropertiesMark (5)
WdRevisionsWrap (3)
WdRevisionType (10)
WdRoutingSlipDelivery (2)
WdRoutingSlipStatus (3)
WdRowAlignment (3)
WdRowHeightRule (3)
WdRulerStyle (4)
WdSalutationGender (4)
WdSalutationType (4)
WdSaveFormat (8)
WdSaveOptions (3)
WdSectionStart (5)
WdSeekView (11)
WdSelectionFlags (5)
WdSelectionType (9)
WdSeparatorType (5)
WdSortFieldType (3)
WdSortFieldTypeHID (4)
WdSortOrder (2)
WdSortSeparator (3)
WdSpecialPane (18)
WdSpellingErrorType (3)
WdSpellingWordType (3)
WdStatistic (6)
WdStatisticHID (1)

WdStoryType (11)
WdStyleType (2)
WdSubscriberFormats (4)
WdSummaryLength (8)
WdSummaryMode (4)
WdTabAlignment (6)
WdTabLeader (4)
WdTabLeaderHID (2)
WdTableFieldSeparator (4)
WdTableFormat (40)
WdTableFormatApply (9)
WdTemplateType (3)
WdTextFormFieldType (6)
WdTextOrientation (3)
WdTextOrientationHID (2)
WdTextureIndex (53)
WdToaFormat (5)
WdTocFormat (7)
WdTofFormat (6)
WdTrailingCharacter (3)
WdUnderline (10)
WdUnits (16)
WdVerticalAlignment (4)
WdViewType (6)
WdWindowState (3)
WdWindowType (2)
WdWordDialog (171)
WdWordDialogHID (3)
WdWordDialogTab (55)
WdWordDialogTabHID (6)
WdWrapSideType (4)
WdWrapType (5)

The VBA Object Browser

Microsoft does supply a tool for viewing the objects, properties, methods, events, and enums in an object model. It is called the Microsoft Object Browser, and it is accessible from the View menu in the VBA IDE (or hit the F2 key). Figure 10-1 shows the Microsoft Object Browser.

The topmost drop-down list box lets you select an object model for viewing (in this case, we are viewing the Word object model). The second list box is for searching the object model. On the left middle, you'll find a list of the classes in the object model. There is one class per object and one class per enum. The right-hand list box shows the properties, methods, and events of the object that is selected in the classes list box. The text box at the bottom gives some information about the selected item.

Figure 10-1. The Microsoft Object Browser

The Object Browser is certainly a useful tool; you will probably want to spend some time experimenting with it. (Perhaps its best feature is that it is easily accessible from the IDE.) However, it gives only a flat one-dimensional view of the object model. For a two-dimensional hierarchical view, I have written the Enhanced Object Browser, a coupon for which is included in the back of this book. In fact, many of the figures in this book (Figure 11-1, for example) are screenshots taken from the Enhanced Object Browser.

11

The Application Object

At last we can begin a detailed look at the major portions of the Word object model, starting with the Application object, which sits atop the object model. Figure 11-1 shows the Application object and its children.

Figure 11-2 shows those children of the Application object that I discuss in this book, in this chapter and later chapters. After discussing some of the properties and methods of the Application object itself, I discuss some of the simpler child objects of Application in this chapter, saving the more involved child objects for later chapters.

Properties and Methods

The Application object has a whopping 139 properties and methods:

Activate	Caption	DefaultTableSeparator
ActiveDocument	CaptionLabels	Dialogs
ActivePrinter	CentimetersToPoints	DisplayAlerts
ActiveWindow	ChangeFileOpenDirectory	DisplayAutoCompleteTips
AddAddress	CheckGrammar	DisplayRecentFiles
AddIns	CheckSpelling	DisplayScreenTips
Application	CleanString	DisplayScrollBars
Assistant	CommandBars	DisplayStatusBar
AutoCaptions	Creator	Documents
AutoCorrect	CustomDictionaries	EnableCancelKey
AutomaticChange	CustomizationContext	FileConverters
BackgroundPrintingStatus	DDEExecute	FileSearch
BackgroundSavingStatus	DDEInitiate	FindKey
BrowseExtraFileTypes	DDEPoke	FocusInMailHeader
Browser	DDERequest	FontNames
Build	DDETerminate	GetAddress
BuildKeyCode	DDETerminateAll	GetSpellingSuggestions
CapsLock	DefaultSaveFormat	GoBack

GoForward
HangulHanjaDictionaries
Height
Help
HelpTool
InchesToPoints
International
IsObjectValid
KeyBindings
KeysBoundTo
KeyString
LandscapeFontNames
Languages
Left
LinesToPoints
ListCommands
ListGalleries
LookupNameProperties
MacroContainer
MailingLabel
MailMessage
MailSystem
MAPIAvailable
MathCoprocessorAvailable
MillimetersToPoints
MountVolume
MouseAvailable
Move
Name

NewWindow
NextLetter
NormalTemplate
NumLock
OnTime
Options
OrganizerCopy
OrganizerDelete
OrganizerRename
Parent
Path
PathSeparator
PicasToPoints
PointsToCentimeters
PointsToInches
PointsToLines
PointsToMillimeters
PointsToPicas
PortraitFontNames
PrintOut
PrintPreview
Quit
RecentFiles
Repeat
ResetIgnoreAll
Resize
Run
ScreenRefresh
ScreenUpdating

Selection
SendFax
ShowClipboard
ShowMe
ShowVisualBasicEditor
SpecialMode
StartupPath
StatusBar
SubstituteFont
SynonymInfo
System
Tasks
Templates
Top
UsableHeight
UsableWidth
UserAddress
UserControl
UserInitials
UserName
VBE
Version
Visible
Width
Windows
WindowState
WordBasic

I discuss many of these properties and methods throughout the remainder of the book when the discussion will seem more relevant. However, I briefly discuss some of these properties and methods in the next section.

The ActiveDocument Property

This ubiquitous property returns a Document object that represents the active document—that is, the document with the focus (or the document that has the focus when Word has the focus). Many of the examples revolve around the active document, so I use this property often. Note that since it is a global property, I do not need to qualify its name with the Application object reference. Thus, the following is acceptable:

```
MsgBox ActiveDocument.Name
```

If there are no documents open when a call is made to the ActiveDocument property, Word will generate an error. You can avoid this by checking the Count property of the Documents collection, as in:

```
If Documents.Count => 1 Then
    MsgBox ActiveDocument.Name
End If
```

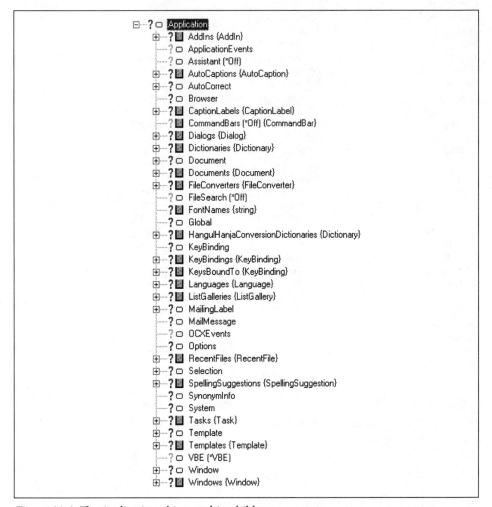

Figure 11-1. The Application object and its children

Since the ActiveDocument property is read-only, you cannot use it to set the active document. Instead, this is done using the *Activate* method of the Document object. For instance, to activate a document named *MyLetter*, execute the code:

```
Documents("MyLetter").Activate
```

The ActivePrinter Property

This property returns or sets the name of the active printer. For instance, on my system, the line:

```
MsgBox Application.ActivePrinter
```

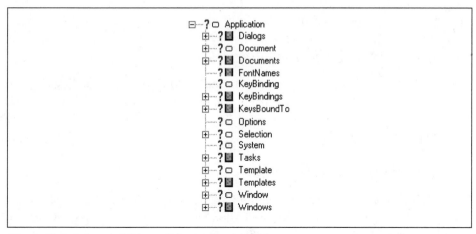

Figure 11-2. Selected children of the Application object

displays the message "HP Laserjet 4000 PS on LPT1." On the other hand, to change the default printer to an Epson Stylus 800 Color, you would use the code:

```
Application.ActivePrinter = "EPSON Stylus 800 COLOR"
```

In view of the fact that the ActivePrinter property can be used to set the active printer, this raises the issue of how to determine the installed printers on a given computer. Unfortunately, VBA does not seem to provide a way to do this. (Visual Basic has a Printers collection, but Visual Basic for Applications does not.)

There are several ways to get a list of installed printers, but they all involve reaching below the VBA programming level to the Windows API. This is a collection of about 1,000 functions that are used primarily by Windows programmers in Visual C++ (or Visual Basic) to access the Windows operating system at a lower level than VBA programmers would normally do.

To be sure, programming with the Windows API functions is significantly more complicated than programming the higher-level Word VBA language. This is not to say, however, that it is beyond the abilities of a Word VBA programmer. It just requires a much longer learning curve and is much more frustrating, since errors tend simply to crash the application (or the computer). The Windows API functions do not issue error messages! Indeed, I would recommend limited use of the Windows API to experienced VBA programmers when it is useful, since it can add considerable power to VBA programs.

In any case, since the issue of getting the installed printers can be important to Word VBA programmers at any level, I have included Appendix C, *Getting the Installed Printers*, which describes a program for getting this information. Even if you do not want to take the time to understand all of the details of this program, you can simply type it into your own code and use it as is. (It will also give you a peek at the complexities of Windows API programming.)

The Build and Version Properties

The Build property returns the version and build number of Microsoft Word; the Version property returns just the version number. If you ever need to write code that works only under certain versions of Word, then you will probably need one of these properties.

The ListCommands Method

This method creates a new document and then inserts a table listing all of Word's commands, along with their associated shortcut keys and menu assignments (if any). The syntax is:

```
Application.ListCommands(ListAllCommands)
```

where the Boolean parameter *ListAllCommands* should be set to True to include all Word commands and False to include only commands with customized key or menu assignments.

The OnTime Method

This method starts a background timer that will run a specified macro at a specified date and time. The syntax is:

```
Application.OnTime(When, Name, Tolerance)
```

where *When* is the time at which the macro is to be run, *Name* is the name of the macro to run, and *Tolerance* is the maximum time, in seconds, that can elapse before the macro is cancelled if it has not yet run. (A macro may be delayed by the system for various reasons, such as if a dialog box is displayed.)

For example, the following code runs the macro *Alarm* at midnight or up to 5 minutes thereafter:

```
Application.OnTime "12:00 pm", "Project.Module1.Alarm", 300
```

You can also include a date in the *Time* argument, as in:

```
Application.OnTime "6/30/98 12:00 pm", _
                "Project.Module1.Alarm", 300
```

It is possible to set the macro run time relative to the time at which the *OnTime* instruction executes. This is done by using the *Now* function, which returns the current date and time. For instance, the following code will run the *Alarm* macro in 10 minutes from the time that the *OnTime* method is executed:

```
Application.OnTime Now + TimeValue("00:10:00"), _
    "Project.Module1.Alarm", 300
```

Note the use of the *TimeValue* function to convert a string into a time so it can be added to the return value of the *Now* function.

It is generally important to use a fully qualified macro name, such as:

```
Project.Module1.Alarm
```

to ensure that the correct macro is run. Also, the document or template that contains the macro to run must be available both when the *OnTime* instruction is executed and when the time specified in that instruction arrives. Hence, it is best to store the macro either in the Normal template (which is always available) or another global template that is loaded automatically.

Finally, note that Word can maintain only one background timer at a time, so a second call to *OnTime* before the first one has done its job will cancel the first timer.

The PrintPreview Property

The Boolean PrintPreview property can be used to determine whether Word is in print preview mode or to set the view mode. In particular, you can set PrintPreview to True to place Word in print preview mode and False to return Word to the previous view mode.

The Quit Method

This method quits Microsoft Word. Its syntax is:

```
Application.Quit(SaveChanges, Format, RouteDocument)
```

The optional *SaveChanges* parameter specifies the save action for the document. It can be one of the constants in the following enum:

```
Enum WdSaveOptions
    wdPromptToSaveChanges = -2
    wdSaveChanges = -1
    wdDoNotSaveChanges = 0
End Enum
```

(If you omit the *SaveChanges* argument, Word will prompt the user to save any unsaved changes. If there are no unsaved changes, Word will just quit.) If the document is to be saved, the optional *Format* parameter specifies the save format. It can be one of the following constants:

```
Enum WdOriginalFormat
    wdWordDocument = 0
    wdOriginalDocumentFormat = 1
    wdPromptUser = 2
End Enum
```

Finally, the optional *RouteDocument* parameter should be set to True to route the document to the next recipient, assuming the document has a routing slip. Otherwise, this argument is ignored.

The Selection Property

This often-used property returns the Selection object that represents the current selection, which may simply be the insertion point if no characters are selected. (I discuss Selection objects in detail in Chapter 14, *The Range and Selection Objects.*)

The FontNames Collection

The FontNames collection holds the names of the currently available fonts. The Application object has three properties that return a FontNames collection object: FontNames, PortraitFontNames, and LandscapeFontNames.

To illustrate, the following code will insert the names of all available fonts into the active document at the current insertion point (referred to by the call to the Selection object's *Collapse* method in the code). Note that the constant **vbCr** represents an end of paragraph character, so each font name will appear in its own paragraph:

```
Dim FontName As Variant

' Collapse the selection to an insertion point
Selection.Collapse wdCollapseEnd

For Each FontName In Application.FontNames
    Selection.InsertAfter FontName & vbCr
Next FontName
```

Recall that the loop variable in a **For Each** loop must be either an object variable or a variable of type Variant; it cannot be a String variable, as would otherwise be appropriate here.

The Options Object

The Options object is used to set various Word options. It has a whopping 144 properties, but only one method: *SetWPHelpOptions*, which sets the options for the WordPerfect Help feature.

Here is an example of code that sets three Word options. Note that since the Options property is global, you can use it without qualification; that is, you can write *Options* rather than *Application.Options*:

```
With Options
    .AnimateScreenMovements = False
```

```
    .CheckSpellingAsYouType = False
    .MeasurementUnit = wdPoints
End With
```

The System Object

The System object contains information about the computer upon which the code is running. The System object has one very interesting method: *MSInfo*, which starts the Microsoft System Information application. This one you should try for yourself by entering the code:

```
System.MSInfo
```

The properties of the System object:

Application	HorizontalResolution	PrivateProfileString
ComputerType	LanguageDesignation	ProcessorType
Connect	MacintoshName	ProfileString
Country	MathCoprocessorInstalled	QuickDrawInstalled
Creator	MSInfo	Version
Cursor	OperatingSystem	VerticalResolution
FreeDiskSpace	Parent	

One of the most useful properties of the System object is PrivateProfileString, which provides a way to save and retrieve string data in a special type of text file, typically called an *initialization file* or *INI file* (with an *.ini* file extension), because it is used to store data that is used to initialize settings in an application. As you probably know, INI files played a prominent role in Windows 3.1, but their role in Windows 95 and later has been taken over by the system Registry (definitely a mixed blessing!).

It is also possible to save and retrieve data from the Windows Registry using this property. However, I do not discuss the Registry, since it is my advice to avoid tampering with it unless you have a compelling reason to do otherwise. (If you decide to tamper with the Registry, don't forget to back it up first.)

The format of an INI file is:

```
[Section1]
Key1=Value1
Key2=Value2
...

[Section2]
Key3=Value3
Key4=Value4
...
```

Notice that an INI file contains sections to allow grouping of the data by subject. Under each section, you can add lines of the form KEY=VALUE.

The syntax for the PrivateProfileString property is:

```
System.PrivateProfileString(Filename, Section, Key)
```

where *Filename* is the name of the initialization file to which you want to add or retrieve information. If the path is not included, the Windows directory is used. However, since it is not a good idea to add to the clutter in an already bloated Windows directory, I strongly suggest that you find another location for your INI files.

The *Section* parameter is the name of the section (without the square brackets), and the *Key* parameter is the name of the key. The PrivateProfileString property returns or sets the value portion of the key/value pair.

To illustrate, the following line of code will create an INI file called *d:\word\text.ini* (if it does not already exist), add a **[Fonts]** section (if it does not already exist), and then insert the key/value pair **Start = Arial**:

```
System.PrivateProfileString("d:\word\test.INI", "Fonts", _
                            "Start") = "Arial"
```

Note that if there is already a key/value pair whose key name is **Start**, its value will be replaced without warning.

The following code displays the value from the **Start=** line in the **[Fonts]** section:

```
MsgBox System.PrivateProfileString("d:\word\test.INI", "Fonts", "Start")
```

The Task Object

A Task object represents a currently running Windows application (not just Microsoft Word). Task objects are kept in the Tasks collection.

One of the more useful properties of a Task object is the Name property. For instance, the following code prints (to the Immediate window) the names of all of the currently running tasks:

```
Dim t as Task
For Each t in Tasks
    Debug.Print t.Name
Next t
```

You might find it amusing to run this code on your system. You will probably see some rather bizarre looking tasks.

On a more useful note, the Tasks collection has a method called Exists that indicates whether a certain task is running. For instance, the following code determines whether Microsoft Excel is running. If so, the code activates Excel and maximizes it;

if not, the code starts Excel using the VBA *Shell* function, whose purpose is to run an executable program (the path is correct for my PC):

```
If Tasks.Exists("Microsoft Excel") = True Then
    Tasks("Microsoft Excel").Activate
    Tasks("Microsoft Excel").WindowState = wdWindowStateMaximize
Else
    Shell "I:\Office97\Excel\Excel.exe", vbMaximizedFocus
End If
```

The Template Object

The Template object represents a Word template. Template objects are kept in the Templates collection, which includes all available Word templates at a given moment, that is:

- All templates that are open as documents

- All templates that are attached to open documents

- All global templates that appear in the Templates and Add-ins dialog box (under the Tools menu)

- The Normal template

The Templates collection does not include all *.dot* files on the hard disk.

The AttachedTemplate Property

Note that the Document object has an AttachedTemplate property that returns the Template object that is attached to the document. Thus, the code:

```
MsgBox ActiveDocument.AttachedTemplate.Name
```

will display the name of the template attached to the currently active Word document.

Properties and Methods of the Template Object

The Template object has only two methods: *Save* and *OpenAsDocument*. The latter method is actually quite important, because some of the properties of a template can be accessed only when the template is opened as a document. For example, to access the formatting styles in a template, it must be opened as a document.

To be perfectly clear, the *OpenAsDocument* method will open, as a document, a template that is in the Templates collection, which means the template is already "open" in some sense. To open a template that is on the disk as a document, we must use the *Open* method of the Documents collection. (I discuss this method in Chapter 12, *The Document Object.*)

To illustrate the use of the *OpenAsDocument* method, the following code opens the template that is attached to the active document and checks to see if the template has any text, that is, contains more than just the omnipresent ending paragraph mark:

```
Dim doc as Document

' Open attached template as document
Set doc = ActiveDocument.AttachedTemplate.OpenAsDocument

' Check contents of doc for more than paragraph mark
If doc.Content.Text = vbCr Then
    MsgBox "Template contains no text."
Else
    MsgBox "Template contains text."
End If

doc.Close SaveChanges:=wdDoNotSaveChanges
```

The following code fragment saves a copy of the Normal template as a template named *Backup.dot*:

```
Dim doc as Document

' Open normal template as document
Set doc = NormalTemplate.OpenAsDocument

' Save it and then close it
With doc
    .SaveAs FileName:="Backup.dot"
    .Close SaveChanges:=wdDoNotSaveChanges
End With
```

Among the properties of the Template object are:

Name

Returns the name of the template.

FullName

Returns the full path name of the template file.

Type

Returns the template type, which can be any of the constants in the following enum:

```
Enum WdTemplateType
    wdNormalTemplate = 0
    wdGlobalTemplate = 1
    wdAttachedTemplate = 2
End Enum
```

To illustrate, the following code displays a message box with the full names and types of all of the templates in the Templates collection. Note that I use a `Select`

Case statement to translate the template type, which is an integer, into a text string for display. Note also that I collect the text string for the message in a string variable called **sMsg**, placing the constants **vbCrLf** between templates to create a multiline message:

```
Dim tmpl As Template
Dim sMsg As String    ' For message
Dim sType As String   ' For template type

sMsg = ""             ' Initialize
sType = ""

' Loop through Templates collection
For Each tmpl In Templates

    ' Get the template type as a string
    Select Case tmpl.Type
       Case wdNormalTemplate
          sType = "Normal"
       Case wdGlobalTemplate
          sType = "Global"
       Case wdAttachedTemplate
          sType = "Attached"
    End Select

    ' Add this template to the message
    sMsg = sMsg & tmpl.FullName & ": " & sType & vbCrLf

Next tmpl

' Display template info
MsgBox sMsg, vbOKOnly, "Current Templates"
```

Figure 11-3 shows the result of running this code on my system with the manuscript for this book open. (I keep my templates in a directory called *d:\wordmacs97.*)

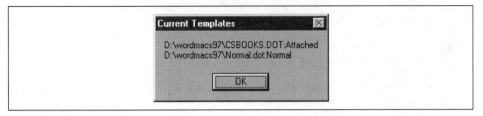

Figure 11-3. Current templates

Creating a Template

The Templates collection does not have an *Add* method, so you cannot create a new template directly. Templates are created by first creating a Word document and then saving it as a template, using the *SaveAs* method. For instance, the following code creates a new document and saves it as a template with name *NewTemplate.dot*:

```
Dim doc As Document
Set doc = Documents.Add
doc.SaveAs "NewTemplate", wdFormatTemplate
```

A template is added to the Templates collection automatically whenever you:

- Use the *Open* method of the Documents collection to open a document based on a template

- Use the *Add* method of the Documents collection to create a new document based on a template

- Use the AttachedTemplate property of the Document object to attach a template to a document, in the process replacing a previously attached template

You can use the NormalTemplate property of the Application object to return a template object that refers to the Normal template. Also, as mentioned earlier, the AttachedTemplate property of the Document object will return the template attached to the document.

Finally, the DefaultFilePath property of the Options object can be used to return or set the location of templates and other documents. The syntax is:

```
Options.DefaultFilePath(Path) = NewPath
```

Here *Path* is the path and name of the directory type to set or retrieve and can be one of the constants in the following enum:

```
Enum WdDefaultFilePath
    wdDocumentsPath = 0
    wdPicturesPath = 1
    wdUserTemplatesPath = 2
    wdWorkgroupTemplatesPath = 3
    wdUserOptionsPath = 4
    wdAutoRecoverPath = 5
    wdToolsPath = 6
    wdTutorialPath = 7
    wdStartupPath = 8
    wdProgramPath = 9
    wdGraphicsFiltersPath = 10
    wdTextConvertersPath = 11
    wdProofingToolsPath = 12
    wdTempFilePath = 13
    wdCurrentFolderPath = 14
    wdStyleGalleryPath = 15
    wdBorderArtPath = 19
End Enum
```

Note that setting the value to the empty string will clear that value, as in:

```
Options.DefaultFilePath(wdStartupPath) = ""
```

The Window Object

A Window object represents a window. Window objects are kept in a Windows collection. Figure 11-4 shows the Windows object and its children. (I discuss Document and Selection objects in Chapters 12 and 14.)

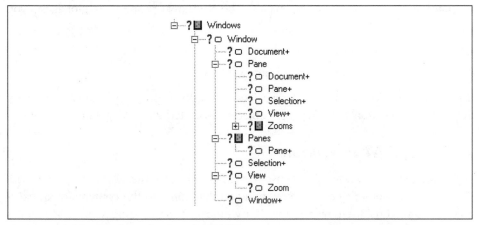

Figure 11-4. The Windows object and its children

Windows, Panes, and Views

In Microsoft Word, each window is associated with a document. Normally, a document window contains a single document pane, but a window can be split into two panes. (Additional panes may exist if comments or footnotes are visible, but I do not deal with these types of panes.)

Many of the visibility-related properties of windows (as opposed to the contents of the windows), such as scrolling and the appearance of rulers and scrollbars, are properties of the Pane objects associated with the window. However, since normally there is only one pane per window, Microsoft was kind enough to define these properties for the Window object as well. Thus, for instance, to scroll down the active window pane, I can write:

```
ActiveWindow.LargeScroll
```

instead of:

```
ActiveWindow.ActivePane.LargeScroll
```

Many of the visibility-related properties of the contents of a window, such as whether hidden text is visible or paragraph marks are visible, are accessed through the View object, which is a child of both the Pane object and the Window object (in keeping with the precept mentioned in the previous paragraph).

Finally, to control the magnification-related properties of a pane, Word defines a Zoom object, which is accessible through the Pane object and the View object.

The Windows Collection

The Application object has a Windows property that returns a Windows collection containing all current Window objects. The Windows property is global, so you can simply write, for example:

```
MsgBox Windows.Count
```

to get the count of the number of open windows.

Note that the Document object also has a Windows property, but this property returns the collection of all Window objects associated with the given document.

Creating a New Window

To create a new Window object, use the *Add* method or the *NewWindow* method. Both of these methods create a new window that contains the contents of an existing window. Thus, the new window is a window for an existing Word document.

The Add method

To open an additional window that duplicates the contents of a currently open window, use the *Add* method of the Windows collection, whose syntax is:

```
Windows.Add(Window)
```

where the optional **Window** parameter is the Window object whose contents you wish to duplicate. If this argument is missing, Word will open a new window for the active document.

Note that when multiple windows are open for a given document, the window caption is appended with a colon and a number (in the Word Window menu).

The NewWindow method

The *NewWindow* method applies to the Application object (and is global) as well as the Window object. When applied to an existing Window object, the *NewWindow* method has the syntax:

```
WindowObject.NewWindow
```

and creates a new window whose contents are identical to the contents of the **WindowObject** window. When applied to the Application object (or globally), a new window is opened for the active window (and hence for the active document).

For instance, the following code opens a new window for the active window:

```
Dim win as Window
Set win = NewWindow
```

The second line could also be replaced by either of the following lines:

```
Set win = ActiveWindow.NewWindow
Set win = Application.NewWindow
```

Properties and Methods of the Window Object

The properties and methods of the Window object are:

Activate	DocumentMap	PrintOut
Active	DocumentMapPercentWidth	Selection
ActivePane	Height	SmallScroll
Application	HorizontalPercentScrolled	Split
Caption	Index	SplitVertical
Close	LargeScroll	StyleAreaWidth
Creator	Left	Top
DisplayHorizontalScrollBar	NewWindow	Type
DisplayRulers	Next	VerticalPercentScrolled
DisplayScreenTips	PageScroll	View
DisplayVerticalRuler	Panes	Width
DisplayVerticalScrollBar	Parent	WindowNumber
Document	Previous	WindowState

Arranging open windows

The most interesting member of the Windows collection is the *Arrange* method, which arranges all open document windows. The syntax is:

```
Windows.Arrange(ArrangeStyle)
```

where **ArrangeStyle** specifies the window arrangement and can be either of the **WdArrangeStyle** constants **wdIcons** or **wdTiled**.

Scrolling properties and methods

The Window object has several properties and methods that relate to scrolling:

The DisplayHorizontalScrollBar and DisplayVerticalScrollBar properties
   These Boolean properties return or set whether horizontal and vertical scrollbars are displayed for the window.

The HorizontalPercentScrolled and VerticalPercentScrolled properties
   These Long properties return or set the horizontal and vertical scroll position as a percentage of the document width. For example, to set the horizontal scroll position of the active window to 50%, write:

```
ActiveWindow.HorizontalPercentScrolled = 50
```

The LargeScroll and SmallScroll methods

The LargeScroll method scrolls a window (or pane) by the specified number of screens. This is equivalent to clicking just before or just after the small square thumbs on the horizontal and vertical scrollbars. The syntax is:

```
expression.LargeScroll(Down, Up, ToRight, ToLeft)
```

where **expression** returns a Window (or Pane) object. The parameters are all optional variants:

Down

The number of screens to scroll the window down.

Up

The number of screens to scroll the window up.

ToRight

The number of screens to scroll the window to the right.

ToLeft

The number of screens to scroll the window to the left.

Note that any of these arguments can be a negative number, which specifies motion in the opposite direction. If no arguments are specified, the window is scrolled down one screen.

The SmallScroll method is analogous to the LargeScroll method, but in this case, each application of the method is equivalent to clicking the small arrows on the scrollbars. (Microsoft refers to this as scrolling a certain number of horizontal or vertical lines). The syntax is:

```
expression.SmallScroll(Down, Up, ToRight, ToLeft)
```

where **expression** is a Window (or Pane) object, and the parameters indicate the number and direction of such "clicks." If no arguments are specified, the window is scrolled down one line.

The PageScroll method

This method scrolls the window (or pane) by full pages. It syntax is:

```
expression.PageScroll(Down, Up)
```

where **expression** is a Window (or Pane) object, **Down** is the number of pages to scroll down, and **Up** is the number of pages to scroll up. If the arguments are missing, the object is scrolled down one page.

Note that this method is available only in page layout view or online layout view. Also, the method does not affect the position of the insertion point.

Special views

Microsoft Word has a few special views that can be quite useful:

The document map

A document map is a vertical region across the left edge of the window that displays an outline of the document, using the heading styles.

The DocumentMap property is a Boolean property that returns or sets whether the document map is visible. The DocumentMapPercentWidth property returns or sets the width of the document map as a percentage of the width of the window.

The style area

When the StyleAreaWidth property is nonzero, Word displays a vertical window on the left that displays the styles for each paragraph. The StyleAreaWidth property returns or sets the width of this style area, in points as a Single. Note that the style area is not visible in page layout view or online layout view.

Additional properties and methods of the Window object

This section lists some additional members of the Window object:

The Activate method and the Active property

This method activates the specified window. The syntax is:

```
Window.Activate
```

For instance, to active the second window, write:

```
Windows(2).Activate
```

To active the second window for a document named *temp.doc*, we would use:

```
Windows("temp.doc:2").Activate
```

We can tell whether a given Window object is the active one by checking the read-only Boolean Active property for the window.

The DisplayRulers and DisplayVerticalRuler properties

The Boolean DisplayRulers property returns or sets whether the rulers are displayed for a window (or pane). It is equivalent to using the Ruler command on the View menu. The property applies in normal as well as page layout view.

If DisplayRulers is True and if the current view is page layout view, then the value of DisplayVerticalRuler determines whether a vertical ruler will be displayed. This property is ignored if DisplayRulers is False, so a vertical ruler cannot be displayed without a horizontal ruler.

The Document property

This read-only property returns a Document object associated with the window (or pane).

The PrintOut method

This method is used to print the contents of a window. I discuss this method in detail when I discuss the Document object (Chapter 12), to which the method also applies.

The Selection property

This property returns the Selection object that represents a selected range or the insertion point in the window. Note that each open window has its own selection or insertion point. Thus, for example, the following code:

```
Debug.Print Windows(1).Selection.Text
Debug.Print Windows(2).Selection.Text
```

will print (to the Immediate window) the selections in each of the first two windows.

The Type property

This read-only property returns the type of the window. If the window is associated with a Word document (*.doc* file), the window's type is `wdWindowDoc-ument`. If the window is associated with a Word template (*.dot* file), then the window's type is `wdWindowTemplate`.

The WindowNumber property

If there is more than one window associated with a document, the window number is shown in the window's menu item in the Window menu and also in the titlebar for the window. (This number is preceded by a colon.) This read-only property returns that window number. (If there is only one window associated with a document, this property returns the number 1.)

The WindowNumber property should not be confused with the Index property, which returns the index of the Window object within the Windows collection.

The WindowState property

This property returns or sets the state of the window. It can be one of the constants in the following enum:

```
Enum WdWindowState
    wdWindowStateNormal = 0
    wdWindowStateMaximize = 1
    wdWindowStateMinimize = 2
End Enum
```

The `wdWindowStateNormal` constant indicates a window that is neither maximized nor minimized. This property can only be applied to the active window. If it is applied to an inactive window, Word will generate an error message. Therefore, you should always check the Active property and if necessary apply the *Activate* method before setting this property.

The Pane Object

In Word, a window can be split into two panes. Each pane is represented by a Pane object. The panes for a given window are stored in the window's Panes collection. The Panes property of the Window object returns this Panes collection.

Note that a document window can be split into at most two window panes. However, if the view is not page layout view, the Panes collection can contain Pane objects for such things as comments or footnotes. I confine our discussion to splitting a window into two document panes.

To retrieve the active pane (the pane with the focus), use the ActivePane property of the Window object.

Creating New Panes

To split a window, use the *Add* method of the Panes collection, the Split property of the Window object, or the SplitVertical property of the Window object.

The Add method

This method adds a new pane to a window. Its syntax is:

```
Panes.Add(SplitVertical)
```

where *SplitVertical* is the percentage of the window, measured from top to bottom, that should appear above the split. Note that this method will generate an error if the window has already been split.

The Split property

This Boolean property can be set to True to split a window, or it can be read to see if the window is already split.

The SplitVertical property

This Long property returns or sets the vertical split percentage for the specified window. To remote the split, set this property to 0, which is equivalent to setting the Split property to False.

Properties and Methods of the Pane Object

Many of the members of the Pane object are also members of the Window object. This is helpful, since when the window is not split, Word allows you to work directly with the Window object, rather than the single Pane object for that window. The following list shows the members of the Pane object (note that the member HorizontalPercentScrolled also belongs to the Window object):

Activate	DisplayVerticalRuler1	Parent1
Application1	Document1	Previous1
AutoScroll	HorizontalPercentScrolled	Selection1
BrowseToWindow	Index1	SmallScroll1
BrowseWidth	LargeScroll1	VerticalPercentScrolled1
Close1	MinimumFontSize	View1
Creator1	Next	Zooms
DisplayRulers1	PageScroll1	

The AutoScroll method

This method (which is not a method of the Window object) scrolls automatically through the specified pane, continuing to scroll until the user presses a key or clicks the mouse. Its syntax is:

```
PaneObject.AutoScroll(Velocity)
```

where *Velocity* is a Long that specifies the scrolling speed. It can be an integer in the range from –100 to 100, where –100 gives full-speed backward scrolling and 100 gives full-speed forward scrolling.

The View Object

A View object represents many of the viewing attributes of a contents of a window or pane. The View property of the Window or Pane object returns the View object.

The properties and methods of the View object are shown in the following list (I discuss just a few of these members):

Application	SeekView	ShowObjectAnchors
BrowseToWindow	ShowAll	ShowOptionalBreaks
CollapseOutline	ShowAllHeadings	ShowParagraphs
Creator	ShowAnimation	ShowPicturePlaceHolders
Draft	ShowBookmarks	ShowSpaces
EnlargeFontsLessThan	ShowDrawings	ShowTabs
ExpandOutline	ShowFieldCodes	ShowTextBoundaries
FieldShading	ShowFirstLineOnly	SplitSpecial
FullScreen	ShowFormat	TableGridlines
Magnifier	ShowHeading	Type
MailMergeDataView	ShowHiddenText	WrapToWindow
NextHeaderFooter	ShowHighlight	Zoom
Parent	ShowHyphens	
PreviousHeaderFooter	ShowMainTextLayer	

The Type Property

The Type property is used to set (or return) the view type. It can be set to any of the constants in the following enum:

```
Enum WdViewType
    wdNormalView = 1
    wdOutlineView = 2
    wdPageView = 3
    wdPrintPreview = 4
    wdMasterView = 5
    wdOnlineView = 6
End Enum
```

For instance, the following code sets the view for the active window to page layout:

```
ActiveWindow.View.Type = wdPageView
```

The Show Properties

The View object has several properties that determine what items are visible in the window. Here is a partial list (note that all of the properties are read/write Boolean, unless stated otherwise):

The ShowAll property

True to display all nonprinting characters (such as hidden text, tab marks, space marks, and paragraph marks).

The ShowAllHeadings method

Toggles between showing all text (headings and body text) and showing only headings. The method generates an error if the view is not outline view or master document view.

The ShowBookmarks property

True to display square brackets around each bookmark.

The ShowDrawings property

True if objects created with the drawing tools are displayed in page layout view.

The ShowFieldCodes property

True to display field codes.

The ShowHeading method

Shows all headings up to the specified heading level and hides additional headings and body text. The method generates an error if the view is not outline view or master document view. The syntax for this method is:

```
ViewObject.ShowHeading(Level)
```

where *Level* is a Long between 1 and 9, inclusive, that specifies the smallest outline heading level to display.

The ShowHiddenText property
> True to display text formatted as hidden text.

The ShowParagraphs property
> True to display paragraph marks.

The ShowSpaces property
> True to display space characters.

The ShowTabs property
> True to display tab characters.

The ShowTextBoundaries property
> True to display dotted lines around page margins, text columns, objects, and frames in page layout view.

The TableGridlines property
> True to display table gridlines.

The Zoom Object

A Zoom object represents the magnification properties of a view type: normal, outline, page layout, and so on.

There are two ways to access a Zoom object. The Zoom property of the View object returns the Zoom object that represents the magnification status for the view type associated with that view. If you want to change the magnification properties for the current view type of a particular View object of a particular Pane object, this is the way to do so.

For instance, the following code sets the magnification for the current view type of the active pane to 125%:

```
ActiveWindow.ActivePane.View.Zoom.Percentage = 125
```

(I discuss the Percentage property later in this chapter.)

On the other hand, you can also set up view magnifications for the various view types (normal, outline, page layout, and so on) without reference to the current view in a particular pane. This is done using the Zooms collection, which is accessed using the Zooms property of the Pane object.

The Zooms collection is very static and rather boring. It has no *Add* or *Count* methods, and we cannot cycle through the collection using a For Each loop. Nevertheless, the Zooms collection includes a single Zoom object for each view type for the pane, and you can refer to an individual Zoom object in the collection using the constants in the WdViewType enum as an index into the collection. As a reminder, this enum is:

```
Enum WdViewType
    wdNormalView = 1
```

```
      wdOutlineView = 2
      wdPageView = 3
      wdPrintPreview = 4
      wdMasterView = 5
      wdOnlineView = 6
   End Enum
```

Hence:

```
ActiveWindow.ActivePane.Zooms(wdNormalView)
```

is the Zoom object that is associated with the normal view for the active pane, and:

```
ActiveWindow.ActivePane.Zooms(wdPageView)
```

is the Zoom object associated with the page layout view.

Now you can set the properties of each of the six Zoom objects in the Zooms collection for a pane without reference to a View object. For instance, the following code sets the zoom percentage for the normal-view Zoom object for the active pane to 125%:

```
ActiveWindow.ActivePane.Zooms(wdNormalView).Percentage = 125
```

and the following code sets the page layout-view Zoom object for the active pane so that the entire page is visible:

```
ActiveWindow.ActivePane.Zooms(wdPageView).PageFit = wdPageFitFullPage
```

(The PageFit property is discussed in the next section.)

Now, whenever you set the view type for this pane to normal:

```
ActiveWindow.ActivePane.View.Type = wdNormalView
```

the View object will be associated with the normal-view Zoom object, so the magnification will be set to 125%. If you change the view to page layout:

```
ActiveWindow.ActivePane.View.Type = wdPageView
```

the magnification will be set to view the full page.

Properties of the Zoom Object

The main properties of the Zoom object are described in the following list. The Zoom object has no methods:

The PageColumns and PageRows properties

These properties return or set the number of pages to be displayed side-by-side (PageColumns) or up-and-down (PageRows) when the view is page layout or print preview.

The PageFit property

This property returns or sets the view magnification to one of the values in the following enum:

```
Enum WdPageFit
   wdPageFitNone = 0
   wdPageFitFullPage = 1
   wdPageFitBestFit = 2
End Enum
```

The **wdPageFitFullPage** constant specifies that a full page should be visible, but has an effect only when the view is page layout view.

If the PageFit property is set to **wdPageFitBestFit**, the zoom percentage is adjusted so that the width of the page just fits the width of the window. Moreover, the zoom percentage is automatically recalculated every time the size of the document window is changed. If the PageFit property is set to **wdPage-FitNone**, the automatic recalculation is turned off.

The Percentage property

This property returns or sets the magnification for the view as a percentage (a Long). For instance, the following code sets the magnification percentage to 150% for the active window:

```
ActiveWindow.View.Zoom.Percentage = 150
```

12

The Document Object

A Document object represents a Word document. Document objects are kept in the Documents collection, which contains all currently opened documents.

The Documents property of the Application object is global, so we can access the Documents collection simply by writing:

```
Documents
```

For instance, the code:

```
MsgBox Documents.Count
```

displays the number of currently open documents.

Perhaps the most commonly used property of the Application object is the Active-Document property, which returns a Document object that represents the currently active Word document.

Figure 12-1 shows the children of the Document object.

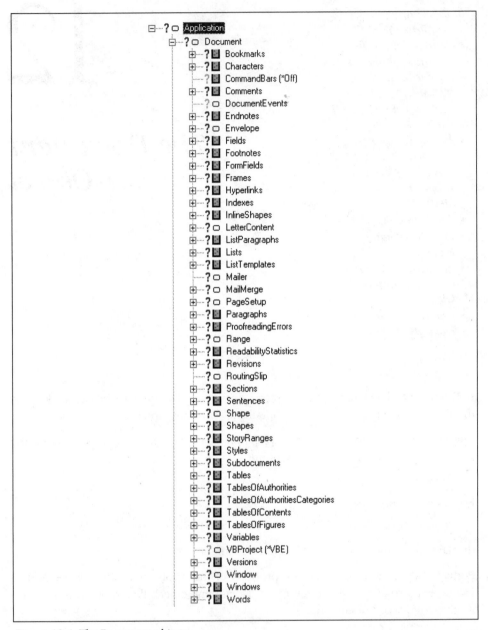

Figure 12-1. The Document object

Figure 12-2 shows the children of the Document object that I discuss specifically, either in this chapter and in subsequent chapters. First, however, I take a look at some of the properties and methods of the Document object.

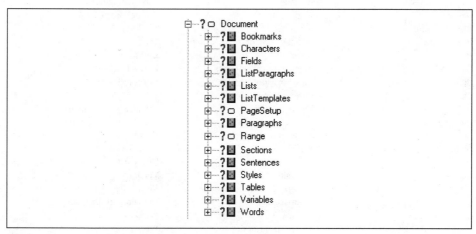

Figure 12-2. Selected children of the Document object

The Document object has a whopping 154 properties and methods (and 15 additional hidden properties and methods):

AcceptAllRevisions	Creator	IsSubdocument
Activate	CustomDocumentProperties	Kind
ActiveWindow	DataForm	ListParagraphs
ActiveWritingStyle	DefaultTabStop	Lists
AddToFavorites	EditionOptions	ListTemplates
Application	EmbedTrueTypeFonts	Mailer
AttachedTemplate	Endnotes	MailMerge
AutoFormat	Envelope	MakeCompatibilityDefault
AutoHyphenation	Fields	ManualHyphenation
AutoSummarize	FitToPages	Merge
Background	FollowHyperlink	Name
Bookmarks	Footnotes	PageSetup
BuiltInDocumentProperties	FormFields	Paragraphs
Characters	FormsDesign	Parent
CheckGrammar	ForwardMailer	Password
CheckSpelling	Frames	Path
Close	FullName	Post
ClosePrintPreview	GetCrossReferenceItems	PresentIt
CodeName	GetLetterContent	PrintFormsData
CommandBars	GoTo	PrintFractionalWidths
Comments	GrammarChecked	PrintOut
Compare	GrammaticalErrors	PrintPostScriptOverText
Compatibility	HasMailer	PrintPreview
ComputeStatistics	HasPassword	PrintRevisions
ConsecutiveHyphensLimit	HasRoutingSlip	Protect
Container	Hyperlinks	ProtectionType
Content	HyphenateCaps	Range
ConvertNumbersToText	HyphenationZone	ReadabilityStatistics
CopyStylesFromTemplate	Indexes	ReadOnly
CountNumberedItems	InlineShapes	ReadOnlyRecommended
CreateLetterContent	IsMasterDocument	Redo

RejectAllRevisions	SendMail	TablesOfFigures
Reload	SendMailer	ToggleFormsDesign
RemoveNumbers	Sentences	TrackRevisions
Repaginate	SetLetterContent	Type
Reply	Shapes	Undo
ReplyAll	ShowGrammaticalErrors	UndoClear
Revisions	ShowRevisions	Unprotect
Route	ShowSpellingErrors	UpdateStyles
Routed	ShowSummary	UpdateStylesOnOpen
RoutingSlip	SpellingChecked	UpdateSummaryProperties
RunAutoMacro	SpellingErrors	UserControl
RunLetterWizard	StoryRanges	Variables
Save	Styles	VBProject
SaveAs	Subdocuments	Versions
Saved	SummaryLength	ViewCode
SaveFormat	SummaryViewMode	ViewPropertyBrowser
SaveFormsData	Tables	Windows
SaveSubsetFonts	TablesOfAuthorities	Words
Sections	TablesOfAuthoritiesCategories	WritePassword
Select	TablesOfContents	WriteReserved
SendFax		

I discuss many of these properties and methods in detail throughout the remainder of the book when the discussion will seem a bit more pertinent. However, this still leaves plenty to discuss here.

Properties That Return Collections

Several properties of the Document object return a child collection object. Here is a list. (I discuss these collections later in this chapter or in subsequent chapters.)

Bookmarks

Returns a Bookmarks collection that represents all the bookmarks in the document.

BuiltInDocumentProperties

Returns a DocumentProperties collection that represents all the built-in document properties for the document.

CustomDocumentProperties

Returns a DocumentProperties collection that represents all the custom document properties for the specified document.

Fields

Returns a Fields collection that represents all the fields in the main story portion of the document.

Sections

Returns a Sections collection that represents all the sections in the document.

Sentences

Returns a Sentences collection that represents all the sentences in the document.

Styles

Returns a Styles collection for the specified document.

Tables

Returns a Tables collection that represents all the tables in the document.

Variables

Returns a Variables collection that represents the variables stored in the document.

Words

Returns a Words collection that represents all the words in the document.

Spelling-Related Properties and Methods

The Document object has several members that relate to spelling and grammar:

CheckGrammar method

Begins a spelling and grammar check for the document and displays the Spelling and Grammar dialog box when errors are encountered.

CheckSpelling method and SpellingChecked property

This method begins a spellcheck for the document and displays the Spelling and Grammar dialog box when errors are encountered (with the Check Grammar checkbox cleared).

Once the *CheckSpelling* method has been executed (or if the user does a spellcheck), Word sets the SpellingChecked property to True. Subsequent calls to *CheckSpelling* will do nothing unless you first set the SpellingChecked property to False.

The SpellingErrors property

The SpellingErrors property returns the ProofreadingErrors collection, which contains Range objects that identify the words in the document that are considered spelling errors.

Note that any reference to this property triggers a behind-the-scenes spellcheck in order to fill the ProofreadingErrors collection (which can take some time). You can verify this simply by creating a new document, filling it with some text that contains some spelling errors and then executing the line:

```
Debug.Print ActiveDocument.SpellingErrors.Count
```

This will cause Word to do a behind-the-scenes spellcheck so Word can report the count of spelling errors.

By way of example, the program in Example 12-1 prints all of the spelling errors in the active document to a new document. Some sample output for this program is shown in Example 12-2.

Example 12-1. The PrintSpellingErrors Procedure

```
Sub PrintSpellingErrors()

Dim doc As Document
Dim pf As ProofreadingErrors
Dim pe As Range
Dim sName As String

' Display waiting message in status bar
StatusBar = "Checking spelling. Please wait. This may take some time." & _
            "Hit Ctrl-Break to interrupt."

' Get spelling errrors and name of active document now
' before we change the active document.
Set pf = ActiveDocument.SpellingErrors
sName = ActiveDocument.FullName

' Create new document.
' The following changes the active document!
Set doc = Documents.Add

' Print header to new document
doc.Range.InsertAfter "Spelling errors for document: " & sName & vbCr
doc.Range.InsertAfter "Spelling error count: " & pf.Count & vbCr

' Loop through spelling errors,
' printing them to new document.
For Each pe In pf

    doc.Range.InsertAfter "Page " & _
        pe.Information(wdActiveEndAdjustedPageNumber) & _
        " / " & pe.Text & vbCr

Next pe

StatusBar = ""

' Save document.
doc.SaveAs "d:\temp\SpellingErrors.doc"

End Sub
```

Example 12-2. Sample Output from the PrintSpellingErrors Procedure

```
Spelling errors for document: Document14
Spelling error count: 3
Page 1 / Subsquent
Page 1 / proprty
Page 1 / debug.print
```

There are a few points of interest in the code in Example 12-1. First, since the spellcheck process may take some time, I use the Word status bar to inform the user of this fact and also of how to interrupt the process.

Second, although I will discuss the *Add* method later, it is important to realize here that adding a new document makes the new document the active one. Hence, I must collect any information about the active document *before* adding the new document. (Alternatively, I could have defined a separate Document variable and pointed it at the active document before using the *Add* method. Then I could access the original document through this variable.)

I have used the Information property of the Range object to report the page number of each spelling error. This property is discussed in more detail in Chapter 14, *The Range and Selection Objects*.

Finally, I conclude the spellcheck discussion with the *ResetIgnoreAll* method of the Application object. This method clears the list of words that were set to be ignored during the previous spellcheck. Hence, after this method is executed, all previously ignored words are included in the spellcheck. This may be important when spellchecking code.

Adding, Opening, and Saving Documents

Document objects have the following expected methods for document housekeeping:

The Add method

The *Add* method of the Documents collection creates a new Word document and adds it to the Documents collection. The new document becomes the active document. The syntax is:

```
DocumentsObject.Add(Template, NewTemplate)
```

where `Template` is the name of the template to be used for the new document. If this argument is omitted, the Normal template is used. The `NewTemplate` parameter can be set to True to open the document as a template. The default value is False.

The Open method

The *Open* method of the Documents collection opens an existing document and adds it to the Documents collection. The syntax is a bit involved:

```
DocumentsObject.Open(FileName, ConfirmConversions, _
    ReadOnly, AddToRecentFiles, PasswordDocument, _
    PasswordTemplate, Revert, WritePasswordDocument, _
    WritePasswordTemplate, Format)
```

All of these parameters are variants, and all except `FileName` are optional.

The parameters that do *not* relate to password protection are:

FileName

> The name of the document (can include a complete path).

ConfirmConversions

> Set to True to display the Convert File dialog box if the file is not in Microsoft Word format.

ReadOnly

> Set to True to open the document as read-only.

AddToRecentFiles

> Set to True to add the filename to the list of recently used files at the bottom of the File menu.

Revert

> Controls what happens if *FileName* is already open. Set the parameter to True to discard any unsaved changes to the open document and reopen the file from disk. Set it to False to activate the open document.

Format

> Specifies the file converter to be used to open the document. It can be one of the following constants:

```
Enum WdOpenFormat
    wdOpenFormatAuto = 0
    wdOpenFormatDocument = 1
    wdOpenFormatTemplate = 2
    wdOpenFormatRTF = 3
    wdOpenFormatText = 4
    wdOpenFormatUnicodeText = 5
End Enum
```

The parameters that relate to password protection are:

PasswordDocument

> If the document that you want to open requires a password to open the document, this parameter should be set to that password. (This applies also to a template file that you want to open as a document.)

WritePasswordDocument

> If the document that you want to open requires a password for modification, this parameter should be set to that password. (This applies also to template files that you want to open as a document.)

PasswordTemplate

> If the document that you want to open is based on a template that requires a password to open, this parameter should be set to that password if you wish the template to be available for opening. (The template needs to be opened if you want to use it in the Style Organizer, for instance.) I will elaborate on this in a moment.

WritePasswordTemplate
> If the document that you want to open is based on a template that requires a password for modification, this parameter should be set to that password if you want the template to be available for modification. This would be the case, for instance, if you create a new style and wish it to be saved in the template.

The issue of password protection of a template is definitely confusing. If a template is password protected for opening, when you try to create a new document based on that template, Word will require the template's password, as expected.

On the other hand, if you attempt to open a document based on that template, Word will prompt you for the template's password, but you can enter any string, or just hit the Esc or Enter key and Word will still open the document! This happens through the user interface as well as through code. In particular, if you set the `PasswordTemplate` parameter to an empty string, Word will prompt the user for a password, but if you set it to an *incorrect nonempty string*, Word will open the document.

Moreover, if you then create a new style in the opened document, for example, and check the Add to Template option, you can save and close the document, but Word will not save the style to the attached template, nor will it warn you that it did not save the style to the attached template! However, it does save the style in the Normal template.

Note that the attached template does appear to be protected; if you try to open the style organizer, for instance, Word will refuse to open the attached template without the correct password.

Some of this behavior may be intentional on Microsoft's part. After all, password-protecting a template does prevent any *new* documents from being created based on that template without the password. An existing document based on that template was presumably created by someone who had the template's password. That person could have password-protected the document itself if desired. So it does not appear that this behavior presents a security problem.

However, it does present other problems. For instance, since Word does not warn you when you try to save a new style in the template, for example, you may think that this style has been saved when it has not. Also, it seems that Word will unexpectedly save the style in the Normal template.

Note also that if you password-protect the template for modification, then Word will refuse to open the document if you type in the wrong password or hit the Enter key, but will open the document if you hit the Esc key. This is clearly a bug.

It certainly would have been nice if Microsoft had explained all of this in some prominent location in its help documentation. (I could not find an explanation of any of this anywhere in Microsoft's documentation.) We are left with a simple caveat: be very careful with template passwords! Do not expect the obvious.

The Close method

The *Close* method closes the specified document. Its syntax is:

```
DocumentObject.Close(SaveChanges, OriginalFormat, _
    RouteDocument)
```

The optional *SaveChanges* parameter specifies the save action for the document and can be one of the constants in the following enum:

```
Enum WdSaveOptions
    wdPromptToSaveChanges = -2
    wdSaveChanges = -1
    wdDoNotSaveChanges = 0
End Enum
```

If the document is to be saved before closing, the optional *OriginalFormat* parameter specifies the save format. It can be one of the following constants:

```
Enum WdOriginalFormat
    wdWordDocument = 0
    wdOriginalDocumentFormat = 1
    wdPromptUser = 2
End Enum
```

Finally, the optional *RouteDocument* parameter should be set to True to route the document to the next recipient, assuming the document has a routing slip. Otherwise, this argument is ignored.

For example, the following line:

```
ActiveDocument.Close SaveChanges:=wdSaveChanges, _
    OriginalFormat:=WdOriginalDocumentFormat
```

closes the active document and saves any changes. Note that the *Close* method can also be applied to the Documents collection to close all of the open documents at the same time.

The Save method

The *Save* method can be applied to a single Document (or Template) object to save that document. The syntax is simply:

```
DocumentObject.Save
```

If the file has not been assigned a filename, Word will display a File Save dialog box.

This method can also be applied to a Documents collection to save every document in the collection. In this case, the syntax is:

```
DocumentsCollection.Save(NoPrompt, OriginalFormat)
```

where *NoPrompt* is set to True to have Word automatically save all documents and False to have Word prompt the user to save each document that has changed since it was last saved. The *OriginalFormat* parameter is the same as for the *Close* method and can be any one of the WdOriginalFormat constants described earlier.

The SaveAs method

This method saves the specified document with a new name or format. This method is rather complex, because its arguments correspond to the myriad options in the Save As dialog box (under the File menu):

```
DocumentObject.SaveAs(FileName, FileFormat, LockComments, Password, _
    AddToRecentFiles, WritePassword, ReadOnlyRecommended, _
    EmbedTrueTypeFonts, SaveNativePictureFormat, SaveFormsData, _
    SaveAsAOCELetter)
```

Here is a brief description of the most common parameters. Note that all of the parameters are optional variants.

FileName

The name for the document. If this argument is omitted, the document is saved under its current name (overwriting the version on disk, as usual).

FileFormat

The format in which the document is saved. It can be one of the constants in the following enum:

```
Enum WdSaveFormat
    wdFormatDocument = 0
    wdFormatTemplate = 1
    wdFormatText = 2
    wdFormatTextLineBreaks = 3
    wdFormatDOSText = 4
    wdFormatDOSTextLineBreaks = 5
    wdFormatRTF = 6
    wdFormatUnicodeText = 7
End Enum
```

LockComments

Set this parameter to True to prevent the document from being changed except for the addition of comments. (This can also be done from Word's Protect Document dialog box, under the Tools menu.)

Password

A password string that will be required to open the document in the future.

AddToRecentFiles

Set to True to add the document to the list of recently used files on the File menu.

WritePassword

A password string that will be required to save changes to the document in the future.

ReadOnlyRecommended

> Set to True to have Word suggest read-only status whenever the document is opened.

EmbedTrueTypeFonts

> Set to True to save (embed) TrueType fonts with the document.

The Saved property

> The Saved property is set to True by Word if the specified document or template has not changed since it was last saved. This property is used by Word to determine whether it should prompt the user to save changes when the document is closed. Note that the property is read/write, so it can be changed in code.

The SaveFormat property

> This read-only property returns the file format of the specified document or file converter. It can be a unique number that specifies an external file converter or one of the constants in the `WdSaveFormat` enum, described earlier.

Password-Related Properties

The Document object has several properties related to document passwords:

HasPassword property

> This read-only property returns True if a password is required to open the specified document.

Password property

> Sets a password (as a string) that must be supplied to open the document. This an example of a relatively rare write-only property. In other words, you can write the password, but not read it!

The WritePassword property

> Sets a password for modifying the document (that is, *writing* to the document, hence the name). It is also a write-only string. Note that a document can still be opened without knowing this password.

Protection-Related Properties and Methods

The Document object has the following several properties related to document protection:

The Protect method and ProtectionType property

> The *Protect* method protects the document from changes. When a document is protected, the user can make only limited changes, such as adding annotations, making revisions, or completing a form.

The syntax of the *Protect* method is:

```
DocumentObject.Protect(Type, NoReset, Password)
```

where the required *Type* parameter specifies the protection type for the document. It can be one of the constants in the following enum:

```
Enum WdProtectionType
    wdNoProtection = -1
    wdAllowOnlyRevisions = 0
    wdAllowOnlyComments = 1
    wdAllowOnlyFormFields = 2
End Enum
```

NoReset is related to any form fields on the document. For more on this, refer to the help documentation. Finally, the optional *Password* parameter can be set to a string password that subsequently will be required in order to unprotect the document.

Note that if a document is already protected, the *Protect* method will cause a run-time error, so the document should first be checked by looking at its ProtectionType property, which can assume any of the **WdProtectionType** constants described earlier. This is illustrated in the following code:

```
If ActiveDocument.ProtectionType = wdNoProtection Then
    ActiveDocument.Protect wdAllowOnlyComments,,"midnight"
End If
```

The UnProtect method

This method removes protection from the document. However, if the document is not currently protected, this method will generate an error, so the ProtectionType property should be checked before using this method.

The syntax for the *UnProtect* method is:

```
DocumentObject.UnProtect(Password)
```

where *Password* is the password string used to protect the document. If the document is protected with a password and an incorrect password is supplied, Word will display a dialog box to prompt the user for the correct password.

The ReadOnly property

This read-only property is True if changes to the document cannot be saved to the original document.

The ReadOnlyRecommended property

If this property is set to True, then Word will display a message box whenever the document is opened, suggesting that it be opened as read-only.

The Name Properties

The Document object has three properties related to the filename of the document, all of them read-only:

The Name property
> Returns the name of the document. This will be the default name if the document has not yet been saved. Since this property is read-only, you cannot change the name of a document by setting this property. (A Word document that is not open can be renamed using the VBA **Name** statement; if the document is open, you can save it under a different name using the *SaveAs* method, but you cannot rename it.)

The FullName property
> Returns the complete path and filename of the document. If the document has not yet been saved, however, this property will return the same value as the Name property.

The Path property
> Returns the path (but not the filename) of the document, without the trailing backslash.

Printing-Related Methods

The *PrintOut* method will print all or part of a document. Its syntax is:

```
DocumentObject.PrintOut(Background, Append, Range, _
    OutputFileName, From, To, Item, Copies, Pages, _
    PageType, PrintToFile, Collate, FileName, _
    ActivePrinterMacGX, ManualDuplexPrint)
```

Note that the *PrintOut* method can also be applied to a Window object to print the contents of the window, or it can be used globally, as in:

```
PrintOut "d:\word\letter.doc"
```

to print the active document. The myriad arguments of the method correspond to the items on the Print dialog box. All of these arguments are optional variants.

In addition to using the *PrintOut* method in this global way, we frequently want to exercise greater control over printing. The following sections examine some of the ways that you can do that.

Printing to a File

To print to a file, set the following parameters of the *PrintOut* method:

PrintToFile
> Set this to True to print to a file.

OutputFileName

>   Set this to the full path and name of the output file.

Append

>   Set this to True to append the document to the output file or False to over-write the contents of the output file.

Restricted Printing

To restrict printing, set the following parameters:

Range

>   The page range for printing. It can be any one of the constants in the following enum:

```
Enum WdPrintOutRange
    wdPrintAllDocument = 0
    wdPrintSelection = 1
    wdPrintCurrentPage = 2
    wdPrintFromTo = 3
    wdPrintRangeOfPages = 4
End Enum
```

From

>   If *Range* is wdPrintFromTo, set this to the starting page number.

To

>   If *Range* is wdPrintFromTo, set this to the ending page number.

Pages

>   If *Range* is wdPrintRangeofPages, set this to the page range to be printed. For instance, the range 2, 6–10 prints page 2 and pages 6 through 10.

PageType

>   The type of pages to be printed. It can be one of the constants in the following enum:

```
Enum WdPrintOutPages
    wdPrintAllPages = 0
    wdPrintOddPagesOnly = 1
    wdPrintEvenPagesOnly = 2
End Enum
```

Item

>   The item to be printed. It can be one of the constants in the following enum:

```
Enum WdPrintOutItem
    wdPrintDocumentContent = 0
    wdPrintProperties = 1
    wdPrintComments = 2
    wdPrintStyles = 3
    wdPrintAutoTextEntries = 4
    wdPrintKeyAssignments = 5
    wdPrintEnvelope = 6
End Enum
```

Other Parameters

The other parameters to the *PrintOut* method are:

Background
> Set to True to have the program continue executing while the document is being printed.

Copies
> The number of copies to be printed.

Collate
> When printing multiple copies of a document, set this to True to print all pages of the document before starting the next copy.

FileName
> When the *PrintOut* method is executed globally, this parameter can be set to the path and filename of the document to be printed. If not set, the active document is printed. (This parameter is ignored when the *PrintOut* method is called from a Document object or Window object.)

PrintPreview

The Document object has *PrintPreview* and *ClosePrintPreview* methods, but the simplest way to change the view mode in and out of print preview is to use the global PrintPreview property. Thus, write:

```
PrintPreview = True
```

to turn on print preview mode and:

```
PrintPreview = False
```

to turn it off.

Additional Members of the Document Object

Some additional members of the Document object include:

The Activate method
> Activates the document, thus making it the active document. For instance, to activate a document named *MyLetter*, execute the code:
>
> ```
> Documents("MyLetter").Activate
> ```

The AttachedTemplate property
> Returns a Template object that represents the template that is currently attached to the document. By setting this property, you can attach a new template to the

document. For instance, the following code attaches the template *FaxDocs* to the current document:

```
ActiveDocument.AttachedTemplate = "FaxDocs.dot"
```

The ComputeStatistics method

This method returns information about the document. It syntax is:

```
DocumentObject.ComputeStatistics(Statistic, IncludeFootnotesAndEndnotes)
```

where *Statistic* is one of the following constants:

```
Enum WdStatistic
    wdStatisticWords = 0
    wdStatisticLines = 1
    wdStatisticPages = 2
    wdStatisticCharacters = 3
    wdStatisticParagraphs = 4
    wdStatisticCharactersWithSpaces = 5
End Enum
```

The parameter *IncludeFootnotesAndEndnotes* is set to True to include footnotes and endnotes when computing the requested information. The default value of this parameter is False.

Incidentally, Word can supply more statistics about a document through the DocumentStatistics dialog box. (I explain how to access this information at the end of Chapter 19, *Built-in Dialog Objects.*)

The Content property

This useful property returns a Range object that represents the main document story. (I show it in action in Chapter 14.)

The CopyStylesFromTemplate method

This method copies styles from the specified template to a document. Its syntax is:

```
DocumentObject.CopyStylesFromTemplate(TemplateFileName)
```

When styles are copied from a template to a document, styles of the same name in the document are redefined to match the styles in the template. Other styles from the template are simply copied to the document, and other styles in the document but not in the template are not affected.

The DefaultTabStop property

This property returns or sets the interval (in points, as a Single) between the default tab stops in the document. (I discuss tab stops at length later in this chapter.)

The EmbedTrueTypeFonts property

Set this property to True to have Word embed TrueType fonts in the document when it is saved. This allows users on other computers to view the document with the same fonts that were used to create the document, in case those fonts are not installed on that computer.

The PageSetup property

This property returns the PageSetup object that is associated with the document. (I discuss PageSetup objects later in this chapter. Suffice it to say now that this object holds all of the page formatting for the document, such as margins and page size.)

The Repaginate method

This method simply repaginates the document. Its syntax is:

```
DocumentObject.Repaginate
```

The UpdateStyles method

This method copies all styles from the attached template into the document, overwriting any existing styles in the document that have the same name. Its syntax is:

```
DocumentObject.UpdateStyles
```

Children of the Document Object

Now that we've examined the properties and methods of the Document object itself, we can begin to look at the children of the Document object.

The Bookmark Object

As you may know, a Word bookmark is a name for a specific range of text within a document or for just a single location (which can be thought of as a range with the same beginning and ending position). Each Word bookmark is represented by a Bookmark object.

Bookmark objects are kept in the Bookmarks collection. Actually, the Bookmarks collection is a child not only of the Document object, but also of the Range and Selection objects. Each of these objects has a Bookmarks property that returns the corresponding Bookmarks collection.

Thus, for instance:

```
MsgBox ActiveDocument.Bookmarks.Count
```

displays the number of bookmarks in the active document, whereas:

```
MsgBox Selection.Bookmarks.Count
```

displays the number of bookmarks in the current selection (of the active window).

Creating a bookmark

To create a bookmark, use the *Add* method of the Bookmarks collection. The syntax is:

```
BookmarksObject.Add(Name, Range)
```

where *BookmarksObject* refers to a Bookmarks collection object and *Name* is the name of the bookmark (which must be a single word). The optional parameter *Range* specifies the range object that the bookmark represents. If *Range* is missing, the bookmark represents the current insertion point only. (The *insertion point* is the location of the blinking cursor.)

For example, the following code creates a bookmark named CurSel and sets it to be the currently selected text in the active document:

```
ActiveDocument.Bookmarks.Add "CurSel", Selection.Range
```

(The expression `Selection.Range` returns the range that is associated with the current selection. This will be discussed fully in Chapter 14.)

Note that if there is already a bookmark named CurSel, this bookmark (but not the range it represents) will be removed *without warning*. To avoid this potential problem, you can use the Exists method, described next, to check for an existing bookmark.

The Exists method

The Exists method of the Bookmarks collection indicates whether a given bookmark exists in a given Bookmarks collection (for a range, selection, or document). The syntax is:

```
BookmarksObject.Exists(Name)
```

where *Name* is the name of a bookmark. The return value is Boolean (True or False). To illustrate, the code in Example 12-3 first asks the user for a bookmark name, then checks to see if a bookmark by that name already exists. If it does, the user is asked to confirm making a change before adding the new bookmark.

Example 12-3. Checking for the Existence of a Bookmark

```
Sub AddBookmark()
   Dim sBkName As String    ' for bookmark name
   ' Ask user for name
   sBkName = InputBox("Enter name of bookmark to add. " & _
                      "Leave blank to cancel.", "Add Bookmark")

   ' Exit if name is blank
   If sBkName = "" Then Exit Sub

   ' Add bookmark with confirmation
   If ActiveDocument.Bookmarks.Exists(sBkName) Then

       ' Bookmark exists, then ask for confirmation
       If MsgBox("Bookmark already exists. OK to change it?", _
               vbQuestion + vbYesNo) = vbYes Then

           ActiveDocument.Bookmarks.Add sBkName, Selection.Range
```

Example 12-3. Checking for the Existence of a Bookmark (continued)

```
        End If
    Else
        ' Bookmark does not exist -- create it
        ActiveDocument.Bookmarks.Add sBkName, Selection.Range
    End If

End Sub
```

The Copy method

The *Copy* method is used to copy an existing bookmark. The syntax is:

```
BookmarkObject.Copy(Name)
```

where *BookmarkObject* refers to a Bookmark object and *Name* is the name of the new bookmark. (Thus, both bookmarks refer to the same location.) The *Copy* method returns a Bookmark object and adds it to the Bookmarks collection.

The Delete method

The *Delete* method deletes an existing bookmark. The syntax is:

```
BookmarkObject.Delete
```

This method provides us with an opportunity to discuss the proper way to delete all of the objects from a collection.

To delete all bookmarks from the active document, you might first try the following code:

```
Dim i As Integer
For i = 1 To ActiveDocument.Bookmarks.Count
    ActiveDocument.Bookmarks(i).Delete
Next i
```

However, at some point this code will produce an error message to the effect that the requested item does not exist. The problem is that as bookmarks are deleted, the remaining bookmarks are reindexed, so that about halfway through the deletion process, the indices will no longer be valid!

The proper way to delete objects from a collection is from the bottom up:

```
Dim i As Integer
For i = ActiveDocument.Bookmarks.Count To 1 Step -1
    ActiveDocument.Bookmarks(i).Delete
Next i
```

Alternatively, a better approach is to use the **For Each** construct, as in:

```
Dim bk As Bookmark
For Each bk In ActiveDocument.Bookmarks
    bk.Delete
Next bk
```

The Empty property

The Empty property is True if the specified bookmark represents an insertion point only and therefore contains no text. In other words, an empty bookmark marks a location only.

The Start, End, and Range properties

Every bookmark has a range associated with it. (If a bookmark represents a location, then its range has the same beginning and ending point.) The Range property returns this range as a Range object. The Start and End properties return or set the starting and ending positions of the bookmark's range, allowing you to change the size of a bookmark. (For more on these properties, see Chapter 14.)

The Name property

This property returns or sets the name of the bookmark.

The Select method

Use the *Select* method as follows:

```
BookmarkObject.Select
```

to select the text contained in a bookmark's range. Note that if the bookmark is empty, the insertion point is moved to the bookmark's location. (In other words, even an empty range is selected.)

For instance, the following code selects a bookmark named BMK1 and changes the text to italic:

```
ActiveDocument.Bookmarks("BMK1").Select
Selection.Font.Italics = True
```

The StoryType property

This property returns the story type (and hence the general location) for the specified bookmark. It can be any one of the constants in the following enum:

```
Enum WdStoryType
    wdMainTextStory = 1
    wdFootnotesStory = 2
    wdEndnotesStory = 3
    wdCommentsStory = 4
    wdTextFrameStory = 5
    wdEvenPagesHeaderStory = 6
    wdPrimaryHeaderStory = 7
    wdEvenPagesFooterStory = 8
    wdPrimaryFooterStory = 9
    wdFirstPageHeaderStory = 10
    wdFirstPageFooterStory = 11
End Enum
```

The Characters, Words, and Sentences Collections

The Document object has a Characters property that returns the Characters collection for the document. As expected, the Characters collection is the collection of all characters in the document. Similarly, the Words property returns the Words collection and the Sentences property returns the Sentences collections. However, the Word object model does not have a Character object, nor does it have a Word or Sentence object. A character, word, or sentence is actually a Range object, so these three collections contain Range objects.

In addition, there is no *Add* method for these three collections, so you cannot add a character, word, or sentence to a Word document directly. Instead, these objects are added automatically by Word when you execute code that inserts text into the document. In other words, Word maintains these collections automatically. The collections do have a read-only Count property for reporting the size of each collection.

Thus, to work with characters, words, or sentences in a document, you actually work with Range objects. For instance, the code:

```
ActiveDocument.Words(1)
```

returns a Range object that represents the first word in the active document. (I discuss Range objects at length in Chapter 14.)

The Fields Collection

A Field object represents a field in a Word document. The Fields property of the Document object returns a Fields collection, which contains all of the Field objects in the document.

To add a field to a document, use the *Add* method of the Fields collection. The syntax is:

```
FieldsObject.Add(Range, Type, Text, PreserveFormatting)
```

where *Range* is the range that is replaced by the Field object. (If the range is a single point, then the field is just inserted at that point.) The *Type* parameter is the type of field desired and is one of the constants in the **wdFieldType** enum shown in the following list. The optional *Text* parameter is any additional text needed for a particular field (see the following example). Finally, *PreserveFormatting* is set to True to have the formatting that is applied to the field preserved during field updates.

wdFieldAddin (81)	wdFieldAutoNum (54)	wdFieldAutoTextList (89)
wdFieldAdvance (84)	wdFieldAutoNumLegal (53)	wdFieldBarCode (63)
wdFieldAsk (38)	wdFieldAutoNumOutline (52)	wdFieldComments (19)
wdFieldAuthor (17)	wdFieldAutoText (79)	wdFieldCompare (80)

wdFieldCreateDate (21)	wdFieldInclude (36)	wdFieldPrivate (77)
wdFieldData (40)	wdFieldIncludePicture (67)	wdFieldQuote (35)
wdFieldDatabase (78)	wdFieldIncludeText (68)	wdFieldRef (3)
wdFieldDate (31)	wdFieldIndex (8)	wdFieldRefDoc (11)
wdFieldDDE (45)	wdFieldIndexEntry (4)	wdFieldRevisionNum (24)
wdFieldDDEAuto (46)	wdFieldInfo (14)	wdFieldSaveDate (22)
wdFieldDocProperty (85)	wdFieldKeyWord (18)	wdFieldSection (65)
wdFieldDocVariable (64)	wdFieldLastSavedBy (20)	wdFieldSectionPages (66)
wdFieldEditTime (25)	wdFieldLink (56)	wdFieldSequence (12)
wdFieldEmbed (58)	wdFieldListNum (90)	wdFieldSet (6)
wdFieldEmpty (-1)	wdFieldMacroButton (51)	wdFieldSkipIf (43)
wdFieldExpression (34)	wdFieldMergeField (59)	wdFieldStyleRef (10)
wdFieldFileName (29)	wdFieldMergeRec (44)	wdFieldSubject (16)
wdFieldFileSize (69)	wdFieldMergeSeq (75)	wdFieldSubscriber (82)
wdFieldFillIn (39)	wdFieldNext (41)	wdFieldSymbol (57)
wdFieldFootnoteRef (5)	wdFieldNextIf (42)	wdFieldTemplate (30)
wdFieldFormCheckBox (71)	wdFieldNoteRef (72)	wdFieldTime (32)
wdFieldFormDropDown (83)	wdFieldNumChars (28)	wdFieldTitle (15)
wdFieldFormTextInput (70)	wdFieldNumPages (26)	wdFieldTOA (73)
wdFieldFormula (49)	wdFieldNumWords (27)	wdFieldTOAEntry (74)
wdFieldGlossary (47)	wdFieldOCX (87)	wdFieldTOC (13)
wdFieldGoToButton (50)	wdFieldPage (33)	wdFieldTOCEntry (9)
wdFieldHTMLActiveX (91)	wdFieldPageRef (37)	wdFieldUserAddress (62)
wdFieldHyperlink (88)	wdFieldPrint (48)	wdFieldUserInitials (61)
wdFieldIf (7)	wdFieldPrintDate (23)	wdFieldUserName (60)
wdFieldImport (55)		

As an example, the following code inserts a Time field at the insertion point, replacing the selected text, if any:

```
ActiveDocument.Fields.Add _
    Range:=Selection.Range, _
    Type:=wdFieldTime, _
    Text:="\@ yyyy-MM-dd", _
    PreserveFormatting:=True
```

The field has the following appearance:

```
{ TIME \@ yyyy-MM-dd \* MERGEFORMAT }
```

However, if I had set the *PreserveFormatting* parameter to False, the resulting field would be

```
{ TIME \@ yyyy-MM-dd }
```

Note that to avoid replacing any existing selection, you can first collapse the selection to a single point, as follows:

```
Selection.Collapse wdCollapseEnd
```

(I discuss the *Collapse* method in detail in Chapter 14.)

Determining field text

To determine the required text for the *Text* field, look at the Field Options dialog box by choosing the Options button in the Field dialog box (under the Insert/Field menu item). For example, Figure 12-3 shows these dialog boxes for the previous sample code.

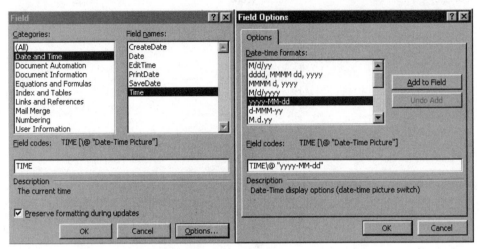

Figure 12-3. Field and Field Options dialog boxes

Some of the more interesting properties of Field object are examined in the following sections.

The Code and Result properties

The Code property of the Field object returns a Range object that represents a field's code, which is everything enclosed by the field delimiters ({}) including the leading space and trailing spaces.

Similarly, the Result property returns a Range object that represents the value of the field. For example, if the first field in the active document is a Date field, then the code:

```
Debug.Print ActiveDocument.Fields(1).Code.Text
Debug.Print ActiveDocument.Fields(1).Result.Text
```

prints:

```
DATE   \* MERGEFORMAT
3/30/98
```

the first line of which is the field code and the second line of which is the field result.

To illustrate one use of these properties, the following code extracts the text from the field containing the cursor and prints it to the debug window. (I use this to get a pure-text version of a Table of Contents or Index field, for example.)

```
Dim fld As Field
Dim sText As String
For Each fld In ActiveDocument.Fields
    If Selection.Range.InRange(fld.Result) Then
        sText = fld.Result.Text
        Exit For
    End If
Next
Debug.Print sText
```

Note the use of the *InRange* method, which tells us when a particular field contains the current selection. (I discuss this method in detail in Chapter 14.)

The Delete method

The *Delete* method, as follows:

```
FieldObject.Delete
```

deletes the referenced Field object.

The DoClick method

The *DoClick* method has the effect of clicking the specified field with the left mouse button. (Some fields are designed to react when clicked upon.) The syntax is:

```
FieldObject.DoClick
```

The Index property

The Index property returns the index of the Field object within the Fields collection. This provides a useful way to identify a particular Field object. Note, however, that when a new field is added to a document, its index reflects its position in the document, which may cause the indices of other fields to change.

The Kind property

The read-only Kind property returns the type of link for a Field object. It can be one of the constants in the following enum:

```
Enum WdFieldKind
    wdFieldKindNone = 0
    wdFieldKindHot = 1
    wdFieldKindWarm = 2
    wdFieldKindCold = 3
End Enum
```

Here are the meanings of these constants:

wdFieldKindHot
> Indicates a field that is automatically updated each time it is displayed or each time the page is reformatted.

wdFieldKindWarm
> Indicates a field that has a result and that can be updated either automatically when the source data changes or manually.

wdFieldKindCold
> Indicates a field that does not have a result, such as XE (Index Entry) fields and TC (Table of Contents Entry) fields or Private fields.

wdFieldKindNone
> Indicates an invalid field.

The Locked property

Setting this property to True locks the given field so it can no longer be updated. This property also applies to the Fields collection, allowing you to lock or unlock all of the fields in a document at one time.

The Next and Previous properties

These properties return the next and previous Field objects in the Fields collection, which is by order of appearance in the document. These read-only properties are useful for iterating through the Fields collection.

The ShowCodes property

The ShowCodes property can be set to True to show the field codes for a field, rather than the field values. For example, the code:

```
ActiveDocument.Fields(2).ShowCodes = True
```

causes Word to display the code for the second field in the active document without affecting the other fields in the document. (The View Field Codes option in the Options dialog box affects all fields in the document.)

This property should not be confused with the ShowFieldCodes property, which reports the status of the View Field Codes option, and the *ToggleFieldCodes* method, which toggles this setting. *ShowFields* affects only a single field.

The Type property

This property returns or sets the type for the given field and can be any of the `wdFieldType` constants listed earlier in this chapter.

The Update method

This method updates the value of the specified field and returns True if the update was successful. The *Update* method can also be applied to a Fields collection, updating all fields in the collection. In this case, the method returns 0 if no errors occur or returns the index of the first field that produced an error.

As a final note, many Word objects (35, to be exact) have a Name property that the programmer can set for identification purposes. Although this property can be very useful, Field objects do not have such a property. (Are you listening, Microsoft?)

List-Related Objects

The Document object has a number of objects (ListParagraphs, Lists, and ListTemplates) that can be used to control Word lists programmatically. Since this is a rather involved topic, I devote an entire chapter (Chapter 17, *The List Object*) to lists.

The PageSetup Object

Several Word objects (the Document, Range, Section, Sections, and Selection objects) have a PageSetup property that returns a PageSetup object. The PageSetup object represents the page formatting that applies to the parent object. For instance, the PageSetup object obtained from a Document object represents the page-level formatting of a document. It corresponds to the Page Setup dialog box under the File menu. The following list shows all of the properties and methods for the PageSetup object:

Application	LineNumbering	RightMargin
BottomMargin	MirrorMargins	SectionStart
Creator	OddAndEvenPagesHeaderFooter	SetAsTemplateDefault
DifferentFirstPageHeaderFooter	Orientation	SuppressEndnotes
FirstPageTray	OtherPagesTray	TextColumns
FooterDistance	PageHeight	TogglePortrait
Gutter	PageWidth	TopMargin
HeaderDistance	PaperSize	VerticalAlignment
LeftMargin	Parent	

Most of the items in this list are self-explanatory, at least as far as their intended purpose (if not their syntax). I discuss only the *SetAsTemplateDefault* method.

The *SetAsTemplateDefault* method, whose syntax is:

```
PageSetupObject.SetAsTemplateDefault
```

sets the given PageSetup object as the PageSetup object for the currently attached template. Hence, this page formatting becomes the default for all documents (present and future) based on the active template.

As an example, the following code changes the left and right margins for the active document and then applies these changes to the page formatting of the attached template, making them the new default settings. Note the use of the very handy *InchesToPoints* function, which converts inches to the point measurement that is required by the margin properties:

```
With ActiveDocument.PageSetup
    .LeftMargin = InchesToPoints(.5)
    .RightMargin = InchesToPoints(.5)
    .SetAsTemplateDefault
End With
```

The Paragraph Object

One of the most important objects in the Word object model is the Paragraph object. Paragraph objects are kept in the Paragraphs collection, which is accessible through the Paragraphs property of the Document object. Following is a list of the properties and methods of the Paragraph object:

Alignment	Next	Shading
Application	NoLineNumber	Space1
Borders	OpenOrCloseUp	Space15
CloseUp	OpenUp	Space2
Creator	Outdent	SpaceAfter
DropCap	OutlineDemote	SpaceBefore
FirstLineIndent	OutlineDemoteToBody	Style
Format	OutlineLevel	TabHangingIndent
Hyphenation	OutlinePromote	TabIndent
Indent	PageBreakBefore	TabStops
KeepTogether	Parent	WidowControl
KeepWithNext	Previous	
LeftIndent	Range	
LineSpacing	Reset	
LineSpacingRule	RightIndent	

The CloseUp method

This method sets the SpaceBefore property to 0. Thus, the following two lines of code have the same effect:

```
ActiveDocument.Paragraphs(1).CloseUp
ActiveDocument.Paragraphs(1).SpaceBefore = 0
```

Note that the *CloseUp* method can be used with a Paragraph, Paragraphs, or ParagraphFormat object, as is the case with many of these properties and methods.

The Format property

This property returns or sets a ParagraphFormat object that represents the formatting of the specified paragraph or paragraphs. (I discuss the ParagraphFormat property later in this chapter.)

The Indent method

The *Indent* method indents the paragraph by one level. This is equivalent to clicking the Increase Indent button on the Formatting toolbar. The Indent method can also be applied to the Paragraphs collection, thereby indenting all paragraphs at one time.

The Range property

The Range property returns a Range object that represents the portion of a document that is contained in the paragraph. The Range object is used to perform many of the actions that we can perform on a paragraph, such as changing the text for the paragraph:

```
para.Range.Text = "new text"
```

or changing the character formatting:

```
para.Range.Font.Name = "Arial"
```

(I discuss the Range object at length in Chapter 14.)

The TabStops property

The TabStops property returns or sets a TabStops collection that represents all the custom tab stops for the specified paragraph (or paragraphs). (I discuss the Tab-Stop object later in this chapter.)

The ParagraphFormat Object

The ParagraphFormat object represents a set of formatting settings that can be applied to a paragraph. It can be obtained from the ParagraphFormat property of a Paragraph object or, as discussed in Chapter 8, *Control Statements*, it can be created independently using the New keyword. In this way, you can create a ParagraphFormat object and use it to format multiple paragraphs.

The properties and methods of the ParagraphFormat object are shown in the following list. Note that all of these members except the Duplicate property are also members of the Paragraph object, which shows that you can also do all paragraph formatting directly on the Paragraph object, rather than use a ParagraphFormat object.

Alignment	LineSpacing	Space1
Application	LineSpacingRule	Space15
Borders	NoLineNumber	Space2
CloseUp	OpenOrCloseUp	SpaceAfter
Creator	OpenUp	SpaceBefore
Duplicate	OutlineLevel	Style
FirstLineIndent	PageBreakBefore	TabHangingIndent
Hyphenation	Parent	TabIndent
KeepTogether	Reset	TabStops
KeepWithNext	RightIndent	WidowControl
LeftIndent	Shading	

Tab Stops

A TabStop object represents a tab setting. A TabStops collection is a set of Tab-Stop objects. Each of the Paragraph, ParagraphFormat, and Paragraphs objects has a TabStops property that returns a TabStops collection.

The TabStops collection

The *Add* method is used to add a TabStop object to a TabStops collection. The syntax is:

```
TabStopsObject.Add(Position, Alignment, Leader)
```

where *Position* is a Single that gives the position of the tab stop (in points) relative to the left margin. The optional **Alignment** parameter can be any of the constants from the following enum:

```
Enum WdTabAlignment
    wdAlignTabLeft = 0
    wdAlignTabCenter = 1
    wdAlignTabRight = 2
    wdAlignTabDecimal = 3
    wdAlignTabBar = 4
    wdAlignTabList = 6
End Enum
```

If this parameter is missing, then **wdAlignTabLeft** is used. The optional *Leader* parameter is the type of leader for the tab stop and can be any of the constants in the following enum:

```
Enum WdTabLeader
    wdTabLeaderSpaces = 0
    wdTabLeaderDots = 1
    wdTabLeaderDashes = 2
    wdTabLeaderLines = 3
End Enum
```

To locate the nearest TabStop object (that is, the nearest tab) to a given position, use the *Before* and *After* methods. The *Before* method has the syntax:

```
TabStopsObject.Before(Position)
```

and returns the previous TabStop object to the left of *Position*, which is a Single giving a ruler location in points. Similarly, the *After* method:

```
TabStopsObject.After(Position)
```

returns the next TabStop object to the right of *Position*.

The *ClearAll* method clears all of the *custom* tab stops from the TabStops collection. Note that the *ClearAll* method does not clear the default tabs. To alter the default tab stop locations, you must use the DefaultTabStop property of the Document object.

Working with the TabStops collection (and TabStop objects) can be a bit tricky. First, it appears that when you insert a custom tab stop into a paragraph (either by code or using Word's graphical environment), Word removes all default tab stops whose positions lie to the left of this custom tab stop. Indeed, this would make sense. However, consider the code in Example 12-4, which prints the tab stop positions in two ways, first using the **For Each** construct and then using an ordinary **For** loop.

Example 12-4. Printing Tab Stop Positions

```
Sub ShowTabStopPositions()

Dim i As Integer
Dim ts As TabStop
Dim tss As TabStops

Set tss = ActiveDocument.Paragraphs(1).TabStops

' Print using For Each
For Each ts In tss
   Debug.Print PointsToInches(ts.Position)
Next

Debug.Print "Count: " & tss.Count

' Print using For loop
For i = 1 To tss.Count
   Set ts = ActiveDocument.Paragraphs(1).TabStops(i)
   Debug.Print PointsToInches(ts.Position)
Next i

End Sub
```

Of course, both of these constructs should produce the same result. However, after inserting a single custom tab stop at position 1.0625, my system displayed the results shown in Example 12-5 in the Immediate window.

Example 12-5. Sample Output from the Routine in Example 12-4

```
1.0625
1.5
2
2.5
3
3.5
4
4.5
5
5.5
6
6.5
7
7.5
8
8.5
Count: 10
1.0625
0.5
1
1.5
2
2.5
3
3.5
4
4.5
```

The first portion of the code prints 16 tab stop positions, starting with the custom stop at 1.0625 (as expected). However, the second portion prints only 10 tab stops, including the default tab stops that appear *before* the custom tab stop. This seems to be an inconsistency. (Adding a second custom tab stop seems to correct the problem with regard to the default tab stops, but not the discrepancy in the number of tab stops.)

The moral of this story is that you should always check your code on some small sample files to see just how it behaves in various circumstances. You may be surprised from time to time!

The TabStop object

The TabStop object represents a single tab stop. Here are some of it its properties and methods:

The Alignment property

Returns or sets the alignment for the specified tab stop. It can be any one of the constants in the `WdTabAlignment` enum described a bit earlier in this chapter.

The Clear method

Removes the specified custom tab stop. Its syntax is:

```
TabStop.Clear
```

It does not apply to default tabs. To alter the default tab stop locations, use the DefaultTabStop property of the Document object.

The CustomTab property

This read-only Boolean property is True if the specified tab stop is a custom tab stop; otherwise, it is False.

The Leader property

Returns or sets the leader for the specified TabStop object. It can be any one of the constants in the **WdTabLeader** enum described earlier in this chapter.

The Previous and Next properties

Return the previous and next TabStop objects in the TabStops collection, respectively. These are the previous and next tab stops in order by position in the paragraph.

The Position property

Returns or sets the position of a tab stop relative to the left margin. This position is given in points as a Single, but the *PointsToInches* function can be used to convert this measurement to inches.

The Style Object

A Style object represents either a built-in or a user-defined Word style. Style objects are contained in a Styles collection, accessed through the Styles property of the Document object. Following is a list of the properties and methods of the Style object:

Application	Font	ListTemplate
AutomaticallyUpdate	Frame	NameLocal
BaseStyle	InUse	NextParagraphStyle
Borders	LanguageID	ParagraphFormat
BuiltIn	LanguageIDFarEast	Parent
Creator	LinkToListTemplate	Shading
Delete	ListLevelNumber	Type
Description		

It might seem as though the Styles property should also be a property of the Template object, since styles are also saved in templates. But it is not. To access the styles of a template, you must first use the *OpenAsDocument* method of the Template object to open a template as a document.

The *UpdateStyles* method of the Document object copies all styles from the attached template into the document. Note that this will overwrite any existing styles in the document that have the same name.

Creating a new style

To create a new user-defined style, use the *Add* method, whose syntax is:

```
StylesObject.Add(Name, Type)
```

where `Name` is the string name for the new style. The `Type` parameter is an optional Variant that gives the type of the new style; the default value is **wdStyle-TypeParagraph**. It can be one of the constants in the following enum:

```
Enum WdStyleType
    wdStyleTypeParagraph = 1
    wdStyleTypeCharacter = 2
End Enum
```

To refer to a particular style in a Styles collection, use the syntax:

```
Styles(index)
```

where *index* can be either an index number, the name of a style (in quotation marks), or a constant from the **WdBuiltinStyle** enum. These constants represent Word's 91 built-in styles:

wdStyleBlockQuotation (-85)	wdStyleHeading4 (-5)	wdStyleListBullet4 (-57)
wdStyleBodyText (-67)	wdStyleHeading5 (-6)	wdStyleListBullet5 (-58)
wdStyleBodyText2 (-81)	wdStyleHeading6 (-7)	wdStyleListContinue (-69)
wdStyleBodyText3 (-82)	wdStyleHeading7 (-8)	wdStyleListContinue2 (-70)
wdStyleBodyTextFirstIndent (-78)	wdStyleHeading8 (-9)	wdStyleListContinue3 (-71)
wdStyleBodyTextFirstIndent2 (-79)	wdStyleHeading9 (-10)	wdStyleListContinue4 (-72)
wdStyleBodyTextIndent (-68)	wdStyleHyperlink (-86)	wdStyleListContinue5 (-73)
wdStyleBodyTextIndent2 (-83)	wdStyleHyperlinkFollowed (-87)	wdStyleListNumber (-50)
wdStyleBodyTextIndent3 (-84)	wdStyleIndex1 (-11)	wdStyleListNumber2 (-59)
wdStyleCaption (-35)	wdStyleIndex2 (-12)	wdStyleListNumber3 (-60)
wdStyleClosing (-64)	wdStyleIndex3 (-13)	wdStyleListNumber4 (-61)
wdStyleCommentReference (-40)	wdStyleIndex4 (-14)	wdStyleListNumber5 (-62)
wdStyleCommentText (-31)	wdStyleIndex5 (-15)	wdStyleMacroText (-46)
wdStyleDate (-77)	wdStyleIndex6 (-16)	wdStyleMessageHeader (-74)
wdStyleDefaultParagraphFont (-66)	wdStyleIndex7 (-17)	wdStyleNavPane (-90)
wdStyleEmphasis (-89)	wdStyleIndex8 (-18)	wdStyleNormal (-1)
wdStyleEndnoteReference (-43)	wdStyleIndex9 (-19)	wdStyleNormalIndent (-29)
wdStyleEndnoteText (-44)	wdStyleIndexHeading (-34)	wdStyleNoteHeading (-80)
wdStyleEnvelopeAddress (-37)	wdStyleLineNumber (-41)	wdStylePageNumber (-42)
wdStyleEnvelopeReturn (-38)	wdStyleList (-48)	wdStylePlainText (-91)
wdStyleFooter (-33)	wdStyleList2 (-51)	wdStyleSalutation (-76)
wdStyleFootnoteReference (-39)	wdStyleList3 (-52)	wdStyleSignature (-65)
wdStyleFootnoteText (-30)	wdStyleList4 (-53)	wdStyleStrong (-88)
wdStyleHeader (-32)	wdStyleList5 (-54)	wdStyleSubtitle (-75)
wdStyleHeading1 (-2)	wdStyleListBullet (-49)	wdStyleTableOfAuthorities (-45)
wdStyleHeading2 (-3)	wdStyleListBullet2 (-55)	wdStyleTableOfFigures (-36)
wdStyleHeading3 (-4)	wdStyleListBullet3 (-56)	wdStyleTitle (-63)

wdStyleTOAHeading (-47)	wdStyleTOC4 (-23)	wdStyleTOC7 (-26)
wdStyleTOC1 (-20)	wdStyleTOC5 (-24)	wdStyleTOC8 (-27)
wdStyleTOC2 (-21)	wdStyleTOC6 (-25)	wdStyleTOC9 (-28)
wdStyleTOC3 (-22)		

The AutomaticallyUpdate property

Word provides a way to redefine a style based on changes that are made to a portion of text that has been formatted with that style. For instance, suppose that a paragraph has **Heading4** style and you make some manual paragraph formatting changes to that text. If you now click on the style combo box and hit the Enter key, you will be presented with the dialog box shown in Figure 12-4. This gives you the choice of updating the style definition to match the new formatting or reapplying the original formatting, thus undoing the changes.

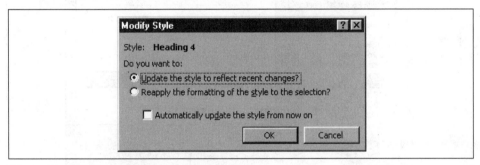

Figure 12-4. The Modify Style dialog box

Setting the AutomaticallyUpdate property to True will cause Word to update the style automatically without displaying this dialog box. Setting the property to False instructs Word to display this dialog box.

The BaseStyle property

A Word style can be based upon another style. The BaseStyle property can be used to return or set this base style. For instance, the following code creates a new style called **NewStyle** and bases it upon the **Chapter** style:

```
Dim st As Style
Set st = ActiveDocument.Styles.Add("NewStyle", wdStyleTypeParagraph)
st.BaseStyle = "Chapter"
```

Note that we can also use the **WdBuiltinStyles** constants to specify the base style.

The BuiltIn property

This read-only Boolean property is True if the specified style is one of Word's built-in styles; otherwise it is False. Note that this property returns True for a built-in style even if the style has been modified.

The Description property

This useful property returns the description of the specified style. This is the text that you see in the Description area of the Style dialog box, as shown in Figure 12-5.

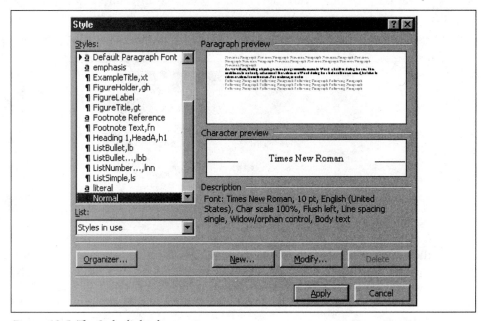

Figure 12-5. The Style dialog box

The InUse property

This read-only Boolean property is True if the specified style is in use. By this, Microsoft means that the style is either a built-in style that has been modified or applied somewhere in the document or is a new style that has been created. (Thus, you can tell which built-in styles have been modified by opening a new document and going directly to the Format Style dialog box.)

It is important to note that the new style does not need to be applied to any text to be considered in use. Thus, the only styles that are *not* in use are any built-in styles that have *never* been applied to any text in the document. Even if a built-in style has been used to format some text and then all such text has been deleted, the style is still marked as being in use.

The Type property

The read-only Type property returns the type for the specified object as one of the following constants:

```
Enum WdStyleType
    wdStyleTypeParagraph = 1
    wdStyleTypeCharacter = 2
End Enum
```

The ParagraphFormat property

Each Style object of type **wdStyleTypeParagraph** (that is, each paragraph style) has a child ParagraphFormat object (accessible through the ParagraphFormat property) that represents the paragraph format settings for the style. Modifying this object modifies the style. Note that if we attempt to use the ParagraphFormat property for a Style object of type **wdStyleTypeCharacter**, Word generates a run-time error. Thus, the Type property should be checked before using the ParagraphFormat property.

The Variable Object

As I have said, a module-level variable remains alive as long as the document (or template) in which it is declared remains open. However, once you close the document (or close all documents that use the template), all module-level variables are destroyed.

To preserve a value associated with a document (or template) even when the document (or template) is no longer open, you have two choices. One is to save the value to a file on the disk and then retrieve it when the document is reopened. This can be done using the System object, as described in Chapter 11, *The Application Object.*

However, when the data are not large, an alternative solution is to use a Variable object, also called a document variable. This is simply a special type of variable that is saved with the document. (Note that to access the Variable objects for a template, you must open the template as a document.)

The Document object has a Variables property that returns a Variables collection containing the document's Variable objects.

The Variable object has but a single method: the *Delete* method. The most interesting properties of a Variable object are Name and Value.

Creating a Variable object

To create a document variable, use the *Add* method of the Variables collection. The syntax is:

```
VariablesObject.Add(Name, Value)
```

For instance, the following line creates a new document variable called *Example-Var* and sets its value to 5:

```
ActiveDocument.Variables.Add "ExampleVar", 5
```

You can then retrieve this variable, even if the document is closed and then reopened, by referring to it as:

```
ActiveDocument.Variables("ExampleVar")
```

Note that if you try to add a document variable with the same name as an existing document variable, Word will issue an error message. Unfortunately, there is no *Exists* method that can be used to determine when a variable name is in use, so you must cycle through all variables to determine this, using code such as the following:

```
Dim v As Variable
Dim bExists As Boolean
bExists = False
For Each v In ActiveDocument.Variables
    If v.Name = "Variable Name" Then
        bExists = True
        Exit For
    End If
Next v
If bExists then
    ' code here for case when name exists
Else
    ' code here for case when name does not exist
End If
```

Finally, note that document variables are generally invisible to the user of Microsoft Word, except that you can display their values by inserting a DOCVARIABLE field with the appropriate variable name.

Example: Printing Document Headings

Having concluded our survey of the Document object and its children, we can now take a look at several sample programs that use them. The first of these is a routine that prints document headings.

As you probably know, Microsoft Word has an outline view that is designed to provide an overview of a Word document by showing only the document headings (and optionally some text). I find the outline view to be of limited use, especially since I have had trouble getting it to display just Heading styles. (For some reason, it seems to want to display some custom styles despite my best efforts to display only Heading styles.)

In any case, the macro in Example 12-6 creates a new document that contains only the headings from the active document. More specifically, the macro first asks the user for a number, *X*. Then it creates a new Word document and inserts into this document those paragraphs in the active document that have style Heading 1 through Heading *X*.

There are a couple of points to observe when looking at this code. First, I use the **Like** operator:

```
If para.Format.Style Like "Heading [0-9]" Then
```

to select styles of the form Heading *X*, where *X* is any single digit.

Second, the **For Each** loop must check each paragraph in the document, which can take some time for a large document (at least several seconds). The first statement within this **For Each** loop is:

```
DoEvents
```

which tells VBA to allow Windows to perform any normal windows housekeeping while the loop is processing. For instance, if you run the program without this statement, all windows on the monitor will seem to be frozen (will not repaint) until the loop finishes. (Try it.)

Finally, since the program can take several seconds to run, I have included code to display a waiting message in the Word status bar:

```
StatusBar = "Printing headings. Please wait..."
```

and also to display a message box at the end of the program to inform the user when the program has finished.

Example 12-6. The PrintHeadings Procedure

```
Sub PrintHeadings()

' Creates a new document with Heading XX
' style paragraphs only from active document.
' User prompted for max level XX.

Dim para As Paragraph, rng As Range
Dim DocA As Document, DocB As Document
Dim iLevel As Integer, iMaxLevel As Integer

' Ask for max level
iMaxLevel = InputBox("Enter maximum level for Heading style.")
If iMaxLevel = 0 Then Exit Sub

StatusBar = "Printing headings. Please wait..."

Set DocA = ActiveDocument

' Create new document
Set DocB = Word.Documents.Add(DocA.AttachedTemplate.Name)
```

Example 12-6. The PrintHeadings Procedure (continued)

```
' Set extra wide page margins
With DocB.PageSetup
    .TopMargin = InchesToPoints(0.25)
    .BottomMargin = InchesToPoints(0.25)
    .LeftMargin = InchesToPoints(0.25)
    .RightMargin = InchesToPoints(0.25)
End With

Set rng = DocB.Range

For Each para In DocA.Paragraphs
    DoEvents
    iLevel = 0

    ' Check for Heading style
    If para.Format.Style Like "Heading [0-9]" Then

        iLevel = Val(Mid(para.Format.Style, 8))
        ' Check for acceptable level
        If iLevel > 0 And iLevel <= iMaxLevel Then
            rng.Collapse wdCollapseEnd
            rng.Text = String(iLevel - 1, vbTab) & _
                Format(iLevel) & ") " & para.Range.Text
        End If

    End If
Next para

' Delete any annoying page breaks
Selection.Find.ClearFormatting
Selection.Find.Replacement.ClearFormatting
With Selection.Find
    .Text = "^m"
    .Replacement.Text = ""
    .Forward = True
    .Wrap = wdFindAsk
    .Format = False
    .MatchCase = False
    .MatchWholeWord = False
    .MatchWildcards = False
    .MatchSoundsLike = False
    .MatchAllWordForms = False
End With
Selection.Find.Execute replace:=wdReplaceAll

' Tell user when done
MsgBox "Done creating new document with headings only."

End Sub
```

Example: Finding Used Styles

As discussed earlier, Word considers a custom style to be in use even if no current text is formatted with that style. However, whenever I turn in a manuscript for
a book, the production editors always want a list of all of the paragraph styles that
I *really* used in that manuscript. They don't care about styles that I might have
used and then removed.

There are actually a couple of ways you could create such a list. One way would
be to start with a list of all InUse styles. Then you could go through the document
looking at the styles of each paragraph, checking off those styles on your list.
However, there may be several thousand paragraphs in a document, and you
would have to search the style list each time. This might be a bit slow.

Alternatively, you could cycle through the document, recording the style of each
paragraph in a string array. Then you would need to eliminate the duplicates,
which is most efficiently done if the array is sorted. The code in Example 12-7
(which lists only paragraph styles) takes this approach. It provides a good example of manipulating arrays.

Example 12-7. Finding Used Styles in a Document

```
Sub FindUsedStyles()

Dim sAllStyles() As String
Dim sUsedStyles() As String
Dim i As Long
Dim idx As Long
Dim cParas As Long
Dim cUsedStyles As Long
Dim sPrevStyle As String
Dim para As Paragraph

' Count of paragraphs in document
cParas = ActiveDocument.Paragraphs.Count

' Redim array to correct size
ReDim sAllStyles(1 To cParas)

' Collect styles in array sAllStyles
idx = 1
For Each para In ActiveDocument.Paragraphs
    sAllStyles(idx) = para.Style
    idx = idx + 1
Next para

' Sort array
SortQuickly sAllStyles, 1, cParas

' Dedup the array to a new array
ReDim sUsedStyles(1 To 10)
```

Example 12-7. Finding Used Styles in a Document (continued)

```
cUsedStyles = 0
sPrevStyle = ""
For i = 1 To cParas
    If sAllStyles(i) <> sPrevStyle Then
        ' Next index in UsedStyle array
        cUsedStyles = cUsedStyles + 1
        ' Add more room to array if necessary
        If UBound(sUsedStyles) > cUsedStyles Then _
            ReDim Preserve sUsedStyles(1 To cUsedStyles + 10)
        ' Add it to used style array
        sUsedStyles(cUsedStyles) = sAllStyles(i)
        ' Set previous style to current style for next time
        sPrevStyle = sAllStyles(i)
    End If
Next i

' Create a new document
' and insert the style names
Documents.Add
For i = 1 To cUsedStyles
    Selection.InsertAfter sUsedStyles(i) & vbCr
    Selection.Collapse wdCollapseEnd
Next i

' Erase the arrays to reclaim space
Erase sAllStyles
Erase sUsedStyles

End Sub
```

Let us take a closer look at a portion of the previous code:

```
' Collect styles in array sAllStyles
idx = 1
For Each para In ActiveDocument.Paragraphs
    sAllStyles(idx) = para.Style
    idx = idx + 1
Next para
```

An alternative to this **For Each** loop is the following **For** loop:

```
Dim paras As Paragraphs
Set paras = ActiveDocument.Paragraphs
For i = 1 To paras.Count
    sAllStyles(i) = paras(i).Style
Next i
```

This code does not require the rather artificial **idx** variable to keep the index of the **sAllStyles** array, so it might be a slightly more readable choice.

However, you may recall that I mentioned in Chapter 8 that the **For Each** loop can be *much* faster than the **For** loop when iterating through a collection. To test this, I did some timing experiments with these two versions. This book started its life as a Word document with over 9800 paragraphs. It took approximately 10 seconds for this example to complete on this manuscript using the `For Each` loop. On the other hand, using the `For` loop, I got tired of waiting after 10 minutes and hit Ctrl-Break. Execution was still within the `For` loop, and the value of the variable i was only 464. Thus, I estimate that it would take over 3 hours to complete using the `For` loop!

You have probably noticed the call to a procedure called *SortQuickly*, which sorts the array **sAllStyles**. This procedure uses a sorting method called *QuickSort*, which is among the fastest known methods in general. In fact, it took less than a second to sort the 9,800 style names for this manuscript!

The *SortQuickly* code is a bit complex, since it actually calls itself! This is referred to as *recursion*. This is not the place to go into the details of recursive procedures or quick sorting, since it has little to do with Word programming, so I just present the code and let you decide whether to use it or the simpler but slower alternative discussed next.

As an alternative to using the *SortQuickly* method, there is another way to handle the sorting. I could create a new Word document, place the **sAllStyles** array in this document (one paragraph per style name), select the entire document, and then ask Word to do the sorting using the *SortAscending* method of the Selection object. (I discuss the *SortAscending* method in Chapter 14.). Finally, you would read the sorted text back into an array. (This might make a good exercise for you.)

In any case, here is the QuickSort procedure:

```
Private Sub SortQuickly(sArray() As String, Fst As Long, _
   Lst As Long)

Dim Tmp As String, i As Long, j As Long

If Fst >= Lst Then Exit Sub

' Swap first element with middle (random) _
' element in case list is already sorted.
j = (Lst + Fst) \ 2
Tmp = sArray(Fst)
sArray(Fst) = sArray(j)
sArray(j) = Tmp

i = Fst + 1

' Find next entry >= first
Do While StrComp(sArray(i), sArray(Fst), 1) = -1
   i = i + 1
Loop

j = Lst
' Find last entry <= first
```

```
Do While StrComp(sArray(Fst), sArray(j), 1) = -1
   j = j - 1
Loop

' Main loop
Do While i < j
   ' Swap out of order pair
   Tmp = sArray(i): sArray(i) = sArray(j): sArray(j) = Tmp

   ' Search for next on left
   i = i + 1
   Do While StrComp(sArray(i), sArray(Fst), 1) = -1
      i = i + 1
   Loop

   ' and on right
   j = j - 1
   Do While StrComp(sArray(Fst), sArray(j), 1) = -1
      j = j - 1
   Loop

Loop

' Swap again
Tmp = sArray(Fst)
sArray(Fst) = sArray(j)
sArray(j) = Tmp

' Call procedure recursively
SortQuickly sArray, Fst, j - 1
SortQuickly sArray, j + 1, Lst

End Sub
```

In this chapter:
- *Adding a New Section*
- *The PageSetup Object*
- *Properties of the Section Object*
- *The HeaderFooter Object*

13

The Section and HeaderFooter Objects

The Section object represents a section in a document, range, or selection. Section objects are stored in the Sections collection. Each of the Document, Range, and Selection objects has a Sections property that returns a Sections collection containing the Section objects for that parent.

Adding a New Section

To add a new section to a document, range, or selection, use the *Add* method of the Sections collection. The syntax is:

```
SectionsObject.Add(Range, Start)
```

The optional variant parameter **Range** refers to a Range object *before* which the section break will be inserted. If this argument is omitted, the section break is inserted at the end of the document. The optional **Start** parameter indicates the type of section break. It can be any of the following WdSectionStart constants:

```
Enum WdSectionStart
    wdSectionContinuous = 0
    wdSectionNewColumn = 1
    wdSectionNewPage = 2
    wdSectionEvenPage = 3
    wdSectionOddPage = 4
End Enum
```

The default value is wdSectionNewPage.

As an alternative to the *Add* method, you can insert a new section using the *Insert-Break* method, which applies to a Range or Selection object. Its syntax is:

```
expression.InsertBreak(Type)
```

where *expression* refers to either a Range or a Selection object, and *Type* can be any of the following **wdBreakType** constants:

```
Enum WdBreakType
    wdSectionBreakNextPage = 2
    wdSectionBreakContinuous = 3
    wdSectionBreakEvenPage = 4
    wdSectionBreakOddPage = 5
    wdLineBreak = 6
    wdPageBreak = 7
    wdColumnBreak = 8
End Enum
```

The default is **wdPageBreak**, so to insert a section, you must specify a different type.

Note that when you insert a section break, it is inserted immediately *before* the specified range or selection. However, for the other types of breaks, the range or selection is actually replaced.

The PageSetup Object

The Sections collection has a PageSetup property that returns a PageSetup object. Although Microsoft does not say this explicitly, experimentation indicates that the settings of the PageSetup object for the Sections collection are accurate for only those settings that are common to all of the sections in the Sections collection.

For instance, if a document has three sections, each with the left margin setting of 1.25, then the LeftMargin property of the PageSetup object will equal 1.25. However, if the right margins of the three sections are not all the same, then the Right-Margin setting of the PageSetup object will contain an "obviously" invalid value. (On my system, it returns 138,888.9 inches.)

As another example, the SectionStart property of the PageSetup object returns or sets on the type of section break. It can be one of the following constants:

```
Enum WdSectionStart
    wdSectionContinuous = 0
    wdSectionNewColumn = 1
    wdSectionNewPage = 2
    wdSectionEvenPage = 3
    wdSectionOddPage = 4
End Enum
```

Now, if we create a document with three sections, each of which has type **wdSectionNewPage**, then the code:

```
MsgBox Sections.PageSetup.SectionStart
```

will display the number 2, as expected (`wdSectionNewPage=2`). On the other hand, if you change the type of one of the sections to, say, `wdSectionContinuous`, the previous code will display the number 9,999,999!

Properties of the Section Object

The Section object has no methods. Its properties are:

Borders	Headers	Parent
Creator	Index	ProtectedForForms
Footers	PageSetup	Range

Notice that the Section object also has a PageSetup property that returns a PageSetup object that represents the page formatting for that particular section only.

The Headers property returns a HeadersFooters collection that contains the headers for the section. The Footers property also returns a HeadersFooters collection, but it represents the footers for the section.

The HeaderFooter Object

A HeaderFooter object represents either a header or a footer. A HeadersFooters collection contains HeaderFooter objects of one type (header or footer) or the other, but not both.

A HeadersFooters collection, whether it be a collection of headers or footers, is indexed by one of the constants in the following enum:

```
Enum WdHeaderFooterIndex
    wdHeaderFooterPrimary = 1
    wdHeaderFooterFirstPage = 2
    wdHeaderFooterEvenPages = 3
End Enum
```

As you can see, there are three types of headers and three types of footers. (I discuss the meaning of a primary header or footer a bit later in this chapter.)

Thus, to obtain the HeaderFooter object that represents the primary header in the first section of the active document, write:

```
ActiveDocument.Sections(1).Headers(wdHeaderFooterPrimary)
```

Similarly, the primary footer in this section is:

```
ActiveDocument.Sections(1).Footers(wdHeaderFooterPrimary)
```

As an example, the following code changes the text in both the primary header and the primary footer:

```
With ActiveDocument.Sections(1)
  .Headers(wdHeaderFooterPrimary).Range.Text = "Header text"
```

```
        .Footers(wdHeaderFooterPrimary).Range.Text = _
            "Footer text"
    End With
```

Note that if the current selection is within a header or footer, the HeaderFooter property of the Selection object will return that HeaderFooter object.

Different Odd and Even Headers or Footers

The PageSetup object has two properties that relate to headers and footers: DifferentFirstPageHeaderFooter and OddAndEvenPagesHeaderFooter.

You can set the DifferentFirstPageHeaderFooter property of the PageSetup object to True to specify a separate first-page header and footer for that portion of the document covered by the PageSetup object. For instance, the following code specifies a separate first-page header and footer for the first section in the active document and then inserts some text in the first-page footer:

```
    With ActiveDocument.Sections(1)
        .PageSetup.DifferentFirstPageHeaderFooter = True
        .Footers(wdHeaderFooterFirstPage).Range. _
            InsertBefore "First page footer text"
    End With
```

The OddAndEvenPagesHeaderFooter property of the PageSetup object is set to True to specify different odd- and even-page headers and footers. When this property is True, the index **wdHeaderFooterPrimary** refers to an odd header or footer.

In particular, the *primary* header (or footer) is defined based on the values of the two properties I have been discussing. The primary header is:

- The only header when DifferentFirstPageHeaderFooter is False and OddAndEvenPagesHeaderFooter is False.

- The nonfirst page header when DifferentFirstPageHeaderFooter is True and OddAndEvenPagesHeaderFooter is False.

- The odd page header when DifferentFirstPageHeaderFooter is False and OddAndEvenPagesHeaderFooter is True.

- The non-first page odd header when DifferentFirstPageHeaderFooter is True and OddAndEvenPagesHeaderFooter is True.

Properties of the HeaderFooter Object

A HeaderFooter object has no methods. Its properties are:

Application	IsHeader	Parent
Creator	LinkToPrevious	Range
Exists	PageNumbers	Shapes
Index		

The Exists property

The Exists property can be used to determine whether a first-page or odd-page header or footer exists. (The primary header and footer always exist.) For example, the following code reports whether a first-page header exists in the first section of the active document:

```
MsgBox ActiveDocument.Sections(1). _
    Headers(wdHeaderFooterFirstPage).Exists
```

The Exists property is more useful than you might think at first. To illustrate, consider the following code:

```
MsgBox ActiveDocument.Sections(1). _
      Headers(wdHeaderFooterEvenPages).Exists
MsgBox ActiveDocument.Sections(1). _
      Headers(wdHeaderFooterEvenPages).IsHeader
```

When applied to a new document, the results are False, followed by True.

This shows that the HeadersFooters collection of headers for a document always contains three HeaderFooter objects, even if you have not specified separate first-page or even-page headers. Thus, the three HeaderFooter objects "exist" in the collection, but their Exists property may be False, indicating that they do not "exist" in the document.

The IsHeader property

The read-only IsHeader property is True if the specified HeaderFooter object is a header; otherwise, it is False.

The LinkToPrevious property

This property can be set to True to link the specified header or footer to the corresponding header or footer in the previous section. In this case, the header or footer automatically receives the same contents as the previous header or footer.

It is important to note that the LinkToPrevious property is set to True by default. This setting allows you to change the contents of all headers or footers of a specific type (primary, first-page, or odd-page) by changing the contents of the first header or footer of that type.

For instance, the following code sets the text for every primary header in the active document (assuming that LinkToPrevious has not been changed to False):

```
ActiveDocument.Sections(1). _
    Headers(wdHeaderFooterPrimary).Range.Text = "whoops"
```

The LinkToPrevious property applies to each type of header and each type of footer separately. Thus, for instance, the LinkToPrevious property could be set to True for the even-page headers but False for the even-page footers.

Finally, note that if the LinkToPrevious property is changed to False after text has been added to each header (of a particular type), the text will remain in all of the headers. In other words, setting the LinkToPrevious property to True automatically inserts text into all headers (or footers), but setting it to False does not automatically remove that text.

Adding page numbers to a header or footer

The PageNumbers property of the HeaderFooter object returns a PageNumbers collection, which holds all of the PageNumber objects for the header or footer. In most cases, a header or footer will contain only a single page number (if any), denoted by `PageNumbers(1)`.

To add a page number to a header or footer, one option is to use the *Add* method of the PageNumbers collection. The syntax is:

```
PageNumbersObject.Add(PageNumberAlignment, FirstPage)
```

The optional `PageNumberAlignment` parameter can be any of the following `WdPageNumberAlignment` constants:

```
Enum WdPageNumberAlignment
    wdAlignPageNumberLeft = 0
    wdAlignPageNumberCenter = 1
    wdAlignPageNumberRight = 2
    wdAlignPageNumberInside = 3
    wdAlignPageNumberOutside = 4
End Enum
```

If `FirstPage` is set to False, a page number is not added to the first page of the header or footer (assuming that the first page of the section is included in the specified header or footer).

The *Add* method inserts a text frame containing a page number field into the specified header or footer. The text frame is positioned according to the `PageNumber-Alignment` parameter.

Note that if the LinkToPrevious property for the HeaderFooter object is set to True, the page numbers will continue sequentially from one section to next.

The *Add* method described previously will insert a page number on the first line, aligned as specified in the `PageNumberAlignment` parameter. However, if you want to place a page number field within some text in a header, for instance, then you can use the Add method of the Fields collection to add a field of type `wdFieldPage` in the appropriate location, as shown in the following code:

```
Dim rng As Range
Set rng = ActiveDocument.Sections(1). _
    Headers(wdHeaderFooterPrimary).Range
rng.ParagraphFormat.Alignment = wdAlignParagraphCenter
rng.Text = "Page number --> "
rng.Collapse wdCollapseEnd
rng.Fields.Add rng, wdFieldPage
rng.Move wdStory
rng.InsertAfter " <-- Page number"
```

which produces a header with the following appearance:

Page number --> # <-- Page Number

Example: Setting Headers

In my opinion, one of the most onerous tasks in a Word document with a lot of sections is to set up running heads (that is, a line of text that appears at the top of each page). Fortunately, a little programming can automate this task.

To illustrate, imagine a document with multiple sections. Each section starts with a paragraph that contains the word "Chapter" followed by the chapter number, as in:

Chapter 12

I want to create headers for this document. The odd-page header should have the form:

Chapter *XX*   Page *YY*

where *XX* is the chapter number and *YY* is the page number. The even-page headers have a similar form, with the two items reversed (so that the page number is always on the outside margin):

Page *YY*   Chapter *XX*

The macro in Example 13-1 does the job.

Example 13-1. The MakeHeaders Macro

```
Sub MakeHeaders()

' Add an odd-page header of the form:
' Chapter #          Page #
' and an even-page header of the form
' Page #             Chapter #
' to each section

Dim rng As Range
Dim sect As Section
Dim sChapter As String
```

Example 13-1. The MakeHeaders Macro (continued)

```
For Each sect In ActiveDocument.Sections

    ' Different odd- and even-page headers
    sect.PageSetup.OddAndEvenPagesHeaderFooter = True

    ' Unlink headers and
    ' add tab stop at right margin
    With sect.Headers(wdHeaderFooterPrimary)
        .LinkToPrevious = False
        .Range.ParagraphFormat.TabStops.ClearAll
        .Range.ParagraphFormat.TabStops.Add _
            sect.PageSetup.PageWidth - _
            sect.PageSetup.RightMargin - _
            sect.PageSetup.LeftMargin, _
            wdAlignTabRight
    End With

    ' Repeat for even-page header
    With sect.Headers(wdHeaderFooterEvenPages)
        .LinkToPrevious = False
        .Range.ParagraphFormat.TabStops.ClearAll
        .Range.ParagraphFormat.TabStops.Add _
            sect.PageSetup.PageWidth - _
            sect.PageSetup.RightMargin - _
            sect.PageSetup.LeftMargin, _
            wdAlignTabRight
    End With

    ' Get Chapter X text from first paragraph
    ' in section.
    sChapter = sect.Range.Paragraphs(1).Range.Text

    ' Trim paragraph mark if present
    If Right(sChapter, 1) = vbCr Then
        sChapter = Left(sChapter, Len(sChapter) - 1)
    End If

    ' Do odd-page (primary) header
    Set rng = sect.Headers(wdHeaderFooterPrimary).Range
    rng.Text = sChapter & vbTab & "Page "
    rng.Collapse wdCollapseEnd
    ' Insert page number
    rng.Fields.Add rng, wdFieldPage

    ' Do even-page (primary) header
    Set rng = sect.Headers(wdHeaderFooterEvenPages).Range
    rng.Text = "Page "
    rng.Collapse wdCollapseEnd
    ' Insert page number
    rng.Fields.Add rng, wdFieldPage
    ' Insert chapter number
    Set rng = sect.Headers(wdHeaderFooterEvenPages).Range
```

Example 13-1. The MakeHeaders Macro (continued)

```
rng.Collapse wdCollapseEnd
rng.InsertAfter vbTab & sChapter

Next sect

End Sub
```

14

The Range and Selection Objects

The Range and Selection objects are the workhorses of the Word object model, as you can probably tell by the relative length of this chapter. One of the reasons that the Range object is so important is that it often provides the gateway to many "properties" of an object. Put more plainly, in many cases what you might expect to be a property of an object is in fact a property of the object's child Range object. For instance, to access the text in the first paragraph in the active document, use:

```
ActiveDocument.Paragraphs(1).Range.Text
```

rather than:

```
ActiveDocument.Paragraphs(1).Text
```

which just produces the error "Method or data member not found" because Text is a property of the Range object, not of the Paragraph object.

Simply put, the Range and Selection objects both represent a contiguous area within a Word document. However, it is important to keep in mind that they represent more than just the text within this area. For instance, a Range object has no less than 65 properties, only one of which is the Text property.

In the next two lists, members marked with an R are unique to the Range object, and those marked with an S are unique to the Selection object. All remaining members with neither an R nor an S are common to both objects. The items marked with an asterisk are discussed in this book. The properties of the Range and Selection objects are:

Application	Case[R]*	Comments*
Bold[R]*	Cells	Creator
BookmarkID	Characters*	Document[S]
Bookmarks*	Columns	Duplicate[R]*
Borders*	ColumnSelectMode[S]	End*

Endnotes
ExtendMode[S]
Fields*
Find*
Flags[S]
Font*
Footnotes
FormattedText*
FormFields
Frames*
GrammarChecked[R]
GrammaticalErrors[R]
HeaderFooter[S]
HighlightColorIndex[R]
Hyperlinks
Information
InlineShapes
IPAtEndOfLine[S]
IsEndOfRowMark

Italic[R]*
LanguageID
LanguageIDFarEast
LanguageIDOther
ListFormat[R]
ListParagraphs[R]
NextStoryRange[R]
Orientation
PageSetup*
ParagraphFormat*
Paragraphs*
Parent
PreviousBookmarkID
*Range[S]
ReadabilityStatistics[R]
Revisions[R]
Rows
Sections*
Sentences*

Shading*
ShapeRange
SpellingChecked[R]
SpellingErrors[R]
Start*
StartIsActive[S]
StoryLength
StoryType
Style*
Subdocuments[R]
SynonymInfo[R]
Tables*
Text*
TextRetrievalMode[R]
Type[S]
Underline[R]*
Words*

The methods of the Range and Selection objects are:

AutoFormat[R]
Calculate
CheckGrammar[R]
CheckSpelling[R]
CheckSynonyms[R]
Collapse*
ComputeStatistics[R]
ConvertToTable*
Copy*
CopyAsPicture
CopyFormat[S]*
CreatePublisher[R]
CreateTextbox[S]
Cut*
Delete
EndKey[S]*
EndOf*
EscapeKey[S]*
Expand*
Extend[S]*
GetSpellingSuggestions[R]
GoTo*
GoToNext*
GoToPrevious*
HomeKey[S]*
InRange*
InsertAfter*
InsertAutoText[R]
InsertBefore*
InsertBreak*
InsertCaption*

InsertCells[S]
InsertColumns[S]
InsertCrossReference
InsertDatabase[R]
InsertDateTime*
InsertFile*
InsertFormula[S]
InsertParagraph*
InsertParagraphAfter*
InsertParagraphBefore*
InsertRows[S]
InsertSymbol*
InStory*
IsEqual*
LookupNameProperties[R]
Move*
MoveDown[S]*
MoveEnd*
MoveEndUntil*
MoveEndWhile*
MoveLeft[S]
MoveRight[S]*
MoveStart*
MoveStartUntil*
MoveStartWhile*
MoveUntil*
MoveUp[S]*
MoveWhile*
Next*
NextField[S]
NextRevision[S]

NextSubdocument
PasteFormat[S]*
PasteSpecial*
Previous*
PreviousField[S]
PreviousRevision[S]
PreviousSubdocument
Relocate[R]
Select*
SelectColumn[S]
SelectCurrentAlignment[S]
SelectCurrentColor[S]
SelectCurrentFont[S]
SelectCurrentIndent[S]
SelectCurrentSpacing[S]
SelectCurrentTabs[S]
SelectRow[S]
SetRange*
Shrink[S]
Sort
SortAscending*
SortDescending*
SplitTable[S]
StartOf*
SubscribeTo[R]
TypeBackspace[S]*
TypeParagraph[S]*
TypeText[S]*
WholeStory*

Figures 14-1 and 14-2 show the children of these objects.

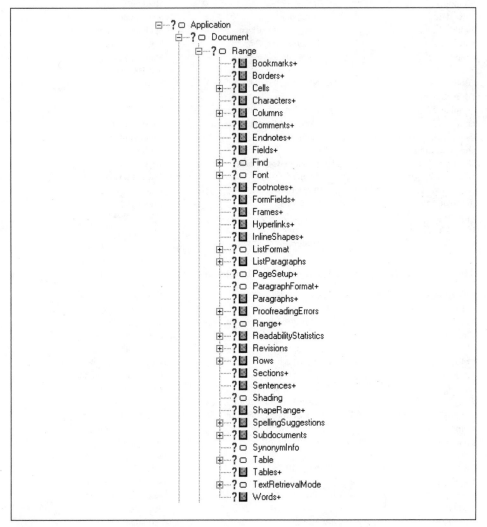

Figure 14-1. The Range object

You should not feel intimidated by the large number of properties and methods of these objects. Many of these members are not used very often, and when they are needed, you can simply look them up in the Word VBA Help system. Moreover, the most commonly used properties and methods can be arranged into a few functional groups, making it much easier to remember them.

The discussion of these objects is divided into three parts. First, I discuss ways to create Range and Selection objects. Then I discuss ways for making changes to a given Range or Selection object (such as expanding, collapsing, and moving the object). Finally, I look at some of the more commonly used properties and methods of these objects, grouped by function.

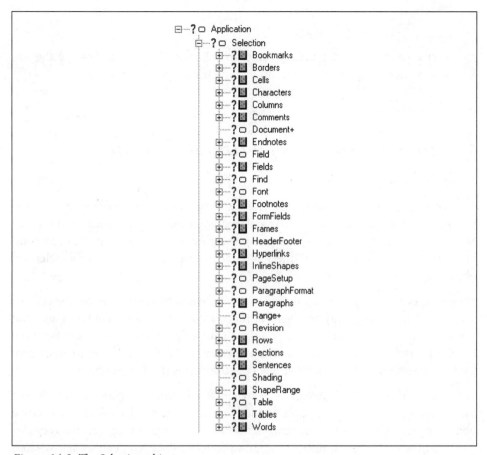

Figure 14-2. The Selection object

I suggest that you read this chapter with an eye toward gaining a general understanding of these objects and their members. Then you can look up the details of any particular member when needed. (Much of the trick to successful Word programming is simply to remember that there is a particular object, property, or method that may do what you need. Then you can look up the details.)

Before plunging in, it is worth mentioning that there are many ways to accomplish most tasks. For instance, here are four ways to create a Range object, rng, that represents the position before the first character in the document:

```
Set rng = ActiveDocument.Range
rng.Collapse wdCollapseStart

Set rng = ActiveDocument.Range
rng.End = 0

Set rng = ActiveDocument.Range
```

```
rng.StartOf wdStory, wdMove

Set rng = ActiveDocument.Range(0,0)
```

As another example, if **rng** already refers to a Range object, then both of the following statements expand the range to include the entire document:

```
rng.WholeStory
rng.Expand wdStory
```

Comparing the Range and Selection Objects

The Range and Selection objects are quite similar in that they have many properties and methods in common. In particular, among the 65 properties of the Range object and 53 properties of the Selection object, a total of 43 properties are common. Among the 61 methods of the Range object and 80 methods of the Selection object, 48 are common.

Nonetheless, there are significant differences between the two types of objects. For instance, there can be only one Selection object per document window pane, but there can be any number of range objects. This makes the Range object far more flexible in many situations and is one reason why Microsoft seems to steer programmers away from the Selection object and towards the Range object.

The most obvious visual difference between Range and Selection objects is that the active Selection object appears highlighted (in reverse video) whereas a Range object has no visible sign. This characteristic of the Range object can be very disconcerting when trying to trace through a program, since you cannot tell when a range is set, changed, or deleted. You can, however, select a Range object, thereby causing it to be highlighted. This is done using the Select method:

```
rng.Select
```

Of course, doing so will lose the current selection, so this may not be a reasonable solution.

An alternative is to use the small subroutine in Example 14-1, which simply changes the font in the range **rng** to emboss style for **rTime** seconds, with or without blinking. You might find this little program useful (as I do) while debugging your code. (For ready access, place it in its own module in your Normal template.)

Example 14-1. Showing a Range While Debugging

```
Public Sub DebugShowRange(rng As Range, rTime As Single, _
                          Blink As Boolean)

Dim StartTime As Variant, Tick As Variant
```

Example 14-1. Showing a Range While Debugging (continued)

```
' Safety net
If rTime < 0.1 Or rTime > 60 Then rTime = 2
' Emboss range
rng.Font.Emboss = True
' Wait rTime seconds, blinking
' every .25 seconds if requested
StartTime = Timer
Tick = StartTime
Do
    DoEvents
    If Blink Then
        If Timer - Tick > 0.25 Then
            rng.Font.Emboss = Not rng.Font.Emboss
            Tick = Timer
        End If
    End If
Loop Until Timer - StartTime >= rTime
' Kill emboss
rng.Font.Emboss = False
End Sub
```

To illustrate, the code:

```
Dim rng as Range
Set rng = ActiveDocument.Paragraphs(1)
ShowRange rng, 3, True
```

causes the range that refers to the first paragraph in the active document to blink in and out of emboss style for three seconds.

Range and Selection Variables

Throughout this discussion, I will use **rng** to denote a variable of type Range and **sel** to denote a variable of type Selection. If you decide to type in the example code, don't forget to declare these variables as:

```
Dim rng as Range
Dim sel as Selection
```

I will also use the expression:

```
(rng or sel)
```

to denote either a Range variable or a Selection variable.

It is not uncommon for a program to use more than one Range object at the same time, so there will be more than one Range variable alive at the same time. On the other hand, since there can be only one Selection object per window pane, it is much less common to create multiple Selection variables.

However, we should at least consider one simple example of manipulating multiple selections. The following code first splits the active window into two panes. Then it selects the first paragraph in pane 1 and the second paragraph in pane 2. These are referred to by the Selection variables `sel1` and `sel2`. Finally, the selection in pane 2 is contracted by the number of characters that appear selected in paragraph 1.

```
ActiveWindow.Split = True

ActiveWindow.Panes(1).Activate
ActiveDocument.Paragraphs(1).Range.Select
Set sel1 = Selection

ActiveWindow.Panes(2).Activate
ActiveDocument.Paragraphs(2).Range.Select
Set sel2 = Selection

sel2.MoveStart wdCharacter, sel1.Characters.Count
```

Figure 14-3 illustrates the effect of this code.

Incidentally, when working with more than one selection at a time, it is useful to know that the Selection object's Active property will return True if the selection to which it is applied is currently the active one. For example:

```
If sel1.Active Then
    ' Code to execute when sel1 is the active selection
```

Creating a Range or Selection Object

There are many ways to create a Range object. Indeed, there are no less than 74 properties and methods of various Word objects that return a Range object, and I discuss several of them shortly.

The procedure for creating a Selection object is a bit different, however. First, I use the *Select* method to select an item (text, bookmark, field, and so on). Then I use the Selection property to return a Selection object that represents that item. For instance, the code:

```
ActiveDocument.Select
Set sel = ActiveDocument.ActiveWindow.Selection
```

first selects the entire document and then sets the variable `sel` to refer to the current selection in the active document (that is, the entire document). As another example, the code:

```
ActiveDocument.Fields(2).Select
ActiveDocument.ActiveWindow.Selection.Delete
```

will select and then delete the second Field object in the active document.

Figure 14-3. Working with two selections

The Selection property applies only to the Application object, the Pane object and the Window object. However, there are many objects that have a Select method:

Bookmark	Frame	Rows
Cell	InlineShape	Selection
Column	MailMergeField	Shape
Columns	OLEControl	ShapeRange
Document	PageNumber	Subdocuments
Field	Range	Table
FormField	Row	

The Selection property is a global property, so it can be referenced without specifying a parent. For instance, the code:

```
Selection.Delete
```

will delete the currently active selection.

I briefly summarize the more common ways to create a Range object before considering them in more detail:

The Range method and the Range property

These return the Range object associated with the object to which they are applied. Some examples of objects that have a Range property or method are: Bookmarks, Cells, Rows, Tables, Documents, Frames, HeaderFooters, Lists, Paragraphs, Sections, and Selections.

The FormattedText property

This property returns a Range object that represents not just the text of the specified object, but also the formatting. (The Text property returns only the object's unformatted text.)

Characters, words, and sentences

Each character, word, or sentence in a Word document is actually a Range object. Thus, for instance, the code:

```
ActiveDocument.Words(1)
```

returns a Range object that consists of the first word in the active document.

The GoTo method

This method returns a Range object that represents the starting position of the target of the *GoTo* method. For instance:

```
Selection.GoTo wdGoToLine, wdGoToAbsolute, 2
```

moves the insertion point to the beginning of the second line (not sentence) in the document and returns this location as a Range object.

The ConvertToText method

The Row, Rows, and Table objects have a *ConvertToText* method that converts table data to text and returns a Range object that represents that text.

The Find object

When the *Execute* method of the Find object is executed successfully, a new Range object is returned.

The Field object

The Field object has two interesting properties that return a Range object: the Code property and the Result property. (I discussed these properties in Chapter 11, *The Application Object.*)

The TextRange property

If you work with frames, then you may need to use the TextRange property of a TextFrame object. This property returns a range containing the text within the TextFrame object.

Now we can take a more detailed look at the properties and methods that return a Range object.

The Entire Document

The Document object has a property called Content and a method called *Range* that return a Range object representing the entire main document story. Thus, the lines:

```
Set rng = ActiveDocument.Content
Set rng = ActiveDocument.Range
```

each create a Range object that refers to the main document story. (The main document story does not include other stories, such as headers/footers and footnotes.)

A Single Point

To insert text into a document without replacing other text, use a Range or Selection object that represents a single location in the document; in other words, a Range or Selection object whose starting and ending points are equal. This is easily obtained from an existing range using the *Collapse* method, whose syntax is:

```
(rng or sel).Collapse(Direction)
```

Here, *Direction* is either **wdCollapseStart** or **wdCollapseEnd**. For example, the following code inserts some text at the beginning of the second paragraph in the active document:

```
Set rng = ActiveDocument.Paragraphs(2).Range
rng.Collapse wdCollapseStart
rng.Text = "Some text. "
```

I often want to insert text at the beginning or ending of a document. The following code creates a single-location Range object at the beginning of the document and inserts some text:

```
Set rng = ActiveDocument.Range
rng.Collapse wdCollapseStart
rng.Text = "Start of Document" & vbCr
```

As I will discuss a bit later, an alternative approach is:

```
Set rng = ActiveDocument.Range(Start:=0,End:=0)
rng.Text = "Start of Document" & vbCr
```

Yet another approach is:

```
Set rng = ActiveDocument.Range
rng.StartOf wdStory, wdMove
rng.Text = "Start of Document" & vbCr
```

To insert text at the end of a document, you can collapse the range to the end using the **wdCollapseEnd** constant, as in:

```
Set rng = ActiveDocument.Paragraphs(2).Range
rng.Collapse wdCollapseEnd
rng.Text = "Some text for beginning of paragraph 3."
```

Note that the text in the previous code is inserted after the second paragraph—that is, at the beginning of the third paragraph. Another alternative is:

```
Set rng = ActiveDocument.Range
rng.EndOf wdStory, wdMove
rng.Text = "End of Document" & vbCr
```

(I discuss the *StartOf* and *EndOf* methods later in this chapter.)

The Range Method and the Range Property

There are several objects (23, to be exact, including the Selection object itself) that have a Range member (method or property). These are shown in the following list. (The Shapes object has a *Range* method, but it does not return a Range object, so it is not included in this list.)

List	HeaderFooter	Section
Cell	Hyperlink	Selection
Comment	Bookmark	Subdocument
Document	InlineShape	Table
Endnote	TableOfFigures	TableOfAuthorities
Footnote	Paragraph	TableOfContents
FormField	Revision	Index
Frame	Row	

The syntax for the Range property is:

```
object.Range
```

This returns a Range object consisting of the contents of the **object** to which the *Range* method is applied.

The syntax for the *Range* method is:

```
object.Range(Start, End)
```

This returns a Range object consisting of the "contents" of the object to which the *Range* method applies. To restrict the range further, you can fill in the optional **Start** and **End** character position parameters. Note that the Document object is the only object in the list with a *Range* method; all of the other objects have a Range property.

The character positions in the *Range* method refer to the point immediately *after* the character. For instance, to refer to a point immediately after the tenth character, set the character position to 10. As a special case, to refer to the beginning of the document (which is not after any character), set the character position to 0. Hence, the code:

```
Set rng = ActiveDocument.Range(0,0)
```

sets **rng** to refer to the beginning of a document. There is a slight subtlety with regard to the end of a document, however. To illustrate, if you were to open a new document and type the following 9 characters:

123456789

the document would actually contain 10 characters; that is:

```
ActiveDocument.Characters.Count
```

returns 10, because the document includes the ending paragraph mark. Since it is not possible to go beyond this ending paragraph mark, we define a range that represents the end of the document by specifying the starting and ending position after the ninth character:

```
set rng = ActiveDocument.Range(9, 9)
```

In general, the code:

```
cChars = ActiveDocument.Characters.Count
set rng = ActiveDocument.Range(cChars - 1, cChars - 1)
```

sets **rng** to refer to the end of a document.

The FormattedText Property

The FormattedText property is very useful, but can be a bit confusing. It may help to contrast this property with the Text property, which returns a String that is the unformatted text contained within the given range (no boldface, italic, and so on).

To illustrate, suppose that the active document consists of the following two lines:

The Merchant of Venice
Hamlet

Then, after executing the following code:

```
Set rng1 = ActiveDocument.Paragraphs(1).Range
Set rng2 = ActiveDocument.Paragraphs(2).Range
rng2.Text = rng1.Text
```

the document will consist of:

The Merchant of Venice
The Merchant of Venice

Note that the second line of text is not italicized, because only the *unformatted* text was replaced in the second paragraph, pointed to by **rng2**. Note also that the Text property is the default property for the Range object, and so you could write the third line of code as:

```
rng2 = rng1
```

Now, the FormattedText property returns a Range object that represents the text along with its formatting (including paragraph formatting when the text includes a paragraph mark). Consider the following code, again acting on our original two-line document:

```
Set rng1 = ActiveDocument.Paragraphs(1).Range
Set rng2 = ActiveDocument.Paragraphs(2).Range
rng2.FormattedText = rng1.FormattedText
```

I might expect the same result as with the previous code, since *FormattedText* returns a Range object and the default property of the Range object is the Text property. Hence, I might expect the third line of code to be equivalent to:

```
rng2.FormattedText.Text = rng1.FormattedText.Text
```

However, this is not the case. The line:

```
rng2.FormattedText = rng1.FormattedText
```

actually produces the output:

> *The Merchant of Venice*
> *The Merchant of Venice*

In other words, the text *and* formatting is transferred from **rng1** to **rng2**. Thus, the FormattedText property has a special use: namely, to transfer text and formatting from one range to another.

To summarize, the code:

```
rng2 = rng1
```

is equivalent to:

```
rng2.Text = rng1.Text
```

and transfers only the unformatted text from **rng1** to **rng2**. The code:

```
Set rng2 = rng1
```

sets **rng2** to point to the range pointed to by **rng1**. However, the code:

```
rng2.FormattedText = rng1.FormattedText
```

transfers both the text and its formatting.

Characters, Words, and Sentences

It is possible to retrieve a Range object from the Characters, Words, or Sentences collections. Each of these collection objects has one method and two properties that return a Range object.

The First and Last properties return a range that represents the first and last items in the collection. For instance, the following code capitalizes each letter in the first word in the second paragraph:

```
Set rng = ActiveDocument.Paragraphs(2).Range.Words.First
rng.Font.AllCaps = True
```

In addition, each of the aforementioned collections has an *Item* method. Thus, for instance:

```
Set rng = ActiveDocument.Words.Item(2)
```

references the second word in the active document.

The GoTo Methods

The Document, Selection, and Range objects have a *GoTo* method. This method returns a Range object that represents the starting position of the target of the *GoTo* method. The syntax of the *GoTo* method is:

```
expression.GoTo(What, Which, Count, Name)
```

where **expression** refers to a Document, Selection, or Range object.

The optional `What` parameter is the target type of the *GoTo* method and can be one of the `WdGoToItem` constants:

wdGoToBookmark	wdGoToGrammaticalError	wdGoToPercent
wdGoToComment	wdGoToGraphic	wdGoToProofreadingError
wdGoToEndnote	wdGoToHeading	wdGoToSection
wdGoToEquation	wdGoToLine	wdGoToSpellingError
wdGoToField	wdGoToObject	wdGoToTable
wdGoToFootnote	wdGoToPage	

The optional `Which` parameter identifies the specific target among those targets that fit the target type and can be any one of the following `WdGoToDirection` constants:

wdGoToAbsolute	wdGoToLast	wdGoToPrevious
wdGoToFirst	wdGoToNext	wdGoToRelative

The `Count` parameter is required if the `Which` parameter is `wdGoToNext`, `wdGoToPrevious`, or `wdGoToAbsolute`. For instance, the code:

```
Selection.GoTo wdGoToLine, wdGoToAbsolute, 2
```

moves the current selection (insertion point) to the beginning of the second line (not sentence) in the document and returns this location as a Range object. Note that the selection is the *beginning* of this line, not the entire line. To select the line itself, use the *Expand* method, as in:

```
Selection.GoTo wdGoToLine, wdGoToAbsolute, 2
Selection.Expand wdLine
```

If the *What* parameter is **wdGoToBookmark**, **wdGoToComment**, **wdGoToField**, or **wdGoToObject**, the *Name* parameter specifies a name. For instance, the following code selects the next Date field in the active document:

```
Selection.GoTo wdGoToField, wdGoToNext, 1, "Date"
```

Note that there is no **wdGoToWord**, **wdGoToSentence**, or **wdGoToCharacter** constant, so you cannot use the *GoTo* method to return a range or selection using these units. To do this, use the *Next* and *Previous* methods, discussed in later sections.

The *GoToNext* and *GoToPrevious* methods are similar to the *GoTo* method with the *Which* parameter set to **wdGoToNext** or **wdGoToPrevious** and the *Count* parameter set to 1. The syntax is:

```
(rng or sel).GoToNext(What)
(rng or sel).GoToPrevious(What)
```

where *What* is a **WdGoToItem** constant from the list earlier in this section.

The ConvertToText Method

The Row, Rows, and Table objects have a *ConvertToText* method that converts table data to text and returns a Range object that represents that text. The syntax is:

```
expression.ConvertToText(Separator)
```

where **expression** represents a Row, Rows, or Table object and the optional **Separator** is a character used to delimit the table columns in the converted text. (The rows are delimited by paragraph marks.) The value of **Separator** can be any one of the **WdTableFieldSeparator** constants in the following enum:

```
Enum WdTableFieldSeparator
    wdSeparateByParagraphs = 0
    wdSeparateByTabs = 1
    wdSeparateByCommas = 2
    wdSeparateByDefaultListSeparator = 3
End Enum
```

As an example, the following code converts the first table in the active document to text:

```
Set tbl = ActiveDocument.Tables(1)
Set rng = tbl.ConvertToText(wdSeparateByParagraphs)
```

The Find Object

When the *Execute* method of the Find object is executed successfully, a new Range object is returned. For example, consider the following code:

```
Set rng = ActiveDocument.Sentences(1)
rng.Find.Text = "donna"
```

```
rng.Find.Execute
If rng.Find.Found Then rng.Select
```

This code first points **rng** to the first sentence of the active document. The next two lines search for the word "donna" in this range. If the search is successful, the variable **rng** then points to the range containing the word "donna". The final line selects that word. (I discuss the Find object in detail in Chapter 15, *The Find and Replace Objects.*)

The Field Object

The Field object has two interesting properties that return a Range object: the Code property and the Result property. (I discussed these properties in Chapter 11.)

Briefly, the Code property returns a Range object that represents a field's code, which is everything that is enclosed by the field delimiters ({,}) including the leading and trailing space characters. Similarly, the Result property returns a Range object that represents the value of the field.

For example, consider a document whose first field is a Date field. Then the code:

```
Set rng = ActiveDocument.Fields(1).Code
Debug.Print rng.Text
Set rng = ActiveDocument.Fields(1).Result
Debug.Print rng.Text
```

prints:

```
 DATE  \* MERGEFORMAT
3/30/98
```

the first line of which is the field code and the second of which is the field result.

The TextRange Property

If you work with frames, then you may need to use the TextRange property of a TextFrame object. This Range returns a range containing the text within the Text-Frame object.

Changing a Range Object

The following list presents a summary of methods that can be used to change a given Range object:

The Next and Previous methods
> Apply to a Range or Selection object and return a Range object that refers to the next or previous item of the type to which they are applied (character, word, sentence, row, column, and so on).

The SetRange method

Sets the starting and ending positions of an existing range or selection.

The Start and End properties

Also set the starting and ending position of an existing range or selection.

The StartOf and EndOf methods

Move the starting or ending position of a range or selection by a specified number of units.

The HomeKey and EndKey methods

These methods of the Selection object mimic the action of the Home and End keys and return a Range object representing the resulting insertion point.

The Collapse method

Collapses the range or selection to which it is applied.

The Expand method

Expands the specified range or selection to encompass a whole unit, such as a word, sentence, or paragraph.

The Extend method

Applies to Selection objects and extends a selection to include a specified character or to include the next complete unit of text, in the following order: word, sentence, paragraph, section, entire document.

The Shrink method

Shrinks the selection to the next smallest *complete* unit of text, in the following order: word, sentence, paragraph, section, entire document.

The WholeStory method

Expands the range or selection to include the entire story.

The Move methods: Move, MoveEnd, MoveStart

Move the specified range or selection or one of its endpoints a specified number of units. (The *Move* method collapses the range or selection to an insertion point before moving.)

The MoveUntil methods: MoveUntil, MoveEndUntil, MoveStartUntil

Similar to the *Move* methods, but move the range or selection (or one of its endpoints) until one of a specified collection of characters is encountered.

The MoveWhile methods: MoveWhile, MoveEndWhile, MoveStartWhile

Similar to the *Move* methods, but move the range or selection (or one of its endpoints) while any one of a specified collection of characters is encountered.

The MoveUp, MoveDown, MoveLeft, and MoveRight methods

Can move a Selection object a specified number of units, optionally extending the selection.

The following sections describe these properties and methods in more detail.

The Next and Previous Methods

The *Next* and *Previous* methods apply to a Range or Selection object and return a Range object. The syntax is:

```
(rng or sel).Next(Unit, Count)
(rng or sel).Previous(Unit, Count)
```

where *Unit* is one of the WdUnits constants in the following list (there are other WdUnits constants, but they cannot be used with *Next* or *Previous*):

wdCell	wdParagraph	wdStory
wdCharacter	wdRow	wdTable
wdColumn	wdSection	wdWord
wdLine (*sel* object only)	wdSentence	

Note that if the *Next* or *Previous* method fails, which will happen when there is no next or previous unit, the method will return Nothing. You must remember to watch out for this possibility, as Example 14-2, which prints the first word from each paragraph in the current selection to the Immediate window, demonstrates.

Example 14-2. The Next Method

```
Dim rng As Range
' Create range object that points
' to start of selection
Set rng = Selection.Range
rng.Collapse Direction:=wdCollapseStart

Do
    ' Stop when rng no longer within selection
    If Not rng.InRange(Selection.Range) Then
        Exit Do
    Else

        ' Expand range to include first word
        rng.Expand wdWord

        ' If rng.Text is paragraph mark only, don't print it
        ' because then we will then get two blank lines
        ' instead of one
        If rng.Text = vbCr Then
            Debug.Print
        Else
            Debug.Print rng.Text
        End If

        ' Set range to start of next paragraph
        Set rng = rng.Next(wdParagraph, 1)

        ' If we come to the end of the document,
        ' Next will fail, so rng will be
        ' set to Nothing. This is the time to quit.
```

Example 14-2. The Next Method (continued)

```
    If rng Is Nothing Then Exit Sub

    rng.Collapse wdCollapseStart

  End If
Loop
```

(Note the use of the *InRange* method, which reports whether one range is contained within another. I discuss this method later in this chapter.)

The SetRange Method

The *SetRange* method sets the starting and ending positions of an existing range or selection. The syntax for the *SetRange* method is:

```
(rng or sel).SetRange(Start, End)
```

where **Start** is the desired starting character position and **End** is the desired ending character position. The character position of the beginning of the document is 0. All characters are counted, including nonprinting characters and hidden characters. For instance, the line:

```
ActiveWindow.Selection.SetRange(0,0)
```

sets the insertion point at the beginning of the active document.

Note that the *SetRange* method differs from the Range method (or property) in that the *SetRange* method redefines the starting and ending positions of an *existing* Range or Selection object, whereas the *Range* method creates a new range, given a starting and ending position.

The Start and End Properties

These properties return or set the starting and ending character positions of a range or selection (as a long integer). For instance, the code:

```
rng.End = rng.End + 1
```

moves the end of the range pointed to by **rng** one character to the right. Also, a quick way to shrink a range to a single insertion point is to write:

```
rng.End = rng.Start
```

or:

```
rng.Start = rng.End
```

The StartOf and EndOf Methods

These methods move the starting or ending position of a range or selection by a specified number of units. The syntax is:

```
(rng or sel).StartOf(Unit, Extend)
(rng or sel).EndOf(Unit, Extend)
```

where *Unit* is a WdUnits constant (listed earlier in this chapter), and *Extend* can be either of the wdMove or wdExtend symbolic constants. When wdMove (the default) is used, *both* ends of the range or selection are moved to the beginning (or end) of the specified unit. Hence, the range is collapsed to a point. When wdExtend is used, only one end of the range or selection is moved.

To illustrate, the following code selects the first character in the active document and then extends that selection to the entire line containing that character:

```
ActiveDocument.Characters(1).Select
Selection.EndOf wdLine, wdExtendNote
```

Note that *StartOf* does not move the beginning of the range if the beginning is already at the start of the specified unit. For instance, if the current range starts at the beginning of a word, then the code:

```
rng.StartOf(wdWord, wdMove)
```

does nothing (and returns 0). A similar statement applies to *EndOf.*

The HomeKey and EndKey Methods

The Selection object has a couple of methods for moving or extending the current selection. The *HomeKey* and *EndKey* methods have the syntax:

```
sel.HomeKey(Unit, Extend)
sel.EndKey(Unit, Extend)
```

The *Unit* parameter can be one of the WdUnits constants wdStory, wdColumn, wdLine, or wdRow. The *Extend* parameter can be either wdMove (the default) or wdExtend. If *Extend* is equal to wdMove, the selection is first collapsed to an insertion point and then moved to the beginning (*HomeKey*) or end (*EndKey*) of the specified unit. If the *Extend* parameter is wdExtend, the beginning (or end) of the selection is extended to the beginning (or end) of the specified unit.

The Collapse Method

This method collapses a Range or Selection object to the start or end of the range. The syntax is:

```
(rng or sel).Collapse(Direction)
```

where *Direction* is one of the constants wdCollapseStart or wdCollapseEnd. This is useful for getting a range that refers to the start (or end) of a document, as in:

```
Set rng = ActiveDocument.Range
rng.Collapse wdCollapseEnd
```

Note that if the rng variable points to an entire paragraph, collapsing the range to the end sets the new range immediately *following* the paragraph mark and hence at the beginning of the next paragraph. (The same is true for selections.)

The Expand Method

The *Expand* method:

```
(rng or sel).Expand(Unit)
```

expands the specified range or selection to encompass whole units, as specified by *Unit*, which is one of the WdUnits constants listed earlier in this chapter. The default value of *Unit* is wdWord.

For instance, consider the code:

```
Selection.Expand wdSentence
```

If the current selection lies within a single sentence, then this code expands the selection to encompass the entire sentence (including the ending space). If the current selection contains portions of two sentences, the selection is expanded just enough to encompass both sentences. In general, if the selection overlaps or includes several sentences, the selection is expanded just enough to encompass only whole sentences.

The Extend Method

The *Extend* method applies only to the Selection object. Its syntax is:

```
sel.Extend(Character)
```

where the optional parameter **Character** may be a single character. (This is case-sensitive.)

The *Extend* method turns on *extend mode*, which means that any movement of the endpoints of the current selection expands the selection. If **Character** is specified, the ending point of the selection is moved forward (toward the end of the document) *through* the next instance of that character in the document and the selection is expanded (because extend mode is now on). If **Character** is not specified, the method simply extends the selection to the next smallest complete unit of text, in the following order: word, sentence, paragraph, section, entire document.

To illustrate, the following code selects the first character in the active document and then extends that selection to include the first # in the document:

```
ActiveDocument.Characters(1).Select
Selection.Extend "#"
```

Note that if the document does not contain the # character, then the second line has no effect.

The Shrink Method

The *Shrink* method also applies only to the Selection object. Its syntax is:

```
sel.Shrink
```

This method shrinks the selection to the next smaller complete unit of text, in the following order: entire document, section, paragraph, sentence, word, insertion point. (The *Shrink* method also applies to the Font object, but in this case, it simply shrinks the point size.) Unfortunately, the *Shrink* method does not have a *Character* parameter.

For instance, the following code selects the first paragraph in the active document and then shrinks the selection to the first sentence in that paragraph (including the trailing space, if there is one):

```
ActiveDocument.Paragraphs(1).Range.Select
Selection.Shrink
```

The WholeStory Method

This method expands a range or selection to include the entire story. (A *story* is a portion of a Word document, identified by its type. For instance, a Word document has a main document story containing the main text of the document, as well as a story for headers and footers, comments, footnotes, and so on. The various types of stories are given by the WdStoryType enum. For more on this, please refer to the StoryType property of the Bookmark object, discussed in Chapter 12, *The Document Object.*) The syntax for the *WholeStory* method is:

```
(rng or sel).WholeStory
```

The same effect is obtained using the *Expand* method as follows:

```
rng.Expand wdStory
```

The Move Methods

The *Move* method has this syntax:

```
(rng or sel).Move(Unit, Count)
```

This method first collapses the specified range or selection to its starting position if `Count` is negative or its ending position if `Count` is positive. Then it moves the collapsed range or selection object the number of units given by `Count`. The `Unit` parameter is a `WdUnits` constant, listed earlier in this chapter. The method returns a long integer indicating the number of units by which the object was actually moved, which may be less than `Count` if the object reaches the beginning or end of the document. If the move was unsuccessful, the return value is 0.

Note that if the range or selection is in the middle of a unit, moving it one unit places it at the beginning or end of the *same* unit. However, since a word includes any trailing spaces (note the plural), moving the insertion point by a single word actually moves it to the beginning of the *next* word.

It is worth remarking that the *Move* method must be applied to a Range object *variable*, not a Range object. For example, the code:

```
ActiveDocument.Paragraphs(1).Range.Move wdWord, 1
```

does nothing (as you would expect), since the paragraph itself cannot be collapsed and moved. On the other hand, the code:

```
Set rng = ActiveDocument.Paragraphs(1).Range
rng.Move wdWord, 1
rng.Expand wdWord
rng.Select
```

resets the *rng* variable (not the Range object) to refer to the start of the first word in the second paragraph and then selects that word.

The *MoveEnd* method:

```
(rng or sel).MoveEnd(Unit, Count)
```

is similar to the *Move* method, but it does not collapse the range or selection. Instead, it merely moves the ending point of the range forward or backward, according to the sign of `Count`. The method returns a long integer indicating the number of units the range (or selection) was actually moved.

Note that if the ending position is moved backward until it passes the starting position, then the starting position will be set equal to the new ending position (this must happen since the starting position cannot be allowed to come after the ending position).

The *MoveStart* method:

```
(rng or sel).MoveStart(Unit, Count)
```

is the analog of the *MoveEnd* method, but moves the starting position instead.

There is a bit of a quirk in the *Move* method, which emphasizes the fact that we should always experiment a bit before declaring our code to be ready for "prime time." To illustrate, consider the following code, which purports simply to loop through the words in the active document, making them bold:

```
Dim wrd As Range

' Get first word
Set wrd = ActiveDocument.Range.Words(1)

' Loop while there are more words
Do
    wrd.Expand wdWord
    wrd.Bold = True
    If wrd.Move(wdWord) = 0 Then Exit Do
Loop
```

There is a problem, however, and this code will never terminate! As I have said, the *Move* method returns the number of units moved, or 0 if the move was unsuccessful, so it would seem that we should get a return value of 0 when the end of the document is reached.

However, imagine that you have just boldfaced the word that lies immediately before the final paragraph mark in the document. On the next loop, the *Move* method will move the insertion point to the beginning of the last "word," which Word considers to be the ending paragraph mark. Then the range wrd will be expanded to encompass this paragraph mark and finally the paragraph mark will be boldfaced.

Now, you might expect that on the next loop, the call to the *Move* method would return 0, since wrd currently encompasses the final paragraph mark. Instead, however, wrd is reset to an insertion point just *before* the last paragraph mark and the Move method returns 1.

To fix the problem, you can add an additional condition that will terminate the loop. This condition says that it should quit when the endpoint of the range wrd is equal to the total number of characters in the document, because this is the point at which wrd encompasses the last paragraph mark in the document.

Note also that in the following corrected version, this condition is placed after the Bold property because we want the last paragraph mark to be boldfaced and before the *Move* method because this method collapses the range wrd to an insertion point, moving the endpoint one character position to the left:

```
Dim wrd As Range
Dim cChars As Long

' Get character count
cChars = ActiveDocument.Characters.Count

' Get first word
Set wrd = ActiveDocument.Range.Words(1)
```

```
' Loop while there are more words
Do
    wrd.Expand wdWord
    wrd.Bold = True
    If wrd.End = cChars Then Exit Do
    If wrd.Move(wdWord, 1) = 0 Then Exit Do
Loop
```

Note also that I have defined a variable **cChars** to hold the total number of characters in the document. If I simply used the condition:

```
If wrd.End = ActiveDocument.Characters.Count Then Exit Do
```

the program would run considerably more slowly, because Word would need to count the number of characters in the document once for each word in the document! (Give it a try.)

The MoveUntil Methods

The *MoveUntil* method has the syntax:

```
(rng or sel).MoveUntil(Cset, Count)
```

This method collapses the range or selection according to the same rules as the *Move* method: to its starting position if *Count* is negative or to its ending position if *Count* is positive. It then moves the collapsed range or selection as described next.

The *Count* parameter is either a number that indicates the maximum number of characters by which the collapsed range or selection is to be moved or is one of the constants **wdForward** or **wdBackward**, which specify a direction but no restriction on distance. If *Count* is positive, the collapsed range or selection is moved forward in the document. If *Count* is negative, the collapsed range or selection is moved backward in the document.

The *Cset* argument is a variant that contains a collection of characters. The characters are case-sensitive. If the move is forward in the document (using **wdForward**), the range is moved to a position just *preceding* the first character in *Cset* that is found in the document. If the move is backward (using **wdBackward**), the range is moved to a position just *following* the first character in *Cset* that is found in the document.

The return value of the *MoveUntil* method needs some explaining. The problem is that there has to be a way to indicate that no characters in *Cset* were found. This is done by returning 0. Hence, if the move was successful (that is, a *Cset* character was found), the return value is one greater than the number of characters that the endpoint was actually moved when *Count* is positive and one less than this (negative) number when *Count* is negative.

The *MoveEndUntil* method:

```
(rng or sel).MoveEndUntil(Cset, Count)
```

is similar to the *MoveUntil* method, but moves only the ending position of the range or selection (no collapsing takes place). As before, the direction of the move is determined by the sign of *Count*.

The *Count* parameter is either the maximum number of characters by which the ending point of the range or selection is to be moved or is one of the constants **wdForward** or **wdBackward**. If *Count* is positive, the ending point of the range or selection is moved forward in the document and the range or selection is expanded. If *Count* is negative, the ending point of range or selection is moved backward and the range or selection is contracted.

The *Cset* argument is a variant that contains a collection of case-sensitive characters. If *Count* is positive, the ending point is moved to a position just *preceding* the first character in *Cset* that is found in the document. If *Count* is negative, the ending point is moved to a position just *following* the first character in *Cset* that is found in the document.

The return value of the *MoveEndUntil* method is the same as the return value of the *MoveUntil* method. As an example, the following code will highlight the text of the active document, starting with the first character in the document and ending just before the first lowercase letter:

```
Set rng = ActiveDocument.Range(0, 0)
rng.MoveEndUntil "abcdefghijklmnopqrstuvwxyz", wdForward
rng.Select
```

The *MoveStartUntil* method:

```
(rng or sel).MoveStartUntil(Cset, Count)
```

is the analog of *MoveEndUntil*, but moves the starting position of the range or selection.

The MoveWhile Methods

The *MoveWhile* method:

```
(rng or sel).MoveWhile(Cset, Count)
```

performs similarly to the *MoveUntil* method, the difference being that the collapsed range or selection is moved *while* (i.e., as long as) it encounters a character in *Cset*. As soon as it encounters a character that is not in *Cset*, the move stops.

The *MoveEndWhile* method:

```
(rng or sel).MoveEndWhile(Cset, Count)
```

performs similarly to the *MoveEndUntil* method, the difference being that the ending position is moved *while* it encounters characters in **Cset**. As soon as it encounters a character that is not in **Cset**, the move stops. (Note that the word *character* refers to all ANSI characters, including spaces.)

As an example, the following code highlights the text of the active document starting with the first character of the document, until it arrives at the first character that is *not* an uppercase letter:

```
Set rng = ActiveDocument.Range(0, 0)
rng.MoveEndWhile "ABCDEFGHIJKLMNOPQRSTUVWXYZ", wdForward
rng.Select
```

The *MoveStartWhile* method:

```
(rng or sel).MoveStartWhile(Cset, Count)
```

is the analog of *MoveEndWhile*, but moves the starting position of the range or selection.

The MoveUp, MoveDown, MoveLeft, and MoveRight Methods

The four methods *MoveUp*, *MoveDown*, *MoveLeft*, and *MoveRight* apply to the Selection object only (not to the Range object). Their syntax is:

```
sel.MoveDown(Unit, Count, Extend)
sel.MoveUp(Unit, Count, Extend)
sel.MoveLeft(Unit, Count, Extend)
sel.MoveRight(Unit, Count, Extend)
```

The **Unit** parameter specifies the units in the move. The **Extend** parameter is either **wdMove** or **wdExtend**, and the **Count** parameter is the number of units to move.

MoveDown or MoveUp

Unit can be one of **wdLine** (the default), **wdParagraph**, **wdWindow**, or **wdScreen**.

If *Extend* is **wdMove**, then the selection is collapsed to its endpoint and moved down or up. If it is **wdExtend**, then the selection is simply extended down or up. The default is **wdMove**.

MoveLeft or MoveRight

Unit can be one of **wdCell**, **wdCharacter** (the default), **wdWord**, or **wdSentence**.

If *Extend* is **wdMove**, the selection is collapsed to the endpoint and moved to the left or right. If it is **wdExtend**, the selection is extended to the left or right. The default is **wdMove**. Note that **wdExtend** cannot be used with **wdCell**.

The return value of each of these methods is the number of units that the selection was actually moved.

Range and Selection Object Properties and Methods

Now that you know how to create or change a Range or Selection object, we will look at some of the properties and methods of these objects that might prompt you to create the object in the first place.

The Text and TextRetrievalMode Properties

As expected, the Text property returns or sets the text in the specified range or selection. In conjunction with this property, you may want to set the TextRetrieval-Mode property. This property returns a TextRetrievalMode object, whose properties in turn affect how text is retrieved using the Text property. Note that the TextRetrievalMode property applies only to the Range object, not the Selection object.

The TextRetrievalMode object has three interesting properties that affect text retrieval. The Boolean IncludeHiddenText property should be set to True to retrieve hidden text along with the ordinary nonhidden text. The Boolean Include-FieldCodes property should be set to True to retrieve field codes along with the text. Finally, the ViewType property can be set to any one of the constants in the following enum:

```
Enum WdViewType
    wdNormalView = 1
    wdOutlineView = 2
    wdPageView = 3
    wdPrintPreview = 4
    wdMasterView = 5
    wdOnlineView = 6
End Enum
```

Note that setting the ViewType property does not affect the view of the text on the screen. It is used *only* to determine what text will be retrieved by the Text property. For instance, if the ViewType property is set to wdOutlineView, then only the text that would be visible in outline view is retrieved by the Text property.

To illustrate, the following code sets the Text property of the range *rng* to include any hidden text within the range, but not any field codes:

```
With rng.TextRetrievalMode
    .IncludeHiddenText = True
    .IncludeFieldCodes = False
End With
Selection.InsertAfter rng.Text
```

Edit Methods

The edit methods correspond to the usual commands on Word's Edit menu. The syntax is:

```
(rng or sel).Copy
(rng or sel).Cut
(rng or sel).Delete
(rng or sel).Paste
```

The *PasteSpecial* method allows you to control the format of the data that is pasted. This method:

```
(rng or sel).PasteSpecial(IconIndex, Link, Placement, _
    DisplayAsIcon, DataType, IconFileName, IconLabel)
```

is considerably more complicated than the *Paste* method; for details, see the Word VBA help file.

The Selection object has two additional edit methods that affect formatting only. The *CopyFormat* method:

```
sel.CopyFormat
```

copies the character formatting of the *first character* in the selection to which it applies. If the selection includes a paragraph mark, the paragraph formatting is also copied.

The *PasteFormat* method:

```
sel.PasteFormat
```

applies the format copied using the *CopyFormat* method to the selection. (This is similar to the Format Painter feature of Word.) It affects formatting only and does not modify the selected text.

Insert Methods

The Range and Selection objects have a variety of *Insert...* methods, used to insert text into a given range or selection:

InsertAfter	InsertCrossReference	InsertParagraphAfter
InsertAutoText (Range object only)	InsertDatabase (Range object only)	InsertParagraphBefore
InsertBefore	InsertDateTime	InsertRows (Selection object only)
InsertBreak	InsertFile	InsertSymbol
InsertCaption	InsertFormula (Selection object only)	
InsertCells (Selection object only)	InsertParagraph	

The following sections briefly discuss some of these methods.

The InsertAfter and InsertBefore methods

The syntax of these methods is:

```
(rng or sel).InsertAfter(Text)
(rng or sel).InsertBefore(Text)
```

and they perform exactly as expected, inserting text either before or after the given range or selection. Note, however, that despite the name, the range or selection is then expanded to include the newly inserted text.

You can insert special characters by using the *Chr$* function or Visual Basic constants such as **vbCr**, **vbLf**, **vbCrLf**, and **vbTab**. Note that **vbCr** is the Word paragraph mark.

If you use the *InsertAfter* method with a range or selection that refers to an entire paragraph, the text is inserted *after* the ending paragraph mark and will thus appear at the beginning of the next paragraph. To insert text at the end of a paragraph, use the *MoveEnd* method to shrink the range, as in the following example:

```
Set rng = ActiveDocument.Paragraphs(1).Range
' Remove ending paragraph mark from range
rng.MoveEnd wdCharacter, -1
rng.InsertAfter " finis."
```

The InsertBreak method

This method performs precisely as though the user had selected the Break item from Word's Insert menu. Its syntax is:

```
(rng or sel).InsertBreak(Type)
```

where *Type* can be one of the **WdBreakType** constants in the following enum:

```
Enum WdBreakType
    wdSectionBreakNextPage = 2
    wdSectionBreakContinuous = 3
    wdSectionBreakEvenPage = 4
    wdSectionBreakOddPage = 5
    wdLineBreak = 6
    wdPageBreak = 7
    wdColumnBreak = 8
End Enum
```

The InsertCaption method

This method, whose syntax is:

```
(rng or sel).InsertCaption(Label, Title, TitleAutoText, Position)
```

inserts a caption immediately preceding or following the specified range or selection.

The parameter *Label* is the caption label to be inserted and can be a string or one of the WdCaptionLabelID constants wdCaptionEquation, wdCaptionFigure, or wdCaptionTable.

The *Title* parameter is the string that is inserted immediately following the label. Alternatively, if a *TitleAutoText* entry is specified, this is inserted in place of the *Title* text. Finally, the *Position* parameter specifies the location of the caption and can be one of the WdCaptionPosition constants, wdCaptionPosition-Above or wdCaptionPositionBelow.

The InsertDateTime method

As the name implies, this method inserts the date and/or time in the given range. Its syntax is:

```
(rng or sel).InsertDateTime(DateTimeFormat, _
    InsertAsField, InsertAsFullWidth)
```

The *DateTimeFormat* parameter specifies the format to be used for displaying the date or time. If this parameter is omitted, the short-date style from the Windows Control Panel is used. If *InsertAsField* is set to True, the information is inserted as a field, rather than as plain text. The *InsertAsFullWidth* parameter is not used in the U.S. English version of Microsoft Word.

Thus, for instance, the line:

```
Selection.InsertDateTime "MMMM dd, yyyy"
```

will insert the date in the following form: June 24, 1998.

The InsertFile method

The syntax of the *InsertFile* method is:

```
(rng or sel).InsertFile(FileName, Range, _
    ConfirmConversions, Link, Attachment)
```

where *FileName* is the path and filename of the file to be inserted. If the path is omitted, Word assumes the file is in the current folder.

To insert only a portion of a file, use the optional *Range* parameter. If the file is a Word document, the *Range* parameter refers to a bookmark. If the file is another type (such as an Excel worksheet), this parameter refers to a named range or a cell range.

Setting the optional *ConfirmConversions* parameter to True makes Word prompt you before converting file types that are in non-Word format. If the optional *Link* parameter is set to True, the file is inserted using an INCLUDETEXT field. Finally, we can set the *Attachment* parameter to True to insert the file as an attachment to a WordMail message.

The InsertParagraph, InsertParagraphAfter, and InsertParagraphBefore methods

The syntax for these methods is:

```
(rng or sel).InsertParagraph
(rng or sel).InsertParagraphAfter
(rng or sel).InsertParagraphBefore
```

Despite the name, the *InsertParagraph* method *replaces* the range or selection with a new paragraph. (We can avoid losing any data by collapsing the range before applying this method.)

The *InsertParagraphAfter* method inserts a new paragraph after the range or selection and then expands the range or selection to include the new paragraph. The *InsertParagraphBefore* method behaves similarly.

Another way to insert a paragraph is to use the *TypeParagraph* method of the Selection object. (This method does not apply to Range objects.) The syntax is:

```
sel.TypeParagraph
```

This method has the same effect as hitting the Enter key. Thus, it will replace an existing selection if there is one.

The InsertSymbol method

The *InsertSymbol* method:

```
(rng or sel).InsertSymbol(CharacterNumber, Font, Unicode)
```

replaces the range or selection with a symbol. The *CharacterNumber* parameter is the character number for the symbol and is equal to the position number of the symbol in the table of symbols obtained by selecting the Symbol menu item from Word's Insert menu (counting from left to right). Note, however, that the first character in the table is character number 32. For example, to specify the Greek letter delta, which is the 37th character in the Symbol font table, we must set *CharacterNumber* equal to 68.

The *Font* parameter is the name of the font that contains the symbol. The optional *Unicode* parameter is set to True to insert the Unicode character specified by *CharacterNumber* and False to insert the ANSI character specified by *CharacterNumber*. The default value is False.

Character and Paragraph Formatting Properties

The Range and Selection objects have several properties that can be used to set or return the formatting of the range or selection. Let us discuss a few of them.

Font-related properties

The Range object has a few font-related properties, namely Bold, Italic, and Underline. (These do not apply to the Selection object.) On the other hand, both objects have a Font property that returns a Font object, which can be used to set font formatting characteristics and also has Bold, Italic, and Underline properties.

The Bold and Italic properties can be set to True, False, or **wdToggle**, which toggles the current state. These properties return True, False or **wdUndefined**, the latter if the range (or selection) contains a mixture of text.

The Underline property returns (and can be set to) a **WdUnderline** constant, which has one of the values in the following list. The default value is **wdUnderlineNone**:

wdUnderlineNone   wdUnderlineThick   wdUnderlineSingle
wdUnderlineDash   wdUnderlineDotted   wdUnderlineWords
wdUnderlineDotDash   wdUnderlineDouble   wdUnderlineWavy
wdUnderlineDotDotDash

The Borders and Shading properties

The Borders property sets or returns a Borders collection, which represents all the borders for the specified object. The Shading property returns a Shading object that refers to the shading for the range. We will not discuss these objects further, however. For more information, see the help documentation.

The Case property

The Case property returns or can be set to a **WdCharacterCase** constant, as described by the following enum:

```
Enum WdCharacterCase
    wdNextCase = -1
    wdLowerCase = 0
    wdUpperCase = 1
    wdTitleWord = 2
    wdTitleSentence = 4
    wdToggleCase = 5
End Enum
```

The Case property applies only to Range objects.

The **wdNextCase** setting causes Word to cycle through three settings: all lowercase, initial uppercase (first letter of each word is uppercase), and all uppercase, just as though the user repeatedly selected the Shift-F3 key combination. The **wdTitleSentence** setting capitalizes the initial letter in the first word of each sentence, and the **wdTitleWord** setting capitalizes the first letter of each word.

The PageSetup property

This read-only property returns a PageSetup object that is associated with the specified range or selection. (This property also applies to Document and Section objects.) I discussed the PageSetup object in Chapter 12.

The ParagraphFormat property

This property returns (or can be set to) a ParagraphFormat object that represents the paragraph settings for the range or selection. We discussed the ParagraphFormat object in Chapter 11.

The Style property

This property returns or sets the style for the range or selection. The Style object was discussed in Chapter 11. We note here that the Style property will return only the first style when applied to a range that includes formatting from more than one style.

Keyboard simulation

The Selection object (but not the Range object) has a number of methods that have the same effect (more or less) as typing at the keyboard. These are:

```
HomeKey
EndKey
EscapeKey
TypeBackspace
TypeParagraph
TypeText
```

For example, the TypeText method inserts text at the insertion point, just as though it was typed at the keyboard. If there is a current selection, it is replaced by the inserted text when the ReplaceSelection property of the Options object is set to True.

Miscellaneous Properties and Methods

I conclude this rather lengthy chapter with some miscellaneous properties and methods of the Range and Selection objects.

Information property

The Range and Selection objects have an Information property that reports certain information about the object. Some of this information, such as whether the Caps Lock is on, is not directly related to the range or selection. The syntax is:

```
(rng or sel).Information(Type)
```

where *Type* is one of the `WdInformation` constants (note that this property may return a number or a Boolean value):

wdActiveEndAdjustedPageNumber	wdNumLock	wdInMasterDocument
wdActiveEndPageNumber	wdOverType	wdInWordMail
wdActiveEndSectionNumber	wdReferenceOfType	wdMaximumNumberOfColumns
wdAtEndOfRowMarker	wdRevisionMarking	wdMaximumNumberOfRows
wdCapsLock	wdSelectionMode	wdNumberOfPagesInDocument
wdEndOfRangeColumnNumber	wdStartOfRangeColumnNumber	wdStartOfRangeRowNumber
wdHorizontalPositionRelative-ToTextBoundary	wdEndOfRangeRowNumber	wdVerticalPositionRelativeToPage
wdInClipboard	wdFirstCharacterColumnNumber	wdVerticalPositionRelativeTo-TextBoundary
wdInCommentPane	wdFirstCharacterLineNumber	wdWithInTable
wdInEndnote	wdFrameIsSelected	wdZoomPercentage
wdInFootnote	wdHeaderFooterType	
wdInFootnoteEndnotePane	wdHorizontalPositionRelativeToPage	
	wdInHeaderFooter	

One of the most useful return values of the Information property is:

```
(rng or sel).Information(wdWithInTable)
```

which is True if the range or selection is entirely within a table.

Selecting a range

As we have seen, the Select method selects the specified range; that is, it sets the Selection object to the specified range. This method is, among other things, very useful when debugging a program that uses Range objects, since they are not visible. By using the *Select* method, you can highlight a given range, thereby making it visible.

Deleting a range or selection

The *Delete* method:

```
(rng or sel).Delete
```

will delete the specified range or selection.

The Selection object also has a *TypeBackspace* method:

```
sel.TypeBackspace
```

that has exactly the same effect as hitting the Backspace key. Thus, it will delete the current selection if there is one or delete the character to the immediate left of the insertion point.

Duplicating a range

To obtain another copy of a Range object, use the Duplicate property. For instance, the code:

```
Set rng2 = rng1.Duplicate
```

creates a second Range object that has the same starting and ending position as the range pointed to by *rng1*. The new range is pointed to by *rng2*. Thus, we have two *distinct* Range objects. This is not the same as:

```
Set rng2 = rng1
```

which simply points a second variable to the *same* Range object.

The IsEqual, InRange, and InStory methods

To tell when two ranges have the same starting and ending positions, use the *IsEqual* method. The syntax is:

```
(rng or sel).IsEqual(rng2)
```

This method returns True if the range or selection specified by *rng* (or *sel*) has the same starting point, ending point, and story type as the range specified by the Range parameter *rng2*.

To determine whether one range (or selection) is contained within another, use the *InRange* method:

```
(rng or sel).InRange(rng2)
```

This method returns True if the range or selection specified by *rng* (or *sel*) is contained within the range specified by *rng2 and* if the story types are the same.

The *InStory* method:

```
(rng or sel).InStory(rng2)
```

returns True if the range or selection specified by *rng* or *sel* lies in the same story as that of *rng2*.

Collection properties

The Range and Selection objects have several properties—all of which are read-only—that return some important collections (these properties also apply to the Document object):

- The Bookmarks property returns the Bookmarks collection, which represents the bookmarks in the range or selection.

- The Characters property returns the Characters collection, which represents the characters in the range or selection.

- The Fields property returns a Fields collection, which represents the fields in the range or selection.

- The Frames property returns the Frames collection, which represents the frames in the range or selection.

- The Paragraphs property returns a Paragraphs collection, which represents the paragraphs in the range or selection.

- The Sections property returns a Sections collection, which represents the sections in the specified range or selection.

- The Sentences property returns a Sentences collection, which represents the sentences in the range or selection.

- The Tables property returns a Tables collection, which represents all the tables in the range or selection.

- The Words property returns a Words collection, which represents the words in the range or selection. Note that punctuation and paragraph marks are included in the Words collection.

The ConvertToTable method

This method has a rather complicated syntax:

```
(rng or sel).ConvertToTable(Separator, NumRows, NumColumns, _
InitialColumnWidth, Format, ApplyBorders, ApplyShading, ApplyFont, _
ApplyColor, ApplyHeadingRows, ApplyLastRow, ApplyFirstColumn, _
ApplyLastColumn, AutoFit)
```

and returns an object of type Table. The purpose of the method is to convert the text in a range or selection into a table. All of the parameters to this method are optional.

The *Separator* parameter specifies the character used to separate the text of each row into columns. It can be a character or one of the **WdTableFieldSeparator** constants in the following enum (the default is **wdSeparatorParagraphs**):

```
Enum WdTableFieldSeparator
    wdSeparateByParagraphs = 0
    wdSeparateByTabs = 1
    wdSeparateByCommas = 2
    wdSeparateByDefaultListSeparator = 3
End Enum
```

The *NumRows* parameter gives the number of rows in the table. If this parameter is omitted, the number of rows is set automatically based on the contents of the range or selection.

The *NumColumns* parameter specifies the number of columns in the table. If this argument is omitted, Word sets the number of columns based on the contents of the range or selection.

The *InitialColumnWidth* parameter sets the initial width of each column, in points. If this parameter is omitted, the column width is adjusted so that the table stretches from margin to margin.

The *Format* parameter specifies one of the predefined formats listed in the Table AutoFormat dialog box (see the Table menu). Its value can be any one of the 40 WdTableFormat constants. I refer the interested reader to the Word VBA help file for details.

To specify a particular item from the format described by the *Format* parameter, set one or more of the Apply parameters: *ApplyBorders*, *ApplyShading*, *Apply-Font*, *ApplyColor*, *ApplyHeadingRows*, *ApplyLastRow*, *ApplyFirstColumn*, *ApplyLastColumn*, and *AutoFit*.

Sorting text

The Range object has three sorting methods. As applied to a Range object or Selection object, the first of these, the Sort method, has the syntax:

```
(rng or sel).Sort(ExcludeHeader, FieldNumber, SortFieldType, SortOrder, _
FieldNumber2, SortFieldType2, SortOrder2, FieldNumber3, SortFieldType3, _
SortOrder3, SortColumn, Separator, CaseSensitive, LanguageID)
```

(The *Sort* method applies not only to Range objects, but also to Table and Column objects, though the syntax varies depending upon the target object.) All parameters are optional.

Set the *ExcludeHeader* parameter to True in order to exclude the first row or paragraph from the sort operation. The default value is False.

The *FieldNumber*, *FieldNumber2*, and *FieldNumber3* parameters are fields that are used in the sorting process. Sorting is done first by *FieldNumber*, then by *FieldNumber2*, and then by *FieldNumber3*.

The *SortFieldType*, *SortFieldType2*, and *SortFieldType3* parameters specify the sort types for the *FieldNumbers* parameters and can be one of the following WdSortFieldType constants: wdSortFieldAlphanumeric, wdSortField-Date, or wdSortFieldNumeric. The default is wdSortFieldAlphanumeric.

The *SortOrder*, *SortOrder2*, and *SortOrder3* parameters specify the sorting order for the *FieldNumbers* parameters and can be one of the WdSortOrder constants:

```
Enum WdSortOrder
    wdSortOrderAscending = 0
    wdSortOrderDescending = 1
End Enum
```

The default value is wdSortOrderAscending.

If the range or selection is within a table and if *SortColumn* is set to True, then only the column specified by the range or selection object is sorted.

The *Separator* parameter specifies the type of field separator and can be one of the following WdSortSeparator constants:

```
Enum WdSortSeparator
    wdSortSeparateByTabs = 0
    wdSortSeparateByCommas = 1
    wdSortSeparateByDefaultTableSeparator = 2
End Enum
```

The default value is wdSortSeparateByCommas. If the range or selection is in a table, this argument is ignored.

The *CaseSensitive* parameter is set to True for a case-sensitive sort. The default value is False.

The *LanguageID* parameter specifies the sorting language. It can be one of the WdLanguageID constants (see Word VBA help).

If you do not need the flexibility of the *Sort* method, you can use the *SortAscending* or *SortDescending* method. The syntax is:

```
(rng or sel).SortAscending
(rng or sel).SortDescending
```

These methods simply sort paragraphs (or table rows) in ascending or descending alphanumeric order. The first paragraph (or table row) is always considered a header record and is not included in the sort.

15

The Find and Replace Objects

Searching (and replacing) is one of the most commonly performed operations. The Word object model provides a Find object and a Replacement object for this purpose. The Range object and the Selection object both have a Find property that returns a Find object, which is used to search within the given range or selection (and possibly beyond).

Searching for Text

Searching for text (or formatting) amounts to little more than setting various properties of the Find object and then executing the object's *Execute* method.

Incidentally, you may be wondering why there is a Find object and not simply a *Find* method. The main reason is that, like the Font object, the Find object retains its settings until they are changed by the programmer and can therefore be used repeatedly. This is especially important when we consider the fact that the Find object has 25 properties. If Find were a method instead of an object, you would potentially need to set all 25 properties each time you made a call to this method!

Here is an example of finding some text using the Find object from a Selection object:

```
With Selection.Find
    .ClearFormatting
    .Text = "To be or not to be"
    .Forward = True
    .Wrap = wdFindContinue
    .Format = False
    .MatchCase = False
    .MatchWholeWord = False
    .MatchWildcards = False
```

```
        .MatchSoundsLike = False
        .MatchAllWordForms = False
    End With
    Selection.Find.Execute
```

Note the use of the `With` construct, which saves some coding when you need to set several properties (or execute methods) for a single object. As I have discussed, the expression:

```
    With Object
        .Property1 = Value1
        .Property2 = Value2
        . . .
        .Propertyn = Valuen
    End With
```

is equivalent to:

```
    Object.Property1 = Value1
    Object.Property2 = Value2
    . . .
    Object.Propertyn = Valuen
```

The main properties and methods of the Find object are:

ClearFormatting	MatchAllWordForms	ParagraphFormat
Execute	MatchCase	Replacement
Font	MatchSoundsLike	Style
Format	MatchWholeWord	Text
Forward	MatchWildcards	Wrap
Found		

Note that several of these properties mirror checkboxes found in the Find dialog box:

Find Property	Check Box in Find Dialog
MatchCase	MatchCase
MatchSoundsLike	Sounds like
MatchWholeWord	Find whole words only
MatchWildcards	Use wildcards

Note also that the *ClearFormatting* method is equivalent to pressing the No Formatting button on the Find dialog box. It is a good idea to execute this method before searching to avoid limiting the search to formatting that may be left over from a previous search.

It is important to understand that Word initially searches only the given selection when the Find object comes from a Selection object or the given range when the Find object comes from a Range object. The behavior of the search with regard to the rest of the document depends upon the setting of the Wrap property, which is discussed in the following section.

Incidentally, the Word help files do not seem to state the default values for the various properties of the Find object, but some experimenting indicates that the following Boolean properties:

MatchCase   MatchWildcards   MatchAllWordForms
MatchWholeWord   MatchSoundsLike

default to False, but that the Boolean property Forward defaults to True. (This also makes sense.) Thus, we could omit them (at our own peril) to shorten the syntax quite a bit:

```
With Selection.Find
    .ClearFormatting
    .Text = "To be or not to be"
    .Forward = True
    .Wrap = wdFindContinue
End With
Selection.Find.Execute
```

The Wrap Property

The Wrap property can be one of the following `WdFindWrap` constants:

wdFindAsk

> After searching the selection or range, Word will display a message asking whether to search the remainder of the document.

wdFindContinue

> The Find operation continues when either the beginning (Forward = False) or end (Forward = True) of the search range or selection is reached.

WdFindStop

> The Find operation ends when the beginning or end of the search range or selection is reached.

The Found Property

After a search, Word will set the Found property of the Find object to reflect the success or failure of the search. This is a Boolean property, so it will be set to either True or False. As an example, the following code acts on the results of the search:

```
With Selection.Find
    .ClearFormatting
    .Text = "find text"
    .Forward = True
    .Wrap = wdFindContinue
    .Format = False
    .MatchCase = False
    .MatchWholeWord = False
    .MatchWildcards = False
```

```
      .MatchSoundsLike = False
      .MatchAllWordForms = False
End With
Selection.Find.Execute

If Selection.Find.Found then
    MsgBox "Text found"
Else
    MsgBox "Text not found"
End
```

Consequences of a Successful Search

It is important to understand that a successful search will have an effect on the current selection or the range object. If a search is successful, then the consequences depend upon whether the Find object comes from a Range object or a Selection object. (If the search is not successful, then nothing happens.)

If the Find object comes from a Selection object, then the found text is selected. Hence, the original selection is no longer selected. If the Find object comes from a Range object, as shown in the following example:

```
Dim rng As Range
' Search entire document
Set rng = ActiveDocument.Content
With rng.Find
    .ClearFormatting
    .Text = "Find text"
    .Forward = True
    .Wrap = wdFindStop
    .Execute
End With
rng.Select
```

then the range is redefined to include just the newly found text. Thus, the original range is lost.

Searching for Formatting

The following example illustrates how to search for formatting (or formatted text). In this case, I search for any italicized text that is centered. As you can see, this is done by setting the corresponding formatting properties of the Find object (Font and ParagraphFormat) and then setting the Format property of the Find object to True. I must also not forget to clear the formatting first, so that only my formatting will be in effect. (By setting the Text property of the Find object to the empty string, all text is found.)

```
Selection.Find.ClearFormatting
Selection.Find.Font.Italic = True
Selection.Find.ParagraphFormat.Alignment = _
```

```
       wdAlignParagraphCenter
Selection.Find.Replacement.ClearFormatting
With Selection.Find
   .Text = ""
   .Replacement.Text = ""
   .Forward = True
   .Wrap = wdFindContinue
   .Format = True
   .MatchCase = False
   .MatchWholeWord = False
   .MatchWildcards = False
   .MatchSoundsLike = False
   .MatchAllWordForms = False
End With
Selection.Find.Execute
```

The following example searches for a particular style, in this case the Heading 1 style:

```
Selection.Find.ClearFormatting
Selection.Find.Style = _
   ActiveDocument.Styles("Heading 1")
With Selection.Find
   .Text = ""
   .Replacement.Text = ""
   .Forward = True
   .Wrap = wdFindContinue
   .Format = True
   .MatchCase = False
   .MatchWholeWord = False
   .MatchWildcards = False
   .MatchSoundsLike = False
   .MatchAllWordForms = False
End With
Selection.Find.Execute
```

The Replace Operation

Performing a search and replace is not much more complicated than performing a simple search. The Find object has a Replacement child object, accessible through the Replacement property. Just set the properties of the Replacement object, including any text or formatting that you want to use for the replacement. Then we run the *Execute* method of the Find object, using the named parameter `Replace`, which can take on one of three values: **wdReplaceAll**, **wdReplace-None**, or **wdReplaceOne**.

Here is an example that replaces each occurrence of the word "find" with the word "replace". Note that we must clear the formatting of both the Find and the Replacement objects.

```
Selection.Find.ClearFormatting
Selection.Find.Replacement.ClearFormatting
```

```
With Selection.Find
    .Text = "find"
    .Replacement.Text = "replace"
    .Forward = True
    .Wrap = wdFindContinue
    .Format = False
    .MatchCase = False
    .MatchWholeWord = False
    .MatchWildcards = False
    .MatchSoundsLike = False
    .MatchAllWordForms = False
End With
Selection.Find.Execute Replace:=wdReplaceAll
```

The Execute Method

The *Execute* method of the Find object actually has a number of parameters that allow an alternative syntax for doing a search and replace. The full syntax of the *Execute* method is:

```
FindObject.Execute(FindText, MatchCase, MatchWholeWord, _
MatchWildcards, MatchSoundsLike, MatchAllWordForms, _
Forward, Wrap, Format, ReplaceWith, Replace)
```

For instance, the previous search and replace could have been coded as follows:

```
Selection.Find.ClearFormatting
Selection.Find.Replacement.ClearFormatting
Selection.Find.Execute _
    FindText:="find", _
    ReplaceWith:="replace", _
    Forward:=True, _
    Wrap:=wdFindContinue, _
    MatchCase:=False, _
    MatchWholeWord:=False, _
    MatchWildcards:=False, _
    MatchSoundsLike:=False, _
    MatchAllWordForms:=False, _
    replace:=wdReplaceAll
```

This syntax seems to be a bit less readable than the previous one, but you may run across it when reading other code.

Example: Repeated Searching

Since the range is redefined after a successful search, the process of repeated searching has a slight complication. The problem is that you cannot simply define a Range object called *rng* to denote the range to search and then use the Find object of *rng*, because a successful search would then change the search range for the next search!

Perhaps it would have been simpler if Microsoft had included a ResultRange object that represented the range of the successful search and left the original search range alone. The ResultRange object could have the Found property, which would be queried to determine whether the search was successful. In any case, in doing a repeated search, you must save the original search range (especially its endpoint) and also keep track of where the next search operation should begin.

The macro in Example 15-1 illustrates one approach to searching repeatedly through a portion of a document. To explain the purpose of this macro, let me set the stage. In the manuscript for this book, the chapter titles have the form:

Chapter *XX* –

where *XX* is a chapter number and – is an en dash. Also, the titles are formatted with style Heading 1. For quickly navigating through the manuscript, I wanted to add a bookmark of the form C*XX* in front of each chapter title. For instance, the bookmark for Chapter 12 should be named C12.

Of course, I could do this manually (for 21 chapters), but the problem is that as the manuscript develops, I may add chapters in the middle, thus changing the chapter numbers. So the best solution is a macro that inserts the bookmarks for me. I can run this whenever the chapter numbers change.

The macro in Example 15-1 also illustrates the use of pattern matching. In particular, the pattern:

```
Chapter?{3,4}^=
```

searches for the word "Chapter" followed by 3 or 4 characters, followed by an en dash. (I used the Find dialog box to help me determine the correct pattern.)

Example 15-1. A Macro to Locate Chapter Titles

```
Sub AddChapterBookmarks()

' Insert a bookmark in front of all
' chapter titles. Chapter XX gets
' bookmark named CXX.

Dim iChapNum As Integer
Dim sChapNum As String
Dim rngToSrch As Range
Dim rngResult As Range

' Set search ranges
Set rngToSrch = ActiveDocument.Range
Set rngResult = rngToSrch.Duplicate

' Loop to find all chapter titles, which
' have style Heading 1 and form
' "Chapter XX -" where XX is a
```

Example 15-1. A Macro to Locate Chapter Titles (continued)

```
' number (1 or 2 digits)
' and - is an en-dash
Do
    With rngResult.Find
        .ClearFormatting
        .Style = "Heading 1"
        .Text = "Chapter?{3,4}^="
        .Forward = True
        .Wrap = wdFindStop
        .MatchWildcards = True
        .Execute
    End With

    ' Exit loop if not found
    If Not rngResult.Find.Found Then Exit Do

    ' Select the chapter title
    rngResult.Select

    ' Get the chapter number
    iChapNum = Val(Mid(Selection.Text, 8))
    sChapNum = Format(iChapNum)

    ' Add bookmark using chapter number
    Selection.Collapse wdCollapseStart
    Selection.Bookmarks.Add "C" & sChapNum

    ' Prepare for next search by
    ' moving the start position over one word
    rngResult.MoveStart wdWord
    ' and extending the end of rngResult
    rngResult.End = rngToSrch.End

Loop Until Not rngResult.Find.Found

End Sub
```

There are a few subtle points in this code, so I will go over them carefully.

First, the code uses two Range objects. The range *rngToSrch* refers to the search range and does not change. The range *rngResult* is used to do the searching and thus changes each time there is a successful search. (Actually, if my code inserts new text into the range *rngToSrch*, then this range will expand to accommodate the new text, so in this case it does change.)

Accordingly, I must first set *rngResult* to point to a range with the same endpoints as the range pointed to by *rngToSrch*. Since I need two different range objects with the same start and endpoints, the appropriate code is:

```
Set rngResult = rngToSrch.Duplicate
```

and not:

```
Set rngResult = rngToSrch
```

(I have discussed this issue in Chapter 14, *The Range and Selection Objects.*)

The next issue is how to prepare for the second (and subsequent) searches. This is done using the code:

```
' Prepare for next search by
' moving the start position over one word
rngResult.MoveStart wdWord
' and extending the end of rngResult
rngResult.End = rngToSrch.End
```

The issue here is that after a successful search, *rngResult* refers only to the word found. I cannot simply restore *rngResult* to its original range, because then I would just repeat the same search and return the same word. Instead, the new search range should begin one word after *rngResult*, so as not to return the same word over and over again. Also, the *endpoint* of the new search range must be restored to its original value, which is the endpoint of the range *rngToSrch*.

Finally, note that it would not do to use a Long variable to capture the search range endpoint, as in:

```
iEnd = rngToSrch.End
```

and then use this to restore the *rngResult* endpoint after each search, as in:

```
rngResult.End = iEnd
```

The reason that this does not work in general is that if my code were to insert or remove some text from the search range, the value *iEnd* would no longer represent the last character in that search range. (Since I am not changing any text in this example, it will work here.) Put another way, I need to save the search range object itself (in *rngToSrch*) and not just the character position of the endpoint of this range.

16

The Table Object

A Table object represents a Word table. The Tables collection contains all of the tables in a range, selection, or document and is returned by the Tables property of the Range, Selection, or Document object. The properties and methods of a Table object are:

Application	Creator	Sort
AutoFormat	Delete	SortAscending
AutoFormatType	Parent	SortDescending
Borders	Range	Split
Cell	Rows	Uniform
Columns	Select	UpdateAutoFormat
ConvertToText	Shading	

To add a new table to a document, use the *Add* method of the Tables collection. The syntax is:

```
TablesObject.Add(Range, NumRows, NumColumns)
```

where *Range* is a range that is *replaced* by the new table. (You can collapse the range to an insertion point using the *Collapse* method discussed in Chapter 13, *The Section and HeaderFooter Objects*, to avoid replacing any text.) The parameters *NumRows* and *NumColumns* specify the number of rows and columns in the table.

Let us take a look at some of the properties and methods of the Table object.

Formatting-Related Properties and Methods

The *AutoFormat* method applies a predefined formatting to a table. The parameters of this method correspond to the options in the Table AutoFormat dialog box (from the Table menu), shown in Figure 16-1.

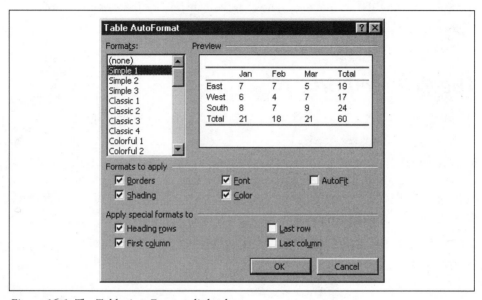

Figure 16-1. The Table AutoFormat dialog box

The syntax for the *AutoFormat* method is:

```
TableObject.AutoFormat(Format, ApplyBorders, ApplyShading, _
ApplyFont, ApplyColor, ApplyHeadingRows, ApplyLastRow, _
ApplyFirstColumn, ApplyLastColumn, AutoFit)
```

The optional **Format** parameter is used to specify a predefined table format. It can be any one of the **WdTableFormat** constants:

wdTableFormat3DEffects1 (32)
wdTableFormat3DEffects2 (33)
wdTableFormat3DEffects3 (34)
wdTableFormatClassic1 (4)
wdTableFormatClassic2 (5)
wdTableFormatClassic3 (6)
wdTableFormatClassic4 (7)
wdTableFormatColorful1 (8)
wdTableFormatColorful2 (9)
wdTableFormatColorful3 (10)
wdTableFormatColumns1 (11)
wdTableFormatColumns2 (12)
wdTableFormatColumns3 (13)
wdTableFormatColumns4 (14)

wdTableFormatColumns5 (15)
wdTableFormatContemporary (35)
wdTableFormatElegant (36)
wdTableFormatGrid1 (16)
wdTableFormatGrid2 (17)
wdTableFormatGrid3 (18)
wdTableFormatGrid4 (19)
wdTableFormatGrid5 (20)
wdTableFormatGrid6 (21)
wdTableFormatGrid7 (22)
wdTableFormatGrid8 (23)
wdTableFormatList1 (24)
wdTableFormatList2 (25)

wdTableFormatList3 (26)
wdTableFormatList4 (27)
wdTableFormatList5 (28)
wdTableFormatList6 (29)
wdTableFormatList7 (30)
wdTableFormatList8 (31)
wdTableFormatNone (0)
wdTableFormatProfessional (37)
wdTableFormatSimple1 (1)
wdTableFormatSimple2 (2)
wdTableFormatSimple3 (3)
wdTableFormatSubtle1 (38)
wdTableFormatSubtle2 (39)

The default value is `wdTableFormatSimple1`. The other parameters are Boolean and match one-for-one with the checkboxes shown in Figure 16-1.

The AutoFormatType property of the Table object returns the type of automatic formatting that has been applied to the table. It is a read-only Long integer that takes on one of the `WdTableFormat` values.

If a predefined format has been applied to a table using the *AutoFormat* method and subsequently the formatting is altered, we can restore the original autoformat using the *UpdateAutoFormat* method, whose syntax is simply:

```
TableObject.UpdateAutoFormat
```

The Cell Method

This method returns a Cell object that represents a cell in a table. The syntax is:

```
TableObject.Cell(Row, Column)
```

where *Row* and *Column* are Long integers that identify the particular cell. A Cell object can be used to format a given cell by adjusting such things as its text (through the Range property), its height, width, shading, and so on. The following is a complete list of the properties and methods of the Cell object:

Application	Height	RowIndex
AutoSum	HeightRule	Select
Borders	Merge	SetHeight
Column	Next	SetWidth
ColumnIndex	Parent	Shading
Creator	Previous	Split
Delete	Range	VerticalAlignment
Formula	Row	Width

The Columns and Rows Properties

The Columns property returns a Columns collection that represents all the table columns in the range, selection, or table. The properties and methods of the Columns collection are:

Add	Delete	Parent
Application	DistributeWidth	Select
AutoFit	First	SetWidth
Borders	Item	Shading
Count	Last	Width
Creator	NewEnum	

and those of the Column object are:

Application	Cells	Index
AutoFit	Creator	IsFirst
Borders	Delete	IsLast

Next	Select	Sort
Parent	SetWidth	Width
Previous	Shading	

Similarly, the Rows property returns a Rows collection that represents all the table rows in the range, selection, or table. The properties and methods of the Rows collection are:

Add	Delete	LeftIndent
Alignment	DistributeHeight	NewEnum
AllowBreakAcrossPages	First	Parent
Application	HeadingFormat	Select
Borders	Height	SetHeight
ConvertToText	HeightRule	SetLeftIndent
Count	Item	Shading
Creator	Last	SpaceBetweenColumns

and those of the Row object are:

Alignment	HeadingFormat	Parent
AllowBreakAcrossPages	Height	Previous
Application	HeightRule	Range
Borders	Index	Select
Cells	IsFirst	SetHeight
ConvertToText	IsLast	SetLeftIndent
Creator	LeftIndent	Shading
Delete	Next	SpaceBetweenColumns

The ConvertToText Method

This method converts the text within a table into plain text and returns a Range object that represents that text. The syntax is:

```
expression.ConvertToText(Separator)
```

where *expression* refers to a Row, Rows, or Table object. The optional *Separator* parameter specifies the character that delimits the text within each row (that is, it delimits the columns). It can be any of the constants in the following enum:

```
Enum WdTableFieldSeparator
    wdSeparateByParagraphs = 0
    wdSeparateByTabs = 1
    wdSeparateByCommas = 2
    wdSeparateByDefaultListSeparator = 3
End Enum
```

It is important to note that when the *ConvertToText* method is applied to a Table object, the table is deleted. For instance, the following code:

```
Set tbl = ActiveDocument.Tables(1)
Set rng = tbl.ConvertToText(wdSeparateByCommas)
MsgBox tbl.Columns.Count
```

produces the error message "Object has been deleted" when it gets to the third line, since the object referred to by `tbl` has been deleted.

This brings up the question of how to test whether an object reference, such as `tbl`, is still valid—that is, still refers to a valid object. Your first thought might be to use the `Nothing` keyword, discussed in Chapter 8, *Control Statements*, to write:

```
If tbl Is Nothing Then ...
```

However, this returns False, even though the object has been deleted, so it does not help. Instead, you must use the IsObjectValid property. This property is global, so you can test whether the `tbl` object still exists by writing:

```
If IsObjectValid(tbl) Then ...
```

Note also that in order to maintain a reference to the converted contents of the table, you must assign the Range object returned by the *ConvertToText* method to a new object variable, as in the second line of the previous example.

Sorting Methods

The *Sort* method can be used to sort an entire table or just a column within a table. (It can also be used to sort text. I discussed this in Chapter 14, *The Range and Selection Objects*.)

The syntax for sorting a table column is:

```
ColumnObject.Sort(ExcludeHeader, SortFieldType, SortOrder, _
                  CaseSensitive, LanguageID)
```

The syntax for sorting an entire table is:

```
TableObject.Sort(ExcludeHeader, FieldNumber, SortFieldType, _
                 SortOrder, FieldNumber2, SortFieldType2, _
                 SortOrder2, FieldNumber3, SortFieldType3, _
                 SortOrder3, CaseSensitive, LanguageID)
```

You can set the *ExcludeHeader* parameter to True to exclude the first row or paragraph from the sort operation. The default value is False.

The *FieldNumber*, *FieldNumber2*, and *FieldNumber3* parameters are fields that are used in the sorting process. Sorting is done first by *FieldNumber*, then by *FieldNumber2*, and finally by *FieldNumber3*.

The *SortFieldType*, *SortFieldType2*, and *SortFieldType3* parameters specify the sort types for the *FieldNumbers* parameters and can be one of the constants in the following enum:

```
Enum WdSortFieldType
    wdSortFieldAlphanumeric = 0
    wdSortFieldNumeric = 1
    wdSortFieldDate = 2
End Enum
```

The default is `wdSortFieldAlphanumeric`.

The *SortOrder*, *SortOrder2*, and *SortOrder3* parameters specify the sorting order for their respective *FieldNumbers* parameters and can be one of the constants in the following enum:

```
Enum WdSortOrder
    wdSortOrderAscending = 0
    wdSortOrderDescending = 1
End Enum
```

The default value is `wdSortOrderAscending`.

The *CaseSensitive* parameter is set to True for a case-sensitive sort. The default value is False.

The *LanguageID* parameter specifies the sorting language. It can be one of the 64 different `WdLanguageID` constants, including `wdEnglishUS` (see Word VBA help for more details).

If you do not need the flexibility of the Sort method, you can use the *SortAscending* or *SortDescending* method. The syntax is:

```
(rng or sel).SortAscending
(rng or sel).SortDescending
```

These methods simply sort table rows in ascending or descending alphanumeric order. The first row is always considered a header record and is not included in the sort.

The Split Method

The *Split* method applies to (among others) the Cell object, the Cells collection object, and the Table object. For a Cell object, the syntax is:

```
CellObject.Split(NumRows, NumColumns)
```

This will split the cell into multiple cells. For a Cells collection, the syntax is:

```
CellsObject.Split(NumRows, NumColumns, MergeBeforeSplit)
```

In this case, the method splits a range of cells. Finally, for the Table object, the syntax is:

```
TableObject.Split(BeforeRow)
```

In this case, the method inserts an empty paragraph immediately above the specified row in the table, thus splitting the table in two. The *Split* method returns a Table object that denotes the lower table. For example, assuming that the insertion point lies within the list of column object members earlier in this chapter, the code:

```
Dim tbl As Table
Dim tbl2 As Table
```

```
Selection.Expand wdTable    ' Select table
Set tbl = Selection.Tables(1)
Set tbl2 = tbl.Split(3)
```

turns that table into two tables, as shown in Figure 16-2.

Application	Index	Select
AutoFit	IsFirst	SetWidth

Borders	IsLast	Shading
Cells	Next	Sort
Creator	Parent	Width
Delete	Previous	

Figure 16-2. A table split into two parts

The various parameters of the *Split* method are:

NumColumns

> The number of columns that the cell or group of cells is to be split into.

NumRows

> The number of rows that the cell or group of cells is to be split into.

MergeBeforeSplit

> Set to True to merge the cells with one another before splitting them.

BeforeRow

> The row at which the table is split. This row becomes part of the lower table. It can be a row number or a Row object.

As another illustration, consider the table shown in Figure 16-3.

Borders	IsLast	Shading
Cells	Next	Sort
Creator	Parent	Width
Delete	Previous	

Figure 16-3. A table before a merge and split

To split the first row of this table into two cells, use the following code (which assumes that the insertion point lies within the table):

```
Dim tbl as Table
' Select the table
Selection.Expand wdTable
```

```
' Return the Table object
Set tbl = Selection.Tables(1)
' Merge then split into 2 cells
tbl.Rows(1).Cells.Split 1, 2, True
```

After this code is run, the resulting table appears as shown in Figure 16-4.

Borders	IsLast	Shading
Cells	Next	Sort
Creator	Parent	Width
Delete	Previous	

Figure 16-4. A table after the first row is split

Example: Creating Tables from Word Lists

I will conclude our discussion of tables with an example, one that was promised in the Preface to the book. Let me first recap the situation.

In writing this book, I was faced with the problem of turning long columns of words into tables. The built-in *ConvertToTable* command was not flexible enough for my needs for three reasons.

First, I wanted the items to be placed in the table in *column-major* order (the first column is filled first), rather than in *row-major* order (the first row is filled first). Second, I wanted to choose the number of columns based on the number of words (cells), so I needed a report on the word count before I made the choice of the number of columns. Finally, I wanted a row at the top of the table for a title.

To illustrate, I wanted to be able to select the following column of words:

Border
Cell
Column
Document
Font
Options
PageSetup
Paragraph
ParagraphFormat
Range
Row
Selection

Style
Table
Template
Window

and then be presented with a dialog box as shown in Figure 16-5. Then, if I entered 3 for the number of columns and hit the OK button, I wanted the table shown in Figure 16-6.

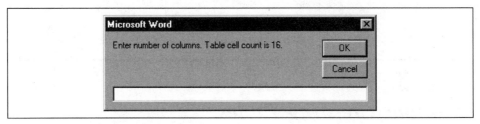

Figure 16-5. Table-making dialog box

Table		
Border	PageSetup	Style
Cell	Paragraph	Table
Column	ParagraphFormat	Template
Document	Range	Window
Font	Row	
Options	Selection	

Figure 16-6. Three-column table produced from a column of text

The code is shown in Example 16-1. (I think that you should get a pretty good idea of what this code does by first reading only the comments.)

Example 16-1. The MakeMultiColumnTable Routine

```
Sub MakeMultiColumnTable()

' Takes selected text and puts it into a table
' with user-defined number of columns.
' Paragraph mark delimits each table entry.
' Adds a title row at the top of the table.

Dim tbl As Table, rng As Range, TitleRow As Row
Dim rText as Range
Dim cCells As Integer, cColumns As Integer
Dim cRows As Integer
Dim iNextCol As Integer, iNextRow As Integer
Dim iNextCell As Integer

' Get count of paragraphs
cCells = Selection.Paragraphs.Count
```

Example 16-1. The MakeMultiColumnTable Routine (continued)

```
' Ask for number of columns
cColumns = Val(InputBox("Enter number of columns. Table cell count: " _
            & cCells))

If cColumns = 0 Then Exit Sub

' Compute the number of rows
cRows = Fix(cCells / cColumns)
If (cCells Mod cColumns) <> 0 Then cRows = cRows + 1

' Create new range object immediately
' after the current selection
Set rng = Selection.Range
rng.Collapse Direction:=wdCollapseEnd

' Make the table
Set tbl = ActiveDocument.Tables.Add(rng, cRows, cColumns)

' Fill the table with the selected paragraphs
iNextCell = 1
' Do first/next column
For iNextCol = 1 To cColumns
    ' Do first/next row
    For iNextRow = 1 To cRows
        ' Get paragraph range
        Set rText = Selection.Paragraphs(iNextCell).Range
        ' Back up one to skip paragraph mark
        rText.MoveEnd Unit:=wdCharacter, Count:=-1
        ' Insert text into cell
        tbl.Cell(iNextRow, iNextCol).Range.InsertAfter rText.Text
        ' Increment cell count and check for end
        iNextCell = iNextCell + 1
        If iNextCell > cCells Then Exit For
    Next iNextRow

    If iNextCell > cCells Then Exit For

Next iNextCol

' Apply autofit formatting
tbl.Columns.AutoFit

' Add new row for title and format it
Set TitleRow = tbl.Rows.Add(tbl.Rows(1))
TitleRow.Cells.Merge
TitleRow.Range.Paragraphs(1).Alignment = _
    wdAlignParagraphCenter
TitleRow.Range.Text = "Table"
tbl.Select

End Sub
```

Example: Closing Up a Table

Let us consider another example of the power of programming when working with tables. One of the tasks that I find myself needing now and then is a way to remove the contents of a cell from a multicolumn table and "close up" the table. For instance, consider the table in Figure 16-7.

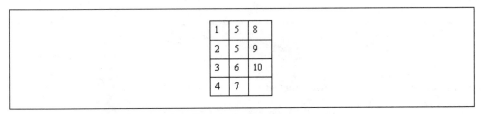

Figure 16-7. A multicolumn table with a duplicate entry

Unfortunately, two cells contain a 5. To remove the entry in row 2 and column 2 and close up the table requires manually moving all of the subsequent entries up one (by columns), to produce the table in Figure 16-8.

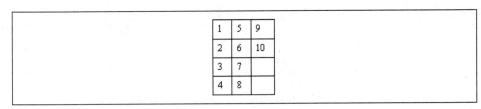

Figure 16-8. A multicolumn table with the duplicate cell removed

However, a little program could do that automatically on any size table! The code to do this is shown in Example 16-2. It requires that the cursor reside within the cell to be removed. Note the error-handling portions of the code, which I discuss next.

Example 16-2. Deleting a Table Cell

```
Public Sub TableDeleteCell()
' Deletes cell contents of current cell
' and moves cells up (column-major)
' Caution: Table must not have merged cells

Dim rng As Range
Dim tbl As Table
Dim cRows As Integer
Dim cCols As Integer
Dim iCurCol As Integer
Dim iCurRow As Integer
Dim iRow As Integer
```

Example 16-2. Deleting a Table Cell (continued)

```
Dim iCol As Integer
Dim CurCell As Cell

On Error GoTo ErrorTableDeleteCells
' Get current col and current row
Selection.Range.Expand wdCell
Set rng = Selection.Range
iCurCol = rng.Cells(1).Column.Index
iCurRow = rng.Cells(1).Row.Index

' Get table, row count and col count
Selection.Range.Expand wdTable
Set rng = Selection.Range
Set tbl = rng.Tables(1)
cRows = tbl.Rows.Count
cCols = tbl.Columns.Count

iCol = iCurCol
iRow = iCurRow
' Close up
Do
    Set CurCell = tbl.Cell(iRow, iCol)

    ' Goto to next cell
    iRow = iRow + 1
    If iRow > cRows Then
       iRow = 1
       iCol = iCol + 1
    End If

    ' If past last cell, then exit do loop
    If (iCol = cCols + 1 And iRow = 1) Then Exit Do

    ' Get range object for next cell
    Set rng = tbl.Cell(iRow, iCol).Range
    ' Remove end of cell character
    rng.MoveEnd wdCharacter, -1
    ' Place in current cell
    CurCell.Range.FormattedText = rng.FormattedText

Loop

' Delete contents of last cell
tbl.Cell(cRows, cCols).Range.Text = ""

Exit Sub

ErrorTableDeleteCells:
    If Err.Number = 5992 Then
       MsgBox "The program will not work on tables with cells that span" & _
               " more than one column.", vbCritical
    Else
```

Example 16-2. Deleting a Table Cell (continued)

```
      MsgBox Err.Number
   End If
Exit Sub

End Sub
```

Note that I move the cell formatting along with the text by using the Formatted-Text property, rather than the Text property. Also, it is important to remove the end-of-cell mark from the formatted range. (In case you are wondering how I knew this, the answer is that I found out the hard way. I forgot to do this when I first wrote the code and was rewarded with a systemwide crash of my PC!)

This code also illustrates the rudiments of error handling. In particular, the program will not work on tables with cells that span more than one column because there is no way to identify individual columns. (I could modify this program to deal with such a case, but I will leave that to you.)

For instance, the program will not work on the table in Figure 16-9.

Header		
1	5	9
2	6	10
3	7	
4	8	

Figure 16-9. A table with a cell spanning multiple columns

If I did not include the error-handling code, then the result of using this procedure on the table would be the error message from VBA shown in Figure 16-10. After issuing the error message, VBA would terminate the procedure.

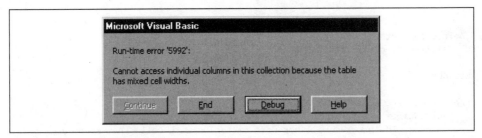

Microsoft Visual Basic

Run-time error '5992':

Cannot access individual columns in this collection because the table has mixed cell widths.

Continue   End   Debug   Help

Figure 16-10. VBA's error message

There is nothing wrong with this message, except perhaps that it is a bit cryptic. (It is not really the cell widths *per se* that matter—it is that some cells span more than one column, making it impossible to identify distinct columns.)

However, if I were intending to give or sell this program to another, then I would have to provide not only a friendlier error message but also a friendlier method of termination of the program. (A buyer of a program should never be presented with the option of debugging the program!)

The line:

```
On Error GoTo ErrorTableDeleteCells
```

tells VBA that if there is an error anywhere in the subsequent code, then execution should be transferred to the label **ErrorTableDeleteCells**. Execution will thus continue with the code:

```
If Err.Number = 5992 Then
    MsgBox "The program will not work on tables with
            cells that span more than one column.", vbCritical
Else
    MsgBox Err.Number
End If
```

This code checks for error number 5992, using the Number property of the Error object. If this error is found, it will issue the message shown in Figure 16-11. Otherwise, I let VBA issue its own error message.

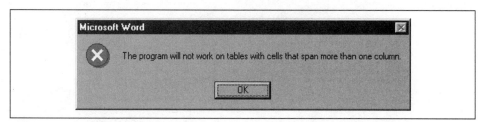

Figure 16-11. The new error message

Admittedly, my message may not be much better than VBA's, but I trust you can see the potential here for vastly improved error handling. Many of VBA's error messages are far too cryptic and should be replaced by more understandable messages. However, there is an even more important reason for error handling. Namely, *you* retain control over the flow of execution, rather than letting VBA take over, issue a fatal error message, and terminate the program.

For instance, there are many cases where you can warn the user about the error and give her a chance to correct the problem and try again. In this particular example, however, there is no way to correct the problem, so I simply issue a friendly error message and terminate the program gracefully.

Note finally that there is an:

```
Exit Sub
```

line immediately *preceding* the error label. This is vital, for otherwise the error-handling code will be executed even if there is no error! Don't forget this line of code.

17

The List Object

Lists play an important role in Word documents, and the Word object model contains objects that give the programmer very powerful control over lists. Figure 17-1 shows most of these objects, which are children of the Document object. The List-Gallery object and ListGalleries collection, which are children of the Application object, are not shown.

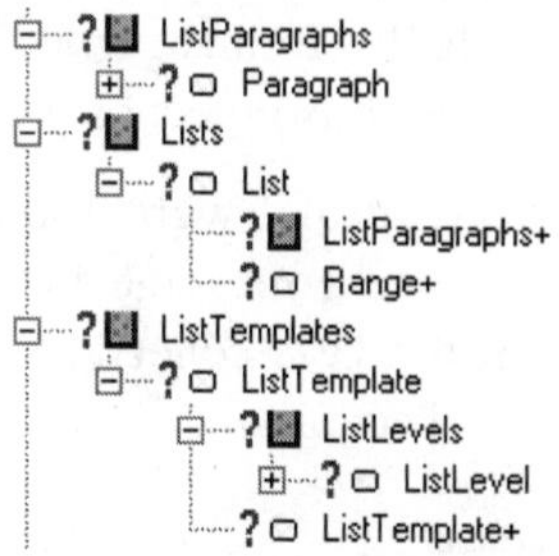

```
⊟···? ▦ ListParagraphs
   ⊞···? ▢ Paragraph
⊟···? ▦ Lists
   ⊟···? ▢ List
         ? ▦ ListParagraphs+
         ? ▢ Range+
⊟···? ▦ ListTemplates
   ⊟···? ▢ ListTemplate
         ⊟···? ▦ ListLevels
            ⊞···? ▢ ListLevel
         ? ▢ ListTemplate+
```

Figure 17-1. List-related objects

The Word object model is a bit confusing when it comes to lists, partly because the Help documentation is decidedly nonpedagogic. To help clarify the situation, I will begin with a few remarks about lists.

List Types

There are three types of lists in Microsoft Word: *single-level bulleted, single-level numbered,* and *multilevel outline-numbered.* The term *outline-numbered* is a bit misleading, since an outline-numbered list can use either bullets or numbers (and need not include any numbers). Nonetheless, this is Microsoft's term, so I will use it as well.

In the case of numbered lists (single- and multilevel), there are options to either restart the numbering or continue the numbering started in a previous list. If there is text between the list you are creating and a previous list, then Word will default to new numbering. If not, Word will continue the numbering from the previous list.

For numbered lists, you can customize the numbering by setting the number format, the amount of indent, and so on. For multilevel lists, this can be done for each level separately.

What Is a List?

Word does not think of lists in the same way as we might. To Word, a document has some paragraphs that are formatted with a list format and some paragraphs that are not. These paragraphs may or may not be consecutive.

The Word object model has a List object, which you might think represents a list. However, according to the Help documentation, a List object represents "a single list format that's been applied to specified paragraphs in a document." In other words, a List object represents a list *format*. I will provide some examples of this in a moment.

The Word object model also has a ListFormat object, which again according to the Help documentation represents "the list formatting attributes that can be applied to the paragraphs in a range." (I discuss this object as well later in this chapter.)

To help understand how Word deals with lists, I will use the code in Example 17-1, which simply displays a message box that shows the number of paragraphs in each List object in the Lists collection (and also tells us how many List objects there are in the Lists collection).

Example 17-1. The ShowLists Procedure

```
Sub ShowLists()
Dim i As Integer
Dim s As String
Dim lst As ListParagraphs
s = ""
For i = 1 To ActiveDocument.Lists.Count
    Set lst = ActiveDocument.Lists(i).Range.ListParagraphs
    s = s & "List " & Format$(i) & ": " & lst.Count & _
            " paragraphs" & vbCrLf
Next i
MsgBox s
End Sub
```

Bulleted Lists

Let us first consider the case of bulleted lists. Consider the two short six-paragraph documents shown in Figures 17-2 and 17-3. Each document has three bulleted paragraphs, followed by a nonbulleted paragraph, followed by two additional bulleted paragraphs. It seems reasonable to say that each document has two distinct *physical* lists.

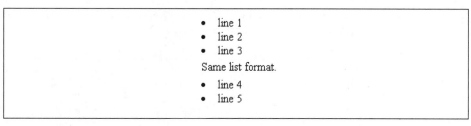

Figure 17-2. Document 1

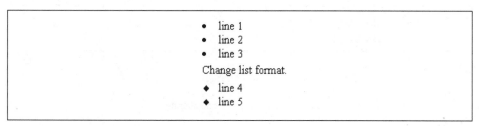

Figure 17-3. Document 2

However, the *ShowLists* procedure displays the result shown in Figure 17-4 for Document 1 and in Figure 17-5 for Document 2.

Figure 17-4. Results of the ShowLists procedure for Document 1

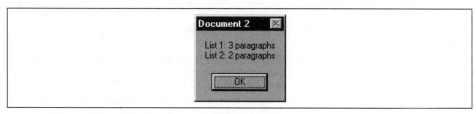

Figure 17-5. Results of the ShowLists procedure for Document 2

Thus, Word considers a single bullet list *format* as a single List object. This is in keeping with the information in the Help documentation that says a List object represents a list *format* that has been applied to the document—the first document has one list format, the second has two list formats. Thus, we see that a single List object may contain paragraphs that are not contiguous.

Numbered Lists

Consider now the case of numbered lists. Figures 17-6 through 17-9 show four more documents, each with multilevel numbered lists.

```
        1.  line 1
        2.  line 2
        3.  line 3
        Same list format, continue numbering.
        4.  line 4
        5.  line 5
```

Figure 17-6. Document 3

```
        1.  line 1
        2.  line 2
        3.  line 3
        Same list format, restart numbering.
        1.  line 4
        2.  line 5
```

Figure 17-7. Document 4

```
        1.  line 1
        2.  line 2
        3.  line 3
        Change list format, continue numbering.
        4)  line 4
        5)  line 5
```

Figure 17-8. Document 5

```
        1.  line 1
        2.  line 2
        3.  line 3
        Change list format, restart numbering.
        1)  line 4
        2)  line 5
```

Figure 17-9. Document 6

In keeping with the definition of List object given in the Help documentation, it would seem that Documents 3 and 4 should each have one List object, because they have one list formatting, and Documents 5 and 6 should each have two List objects, because they have two list formats. However, Figure 17-10 shows the returns from the *ShowLists* procedure.

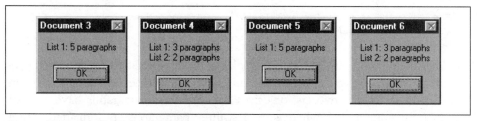

Figure 17-10. Results of the ShowLists procedure

Thus, it seems that when numbered lists are involved, it is a restarting of the numbering that determines a new List object, not a change in the list format. The upshot of this discussion is probably to heed Microsoft's own faint suggestion: "You can manipulate the individual List objects within a document, but for more precise control you should work with the ListFormat object." The fact is that List objects are useful, but you must use them with circumspection.

To illustrate this point, I recently finished a 450-page Word manuscript containing countless lists scattered throughout, with almost 300 paragraphs that are either bulleted or numbered. (In case you are interested, the manuscript is entitled *Understanding Personal Computer Hardware*, published by Springer-Verlag, and should be available by the time you read this. Pardon my commercial.) Here is the result of *ShowLists* on my manuscript:

```
List 1: 279 paragraphs
List 2: 1 paragraphs
List 3: 4 paragraphs
List 4: 3 paragraphs
List 5: 6 paragraphs
```

The first List object represents a bulleted list format, which happens to appear first on page 6 of my manuscript and last on page 416 (and in 279 paragraphs in total).

Now, the seemingly innocuous code to select the first list in the manuscript:

```
ActiveDocument.Lists(1).Range.Select
```

actually selects all text *between* the first and last paragraphs that have this bullet format; that is, it selects 410 pages of text! (Recall that a Range object represents a *contiguous* area within a document.)

Suppose that I had wanted to italicize the paragraphs in List 1. The code:

```
ActiveDocument.Lists(1).Range.Font.Italic = True
```

would be a disaster, since it would italicize 410 pages of text. The proper code to do this job requires the ListParagraphs collection (which I discuss a bit later in this chapter):

```
For Each para In ActiveDocument.Lists(1).ListParagraphs
    para.Range.Font.Italic = True
Next para
```

One final point: two bulleted lists may look identically formatted to the naked eye, but may actually have different formatting. For instance, the list shown in Figure 17-11 is actually two List objects! (The first three paragraphs have Normal style with bulleting added, whereas the last three paragraphs are formatted with a Bullet List style.)

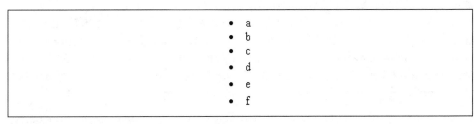

Figure 17-11. A document with two List objects

The List Object

The List object represents a single list format that has been applied to at least one paragraph in a document. The code:

```
MsgBox ActiveDocument.Lists.Count
```

displays the number of List objects in the active document. Here are some of the properties of the List object:

The ListParagraphs property
    Returns a ListParagraphs collection, which is the collection of all paragraph objects in the list that have list formatting. Note that this property also applies to the Document and Range objects, in which case some paragraphs may not have a list formatting.

The Range property
    Returns a Range object that represents all paragraphs that lie between the first and last paragraphs in the list. This includes paragraphs that are not list-formatted. (See the earlier discussion of list objects.)

The SingleListTemplate property

A single list may use more than one list template; that is, it may have formatting from more than one list template. The SingleListTemplate property is True when a list uses only one list template. This is a read-only property. (I discuss list templates a bit later in this chapter.)

The ApplyListTemplate method

Applies a list template (that is, a list format) to the given List object. The syntax is:

```
ListObject.ApplyListTemplate(ListTemplate,_
ContinuePreviousList)
```

where `ListTemplate` is the list template to be applied. The optional `ContinuePreviousList` parameter is True to continue the previous list or False to start a new list with new numbering. (I discuss list templates a bit later in this chapter.)

The ConvertNumbersToText method

To convert the automatic numbering in a list to plain text numbers, we can write:

```
ListObject.ConvertNumbersToText
```

After converting to text, the automatic numbering feature is lost.

The CountNumberedItems method

Returns the number of bulleted or numbered paragraphs and `LISTNUM` fields in the List object. It also applies to Document and ListFormat objects:

```
Msgbox ActiveDocument.Lists(1).CountNumberedItems
```

The RemoveNumbers method

Removes list formatting from the specified list. All indents are removed as well.

The ListTemplate Object and ListGalleries

The ListTemplate object represents a list template, which is an object that specifies all the formatting that defines a list. ListTemplates are kept in a ListTemplates collection.

There are three Word objects that have a ListTemplates property that returns a List-Templates collection: Document objects, Template objects, and ListGallery objects. In other words, ListTemplate objects can be stored in any of these three objects.

ListGallery Objects

One place to keep a ListTemplate object is in a ListGallery object. There are three ListGallery objects representing the three tabs in the Bullets and Numbering dialog box. The collection of these three ListGallery objects is the ListGalleries collection.

In fact, Word supplies an enum to use as the index for the ListGalleries collection:

```
Enum WdListGalleryType
    wdBulletGallery = 1
    wdNumberGallery = 2
    wdOutlineNumberGallery = 3
End Enum
```

Thus, for instance:

```
ListGalleries(wdNumberGallery)
```

is the second ListGallery object and represents the second tab in the Bullets and Numbering dialog box. Note that the type of the ListGallery object determines the type of ListTemplate objects that can be placed in that ListGallery's ListTemplates collection. For instance, the list templates in `ListGalleries(wdNumberGallery)` must be single-level numbered list formats.

The ListGallery object has the following properties and methods (among others):

The ListTemplates property

> Returns a ListTemplates collection that represents all of the list formats for the ListGallery object. As mentioned, this read-only property also applies to Document and Template objects.

The Modified property

> The Modified property has the syntax:

> `ListGalleryObject.Modified(Index)`

> where *Index* is a number between 1 and 7 that specifies the position of the template in the Bullets and Numbering dialog box. (Templates are numbered from left to right, skipping the first position, marked "None".) This is a read-only Boolean property that returns True if the template in the position *Index* is not the built-in Word default template for that position.

The Reset method

> Resets a ListGallery position to the default built-in template. Its syntax is:

> `ListGalleryObject.Reset(Index)`

> where *Index* is a number between 1 and 7 that specifies the position of the template in the Bullets and Numbering dialog box.

The ListTemplate Object

The ListTemplate object has the following list-related properties and methods:

The ListLevels property
> Returns the ListLevels collection, which contains ListLevel objects. (I discuss ListLevel objects a bit later in this chapter.)

The OutlineNumbered property
> This property is True if the ListTemplate object is outline numbered (multi-level), as opposed to single-level. You can set this property to False to change a multilevel numbered list to a single-level numbered list. However, we cannot set this property for a ListTemplate object returned from a ListGallery object.

The Convert method
> This method converts a multilevel list to a single-level list or vice versa. The syntax is:
>
> ```
> ListTemplateObject.Convert
> ```

The ListLevel Object

As mentioned previously, each ListTemplate object has a ListLevels collection. The ListLevel objects in this collection are the objects that really define the formatting of a ListTemplate object. This is evident by looking at the various properties of a ListLevel object, which I do later in this section.

Note first that if the ListTemplate object represents a single-level format, then its ListLevels collection contains only one ListLevel object. A multilevel list format may have up to nine levels. Hence, there may be up to nine ListLevel objects in a ListLevels collection.

Figure 17-12 shows the Customize Outline Numbered List dialog box, which contains settings corresponding to the properties of the ListLevel object. These include the following:

The Alignment property
> Returns or sets the alignment for the corresponding list level. Its value can be one of the constants in the **WdListLevelAlignment** enum:
>
> ```
> Enum WdListLevelAlignment
>    wdListLevelAlignLeft = 0
>    wdListLevelAlignCenter = 1
>    wdListLevelAlignRight = 2
> End Enum
> ```

The Font property
> Returns or sets a Font object that represents the character formatting of the corresponding list level.

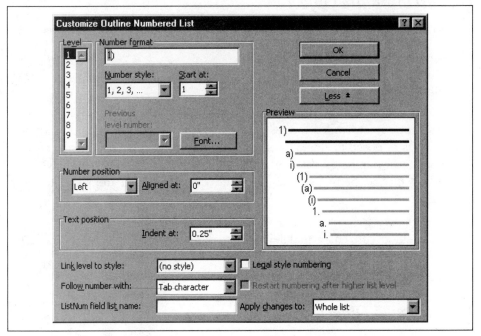

Figure 17-12. The Customize Outline Numbered List dialog box

The Index property

This read-only property specifies the level of the ListLevel object in the List-Template object. Thus, if a ListLevel object has index 2, for example, then it represents the second level in the list. The value of *Index* is a number between 1 and 9. Note that `ListLevels(i)` is the ListLevel object with index *i*. Thus, the index of a ListLevel object in the ListLevels collection is actually the level of the ListLevel object. (In general, the index of a member of a collection cannot be relied upon to have any particular meaning—it simply identifies the object among the members of the collection. When an object is removed from a collection, the indices of other object may change. However, this case is an exception.)

The LinkedStyle property

Returns or sets the name of the Word style (if any) that is linked to the ListLevel object.

The NumberFormat property

Returns or sets a string that represents the numbering format for the list level. You can use a percent sign (%) to specify the variable that holds the numbering. For instance, to obtain the numbering format:

Section I
Section II

Section III

. . .

you would set the NumberFormat property as follows:

```
ListLevel(Index).NumberFormat = "Section %1"
```

Then you would set the NumberStyle property to **wdListNumberStyleUppercaseRoman** (see the entry for the NumberStyle property later in this list).

Note that if the NumberStyle property is set to **wdListNumberStyleBullet**, then the string for the NumberFormat property should contain only one character, which is used for the bullet.

The NumberPosition property

Returns or sets the position (in points, as a Single) of the number or bullet for the ListLevel object.

The NumberStyle property

Returns or sets the number style for the specified object. Its value can be any of the constants in the following enum:

```
Enum WdListNumberStyle
    wdListNumberStyleArabic = 0
    wdListNumberStyleUppercaseRoman = 1
    wdListNumberStyleLowercaseRoman = 2
    wdListNumberStyleUppercaseLetter = 3
    wdListNumberStyleLowercaseLetter = 4
    wdListNumberStyleOrdinal = 5
    wdListNumberStyleCardinalText = 6
    wdListNumberStyleOrdinalText = 7
    wdListNumberStyleArabicLZ = 22
    wdListNumberStyleBullet = 23
    wdListNumberStyleLegal = 253
    wdListNumberStyleLegalLZ = 254
    wdListNumberStyleNone = 255
End Enum
```

The ResetOnHigher property

This Boolean property can be set to True to force the specified list level to restart its numbering (at the beginning) whenever it follows a higher list level. It can be set to False to force the numbering to continue each time the list level appears. This feature allows lists to be interleaved. The two lists in Figure 17-13 illustrate the difference, using the second list level.

The StartAt property

Returns or sets the starting number for the specified ListLevel object.

The TabPosition property

Returns or sets the tab position (in points, as a Single) for the ListLevel object.

The TextPosition property

Returns or sets the position for the second line of wrapping text for the specified ListLevel object.

```
1)  Line 1
    a) Line 2
2)  Line 3
    a) Line 4 (ResetOnHigher is True—second list level restarts numbering)
3)  Line 5



1)  Line 1
    a) Line 2
2)  Line 3
    b) Line 4 (ResetOnHigher is False—second list level continues numbering. List is
       interleaved.)
3)  Line 5
```

Figure 17-13. Noninterleaved and interleaved lists

The TrailingCharacter property

Returns or sets the character inserted after the number for the list level. It can be any of the constants in the following enum:

```
Enum WdTrailingCharacter
    wdTrailingTab = 0
    wdTrailingSpace = 1
    wdTrailingNone = 2
End Enum
```

The ListTemplates Collections

We have seen that ListTemplate objects can be kept in ListTemplate collections associated with either a ListGallery object, a Document object, or a Template object. Moreover, a ListGallery object contains exactly seven ListTemplate objects, which must be of a specific gallery type: bulleted, numbered single-level, or numbered outline.

The *Add* method can be used to create and add new ListTemplate objects to a ListTemplates collection. The syntax is:

```
ListTemplatesObject.Add(OutlineNumbered, Name)
```

where *OutlineNumbered* is True for a multilevel list template and *Name* is an optional name for the list template.

Note that the *Add* method does not apply to a ListTemplates collection obtained from a ListGallery object. (ListGallery objects have seven list templates—period.) Indeed, you are restricted either to modifying the formatting of a ListFormat object from a list gallery or to resetting the format to its default. You cannot move, remove, or replace these ListFormat objects.

While I am on the subject, Word does not seem to have supplied any method for removing a ListTemplate object from any ListTemplates collection, so you should add ListTemplate objects carefully. Also, Microsoft does not seem to want to explain how Word itself manages the various ListTemplates collections.

If you change the formatting of an existing list in a document, Word will add a new ListTemplate to the document's ListTemplates collection. However, if you then delete the list, Word does not remove the ListTemplate object. (The document that I am using to write this book currently has 102 pages and its ListTemplates collection has a whopping 82 ListTemplate objects!)

As an example, the following code create a new ListTemplate object and adds it to the active document's ListTemplates collection. The name of the list format is "TestTemplate."

```
Dim lst As ListTemplate
Set lst = ActiveDocument.ListTemplates.Add()
With lst
    .OutlineNumbered = True
    .Name = "TestTemplate"
    .ListLevels(1).Font.Size = 18
    .ListLevels(1).NumberStyle = _
        wdListNumberStyleCardinalText
    .ListLevels(2).Font.Size = 14
    .ListLevels(2).NumberStyle = _
        wdListNumberStyleCardinalText
    .ListLevels(3).Font.Size = 10
    .ListLevels(3).NumberStyle = _
        wdListNumberStyleCardinalText
End With
```

The following code applies the list formatting to the currently selected list:

```
Selection.Range.ListFormat.ApplyListTemplate _
    ActiveDocument.ListTemplates("TestTemplate")
```

Figure 17-14 shows the result of applying it to the selected text.

One. Select the Customize option from the Tools menu.

Two. Make sure the toolbar you want to customize is visible. If not, click on the Toolbars tab and make sure that a check appears next to its name.

Three. Click on the Commands tab.

Four. Select Macros from the Commands menu.

Five. Select the name of the macro that you want to assign to the toolbar and drag it to the position on the toolbar where you'd like it to appear.

Figure 17-14. Applying the TestTemplate list

The ListFormat Object

The ListFormat object is a child of the Range object and is used to access various list-related properties and methods for the paragraphs in a given range. In a sense, it is the conduit to the list-related properties of a range. The ListFormat object for a given range is obtained through the ListFormat property, as in:

```
rng.ListFormat
```

The Apply...Default methods

The *ApplyBulletDefault, ApplyNumberDefault,* and *ApplyOutlineNumberDefault* methods apply (or remove) the default bulleted, numbered, or outline numbered format to the specified range. If the range is already so formatted, the formatting is removed.

Unfortunately, Microsoft does not make clear what is meant by the *default* list format for each type, but it appears to be the format that was last used to apply list formatting of that type. In any case, to apply a specific list format, you can use the *ApplyListTemplate* method, described next.

The ApplyListTemplate method

This method applies a list formatting from a specified ListTemplate object to the specified range. The syntax is:

```
ListFormatObject.ApplyListTemplate(ListTemplate, _
        ContinuePreviousList, ApplyTo)
```

where **ListTemplate** is the ListTemplate object to be applied, the optional **ContinuePreviousList** is set to True to continue the numbering from the previous list or False to start new numbering, and the optional **ApplyTo** is set to one of the constants in the following enum:

```
Enum WdListApplyTo
    wdListApplyToWholeList = 0
    wdListApplyToThisPointForward = 1
    wdListApplyToSelection = 2
End Enum
```

For example, the following code applies the sixth bullet format in the Bullet List Gallery to the selected text:

```
Selection.Range.ListFormat.ApplyListTemplate _
ListGalleries(wdBulletGallery).ListTemplates(6)
```

The ConvertNumbersToText method

This method changes the list numbers and optionally any **LISTNUM** fields in the specified range into text. After invoking this method, automatic list numbering is no longer available. The syntax is:

```
ListFormatObject.ConvertNumbersToText(NumberType)
```

where the optional parameter *NumberType* specifies the type of number to be converted and can be one of the constants in the following enum:

```
Enum WdNumberType
    wdNumberParagraph = 1
    wdNumberListNum = 2
    wdNumberAllNumbers = 3
End Enum
```

The constant **wdNumberParagraph** refers to the automatic numbering that is applied via a list format. The constant **wdListNum** refers to any LISTNUM fields that are included in the list.

The *ConvertToNumbers* method is useful when exporting a Word document to a format that does not support automatic list numbering (such as rich text format), but we want to keep the existing numbering.

The CountNumberedItems method

This method returns the number of bulleted or numbered items (and LISTNUM fields) in the specified range. (The method also applies to Document and List objects.) Its syntax is:

```
ListFormatObject.CountNumberedItems(NumberType, Level)
```

where *NumberType* is the same as in the *ConvertToNumbers* method and *Level* is an optional parameter that specifies the level for which you want to apply the method. If *Level* is omitted, all levels are counted.

The List property

If each paragraph in the specified range lies within a *single* List object, the List property returns that List object. It is read-only. As an example, consider the four-line document shown in Figure 17-15.

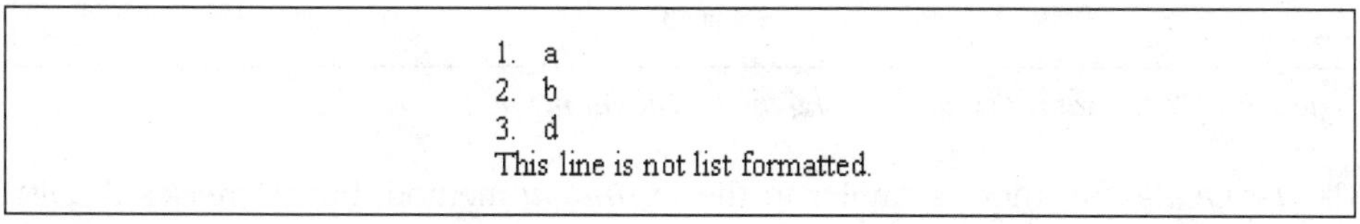

```
    1. a
    2. b
    3. d
    This line is not list formatted.
```

Figure 17-15. A simple four-line document

If I highlight the second and third lines, for instance, then the code:

```
MsgBox Selection.Range.ListFormat.List.CountNumberedItems
```

returns the number 3, since the List object contains three numbered lines. However, if I highlight the second, third, and fourth lines, the code produces an error message, since the specified range (that is, the selection) is not contained *completely* within a single List object, and so:

```
Selection.Range.ListFormat.List
```

is set to Nothing. Thus, to avoid errors, it is important to explicitly test for Nothing, as in:

```
If Not Selection.Range.ListFormat.List Is Nothing Then
    MsgBox Selection.Range.ListFormat.List.CountNumberedItems
End If
```

The ListIndent, ListOutdent, and ListLevelNumber methods

The *ListIndent* method increases the list level of the paragraphs in the specified range by one level. Its syntax is:

```
ListFormatObject.ListIndent
```

The *ListIndent* method makes the most sense when applied to a multilevel list. For instance, if the insertion point is on the second line in the multilevel list shown in Figure 17-16, then the code:

```
Selection.Range.ListFormat.ListIndent
```

results in the list shown in Figure 17-17.

```
                    1)  line1
                    2)  line2
                    3)  line3
```

Figure 17-16. A list before calling the ListIndent method

```
                    1)  line1
                        a)  line2
                    2)  line3
```

Figure 17-17. The same list after calling the ListIndent method

The *ListOutdent* method is similar to the *ListIndent* method, but decreases the list level instead of increasing it. The syntax is:

```
ListFormatObject.ListOutdent
```

The ListLevelNumber property returns or sets the list level (as a Long integer) for the first paragraph in the specified range.

The ListString and ListValue properties

The read-only ListString property returns a string that shows how the list numbering appears for the first paragraph in the specified range. For example, if the second line is the list in Figure 17-18 is selected, the code:

```
Selection.Range.ListFormat.ListString
```

returns the string "Two.".

```
                              One.   line1
                              Two.   line2
                              Three. line3
```

Figure 17-18. A three-item list

Note that for bulleted lists, the previous code returns the ANSI character code for the bullet, but you must apply the correct font (which is usually Symbol or Wingdings) to see the actual bullet.

The read-only ListValue property returns the numeric value corresponding to the string value returned by the ListString property. For instance, consider the list in Figure 17-19. If the insertion pointer is on the line with the text "line3," then the ListValue property is equal to 2, because "b" is the second item in the alphabet.

If the paragraph in question has a bulleted format, then *ListValue* returns 1.

```
                        1)  line1
                            a)  line2
                            b)  line3
                            c)  line4
                                i)   line5
                        2)  line6
```

Figure 17-19. A nested list

The ListTemplate property

If each paragraph in the specified range is formatted with a *single* ListTemplate object, the ListTemplate property returns that ListTemplate object. This is a read-only property.

The ListType property

This property returns the type of lists that are contained in the specified range. It can be any one of the constants in the following enum:

```
Enum WdListType
   wdListNoNumbering = 0
```

```
      wdListListNumOnly = 1
      wdListBullet = 2
      wdListSimpleNumbering = 3
      wdListOutlineNumbering = 4
      wdListMixedNumbering = 5
   End Enum
```

For instance, if I highlight the two lists shown in Figure 17-20, then the code:

```
   Selection.Range.ListFormat.ListType
```

returns the number 5 (or **wdListMixedNumbering**).

•   line1
              •   line2
 	
             1)   line3
             2)   line4

Figure 17-20. Lists of two different types

The RemoveNumbers method

This method removes numbers or bullets from the specified range. The syntax is:

```
   ListFormatObject.RemoveNumbers(NumberType)
```

where *NumberType* is one of the constants in the following enum:

```
   Enum WdNumberType
      wdNumberParagraph = 1
      wdNumberListNum = 2
      wdNumberAllNumbers = 3
   End Enum
```

See the *ConvertNumbersToText* method for more on these constants.

The SingleList property

This read-only property is True if the specified range contains only one List object.

The SingleListTemplate property

This read-only property is True if the entire range uses a single list template.

Example: Looking at Lists

By way of example, let me share with you an issue I had to deal with recently concerning the 450-page manuscript I mentioned earlier. After sending the manuscript to the publisher, the editor requested that I add a half-line spacing between each bulleted item to improve readability. This was easy enough to do—I just changed the List Bullet style that I used to create bulleted lists. However, having worked with computers for some time, I knew enough to check each list visually to make sure everything came out as expected.

Now, it is easy to iterate through each list paragraph in the document. The following code will do the job:

```
Dim para As Paragraph
For Each para in  ActiveDocument.ListParagraphs
    para.Range.Select
Next para
```

The problem here is that the list paragraphs will go flying by without allowing me to check each paragraph.

The solution is to write a macro that uses a static variable that remembers the index of the current list paragraph. (Recall that a static variable retains its value as long as the document to which the code is attached is open or as long as there is an open document that uses the template to which the code is attached.) Then, when the macro is executed repeatedly, it goes from one list to the next. By assigning a hotkey or a toolbar button to this macro, it is easy to check each list paragraph. The code is shown in Example 17-2.

Example 17-2. Iterating List Paragraphs

```
Sub FindNextList()

Dim i As Integer
Static Idx As Integer

' Idx is initialized to 0!
If Idx >= ActiveDocument.ListParagraphs.Count Then
   MsgBox "Done"
   Exit Sub
End If
ActiveDocument.ListParagraphs(Idx + 1).Range.Select
Idx = Idx + 1

End Sub
```

Note the use of the index **Idx** in the preceding code. I had to make some adjustments because an integer variable is initialized to 0, but the ListParagraphs collection is 1-based.

18

Shortcut Key Bindings

A KeyBinding object represents a custom key assignment in the current context: document, template, or application (normal template). Note that custom key assignments can be made in the Customize Keyboard dialog box (see Figure 18-1) as well. KeyBinding objects are members of the KeyBindings collection.

A *key binding* consists of several things, as reflected in the Customize keyboard dialog box shown in Figure 18-1. First, a key binding requires a Word command (such as *FileOpenFile*) that is executed when the keystrokes are invoked. This command may require a command parameter (such as a filename). Second, a key binding requires a key combination (such as Alt-O,1) that invokes the command. As you will learn, this key combination is described by a key code.

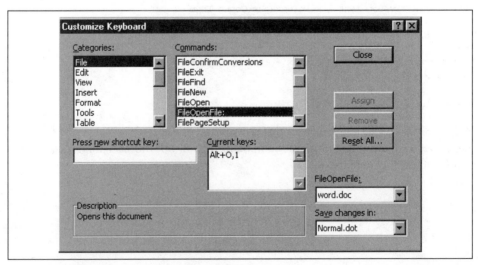

Figure 18-1. The Customize Keyboard dialog box

I will describe a couple of examples before discussing the individual properties and methods of the KeyBinding and other objects.

Finding a Key Binding

It is time to fulfill a promise given in the Preface to show you how to find renegade shortcut key assignments. But first, let me review the situation. While experimenting with the material for this chapter, I created a shortcut for the *FileOpen-File* command and assigned it the hotkey combination Alt-O,1, forgetting that Alt-O is used to invoke the Format menu.

Then my work on the book (and on the computer in general) was interrupted for several days. When I returned to work, at some point I hit Alt-O, expecting to get the Format menu. But nothing happened. I had to figure out why.

The first thing that occurred to me is that I had reassigned the Alt-O key, but I couldn't remember how. This left me with three choices. First, I could painstakingly search through each of the hundreds of commands and macros using the Customize Keyboard dialog box, trying to find a keystroke assignment that begins with Alt-O. This was my *last* choice. Second, I could invoke the FindKey method (discussed later in this chapter), which searches for a command that corresponds to a given hotkey combination. The problem with this choice is that I would need to know the *exact* keystroke combination. I did try searching for Alt-O, but this returned nothing.

The final (and best) choice was to use the short program in Example 18-1, which makes a list of all of the current key bindings. My advice: Keep this program handy. (The example I give at the end of this chapter is a little more complete than the code in Example 18-1.)

Example 18-1. Listing All Current Key Bindings

```
Public Sub ShowKeyBindings()

Dim kb As KeyBinding

' Print heading
Selection.InsertAfter KeyBindings.Count & _
    " key bindings in context: " & CustomizationContext & vbCr

' Start the For loop, printing KeyString and Command
Selection.Collapse wdCollapseEnd
For Each kb In KeyBindings
    Selection.InsertBefore kb.KeyString & vbTab & _
        kb.Command & " (" & kb.CommandParameter & ")" & vbCr
    Selection.Collapse wdCollapseEnd
Next kb

End Sub
```

A portion of the output of this code on my PC is shown in Example 18-2. Note the last line.

Example 18-2. Output from the ShowKeyBindings Routine

```
F12     Bold ()
Shift+F2    Italic ()
Shift+F9    Times New Roman ()
Shift+F11   Normal ()
Shift+F12   Code ()
Ctrl+*   ShowAll ()
Alt+1    Heading 1 ()
Alt+2    Heading 2 ()
Alt+3    Heading 3 ()
Alt+4    Heading 4 ()
Alt+9    Arial ()
Alt+O,1   FileOpenFile (D:\word\Word.doc)
```

Creating a Key Binding

To create a key binding and add it to the KeyBindings collection, use the *Add* method of the KeyBindings collection. The syntax for this *Add* method is:

```
KeyBinding.Add(KeyCategory, Command, KeyCode, KeyCode2, CommandParameter)
```

The parameters of this method are described in detail later in this chapter, since they are also properties of the KeyBinding object.

To illustrate, the following code:

```
KeyBindings.Add wdKeyCategoryFont, "Arial", _
    BuildKeyCode(wdKeyAlt, wdKey9)
```

adds a new key binding with shortcut key Alt-9, whose command changes the font to Arial.

The KeyBinding Object

The following list describes some of the properties and methods of a KeyBinding object:

The Clear method

Removes the key binding from the KeyBindings collection and also resets a built-in command to its default key assignment. The syntax is:

```
KeyBinding.Clear
```

The *ClearAll* method of the KeyBindings collection can be used to clear all custom key bindings and reset the default key bindings.

The Command property

This read-only property returns the command assigned to the specified key combination as a string. A list of the more than 1,000 commands is available from the Customize menu item (under the Tools menu). Those commands whose names are followed by a colon require a command parameter. In addition to the well-known Word commands such as New, Open, Print, Bold, and Italic, there are a great many commands that most Word users have never encountered, such as Auto Correct Exceptions, Bookshelf Lookup Reference, Control Run, and so on.

The CommandParameter property

This read-only property returns a string containing the command parameter for the key binding. If the command in question takes no parameters, this property returns an empty string.

For instance, the `FileOpenFile` command (which opens a specific file) requires a string parameter that specifies the filename (and path) for the file to open. The `Symbol` command requires a string of the form:

```
Chr(x) & FontName
```

where *x* is a character code and *FontName* is the name of a symbol font, as in:

```
Chr(125) & " Symbol"
```

For more on commands that take parameters, see the *Add* command in Word Help.

The Context and CustomizationContext properties

The read-only Context property returns the storage location of the key binding—a Document, Template, or Application object. In particular, if the key binding is built-in, then the *Context* method returns the Application object. Otherwise, it returns the object that reflects the context in effect when the KeyBinding object was created and added to the KeyBindings collection.

The CustomizationContext property of the Application object can be used to set (or read) a Template or Document object that represents the location in which to store key bindings. It corresponds to the "Save in" drop-down combo box on the Commands tab in the Customize dialog box of the Tools menu.

The Disable method

This method, with syntax:

```
KeyBinding.Disable
```

disables the key combination in the KeyBinding object so that it no longer invokes the corresponding command. This is the equivalent of clicking the Remove button in the Customize Keyboard dialog box.

Note that the *Clear* method is used to permanently reset a built-in command to its Word default key assignment.

The Execute method

This method runs the command associated with the key binding. Its syntax is:

```
KeyBinding.Execute
```

The KeyCategory property

This read-only property returns the type of command assigned to the key binding. It can be any one of the constants in the following enum:

```
Enum WdKeyCategory
    wdKeyCategoryAutoText = 4
    wdKeyCategoryCommand = 1
    wdKeyCategoryDisable = 0
    wdKeyCategoryFont = 3
    wdKeyCategoryMacro = 2
    wdKeyCategoryNil = -1
    wdKeyCategoryPrefix = 7
    wdKeyCategoryStyle = 5
    wdKeyCategorySymbol = 6
End Enum
```

The KeyCode and KeyCode2 properties

Every key combination is identified by a unique **Long** integer, called a *key code*. The KeyCode and KeyCode2 properties return this key code for the first and (optional) second keys in a key binding. These properties are read-only.

The key codes are built (by addition) from the constants in the **WdKey** enum:

wdKey0 (48)	wdKeyF (70)	wdKeyN (78)
wdKey1 (49)	wdKeyF1 (112)	wdKeyNumeric0 (96)
wdKey2 (50)	wdKeyF10 (121)	wdKeyNumeric1 (97)
wdKey3 (51)	wdKeyF11 (122)	wdKeyNumeric2 (98)
wdKey4 (52)	wdKeyF12 (123)	wdKeyNumeric3 (99)
wdKey5 (53)	wdKeyF13 (124)	wdKeyNumeric4 (100)
wdKey6 (54)	wdKeyF14 (125)	wdKeyNumeric5 (101)
wdKey7 (55)	wdKeyF15 (126)	wdKeyNumeric5Special (12)
wdKey8 (56)	wdKeyF16 (127)	wdKeyNumeric6 (102)
wdKey9 (57)	wdKeyF2 (113)	wdKeyNumeric7 (103)
wdKeyA (65)	wdKeyF3 (114)	wdKeyNumeric8 (104)
wdKeyAlt (1024)	wdKeyF4 (115)	wdKeyNumeric9 (105)
wdKeyB (66)	wdKeyF5 (116)	wdKeyNumericAdd (107)
wdKeyBackSingleQuote (192)	wdKeyF6 (117)	wdKeyNumericDecimal (110)
wdKeyBackSlash (220)	wdKeyF7 (118)	wdKeyNumericDivide (111)
wdKeyBackspace (8)	wdKeyF8 (119)	wdKeyNumericMultiply (106)
wdKeyC (67)	wdKeyF9 (120)	wdKeyNumericSubtract (109)
wdKeyCloseSquareBrace (221)	wdKeyG (71)	wdKeyO (79)
wdKeyComma (188)	wdKeyH (72)	wdKeyOpenSquareBrace (219)
wdKeyCommand (512)	wdKeyHome (36)	wdKeyOption (1024)
wdKeyControl (512)	wdKeyHyphen (189)	wdKeyP (80)
wdKeyD (68)	wdKeyI (73)	wdKeyPageDown (34)
wdKeyDelete (46)	wdKeyInsert (45)	wdKeyPageUp (33)
wdKeyE (69)	wdKeyJ (74)	wdKeyPause (19)
wdKeyEnd (35)	wdKeyK (75)	wdKeyPeriod (190)
wdKeyEquals (187)	wdKeyL (76)	wdKeyQ (81)
wdKeyEsc (27)	wdKeyM (77)	wdKeyR (82)

wdKeyReturn (13)	wdKeySlash (191)	wdKeyW (87)
wdKeyS (83)	wdKeySpacebar (32)	wdKeyX (88)
wdKeyScrollLock (145)	wdKeyT (84)	wdKeyY (89)
wdKeySemiColon (186)	wdKeyTab (9)	wdKeyZ (90)
wdKeyShift (256)	wdKeyU (85)	wdNoKey (255)
wdKeySingleQuote (222)	wdKeyV (86)	

Microsoft has been kind enough to supply a global method called *BuildKey-Code* that computes (by addition) the key code for a keystroke combination. The syntax of the *BuildKeyCode* method is:

```
Application.BuildKeyCode(Arg1, Arg2, Arg3, Arg4)
```

where *Arg1* is a required constant, and *Arg2–Arg4* are optional constants from the WdKey enum listed previously.

For example, to return the key code for the F3 key, write:

```
BuildKeyCode(wdKeyF3)
```

which returns the value 114. To return the key code for Alt-Shift-Tab, write:

```
BuildKeyCode(wdKeyAlt, wdKeyShift, wdKeyTab)
```

which returns 1,289 (= 1024 + 256 + 9). In short, *BuildKeyCode* looks up each argument in Table 3 and returns the sum.

The KeyString property

Returns the string version of the key combination for the key binding. For example, if the key code is:

```
BuildKeyCode(wdKeyAlt, wdKeyShift, wdKeyA)
```

then KeyString returns the string "ALT+SHIFT+A". This property is read-only.

The Rebind method

The *Rebind* method changes the command that is currently assigned to the specified key binding. Its syntax is:

```
KeyBinding.Rebind(KeyCategory, Command, CommandParameter)
```

The parameter *KeyCategory* is the key category of the key binding and can be any one of the constants in the following enum:

```
Enum WdKeyCategory
   wdKeyCategoryAutoText = 4
   wdKeyCategoryCommand = 1
   wdKeyCategoryDisable = 0
   wdKeyCategoryFont = 3
   wdKeyCategoryMacro = 2
   wdKeyCategoryNil = -1
   wdKeyCategoryPrefix = 7
   wdKeyCategoryStyle = 5
   wdKeyCategorySymbol = 6
End Enum
```

The *Command* parameter is the name of the new command, and the *Command-Parameter* parameter is the command's parameter, if required.

Finding a Key Binding

If you have a key code combination in mind and are looking for a corresponding key binding, you can use the FindKey property of the Application object or the *Key* method of the KeyBindings or KeysBoundTo collections.

The FindKey property has the syntax:

```
Application.FindKey(KeyCode, KeyCode2)
```

and returns a KeyBinding object that represents the key combination defined by *KeyCode* (required) and *KeyCode2* (optional). It is read-only.

The *Key* method is a method of the KeyBindings or KeysBoundTo collections that also returns a KeyBinding object representing the key combination. If the key combination doesn't exist, this method returns **Nothing**. The syntax is:

```
kb.Key(KeyCode, KeyCode2)
```

where *kb* refers to a KeyBindings or KeysBoundTo object.

The KeysBoundTo Collection

The KeysBoundTo collection is the collection of KeyBinding objects that are assigned to a specific command, style, macro, or other item in the current context. To obtain this collection, you can apply the KeysBoundTo property to the Application object, as follows:

```
Application.KeysBoundTo(KeyCategory, Command, CommandParameter)
```

For example, the following code displays the key combinations assigned to the *FileNew* command in the Normal template:

```
Dim kb as KeyBinding
Dim s as string
CustomizationContext = NormalTemplate
For Each kb In KeysBoundTo(wdKeyCategoryCommand,"FileNew")
    s = s & kb.KeyString & vbCr
Next kb
MsgBox s
```

The KeysBoundTo collection has a Context property that returns the context in which the key bindings are held. Thus, for example, the following code displays the name of the document or template where the shortcut keys for the macro named "Macro1" are stored:

```
Set kb = KeysBoundTo(wdKeyCategoryMacro, "Macro1")
MsgBox kb.Context.Name
```

Example: Listing Key Bindings

In this example, I want to create a program that will list all current key bindings in a table. Also, I want the code to check the active document for text. If it contains text, I should warn the user about this fact and allow him to abort.

I could create the table on the fly, but for variety, I will instead place two bookmarks in the document where the table should begin and end. Then I will convert the text between these bookmarks into a table. The code is shown in Example 18-3.

Example 18-3. Listing All Current Key Bindings

```
Public Sub ListKeyBindings()

Dim kb As KeyBinding
Dim s As String
Dim tbl As Table

' Check active document for text
' and warn user.
If ActiveDocument.Content <> vbCr Then
    If MsgBox("Active doc has content. Proceed?", _
        vbQuestion + vbYesNo) = vbNo Then Exit Sub
End If

' Print Heading
Selection.InsertAfter KeyBindings.Count & _
    " key bindings in context: " & CustomizationContext _
    & vbCr & vbCr

' Collapse selection to end of document
Selection.Collapse wdCollapseEnd

' Insert start of table bookmark
ActiveDocument.Bookmarks.Add "StartOfTable"

' Print table heading
Selection.InsertAfter "KeyString" & vbTab & _
    "KeyCategory" & vbTab & "Command" & vbTab _
    & "KeyCode" & vbTab & "KeyCode2" _
    & vbTab & "CommandParameter" & vbCr

' Start the For loop, printing key binding data
Selection.Collapse wdCollapseEnd
For Each kb In KeyBindings
    s = kb.KeyString & vbTab & kb.KeyCategory _
        & vbTab & kb.Command & vbTab & kb.KeyCode _
        & vbTab & kb.KeyCode2 & vbTab _
        & kb.CommandParameter & vbCr
    Selection.InsertAfter s
    Selection.Collapse wdCollapseEnd
Next kb
```

Example 18-3. Listing All Current Key Bindings (continued)

```
' Collapse selection to end of document
Selection.Collapse wdCollapseEnd

' Insert end of table bookmark
ActiveDocument.Bookmarks.Add "EndOfTable"

' Select text between bookmarks
ActiveDocument.Bookmarks("StartofTable").Select
With Selection
    .ExtendMode = True
.GoTo wdGoToBookmark,,, "EndOfTable"
    .ExtendMode = False
End With

Set tbl = _
    Selection.ConvertToTable(Separator:=wdSeparateByTabs)
tbl.Columns.AutoFit
Selection.Collapse wdCollapseEnd

End Sub
```

In this chapter:
- *The Show Method*
- *The Display and Execute Methods*
- *The DefaultTab Property*
- *The Type Property*
- *The Update Method*
- *Example: Printing Document Statistics*

19

Built-in Dialog Objects

The Word object model contains a Dialog object for each of Word's almost 200 built-in dialog boxes. These Dialog objects are kept in the Dialogs collection and are indexed by the 171 `WdWordDialog` constants:

WdDialogConnect (420)
WdDialogControlRun (235)
WdDialogConvertObject (392)
WdDialogCopyFile (300)
WdDialogCreateAutoText (872)
WdDialogDocumentStatistics (78)
WdDialogDrawAlign (634)
WdDialogDrawSnapToGrid (633)
WdDialogEditAutoText (985)
WdDialogEditCreatePublisher (732)
wdDialogEditFind (112)
wdDialogEditGoTo (896)
wdDialogEditGoToOld (811)
wdDialogEditLinks (124)
wdDialogEditObject (125)
wdDialogEditPasteSpecial (111)
wdDialogEditPublishOptions (735)
wdDialogEditReplace (117)
wdDialogEditSubscribeOptions (736)
wdDialogEditSubscribeTo (733)
wdDialogEditTOACategory (625)
wdDialogFileDocumentLayout (178)
wdDialogFileFind (99)
wdDialogFileMacCustomPageSetupGX (737)
wdDialogFileMacPageSetup (685)
wdDialogFileMacPageSetupGX (444)
wdDialogFileNew (79)
wdDialogFileOpen (80)
wdDialogFilePageSetup (178)
wdDialogFilePrint (88)
wdDialogFilePrintOneCopy (445)

wdDialogFilePrintSetup (97)
wdDialogFileRoutingSlip (624)
wdDialogFileSaveAs (84)
wdDialogFileSaveVersion (1007)
wdDialogFileSummaryInfo (86)
wdDialogFileVersions (945)
wdDialogFontSubstitution (581)
wdDialogFormatAddrFonts (103)
wdDialogFormatBordersAndShading (189)
wdDialogFormatBulletsAndNumbering (824)
wdDialogFormatCallout (610)
wdDialogFormatChangeCase (322)
wdDialogFormatColumns (177)
wdDialogFormatDefineStyleBorders(185)
wdDialogFormatDefineStyleFont (181)
wdDialogFormatDefineStyleFrame(184)
wdDialogFormatDefineStyleLang (186)
wdDialogFormatDefineStylePara (182)
wdDialogFormatDefineStyleTabs (183)
wdDialogFormatDrawingObject (960)
wdDialogFormatDropCap (488)
wdDialogFormatFont (174)
wdDialogFormatFrame (190)
wdDialogFormatPageNumber (298)
wdDialogFormatParagraph (175)
wdDialogFormatPicture (187)
wdDialogFormatRetAddrFonts (221)
wdDialogFormatSectionLayout (176)
wdDialogFormatStyle (180)
wdDialogFormatStyleGallery (505)
wdDialogFormatTabs (179)

wdDialogFormFieldOptions (353)
wdDialogHelpAbout (9)
wdDialogHelpWordPerfectHelp (10)
wdDialogHelpWordPerfectHelpOptions (511)
wdDialogInsertAddCaption (402)
wdDialogInsertAutoCaption (359)
wdDialogInsertBookmark (168)
wdDialogInsertBreak (159)
wdDialogInsertCaption (357)
wdDialogInsertCaptionNumbering(358)
wdDialogInsertCrossReference (367)
wdDialogInsertDatabase (341)
wdDialogInsertDateTime (165)
wdDialogInsertField (166).
wdDialogInsertFile (164)
wdDialogInsertFootnote (370)
wdDialogInsertFormField (483)
wdDialogInsertIndex (170)
wdDialogInsertIndexAndTables (473)
wdDialogInsertMergeField (167)
wdDialogInsertObject (172)
wdDialogInsertPageNumbers (294)
wdDialogInsertPicture (163)
wdDialogInsertSubdocument (583)
wdDialogInsertSymbol (162)
wdDialogInsertTableOfAuthorities (471)
wdDialogInsertTableOfContents (171)
wdDialogInsertTableOfFigures (472)
wdDialogLetterWizard (821)
wdDialogListCommands (723)
wdDialogMailMerge (676)
wdDialogMailMergeCheck (677)
wdDialogMailMergeCreateDataSource (642)
wdDialogMailMergeCreateHeaderSource (643)
wdDialogMailMergeFindRecord (569)
wdDialogMailMergeHelper (680)
wdDialogMailMergeInsertAsk (4047)
wdDialogMailMergeInsertFillIn (4048)
wdDialogMailMergeInsertIf (4049)
wdDialogMailMergeInsertNextIf (4053)
wdDialogMailMergeInsertSet (4054)
wdDialogMailMergeInsertSkipIf (4055)
wdDialogMailMergeOpenDataSource (81)
wdDialogMailMergeOpenHeaderSource (82)
wdDialogMailMergeQueryOptions (681)
wdDialogMailMergeUseAddressBook (779)
wdDialogMarkCitation (463)
wdDialogMarkIndexEntry (169)
wdDialogMarkTableOfContentsEntry (442)
wdDialogNewToolbar (586)
wdDialogNoteOptions (373)
wdDialogOrganizer (222)
wdDialogTableAutoFormat (563)
wdDialogTableDeleteCells (133)
wdDialogTableFormatCell (612)

wdDialogTableFormula (348)
wdDialogTableInsertCells (130)
wdDialogTableInsertRow (131)
wdDialogTableInsertTable (129)
wdDialogTableSort (199)
wdDialogTableSplitCells (137)
wdDialogTableToText (128)
wdDialogTextToTable (127)
wdDialogToolsAcceptRejectChanges (506)
wdDialogToolsAdvancedSettings (206)
wdDialogToolsAutoCorrect (378)
wdDialogToolsAutoCorrectExceptions (762)
wdDialogToolsAutoManager (915)
wdDialogToolsAutoSummarize (874)
wdDialogToolsBulletsNumbers (196)
wdDialogToolsCompareDocuments (198)
wdDialogToolsCreateDirectory (833)
wdDialogToolsCreateEnvelope (173)
wdDialogToolsCreateLabels (489)
wdDialogToolsCustomize (152)
wdDialogToolsCustomizeKeyboard (432)
wdDialogToolsCustomizeMenuBar (615)
wdDialogToolsCustomizeMenus (433)
wdDialogToolsEnvelopesAndLabels (607)
wdDialogToolsHighlightChanges (197)
wdDialogToolsHyphenation (195)
wdDialogToolsLanguage (188)
wdDialogToolsMacro (215)
wdDialogToolsMacroRecord (214)
wdDialogToolsManageFields (631)
wdDialogToolsMergeDocuments (435)
wdDialogToolsOptions (974)
wdDialogToolsOptionsAutoFormat (959)
wdDialogToolsOptionsCompatibility (525)
wdDialogToolsOptionsEdit (224)
wdDialogToolsOptionsFileLocations (225)
wdDialogToolsOptionsGeneral (203)
wdDialogToolsOptionsPrint (208)
wdDialogToolsOptionsSave (209)
wdDialogToolsOptionsSpellingAndGrammar (211)
wdDialogToolsOptionsTrackChanges (386)
wdDialogToolsOptionsUserInfo (213)
wdDialogToolsOptionsView (204)
wdDialogToolsProtectDocument (503)
wdDialogToolsProtectSection (578)
wdDialogToolsRevisions (197)
wdDialogToolsSpellingAndGrammar (828)
wdDialogToolsTemplates (87)
wdDialogToolsThesaurus (194)
wdDialogToolsUnprotectDocument (521)
wdDialogToolsWordCount (228)
wdDialogUpdateTOC (331)
wdDialogViewZoom (577)
wdDialogWindowActivate (220)

As we will see, Dialog objects gives us *programmatic* access to Word's built-in dialog boxes. This enables us to not only set some of the values in a Word dialog box before the user sees it, but also to retrieve values from the user. For instance, in order to ask the user for a font name, it is easier to display the Format Font dialog box than to create a custom dialog box and fill it with all available font names. (You will see an example of this soon.)

For example, the Open dialog box in Figure 19-1 is:

```
Dialogs(wdDialogFileOpen)
```

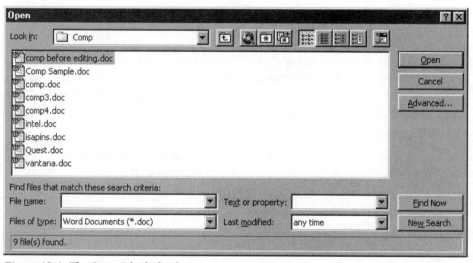

Figure 19-1. The Open File dialog box

You can access and set many of the controls on the Word dialog boxes by using named arguments. These arguments are listed in the Word VBA help file under "Built-in Word dialog boxes." For instance, the **wdDialogDocumentStatistics** dialog box has the following named arguments:

FileName	LastSavedBy	Words
Directory	Revision	Characters
Template	Time	Paragraphs
Title	Printed	Lines
Created	Pages	FileSize
LastSaved		

Hence, the following code displays the date and time that the active document was last saved:

```
MsgBox Dialogs(wdDialogDocumentStatistics).LastSaved
```

At the end of this chapter, I present an application that creates a new document containing the statistics for a given document.

The following sections explain some of the most useful properties and methods of the Dialog object.

The Show Method

The *Show* method displays a dialog box. Moreover, when the dialog box is dismissed, *any appropriate actions indicated by the fields in the dialog box are carried out.* Thus, it is the *Show* method that makes Dialog objects useful to the Word programmer, for it provides a method not only to get user input, but also to perform various actions with very little coding. (You will see an example of this soon.) Note that no actions are taken if the user dismisses the dialog box using the Cancel button.

The *Show* method has the syntax:

```
DialogBoxObject.Show(TimeOut)
```

where `DialogBoxObject` refers to a Dialog object. The parameter `TimeOut` is an optional variant that represents the amount of time, in approximate milliseconds, the dialog box will remain displayed before automatically closing. If `TimeOut` is missing, the dialog box remains displayed until the user dismisses it by clicking a command button.

The return value of the *Show* method indicates which button was used to dismiss the dialog box. The possible values are shown in Table 19-1.

Table 19-1. Return Values for the Show Method

Return Value	Meaning
−2	Close button
−1	OK button or a timeout
0	Cancel button
> 0	Command button (1 = first button, 2 = second button, etc.)

To illustrate, the following code opens the Find dialog box with its Match Case box checked and then responds appropriately when the user selects a button:

```
Dim dial As Dialog
Set dial = Dialogs(wdDialogEditFind)
dial.MatchCase = True
dial.Show
```

The Display and Execute Methods

The *Display* method has syntax:

```
DialogBox.Display(TimeOut)
```

and differs from the *Show* method in only one way: after the dialog box is dismissed, no actions are taken. This method is used to prompt the user with a dialog box.

Note that if the user makes any changes in a dialog box while it is displayed, these changes will not be applied unless we use the *Execute* method. For instance, the following code displays the Font formatting dialog box. Once the user has dismissed the dialog, it checks to see if the font was changed to Tahoma. If so, it asks the user if she is sure and then either makes the change or discards it:

```
Dim dial As Dialog
Set dial = Dialogs(wdDialogFormatFont)
dial.Display
If dial.Font = "Tahoma" Then
    If MsgBox("You have selected Tahoma. Are you sure?", _
        vbYesNo) = vbYes Then
        dial.Execute
    End If
Else
    dial.Execute
End If
```

The DefaultTab Property

This property returns or sets the active tab when a dialog box is displayed. Its value can be any of the **WdWordDialogTab** constants:

wdDialogFilePageSetupTabLayout
wdDialogFilePageSetupTabMargins
wdDialogFilePageSetupTabPaperSize
wdDialogFilePageSetupTabPaperSource
wdDialogFormatBordersAndShadingTabBorders
wdDialogFormatBordersAndShadingTabPageBorder
wdDialogFormatBordersAndShadingTabShading
wdDialogFormatBulletsAndNumberingTabBulleted
wdDialogFormatBulletsAndNumberingTabNumbered
wdDialogFormatBulletsAndNumberingTab-
    OutlineNumbered
wdDialogFormatDrawingObjectTabColorsAndLines
wdDialogFormatDrawingObjectTabPicture
wdDialogFormatDrawingObjectTabPosition
wdDialogFormatDrawingObjectTabSize
wdDialogFormatDrawingObjectTabTextbox
wdDialogFormatDrawingObjectTabWrapping
wdDialogFormatFontTabAnimation
wdDialogFormatFontTabCharacterSpacing
wdDialogFormatFontTabFont
wdDialogFormatParagraphTabIndentsAndSpacing
wdDialogFormatParagraphTabTextFlow
wdDialogInsertIndexAndTablesTabIndex
wdDialogInsertIndexAndTablesTabTableOfAuthorities
wdDialogInsertIndexAndTablesTabTableOfContents
wdDialogInsertIndexAndTablesTabTableOfFigures
wdDialogInsertSymbolTabSpecialCharacters
wdDialogInsertSymbolTabSymbols

wdDialogLetterWizardTabLetterFormat
wdDialogLetterWizardTabOtherElements
wdDialogLetterWizardTabRecipientInfo
wdDialogLetterWizardTabSenderInfo
wdDialogNoteOptionsTabAllEndnotes
wdDialogNoteOptionsTabAllFootnotes
wdDialogOrganizerTabAutoText
wdDialogOrganizerTabCommandBars
wdDialogOrganizerTabMacros
wdDialogOrganizerTabStyles
wdDialogToolsAutoCorrectExceptionsTabFirstLetter
wdDialogToolsAutoCorrectExceptionsTabInitialCaps
wdDialogToolsAutoManagerTabAutoCorrect
wdDialogToolsAutoManagerTabAutoFormat
wdDialogToolsAutoManagerTabAutoFormatAsYouType
wdDialogToolsAutoManagerTabAutoText
wdDialogToolsEnvelopesAndLabelsTabEnvelopes
wdDialogToolsEnvelopesAndLabelsTabLabels
wdDialogToolsOptionsTabCompatibility
wdDialogToolsOptionsTabEdit
wdDialogToolsOptionsTabFileLocations
wdDialogToolsOptionsTabGeneral
wdDialogToolsOptionsTabPrint
wdDialogToolsOptionsTabProofread
WdDialogToolsOptionsTabSave
WdDialogToolsOptionsTabTrackChanges
WdDialogToolsOptionsTabUserInfo
WdDialogToolsOptionsTabView

The Type Property

The Type property is a read-only property that returns a Long representing the `WdWordDialog` constant in the list earlier in this chapter that corresponds to the given Dialog object.

The Update Method

The *Update* method simply updates the values in a dialog box. This is useful if we assign a variable of type Dialog to a Dialog object and then subsequently one of the settings in the Dialog box is changed. To illustrate, the following code first assigns the `dial` variable to the Font Dialog object. Then it changes the current font for the selected text. At this point, the Dialog object pointed to by `dial` is not updated to reflect the new font. The *Update* method updates this object:

```
Dim dial as Dialog
Set dial = Dialogs(wdDialogFormatFont)
. . .
Selection.Font.Name = "Arial"
. . .
dial.Update
dial.Show
```

By the way, it is not entirely clear what is going on behind the scenes here. For if you insert the following code immediately after the `Selection.Font.Name` line:

```
Set dial2 = Dialogs(wdDialogFormatFont)
dial2.Display
dial.Display
```

you will see a dialog box (the one referred to by `dial2`) that shows the new font, followed by a dialog box (referred to by `dial`) that shows the old font. Thus, there appear to be two distinct Dialog objects with index `wdDialogFormatFont`—one pointed to by `dial` and one pointed to by `dial2`!

In any case, I can say for sure that whenever we need to rely on current information from a variable of type Dialog, it is important to first call the *Update* method.

Example: Printing Document Statistics

I will now present the application mentioned earlier. In particular, the code in Example 19-1 gathers statistics about the active document and places that data in a table in a new document. The only point to note is that I must reference the Dialog object *before* creating a new document, since that new document will become the active document and I will lose the statistics on the original document.

Example 19-1. The PrintStatistics Routine

```
Sub PrintStatistics()
' Prints statistics on the active document
' to a table in a new document
Dim dial As dialog
Dim tbl As Table
Dim sName As String
Dim sProp As String

' Get this now, before the active document changes
Set dial = Dialogs(wdDialogDocumentStatistics)

' Create new document
Documents.Add

' Insert document heading
Selection.InsertAfter "Document Statistics.  Created " & _
    Now() & vbCr & vbCr
' Give it a nice style
Selection.Style = wdStyleHeading1
Selection.Collapse wdCollapseEnd

' Create a table with 2 columns
Set tbl = ActiveDocument.Tables.Add(Range:=Selection.Range, NumRows:=1 _
        NumColumns:=2)

' Print the document statistics to the table
' adding rows as we go
tbl.Cell(1, 1).Select

Selection.Text = "File Name"
Selection.Font.Bold = True
Selection.Move wdCell
Selection.Text = dial.FileName

' DoNextRow adds a new row and
' fills it with the next piece of data
DoNextRow tbl, "Directory", dial.Directory
DoNextRow tbl, "Template", dial.Template
DoNextRow tbl, "Title", dial.Title
DoNextRow tbl, "Created", dial.Created
DoNextRow tbl, "LastSaved", dial.LastSaved
DoNextRow tbl, "LastSavedBy", dial.LastSavedBy
DoNextRow tbl, "Revision", dial.Revision
DoNextRow tbl, "Time", dial.Time
DoNextRow tbl, "Printed", dial.Printed
DoNextRow tbl, "Pages", dial.Pages
DoNextRow tbl, "Words", dial.Words
DoNextRow tbl, "Characters", dial.Characters
DoNextRow tbl, "Paragraphs", dial.Paragraphs
DoNextRow tbl, "Lines", dial.Lines
DoNextRow tbl, "FileSize", dial.FileSize
```

Example 19-1. The PrintStatistics Routine (continued)

```
tbl.Columns.AutoFit

End Sub


Private Sub DoNextRow(uTable As Table, _
    sName As String, sProp As String)


uTable.Rows.Add
Selection.Move wdCell
Selection.Text = sName
Selection.Font.Bold = True
Selection.Move wdCell
Selection.Text = sProp

End Sub
```

The outcome of this macro on the manuscript for this book is as follows:

File Name	Word.doc
Directory	D:\word
Template	D:\wordmacs97\CSBOOKS.DOT
Title	Programming Microsoft Word
Created	04/09/98 10:29 PM
LastSaved	05/18/98 2:27 PM
LastSavedBy	sr
Revision	2,732
Time	8,271 Minutes
Printed	05/10/98 1:37 PM
Pages	351
Words	77,724
Characters	404,168
Paragraphs	7,924
Lines	13,936
FileSize	1,767,424 Bytes

Incidentally, you could expand this code to include document properties that are available from the DocumentProperties collection of the Microsoft Office object model. (For this, you'd have to add a reference to the Microsoft Office 8.0 object library by opening the References dialog from the Tools menu.) I will leave the details of this to you, but just mention that the following code will print the built-in document properties of the active document to the Immediate window:

```
Dim d As DocumentProperty
On Error Resume Next
```

```
For Each d In ActiveDocument.BuiltInDocumentProperties
    Debug.Print d.Name & " - " & d.Value
Next
```

The reason for the **On Error** line in this code is the following: Word does not support all of the built-in document properties in the BuiltInDocumentProperties collection (remember that this is an Office object, not a Word object). Moreover, Word will interrupt the previous code with an error message when it comes to a property that it does not support. The line:

```
On Error Resume Next
```

tells Word to continue even when it encounters an error.

The output from this program on the manuscript for this book is shown in Example 19-2.

Example 19-2. Information from the Office DocumentProperties Collection

```
Title - Programming Microsoft Word
Subject - Programming Micrsoft Word
Author - Dr. Steven Roman
Keywords - Word, Programming
Comments - No comments
Template - Csbooks.dot
Last author - sr
Revision number - 2730
Application name - Microsoft Word 8.0
Last print date - 5/10/98 1:37:00 PM
Creation date - 4/9/98 10:29:00 PM
Last save time - 5/18/98 2:20:00 PM
Total editing time - 8267
Number of pages - 351
Number of words - 78431
Number of characters - 409648
Security - 0
Category - Book
Format -
Manager - Me
Company - None
Number of bytes - 1763328
Number of lines - 13919
Number of paragraphs - 7988
Hyperlink base -
Number of characters (with spaces) - 483352
```

20

In this chapter:
- *What Is a UserForm Object?*
- *Example: Adding a Closing to a Letter*
- *Example: A Fax Cover Sheet*
- *Example: Quick Selection*

Custom Dialog Boxes

Not only does Word have a large number of built-in dialog boxes for gathering user input, but Word also makes it possible to create custom dialog boxes to communicate with the user.

Custom dialog boxes are also called forms or UserForms. My intention here is to present an introduction to the subject, which will provide a good jumping-off point for further study.

Generally speaking, most Word applications will require only very simple forms (if any). For example, you might want to display a form with a text box for text input or some option buttons to select from several choices and some command buttons to execute procedures.

Actually, Microsoft's Visual Basic is a more appropriate programming environment than Microsoft Office for creating applications that involve complex forms, since it was designed specifically for that purpose. (Also, it is possible to access any of the Office object models from within Visual Basic.)

What Is a UserForm Object?

A UserForm object can be thought of as a standard code module with a visual interface (a form) that is used to interact with the user (hence the term User-Form). However, you must be a bit careful not to take this description too literally. For instance, procedures (even public ones) that are declared in the General section of a UserForm module are generally intended to support objects (or code) on the form itself, whereas public procedures declared in a standard module are generally intended to support code anywhere in the project (not just in their own module).

To illustrate the point, suppose you declare a public procedure called *ProcedureA* in the General section of a UserForm module called UserForm1. Even though this procedure is public, you cannot access it from another module (even within the same project) by simply writing:

```
ProcedureA
```

as you could if the procedure was defined within a standard module. Instead, you must use the qualified name:

```
UserForm1.ProcedureA
```

Creating a UserForm Object

To create a user form at design time, just select the project in which the form will reside and choose UserForm from the Insert menu. (Forms can be created at run time using the *Add* method of the UserForms collection, but I limit the focus here to creating forms at design time.)

Figure 20-1 shows the design environment when a UserForm object is selected in the Project window. Note that the window on the top right in Figure 20-1 contains the dialog box, where I have placed a text box control and two command button controls. There is also a floating Toolbox window that contains icons used to add various controls to the form.

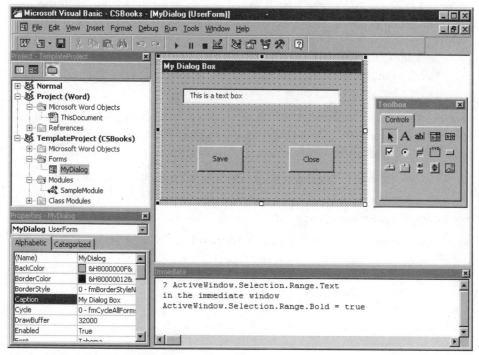

Figure 20-1. A UserForm dialog box

To place a control on a form, simply click on the icon in the Toolbox and then drag a rectangle on the form. This rectangle is replaced by the control. We can change the properties of the form itself (or of any controls on the form) by selecting the object and making the changes in the Properties window. (Note the change to the form's caption in Figure 20-1, which was done by modifying the form's Caption property.)

Windows Controls

If you have been using Microsoft Windows for some time (as we presume you have, since you are reading this book), then you are quite familiar with controls at the user level. The following are examples of controls:

> Command buttons
> Text boxes
> List boxes
> Combo boxes
> Option buttons
> Checkboxes
> Labels
> Tabs
> Scrollbars

All of the controls listed here have a visual interface for interaction with the user. However, some controls do not have a visual interface. One example is the Timer control, which can be set to fire an event at regular intervals. Thus, the programmer can write code that will execute at regular intervals. (I discussed the concept of an event in the section on the Open, Close, and New events for a document or template in Chapter 3, *The Visual Basic Editor, Part I.*)

Generally speaking, a control (full name: ActiveX control) can be thought of as a special type of code component that can be placed within a larger container object (such as a form) and that has the following properties:

- Controls generally (but not always) provide a visual interface for communication with the user.

- Controls have methods that can be invoked by the user.

- Controls have properties that can be read and set by the user.

- Controls have events for which the user can write event code.

Adding UserForm Code

In general, the VBA programmer adds two types of code to a UserForm module: event code that underlies the various controls on the form (and perhaps the form itself) and additional procedures that perform utility functions needed by the application. The latter code is added to the general section of the UserForm code module.

To illustrate the point with a very simple example, suppose you want to create an application that sorts selected text. Your form might look something like the one shown in Figure 20-2.

Figure 20-2. A sort dialog box

When the user clicks the Sort button, you will ask him to confirm the sort operation and then act accordingly.

Now, when the Sort button is selected by the user, VBA fires the Click event for this button. If the button is named *cmdSort*, then VBA provides the event code shell:

```
Private Sub cmdSort_Click()

End Sub
```

Clearly, you want to perform the sorting operation when this event is fired. However, it would not be a good idea to place the actual code to perform the sort in this event code shell. Instead, you write a separate sorting procedure to do the sorting and place it in the General section of the UserForm module or perhaps make it a public procedure in a separate standard code module within the project, as follows:

```
Public Sub SortText(SortMethod As String)
    ' code here to sort text
End Sub
```

There are several reasons why it is better to place the sorting code in a separate procedure. This code modularity makes it easier to:

- Use the code in other locations in the application
- Move the code to other applications

- Find and repair bugs in the code
- Make improvements or additions to the code
- Just plain read the code

Once the sorting procedure is complete, you can add the following code to the Click event:

```
Private Sub cmdSort_Click()

If MsgBox("Sort currently selected text?", _
    vbQuestion + vbYesNo) = vbYes Then SortText

End Sub
```

Incidentally, the Click event for the Cancel button is often just the following:

```
Private Sub cmdCancel_Click()
    Unload Me
End Sub
```

All this does is unload the form.

Example: Adding a Closing to a Letter

Perhaps the best way to get a feel for creating and using UserForm objects is to go through some examples, which I suggest that you follow along with on your PC. In this example, we create an application that inserts an ending in a Word letter. There are three types of endings: friendly, formal, and hostile. We want the user to be able to select between these three alternatives and click a command button to automatically insert the ending. We also want the user to be able to type in a name in a text box. This name will be used in the ending as well. (In this way, more than one user can use the application.)

Add a UserForm Object and Set Its Properties

The first step is to choose the project in which to place the UserForm object. The most logical choice would be a template that is used for writing letters, or, if no such template exists, then the project for the Normal template, making the form available to all documents.

Once you've chosen the template in which your code will reside, switch to the VBA Editor, select the desired project, and use the Insert menu to add a UserForm to the project. Once the form is visible (as in Figure 20-1), we can make use of the Properties window to make the changes shown in Table 20-1 to its properties.

Table 20-1. Nondefault UserForm Properties

Property	Value
Name	frmLetterEnding
Caption	Letter Ending
StartUpPosition	CenterScreen

Add Controls to the Form

The next step is to place a few controls on the form. (See Figure 20-3 for the form with its controls.) We want to use option buttons for the ending type. Option buttons must be enclosed within a frame control so they can work together; that is, so that when one option button is selected, the others are deselected automatically. Place the frame control on the form and set its properties as shown in Table 20-2.

Table 20-2. Nondefault Properties of the Frame Control

Property	Value
Name	fraType
Caption	Choose Type of Ending

Next, we must add the option buttons to the inside of the frame. Make sure that the frame is selected, click the Option Button icon on the Toolbox, and drag a small rectangle within the Frame control. Position the option button to the left side of the frame. (You can adjust the size of the form itself and all of its controls using the mouse.) Set the properties of the option button as shown in Table 20-3. Note the Accelerator property listed in Table 20-3: it defines the accelerator key, which is used in combination with the Alt key to toggle the state of the option button.

Table 20-3. Nondefault Properties of the Friendly Option Button

Property	Value
Name	optFriendly
Caption	Friendly
Accelerator	F
AutoSize	True

To add the other two option buttons, you can select *optFriendly* and choose Copy from the Edit menu. Then make sure that the frame is selected and choose Paste. You will get a new option button whose properties are identical to *optFriendly* except for its name. (In particular, it has the same size as the previous control.) Set the properties of the new option button as shown in Table 20-4.

Table 20-4. Nondefault Properties of the Formal Option Button

Property	Value
Name	optFormal
Caption	Formal
Accelerator	R

Finally, do the same for the third option button, setting its properties as shown in Table 20-5.

Table 20-5. Nondefault Properties of the Hostile Option Button

Property	Value
Name	optHostile
Caption	Hostile
Accelerator	H

Next, use the menu items under the Format menu to arrange the three option buttons nicely:

1. Select one option button by clicking on it, and then select the other two by clicking on them while pressing the Ctrl key. When you're finished, all three option buttons should be selected.

2. Use the Align menu option to align the option buttons in the middle.

3. Use the Horizontal Spacing option to give the buttons equal horizontal spacing.

The next step is to add a Label control. Position the control as in Figure 20-3 and change its properties as shown in Table 20-6.

Table 20-6. Nondefault Properties of the Label Control

Property	Value
Name	lblName
Caption	Name
Accelerator	N

Then add a Textbox control, position it as in Figure 20-3, and change its Name property to *txtName*. Add two command buttons, position them as in Figure 20-3, and set their properties as shown in Table 20-7.

Finally, we must check the TabIndex properties of each control. This integer property determines the tab order, which is the order that the controls receive the focus

Table 20-7. Nondefault Properties of the CommandButton Controls

Property	First Button	Second Button
Name	cmdAddEnding	cmdCancel
Caption	Add Ending	Cancel
Accelerator	A	C

as we repeatedly hit the Tab key. Since we created the controls in order, the tab index should be fine. However, there are two points to check. First, the control with tab index 0 gets the focus when the form is first loaded. We don't care too much about that in this example, since all controls are reachable via an accelerator key.

The second issue is much more important. The purpose of giving a label control an accelerator key is to be able to activate the control associated with the label—in this case, the text box control *txtName*. (A label control cannot receive the focus.) For this to happen, the tab index of *txtName* must be one greater than the tab index of the label *lblName*.

Your finished form should resemble the form shown in Figure 20-3.

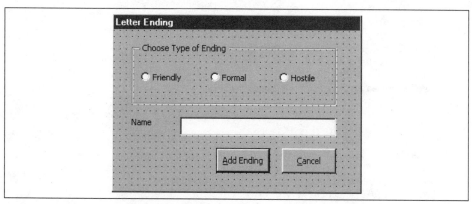

Figure 20-3. Letter Ending custom dialog box

Add Code to the Form

Now that the form is properly populated with controls, we can add the code that underlies the form. To add code to an event associated with a control, just double-click the control to raise the code window. Then use the Procedures list box at the top of the code window to select the event to which you want to add code.

The code for the Click event of the Cancel button, which is shown in Example 20-1, simply unloads the form.

Example 20-1. The Cancel Button's Click Event Procedure

```
Private Sub cmdCancel_Click()
   Unload Me
End Sub
```

The code for the Click event of the AddEnding button, which is shown in Example 20-2, calls the *AddEnding* procedure, which does all of the work in this application. The *AddEnding* procedure is shown in Example 20-3.

Example 20-2. The Add Ending Button's Click Event Procedure

```
Private Sub cmdAddEnding_Click()
   AddEnding
End Sub
```

Example 20-3. The AddEnding Procedure

```
Sub AddEnding()

   Dim rng As Range        ' for text insertion
   Dim sText As String     ' text to insert

   ' Check to see if text box is empty
   ' If so, warn user and exit
   If txtName.Text = "" Then
      MsgBox "Please fill in your name."
      Exit Sub
   End If

   ' Compose text based on ending type
   If optFriendly.Value = True Then

      sText = "Thanks a lot."
      sText = sText & vbCrLf & vbCrLf & "Catch you later,"
      sText = sText & vbCrLf & vbCrLf & vbCrLf & txtName

   ElseIf optFormal.Value = True Then

      sText = "Thank you for your cooperation."
      sText = sText & vbCrLf & vbCrLf & "Yours truly,"
      sText = sText & vbCrLf & vbCrLf & vbCrLf & txtName

   ElseIf optHostile.Value = True Then

      sText = "Bugger off."
      sText = sText & vbCrLf & vbCrLf & "Sincerely,"
      sText = sText & vbCrLf & vbCrLf & vbCrLf & txtName

   Else

      ' No option chosen, warn the user and exit
      MsgBox "Please check an ending type."
```

Example 20-3. The AddEnding Procedure (continued)

```
    Exit Sub

End If

' Insert the text, preceded by 2 paragraph marks
Set rng = ActiveDocument.Range
rng.Collapse wdCollapseEnd
rng.Text = vbCr & vbCr & sText

End Sub
```

Activating the Application

Now that we have completed our application, we need a convenient way to activate it from a Word document. For this, we simply create a macro. That is, we create a new standard module, called *LetterEnding*, that contains the code in Example 20-4.

Example 20-4. The LetterEnding Routine to Invoke the frmLetterEnding

```
Sub LetterEnding()
   frmLetterEnding.Show
End Sub
```

Now when we invoke this macro, it will display the `frmLetterEnding` dialog box. (The *Show* method of a form simply displays that form.) Of course, we can attach the macro to a custom menu item or command button on a toolbar. (I discuss how to do this programmatically in Chapter 21, *Menus and Toolbars.*)

Example: A Fax Cover Sheet

A little programming makes it easy to automate the process of creating fax cover sheets. In particular, we want a dialog box that opens automatically whenever the user creates a new document based on the fax cover sheet template, so we will include the UserForm module in this template's project.

The first step is to create the template, as shown in Figure 20-4. Note that I have placed bookmarks in some of the table cells, as indicated by the words (Bkm) in Figure 20-4. (These words are not meant to be in the actual document, but are there to indicate where the bookmarks are placed.) These bookmarks are used by our code to place additional text. Their names are (from top to bottom in Figure 20-4) To, ToCompany, ToPhone, ToFax, Pages, Re, and Comments.

In order to get the form to open automatically when a new document is created, place code to execute the *Show* method of the form in the Document_New event for the template, as Example 20-5 shows.

Example 20-5. Inovking the Fax User Form

```
Private Sub Document_New()
    frmFaxCover.Show
End Sub
```

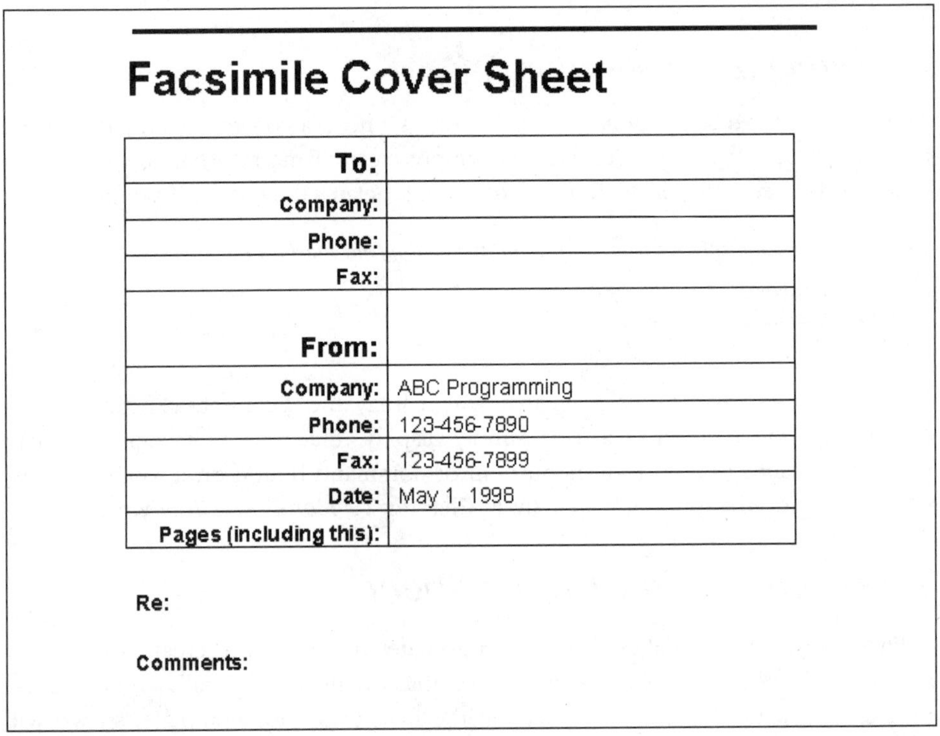

Facsimile Cover Sheet

To:	
Company:	
Phone:	
Fax:	
From:	
Company:	ABC Programming
Phone:	123-456-7890
Fax:	123-456-7899
Date:	May 1, 1998
Pages (including this):	

Re:

Comments:

Figure 20-4. A fax cover sheet

The dialog box is shown in Figure 20-5. Its controls and their non-default properties are shown in Table 20-8.

Table 20-8. Controls and Their Nondefault Properties for the Fax Cover Sheet

Control	Property	Value
UserForm	Name	frmFAXCover
	Caption	Fax
Frame	Caption	To:
Label	Accelerator	N
	Caption	Name:

Table 20-8. Controls and Their Nondefault Properties for the Fax Cover Sheet (continued)

Control	Property	Value
TextBox	Name	txtToName
Label	Accelerator	C
	Caption	Company:
TextBox	Name	txtToCompany
Label	Accelerator	P
	Caption	Phone:
TextBox	Name	txtToPhone
Label	Accelerator	F
	Caption	Fax:
TextBox	Name	txtToFax
Label	Accelerator	O
	Caption	From:
TextBox	Name	txtFromName
Label	Accelerator	R
	Caption	Re:
TextBox	Name	txtRe
Label	Accelerator	A
	Caption	Pages (including this one):
TextBox	Name	txtPages
CommandButton	Name	cmdOK
	Caption	OK
	Default	True
CommandButton	Name	cmdCancel
	Caption	Cancel
	Cancel	True
CommandButton	Name	cmdClear
	Accelerator	C
	Caption	Clear Fields

After the user has filled in the controls in the fax dialog box and hit the OK button, our code places the filled-in text in the appropriate locations in the document, using the predefined bookmarks. Example 20-6 contains is the entire code for the fax application.

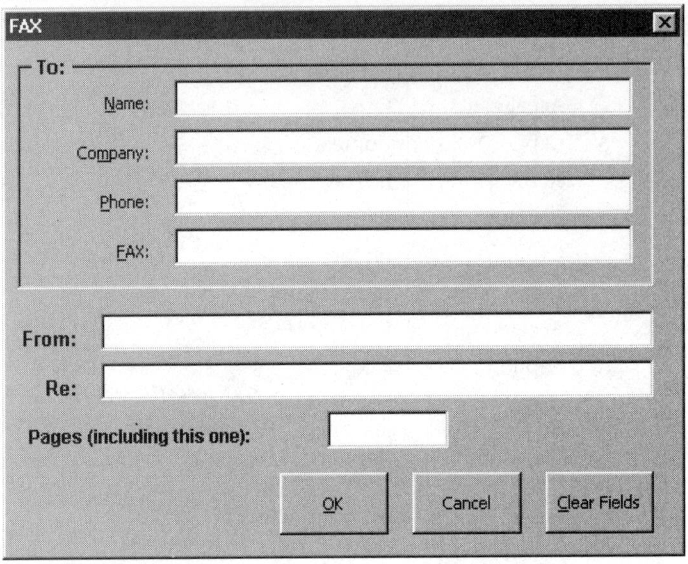

Figure 20-5. The fax dialog box

Example 20-6. Code for the Fax Application

```
Private Sub cmdCancel_Click()
    Unload Me
End Sub

Private Sub cmdClear_Click()
    txtFromName = ""
    txtToName = ""
    txtToCompany = ""
    txtToPhone = ""
    txtToFax = ""
    txtRe = ""
    txtPages = ""
End Sub

Private Sub cmdOK_Click()
    Dim rng As Range

    Set rng = ActiveDocument.Bookmarks("To").Range
    rng.InsertAfter txtToName

    Set rng = ActiveDocument.Bookmarks("ToCompany").Range
    rng.InsertAfter txtToCompany

    Set rng = ActiveDocument.Bookmarks("ToPhone").Range
    rng.InsertAfter txtToPhone

    Set rng = ActiveDocument.Bookmarks("ToFax").Range
```

Example 20-6. Code for the Fax Application (continued)

```
    rng.InsertAfter txtToFax

    Set rng = ActiveDocument.Bookmarks("From").Range
    rng.InsertAfter txtFromName

    Set rng = ActiveDocument.Bookmarks("Re").Range
    rng.InsertAfter txtRe

    Set rng = ActiveDocument.Bookmarks("Pages").Range
    rng.InsertAfter txtPages

    Selection.GoTo What:=wdGoToBookmark, Name:="Comments"

    Unload Me
End Sub
```

Example: Quick Selection

In this example, we create a simple but useful item selection program. The purpose of this program is to make selecting an item such as a word, sentence, line, paragraph, field, column, or table as easy as possible.

In particular, by pressing a hotkey (I use Alt-S), the dialog box in Figure 20-6 will appear. While this dialog box is showing, a single key (no need even to use the Alt key) will make a selection. For instance, striking the S key will select (highlight) the sentence that contains the insertion point.

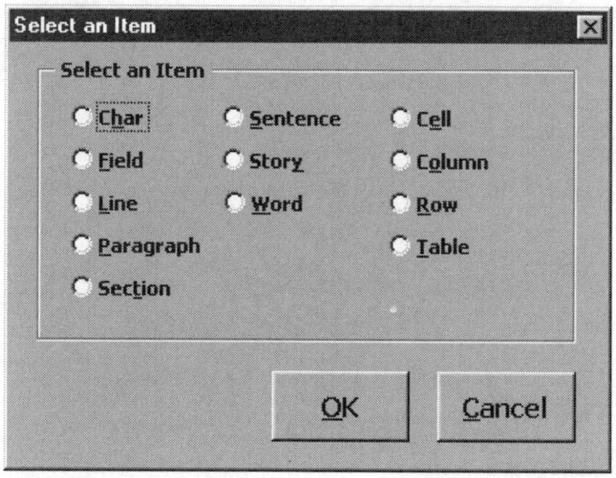

Figure 20-6. Select an Item dialog box

The form is similar in design to the form used in the letter closing example, so I will leave the details to you. The entire code is listed in Example 20-7.

Example 20-7. Source Code for the Select an Item Dialog Box

```
Private Sub cmdCancel_Click()
   Unload Me
End Sub

Private Sub cmdOK_Click()
Dim fld As Field
If optItemCell Then
   Selection.Expand wdCell
ElseIf optItemCharacter Then
   Selection.Expand wdCharacter
ElseIf optItemColumn Then
   Selection.Expand wdColumn
ElseIf optItemField Then
   For Each fld In ActiveDocument.Fields
      If Selection.Range.InRange(fld.Result) Then
         fld.Select
         Exit For
      End If
   Next
ElseIf optItemLine Then
   Selection.Expand wdLine
ElseIf optItemParagraph Then
   Selection.Expand wdParagraph
ElseIf optItemRow Then
   Selection.Expand wdRow
ElseIf optItemSection Then
   Selection.Expand wdSection
ElseIf optItemSentence Then
   Selection.Expand wdSentence
ElseIf optItemStory Then
   Selection.Expand wdStory
ElseIf optItemTable Then
   Selection.Expand wdTable
ElseIf optItemWord Then
   Selection.Expand wdWord
End If
Unload Me
End Sub

Private Sub cmdOK_KeyPress(ByVal KeyAscii As MSForms.ReturnInteger)
Dim fld As Field
Select Case Chr$(KeyAscii)
   Case "e", "E"
      Selection.Expand wdCell
   Case "h", "H"
      Selection.Expand wdCharacter
   Case "o", "O"
      Selection.Expand wdColumn
   Case "f", "F"
      For Each fld In ActiveDocument.Fields
         If Selection.Range.InRange(fld.Result) Then
            fld.Select
```

Example 20-7. Source Code for the Select an Item Dialog Box (continued)

```
            Exit For
        End If
     Next
   Case "l", "L"
       Selection.Expand wdLine
   Case "p", "P"
       Selection.Expand wdParagraph
   Case "r", "R"
       Selection.Expand wdRow
   Case "i", "I"
       Selection.Expand wdSection
   Case "s", "S"
       Selection.Expand wdSentence
   Case "y", "Y"
       Selection.Expand wdStory
   Case "t", "T"
       Selection.Expand wdTable
   Case "w", "W"
       Selection.Expand wdWord
End Select
Unload Me
End Sub
```

The first thing to observe is that almost all selecting is done simply with the *Expand* method of the Selection object. However, there is no constant (such as **wdField**) for expanding to the Field object that contains the current selection, so I had to write a bit more code, to wit:

```
For Each fld In ActiveDocument.Fields
    If Selection.Range.InRange(fld.Result) Then
        fld.Select
        Exit For
    End If
Next
```

This **For** loop simply cycles through all Field objects in the document, looking for the one whose Result Range object contains the current selection's Range object. It then selects this field.

The OK button's Click event looks for an option button that is selected and then executes the appropriate code (usually the *Expand* method). For this to work, the user must use an Alt-key combination, such as Alt-W, to select an option button.

However, we want to spare the user the need to involve the Alt key. This is done by using the KeyPress event of the OK button. The KeyPress event for a control is fired whenever a key is pressed and the control has the focus. By assigning the OK button a tab index of 0, we ensure that this control gets the focus when the form is initially made visible. Hence, its KeyPress event will fire.

Within this event, simply place a `Select Case` statement to deal with the possible keystrokes. Note that the KeyPress event has a parameter called *KeyAscii* that gives the ASCII value of the key pressed. I use the *Chr* function to convert the ASCII value to a character. This makes the program more readable.

As an aside, note that the KeyPress event responds to ordinary alphanumeric keys. To write code that will fire when the user strikes other types of keys, such as the arrow keys, use the KeyDown event.

Finally, we want to be able to display this dialog box quickly and easily from within Word by pressing a hotkey (such as Alt-S). This can be done by creating a macro whose sole purpose is to invoke the *Show* method of the form. If the form has been named `frmSelectItem`, then the following code will do the job:

```
Sub SelectItem()
    frmSelectItem.Show
End Sub
```

Then use Word's Customize Keyboard dialog box to assign a hotkey to this macro.

21

Menus and Toolbars

In this chapter, I discuss methods for programmatically controlling menus and toolbars. Even though the subject of menus and toolbars is fairly straightforward, it can seem very confusing, especially since the documentation (from Microsoft and others) is, in my opinion, very unenlightening. Let me see if I can clarify the subject.

An Overview

Actually, Word's menu and toolbar objects do not belong to the Word object model. Instead, the menus and toolbars throughout Microsoft Office belong to the Office object model. The portion of the Office object model that relates to menus and toolbars is actually quite small, containing only two objects and their corresponding collections:

- CommandBar objects and CommandBars collections

- CommandBarControl objects and CommandBarControls collections

To help set the notation, Figure 21-1 shows the components of the Office menu structure.

Toolbars, menubars, menus, submenus, and shortcut menus (which are menus that pop up at various locations on the screen in response to a right mouse-click) are all CommandBar objects.

It is important to realize is that the "items" that you see on a toolbar, menubar, menu, or submenu are actually controls, called *command bar controls*; that is, they are CommandBarControl objects. As you will see, there are various types of command bar controls, falling into two broad categories: custom command bar controls (including custom text boxes, drop-down list boxes, and combo boxes) and

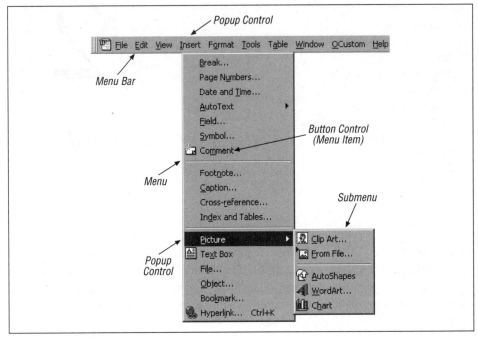

Figure 21-1. An Office menu

built-in command bar controls. Note that command bar controls are not the same as the controls that you can place on a UserForm object—they are designed specifically for toolbars and menus.

There are two special types of custom command bar controls that are not typical of other types of controls:

- A command bar control of type `msoControlPopup` is a control whose sole purpose is to pop up a menu (when the control is on a menubar) or a submenu (when the control is on a menu). These controls are naturally referred to as *popup controls* (see Figure 21-1). Popup controls that are located on a menubar take on the appearance of a recessed button when the mouse pointer is over the control. Popup controls on a menu or submenu have a small arrow on the far right to identify them.

- A command bar control of type `msoControlButton`, called a *button control*, also has two appearances but only one function. When placed on a toolbar, a button control looks like a command button (when the mouse pointer is over the control), and when placed on a menu or submenu, it looks like a "typical" menu item. In either case, when a button control is activated (using an accelerator key or mouseclick), a macro is executed. Button controls have a string property called OnAction, which you can set to the name of the macro that you want executed when the control is activated.

Finally, there are a few wrinkles in the process of menu creation. In particular, you might think at first that adding a new menu should be done using the *Add* method of the CommandBars collection, specifying the name of the parent menu and the location of the new menu on the parent. After all, a menu is a CommandBar object, and this procedure would be consistent with other cases of adding objects to a collection.

However, this is not how it is done. Instead, you create a new menu (or sub-menu) by adding a command bar control of type `msoControlPopup` to the Com-mandBarControls collection of the parent menu (and specifying the new control's position on the parent). Actually, this does make more sense when you consider the fact that menus may contain not only submenus (that is, popup controls), but also other types of controls, such as text boxes and list boxes.

One word of advice before proceeding: when creating a new toolbar or menu, you can set one of the parameters to make the object temporary, meaning that it will be destroyed when Word is closed. In this way, if anything unexpected hap-pens, it is easy to recover—just close Word and reopen it. Alternatively, by open-ing the Customize dialog box (from the Tools menu), you can delete menu items by dragging them off of the menu and delete toolbars using the Delete button.

Also, as usual, experimenting should be done on a template used just for that pur-pose (and back up your Normal template). If you find that you have some extra toolbars or menus, you can always open the Customize dialog box under the Tools menu. When that dialog box is open, you can delete toolbars and remove menu items with the mouse.

CustomizationContext

Before customizing the menu and toolbar system, you must set the context in which the changes will be saved. This is done by setting the CustomizationCon-text property of the Application object to a Template or Document object.

For example, the line:

```
CustomizationContext = NormalTemplate
```

sets the customization context to the Normal template so that all changes will be saved in this template. The line:

```
CustomizationContext = ActiveDocument.AttachedTemplate
```

sets the customization context to the attached template of the active document.

The CommandBars Collection

The topmost object that relates to menus and toolbars is the CommandBars collection, which contains all of the application's CommandBar objects. The CommandBars collection is accessible through the CommandBars property of the Application object; that is

```
Application.CommandBars
```

(CommandBars is also a global property, so it can be used without the qualifying word "Application.") The following code will print a list of all of the CommandBar objects to the Immediate window. I think you will be surprised at the large number of these objects, most of which are not currently visible:

```
Dim sType as string, cbar as CommandBar
For Each cbar In CommandBars
  Select Case cbar.Type
  Case msoBarTypeNormal
    sType = "Normal"
  Case msoBarTypeMenuBar
    sType = "Menu bar"
  Case msoBarTypePopup
    sType = "Popup"
  End Select
  Debug.Print cbar.Name & "," & sType & "," & cbar.Visible
Next
```

The CommandBar Object

As you have seen, the principal object related to menus and toolbars is the CommandBar object. Menubars, menus, submenus, shortcut menus, and toolbars are CommandBar objects. Note, however, that Office VBA does not treat each of these CommandBar objects in the same way. For instance, the Count property of the CommandBars collection counts only menubars, toolbars and shortcut menus. It does not count menus or submenus. Also, as mentioned earlier, the *Add* method of the CommandBars collection allows can be used to create toolbars or menubars, but not menus or submenus.

The CommandBar object has a Type property that can assume one of the constants in the following enum:

```
Enum MsoBarType
    msoBarTypeNormal = 0     ' toolbar
    msoBarTypeMenuBar = 1    ' menubar
    msoBarTypePopup = 2      ' menu, submenu or shortcut menu
End Enum
```

Creating a New Menubar or Toolbar

As we have said, one way in which menubars and toolbars differ from menus and submenus is in their creation. To create a new menubar or shortcut menu, we use the Add method of the CommandBars collection. The syntax for the *Add* method is:

```
CommandBarsObject.Add(Name, Position, MenuBar, Temporary)
```

The optional *Name* parameter is the name of the new command bar. If this argument is omitted, Word VBA assigns a default name (such as "Custom 1") to the command bar. The optional *Position* parameter gives the position of the new command bar. This can be set to msoBarLeft, msoBarTop, msoBarRight, mso-BarBottom, or msoBarFloating (for a floating command bar), or msoBarPopup (for a shortcut menu). (Note, however, that Word does not provide a way to display custom shortcut menus.)

The optional Boolean *MenuBar* parameter is set to True for a menubar and False for a toolbar. The default value is False, so if the argument is omitted, a toolbar is created. Note that if you create a new menubar and make it visible, it will replace the existing Word menubar! (If this happens, you can still save a document using the Ctrl-S key combination and exit Word using the Alt-F4 keys.)

Setting the optional *Temporary* parameter to True makes the new command bar temporary. Temporary command bars are deleted when Word is closed. The default value is False.

To illustrate, the following code creates a new floating toolbar called "Custom Toolbar" and makes it visible:

```
Dim cbar As CommandBar
Set cbar = CommandBars.Add("Custom Toolbar", _
    msoBarFloating, False, True)
cbar.Visible = True
```

Command Bar Controls

Initially, one of the most confusing aspects of the Office menu system is that the items that appear on a menubar are not menus, or even names of menus. Rather, they are controls of type CommandBarControl. Command bar controls can be added to a menubar, toolbar, menu, submenu, or shortcut menu.

Every command bar control is an object of type CommandBarControl. In addition, every command bar control is an object of one of the following three object types:

- CommandBarButton
- CommandBarComboBox
- CommandBarPopup

This allows the various types of command bar controls to possess a common set of properties and methods (those of the CommandBarControl object), as well as an additional set of properties and methods that reflects the diversity of these controls. (After all, text boxes are quite different from popup controls, for instance.)

Creating a New Command Bar Control

To create and add a command bar control to a command bar, use the *Add* method of the CommandBarControls collection. This method returns a CommandBarButton, CommandBarComboBox, or CommandBarPopup object, depending on the value of the *Type* parameter (see later in this section). The syntax is:

```
CommandBarControlsObject.Add(Type, Id, Parameter, _
                     Before, Temporary)
```

Type is the type of control to be added to the specified command bar. Table 21-1 shows the possible values for this parameter, along with the corresponding control and the return type of the *Add* method.

Table 21-1. msoControlType Values for the Type Parameter

Type Parameter (Value)	Control	Returned object
msoControlButton (1)	Button	CommandBarButton
msoControlEdit (2)	Text box	CommandBarComboBox
msoControlDropdown (3)	List box	CommandBarComboBox
msoControlComboBox (4)	Combo box	CommandBarComboBox
msoControlPopup (10)	Popup	CommandBarPopup

The optional *Before* parameter is a number that indicates the position of the new control on the command bar. The new control will be inserted before the control that is at this position. If this argument is omitted, the control is added at the end of the command bar.

To add a custom control of one of the types listed in Table 21-1, set the *Id* parameter to 1 or leave it out. You can also use a built-in Word control, for which you would set the *Id* parameter to the ID number of the control (and leave out the *Type* argument). (I discuss built-in control IDs, and consider some examples, a bit later in this chapter.)

As with command bars, you can set the optional *Temporary* parameter to True to make the new command bar control temporary. It will then be deleted when Word is closed.

Note that a CommandBar object does not have a CommandBarControls property, as you might expect. In order to return a CommandBarControls object, use the Controls property, as in:

```
CommandBars("Menu bar").Controls
```

Built-in Command Bar Control IDs

As you saw in the toolbar example, it is possible to place built-in command bar controls on toolbars (or menus). This is done using the *Id* parameter of the *Add* method of the CommandBarControls collection.

I can now address the issue of how to determine the IDs for the built-in controls. One approach to finding the ID of a particular control is to use the FindControl method to locate the control and then to get its ID using the ID property. If you would like to browse through the built-in command bar controls, try running the procedure in Example 21-1, which creates a file and fills it with a list of all names and IDs. (On my PC, the list contains 1,205 items!)

Example 21-1. Getting the Names and IDs of Command Bar Controls

```
Sub GetIDs()
    Dim fr As Integer
    Dim cbar As CommandBar
    Dim ctl As CommandBarControl
    Dim i As Integer
    Const maxid = 4000
    fr = FreeFile
    Open "d:\word\ids.txt" For Output As #fr
    ' Create temporary toolbar
    Set cbar = CommandBars.Add("temporary", msoBarTop, _
        False, True)
    For i = 1 To maxid
        On Error Resume Next ' skip if cannot add
        cbar.Controls.Add ID:=i
    Next i
    On Error GoTo 0
    For Each ctl In cbar.Controls
        Print #fr, ctl.Caption & " (" & ctl.ID & ")"
    Next
    cbar.Delete
    Close #fr
End Sub
```

Example: Creating a Menu

The program in Example 21-2 creates the menu system shown in Figure 21-2 on Word's main menubar. Note that the macros that are invoked by the selection of the menu items are named *ExampleMacro1* and *ExampleMacro2*; in order to successfully install the custom menu without generating a syntax error, you must define these two procedures.

Example 21-2. Creating a System Menu

```
Sub CreatePopup()

Dim cbpop As CommandBarControl
```

Example 21-2. Creating a System Menu (continued)

```
Dim cbctl As CommandBarControl
Dim cbsub As CommandBarControl

' Create a popup control on the main menubar
Set cbpop = CommandBars("Menu bar"). _
   Controls.Add(Type:=msoControlPopup)
cbpop.Caption = "&Custom"
cbpop.Visible = True

' Add a menu item
Set cbctl = cbpop.Controls.Add(Type:=msoControlButton)
cbctl.Visible = True
' Next is required for caption
cbctl.Style = msoButtonCaption
cbctl.Caption = "MenuItem&1"
' Action to perform
cbctl.OnAction = "ExampleMacro1"

' Add a popup for a submenu
Set cbsub = cbpop.Controls.Add(Type:=msoControlPopup)
cbsub.Visible = True
cbsub.Caption = "&SubMenuItem1"

' Add a menu item to the submenu
Set cbctl = cbsub.Controls.Add(Type:=msoControlButton)
cbctl.Visible = True
' Next is required for caption
cbctl.Style = msoButtonCaption
cbctl.Caption = "SubMenuItem&2"
' Action to perform
cbctl.OnAction = "ExampleMacro2"

End Sub
```

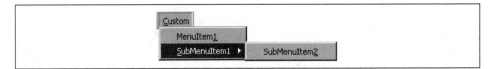

Figure 21-2. A sample custom menu

Note the use of the ampersand character (&) in the Caption properties. This character signals a hotkey (or accelerator key). Thus, "&Custom" appears as Custom in the menubar and can be invoked using the keystroke combination Alt-C.

Example: Creating a Toolbar

Let us construct a custom toolbar with four different types of controls, as shown in Figure 21-3. This will illustrate the use of Word's built-in command controls. The code in Example 21-3 (as well as in Examples 20-4 and 20-5) does the job. I will discuss various portions of the code after you have glanced at it.

Example 21-3. Constructing a Custom Toolbar

```
Sub CreateToolbar()

Dim cbar As CommandBar, cbctl As CommandBarControl

' Create a floating toolbar
Set cbar = CommandBars.Add(Name:="Toolbar Example", _
    Position:=msoBarFloating)
cbar.Visible = True

' Add a custom button control to execute a macro
Set cbctl = cbar.Controls.Add(Type:=msoControlButton)
cbctl.Visible = True
cbctl.Style = msoButtonCaption
cbctl.Caption = "CustomButton"
' Run the following macro
cbctl.OnAction = "ExampleMacro"

' Add built-in Find... control
Set cbctl = cbar.Controls.Add(ID:=141)
' Icon for button
cbctl.FaceId = 141
cbctl.Visible = True

' Add built-in spell checking button
Set cbctl = cbar.Controls.Add(ID:=2)
cbctl.FaceId = 2
cbctl.Visible = True

' Add a list box
Set cbctl = cbar.Controls.Add(Type:=msoControlDropdown)
' Add a tag so macro can find it
cbctl.Tag = "ComposerList"
cbctl.Visible = True
cbctl.Caption = "ListCaption"
' Set list properties of the list box
With cbctl
    .AddItem "Chopin", 1
    .AddItem "Mozart", 2
    .AddItem "Bach", 3
    .DropDownLines = 0
    .DropDownWidth = 75
    ' select nothing to start
    .ListIndex = 0
End With
' Set macro to execute when an item
' is selected
cbctl.OnAction = "ExampleListMacro"

End Sub
```

The first line of the procedure creates a floating toolbar whose name is "Toolbar Example." The name is important, since we will use it later for identification.

Figure 21-3. A custom toolbar

Next, I add a custom button control (*Id* argument missing) and assign it the macro *ExampleMacro*, whose code, which is shown in Example 21-4, simply tells me that I pushed the button.

Example 21-4. The ExampleMacro Procedure

```
Sub ExampleMacro()
   MsgBox "Custom button pressed"
End Sub
```

Next, I add a built-in Find... custom control, whose *Id* happens to be 141. (I will discuss how to find built-in control IDs a bit later.) This custom control automatically displays the Find dialog box. Note that I set the *FaceId* to 141 as well. This displays the default icon (binoculars), but you could choose another icon if desired.

Then I add the built-in Spelling custom control, which checks the spelling of the active document.

Finally, I add a custom list box and populate it with the names of three composers. Note that I set the Tag property of this list box. The reason is that I want to be able to find the list box from within the macro that is assigned to the OnAction property, which, in this case, is shown in Example 21-5.

Example 21-5. The ExampleListMacro Procedure

```
Sub ExampleListMacro()
   Dim cbctl As CommandBarControl
   ' Find the list box control
   Set cbctl = CommandBars("Toolbar Example"). _
      FindControl(Tag:="ComposerList")
   If Not cbctl Is Nothing Then
      MsgBox "You selected " & cbctl.List(cbctl.ListIndex)
   End If
End Sub
```

In this macro, I use the *FindControl* method to locate the list box control via its tag, on the toolbar. Once I have located the list box, I can get the currently selected item (which I simply display for this example).

The *FindControl* method has the syntax:

```
CommandBarsObject.FindControl(Type, Id, Tag, Visible, _
   Recursive)
```

and permits you to search for a command bar control by type, ID, or tag. You also have the option of searching only visible controls and searching recursively through submenus.

In particular, the optional *Type* parameter is the type of control to be searched for. It can be any of the constants in the following `msoControlType` enum:

```
Enum MsoControlType
    msoControlCustom = 0
    msoControlButton = 1
    msoControlEdit = 2
    msoControlDropdown = 3
    msoControlComboBox = 4
    msoControlButtonDropdown = 5
    msoControlSplitDropdown = 6
    msoControlOCXDropdown = 7
    msoControlGenericDropdown = 8
    msoControlGraphicDropdown = 9
    msoControlPopup = 10
    msoControlGraphicPopup = 11
    msoControlButtonPopup = 12
    msoControlSplitButtonPopup = 13
    msoControlSplitButtonMRUPopup = 14
    msoControlLabel = 15
    msoControlExpandingGrid = 16
    msoControlSplitExpandingGrid = 17
    msoControlGrid = 18
    msoControlGauge = 19
    msoControlGraphicCombo = 20
End Enum
```

Note that if two or more controls fit the search criteria, *FindControl* returns the first control that it finds. Also, if no control fits the criteria, *FindControl* returns `Nothing`, so you can check this as I have done in this program.

IV

Appendixes

Programming Word from Another Application

In this appendix, I describe briefly how the Word object model can be programmed from within certain other applications, including Microsoft Access, Excel, and PowerPoint. A well-known technique that Microsoft refers to as *Automation* (formerly called OLE Automation) allows one application to gain access to the objects of another. An application that "exposes" its objects is called an *Automation server*. An application that can access the objects of an Automation server is called an *Automation controller* or *Automation client*. Since Microsoft Word, Access, and Excel are both Automation servers and Automation controllers, as a VBA programmer, you can program any of these applications from within any other.

Setting a Reference to the Word Object Model

The first step in communicating with the Word object model is to set a reference to its object library. Each of the client applications (Word, Access, PowerPoint, and Excel) has a References menu item under the Tools menu. Selecting this item displays the References dialog box shown in Figure A-1. From here, you can select the object models that you want to access from within the Automation controller. (Note the second entry under Available References.)

Getting a Reference to the Word Application Object

Once the proper references are set, you can declare an object variable of type Application:

```
Dim Wrd As Word.Application
```

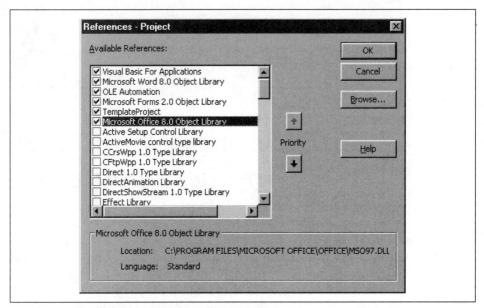

Figure A-1. The References dialog box

which the Automation client will understand, because it can now check the server's object library. Note that you need to qualify the object name, since other object models have an Application object as well.

Next, you can start the Word Automation server, create a Word Application object, and get a reference to that object. This is done in the following line:

```
Set Wrd = New Word.Application
```

At this point, you have complete access to Word's object model. It is important to note, however, that the previous line starts the Word Automation server, but does not start Word's graphical user interface, so Word will be running invisibly. To make Word visible, you just set its Visible property to True:

```
Wrd.Visible = True
```

You can now program as though you were within the Word VBA IDE. For instance, the following code creates a new document, adds some content to it, and saves the document:

```
Dim doc as Word.Document
Set doc = Wrd.Documents.Add
doc.Content = "To be or not to be"
doc.Save
```

Note that the Word server will not terminate by itself, even if the **Wrd** variable is destroyed. If you have made Word visible, then you can close it programmatically, as well as from the user interface in the usual way (choosing Exit from the File menu, for instance). But if the Word server is invisible, it must be closed using the *Quit* method:

```
Wrd.Quit
```

(If you fail to terminate the Word server, it will remain running invisibly, taking up system resources, until the PC is restarted.)

An Alternative Approach

The previous approach for programming Word from within another application is the preferred approach, since it is the most efficient. However, there is an alternative approach that you may encounter, so I will discuss it briefly. As before, I assume that a reference has been set to the Word object library.

The CreateObject Function

The *CreateObject* function can start an Automation server, create an object, and assign it to an object variable. Thus, you can write:

```
Dim Wrd as Word.Application
Set Wrd = CreateObject("Word.Application")
```

This approach will execute more slowly than the previous approach using the New keyword, but it is perfectly valid.

As before, you must remember to close Word using the *Quit* method (or through normal means if Word is visible).

The GetObject Function

If Word is already running, the *CreateObject* function will start a second copy of the Word server. To use the currently running version, use the *GetObject* function to set a reference to the Application object of a running copy of Word. This is done as follows:

```
Set Wrd = GetObject(, "Word.Application")
```

(The first parameter of *GetObject* is not used here.)

One of the problems with using *GetObject* is that it will produce an error if Word is not running, so it is somewhat unpredictable, for you cannot be sure that the user has not closed Word. Thus, you need some code that will start Word if it is not running or use the existing copy of Word if it is running.

The trick to this is to know that if *GetObject* fails to find a running copy of Word, it then issues error number 429 ("ActiveX component can't create object"). Thus, the following code does the trick:

```
Dim Wrd As Word.Application
On Error Resume Next
' Try to get reference to running Word
Set Wrd = GetObject(, "Word.Application")
If Err.Number = 429 Then
    ' If error 429, then create new object
    Set Wrd = CreateObject("Word.Application")
ElseIf Err.Number <> 0 Then
    ' If another type of error, report it
    MsgBox "Error: " & Err.Description
    Exit Sub
End If
```

No Object Library Reference

I have been assuming that the client application has a reference to the server's object library. However, it is still possible for a client application (an Automation client) to program the objects of an Automation server (such as Word) without such a reference. Under these circumstances, you cannot refer to objects by name in code, since the client will not understand these names. Instead, you must use the generic Object data type, as in the following code:

```
Dim Wrd As Object
Dim doc As Object
Set Wrd = CreateObject("Word.Application")
Wrd.Visible = True
Set doc = Wrd.Documents.Add
doc.Content = "To be or not to be"
doc.Save
```

This code will run even more slowly than the previous code which, in turn, is slower than the first version.

Thus, there are three versions of Automation:

- Using the **New** keyword syntax (requires an object library reference).

- Using *CreateObject* and specific object variable declarations (requires an object library reference).

- Using *CreateObject* with generic **As Object** declarations (does not use an object library reference).

These versions of automation are sometimes referred to by the names *very early binding*, *early binding*, and *late binding*, respectively (although you may hear these terms used somewhat differently).

The reason for these terms has to do with the time at which VBA can associate (or *bind*) the object, property, and method names in our code to the actual addresses of these items. In very early binding, all bindings are done at compile time by VBA—that is, *before* the program runs. In early binding, some of the bindings are done at compile time and others are done at run time. In late binding, all bindings are done at run time.

The issue is now evident. The more binding that needs to be done at run time, the more slowly the program will run. Thus, very early binding is the most efficient, followed by early binding and then late binding.

B

The Shape Object

In this appendix, I take a brief look at the issue of drawing pictures using VBA code. Since this subject is not fundamental to Word VBA programming, I will be very brief, but this introduction will give you the necessary background for further study using the VBA help files.

The Shape and InLineShape Objects

Each Word document has two layers: the *text layer* and the *drawing layer*. A Shape object is a drawing object that is placed in the drawing layer of a document. As you will see, a Shape object is anchored to a Range object (on the text layer) and its position is determined by giving its distance from that Range object.

On the other hand, an InLineShape object is a drawing object that is placed on the text layer. It is therefore treated like a character, in the sense that it moves with the surrounding text. Note that InLineShape objects are restricted to pictures, OLE objects, and ActiveX controls only, whereas there are many other types of Shape objects.

As usual, the Shape objects for a document are stored in a Shapes collection and the InLineShape objects are stored in the InLineShapes collection.

Z-Order

Every Shape object has an order, called its *z-order*, that indicates the object's relative position with respect to an imaginary z-axis that comes directly out of the monitor at right angles towards the user, as pictured in Figure B-1.

The read-only ZOrderPosition property of a Shape object reports the current z-order of the object, which, incidentally, is the same as the object's index within

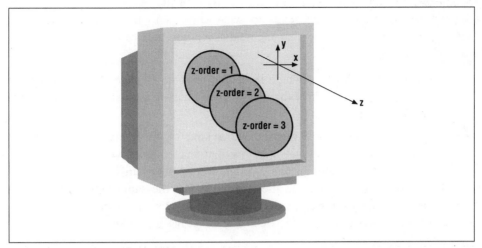

Figure B-1. An illustration of z-order

the Shapes collection. Shape objects with a larger z-order appear on top of objects with a smaller z-order. Hence, the Shape object with z-order equal to 1 is `Shapes(1)` and lies at the bottom of the pile!

The *ZOrder* method sets the z-order of a Shape object relative to other objects. Note that the method does not set the absolute z-order. The syntax is:

```
ShapeObject.ZOrder(ZOrderCmd)
```

where **ZOrderCmd** is one of the constants in the following enum (from the Microsoft Office object model):

```
Enum MsoZOrderCmd
    msoBringToFront = 0
    msoSendToBack = 1
    msoBringForward = 2
    msoSendBackward = 3
    msoBringInFrontOfText = 4
    msoSendBehindText = 5
End Enum
```

Thus, the z-order can be set only in the following ways:

- Move the object to the front of the z-order.

- Move the object to the back of the z-order.

- Move the object one forward in the z-order; that is, increase its index by 1.

- Move the object one backward in the z-order; that is, decrease its index by 1.

The *ZOrder* method permits placing an object with respect to the text layer as well, using the **msoBringInFrontOfText** and **msoSendBehindText** constants.

A little experimenting to determine the behavior of the text layer with respect to the z-order of Shape objects leads to what appears to be an inconsistency. It seems reasonable to assume that the text layer has one of two behaviors with respect to z-order:

- The text layer might be a single layer that must fit "between" two z-orders. In this case, we could think of the text layer has having a fractional z-order of the form 0.5, 1.5, 2.5, and so on.

- Alternatively, each shape might have a kind of "property" that determines whether text appears above or below that shape. Moreover, this property is totally unrelated to the shape's z-order. Hence, text can appear on top of a shape that appears higher in the z-order and at the same time underneath a shape that appears lower in the z-order, as shown in Figure B-2, where the word "Text" is partially hidden by a shape that has a smaller z-order.

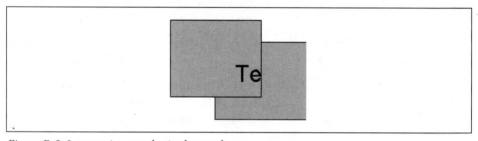

Figure B-2. Interpreting z-order in the text layer

In an attempt to determine which (if indeed either) of these hypotheses is accurate, the following code creates two shapes, `shSquare` (a dark square) and `shRect` (a shaded rectangle), as shown in Figure B-3. (We will discuss the syntax of this code a bit later.)

```
Dim shSquare As Shape
Dim shRect As Shape
Dim rng As Range

Set rng = Selection.Range
Set shSquare = ActiveDocument.Shapes.AddShape _
    (msoShapeRectangle, 0, 0, 72, 72, rng)
Set shRect = ActiveDocument.Shapes.AddShape _
    (msoShapeRectangle, 0, 0, 144, 36, rng)
' Shade each shape
shSquare.Fill.ForeColor.RGB = RGB(196, 196, 196)
shRect.Fill.ForeColor.RGB = RGB(216, 216, 216)
```

The following code sends both shapes behind the text layer and then makes certain that `shSquare` lies behind `shRect`:

```
shSquare.ZOrder msoSendBehindText
shRect.ZOrder msoSendBehindText
```

```
shSquare.ZOrder msoSendToBack

' report z-orders
Debug.Print shSquare.ZOrderPosition
Debug.Print shRect.ZOrderPosition
```

After executing this code, the situation is as shown in Figure B-3, where the square is behind the rectangle, both of which are behind the text, as expected. Also, the z-orders are as expected:

```
shSquare.ZOrderPosition = 1
shRect.ZOrderPosition = 2
(TextLayer.ZOrderPosition = 2.5???)
```

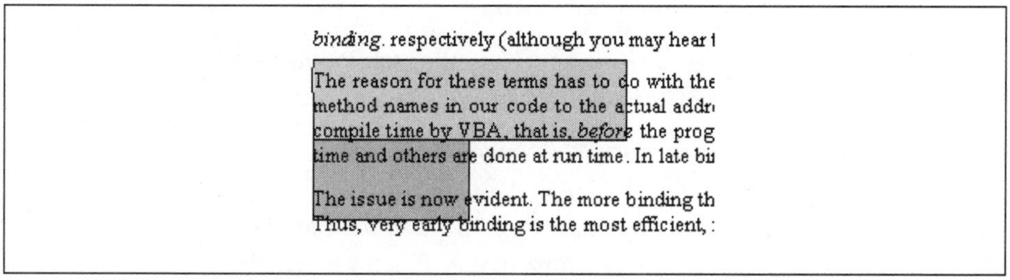

Figure B-3. Shape objects behind the text

Next, I bring the square above the text layer using the code

```
shSquare.ZOrder msoBringInFrontOfText

' report z-orders
Debug.Print shSquare.ZOrderPosition
Debug.Print shRect.ZOrderPosition
```

The result is shown in Figure B-4 and tends to support the view that the text layer has a fractional z-order and now lies above the rectangle but below the square.

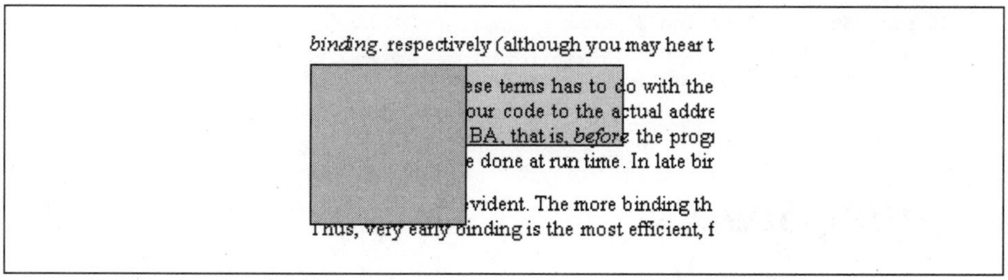

Figure B-4. Evidence of a fractional z-order

In view of Figure B-4, you might expect the z-orders to be:

```
shSquare.ZOrderPosition = 2
shRect.ZOrderPosition = 1
(TextLayer.ZOrderPosition = 1.5???)
```

However, the actual values reported by the `Debug.Print` statements are:

```
shSquare.ZOrderPosition = 1
shRect.ZOrderPosition = 2
```

which is contrary to the appearance of the two shapes—never mind the text layer!

Creating InLineShapes

As I have said, an inline shape is a shape that is placed in the text layer of a document and moves with the surrounding text. Inline shapes are restricted to pictures, OLE objects, and ActiveX controls. We will content ourselves with a single example of placing pictures in a document.

To add an inline picture to a document, use the *AddPicture* method of the InLineShapes collection. The syntax is:

```
InLineShapesObject.AddPicture(FileName, LinkToFile, _
    SaveWithDocument, Range)
```

The *FileName* parameter is the name of the picture file. The optional *LinkToFile* is set to True to link the picture to the file from which it was created and False to use an independent copy of the original picture. The default value is False. If the picture is linked, the optional *SaveWithDocument* is set to True to save the linked picture with the document. The default value is False. The parameter *Range* is the range that will be replaced by the picture (unless, of course, the range is an insertion point).

To illustrate, the following code places a picture with the word ATTENTION! in front of each paragraph that has style Heading 2, turning Figure B-5 into Figure B-6:

```
Dim para As Paragraph
For Each para In ActiveDocument.Paragraphs
If para.Style = "Heading 2" Then
    ActiveDocument.InlineShapes.AddPicture _
        "d:\word\atten.bmp", , , para.Range
End If
Next para
```

Creating Shapes

Word has several methods for creating shapes (that is, for adding a shape to the Shapes collection), depending upon the type of shape desired. Among the possibilities are: *AddCallout*, *AddCurve*, *AddLabel*, *AddLine*, *AddPicture*, *AddPolyLine* (polygonal line), *AddTextbox*, *AddShape*, and *AddTextEffect*.

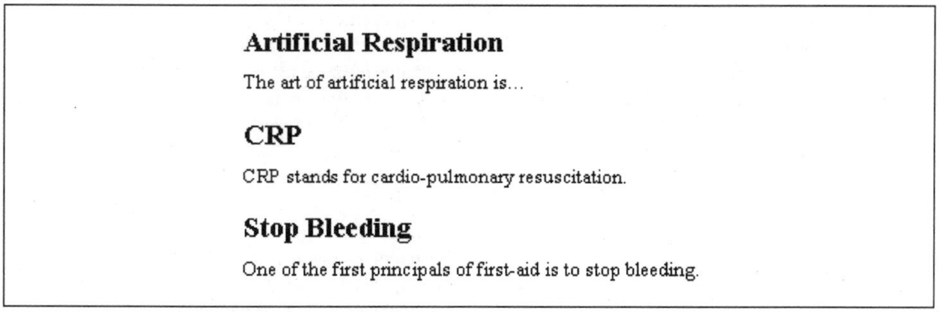

Artificial Respiration

The art of artificial respiration is...

CRP

CRP stands for cardio-pulmonary resuscitation.

Stop Bleeding

One of the first principals of first-aid is to stop bleeding.

Figure B-5. Text before calling the AddPicture method

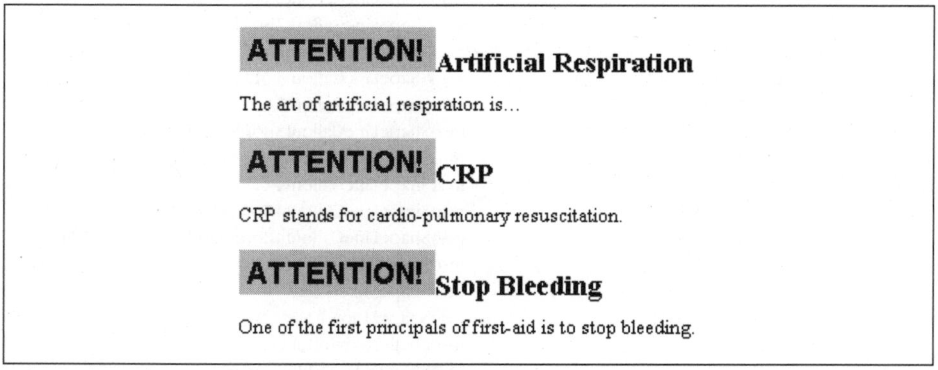

ATTENTION! **Artificial Respiration**

The art of artificial respiration is...

ATTENTION! **CRP**

CRP stands for cardio-pulmonary resuscitation.

ATTENTION! **Stop Bleeding**

One of the first principals of first-aid is to stop bleeding.

Figure B-6. Inserting an image with AddPicture

AutoShapes

An *AutoShape* is a Shape object that represents a built-in drawing. To add a new AutoShape object, use the *AddShape* method, whose syntax is:

```
ShapesCollection.AddShape(Type, Left, Top, Width, Height, Anchor)
```

The parameter *Type* is the type of AutoShape to create. It can be any one of the MsoAutoShapeType constants:

msoShape16pointStar (94)
msoShape24pointStar (95)
msoShape32pointStar (96)
msoShape4pointStar (91)
msoShape5pointStar (92)
msoShape8pointStar (93)
msoShapeActionButtonBackorPrevious (129)
msoShapeActionButtonBeginning (131)
msoShapeActionButtonCustom (125)
msoShapeActionButtonDocument (134)
msoShapeActionButtonEnd (132)
msoShapeActionButtonForwardorNext (130)

msoShapeActionButtonHelp (127)
msoShapeActionButtonHome (126)
msoShapeActionButtonInformation (128)
msoShapeActionButtonMovie (136)
msoShapeActionButtonReturn (133)
msoShapeActionButtonSound (135)
msoShapeArc (25)
msoShapeBalloon (137)
msoShapeBentArrow (41)
msoShapeBentUpArrow (44)
msoShapeBevel (15)
msoShapeBlockArc (20)

msoShapeCan (13)

msoShapeChevron (52)

msoShapeCircularArrow (60)

msoShapeCloudCallout (108)

msoShapeCross (11)

msoShapeCube (14)

msoShapeCurvedDownArrow (48)

msoShapeCurvedDownRibbon (100)

msoShapeCurvedLeftArrow (46)

msoShapeCurvedRightArrow (45)

msoShapeCurvedUpArrow (47)

msoShapeCurvedUpRibbon (99)

msoShapeDiamond (4)

msoShapeDonut (18)

msoShapeDoubleBrace (27)

msoShapeDoubleBracket (26)

msoShapeDoubleWave (104)

msoShapeDownArrow (36)

msoShapeDownArrowCallout (56)

msoShapeDownRibbon (98)

msoShapeExplosion1 (89)

msoShapeExplosion2 (90)

msoShapeFlowchartAlternateProcess (62)

msoShapeFlowchartCard (75)

msoShapeFlowchartCollate (79)

msoShapeFlowchartConnector (73)

msoShapeFlowchartData (64)

msoShapeFlowchartDecision (63)

msoShapeFlowchartDelay (84)

msoShapeFlowchartDirectAccessStorage (87)

msoShapeFlowchartDisplay (88)

msoShapeFlowchartDocument (67)

msoShapeFlowchartExtract (81)

msoShapeFlowchartInternalStorage (66)

msoShapeFlowchartMagneticDisk (86)

msoShapeFlowchartManualInput (71)

msoShapeFlowchartManualOperation (72)

msoShapeFlowchartMerge (82)

msoShapeFlowchartMultidocument (68)

msoShapeFlowchartOffpageConnector (74)

msoShapeFlowchartOr (78)

msoShapeFlowchartPredefinedProcess (65)

msoShapeFlowchartPreparation (70)

msoShapeFlowchartProcess (61)

msoShapeFlowchartPunchedTape (76)

msoShapeFlowchartSequentialAccessStorage (85)

msoShapeFlowchartSort (80)

msoShapeFlowchartStoredData (83)

msoShapeFlowchartSummingJunction (77)

msoShapeFlowchartTerminator (69)

msoShapeFoldedCorner (16)

msoShapeHeart (21)

msoShapeHexagon (10)

msoShapeHorizontalScroll (102)

msoShapeIsoscelesTriangle (7)

msoShapeLeftArrow (34)

msoShapeLeftArrowCallout (54)

msoShapeLeftBrace (31)

msoShapeLeftBracket (29)

msoShapeLeftRightArrow (37)

msoShapeLeftRightArrowCallout (57)

msoShapeLeftRightUpArrow (40)

msoShapeLeftUpArrow (43)

msoShapeLightningBolt (22)

msoShapeLineCallout1 (109)

msoShapeLineCallout1AccentBar (113)

msoShapeLineCallout1BorderandAccentBar (121)

msoShapeLineCallout1NoBorder (117)

msoShapeLineCallout2 (110)

msoShapeLineCallout2AccentBar (114)

msoShapeLineCallout2BorderandAccentBar (122)

msoShapeLineCallout2NoBorder (118)

msoShapeLineCallout3 (111)

msoShapeLineCallout3AccentBar (115)

msoShapeLineCallout3BorderandAccentBar (123)

msoShapeLineCallout3NoBorder (119)

msoShapeLineCallout4 (112)

msoShapeLineCallout4AccentBar (116)

msoShapeLineCallout4BorderandAccentBar (124)

msoShapeLineCallout4NoBorder (120)

msoShapeMixed (-2)

msoShapeMoon (24)

msoShapeNoSymbol (19)

msoShapeNotchedRightArrow (50)

msoShapeNotPrimitive (138)

msoShapeOctagon (6)

msoShapeOval (9)

msoShapeOvalCallout (107)

msoShapeParallelogram (2)

msoShapePentagon (51)

msoShapePlaque (28)

msoShapeQuadArrow (39)

msoShapeQuadArrowCallout (59)

msoShapeRectangle (1)

msoShapeRectangularCallout (105)

msoShapeRegularPentagon (12)

msoShapeRightArrow (33)

msoShapeRightArrowCallout (53)

msoShapeRightBrace (32)

msoShapeRightBracket (30)

msoShapeRightTriangle (8)

msoShapeRoundedRectangle (5)

msoShapeRoundedRectangularCallout (106)

msoShapeSmileyFace (17)

msoShapeStripedRightArrow (49)

msoShapeSun (23)

msoShapeTrapezoid (3)

msoShapeUpArrow (35)

msoShapeUpArrowCallout (55)
msoShapeUpDownArrow (38)
msoShapeUpDownArrowCallout (58)
msoShapeUpRibbon (97)

msoShapeUTurnArrow (42)
msoShapeVerticalScroll (101)
msoShapeWave (103)

The parameters *Left* and *Top* specify the position (in points as a Single) of the upper-left corner of the bounding box for the AutoShape object, measured relative to the anchor.

The *Width* and *Height* parameters specify the width and height (in points as a Single) of the bounding box for the AutoShape.

Finally, the optional *Anchor* parameter specifies a Range object that is used to locate the AutoShape object. If *Anchor* is specified, then the anchoring point for the AutoShape is the beginning of the *first* paragraph in the range. If *Anchor* is omitted, the AutoShape is positioned relative to the top and left edges of the page.

Incidentally, the type of a Shape object can be changed by setting the AutoShapeType property. The short program in Example B-1 will display each AutoShape, along with its AutoShapeType, for 0.5 seconds. (It should be run on a blank document whose left margin is set to 2 inches. You can interrupt this program at any time by hitting Ctrl-Break.)

Example B-1. Displaying AutoShapes

```
Sub DisplayAutoShapes()

Dim sh As Shape
Dim rng As Range
Dim i As Integer

Set rng = Selection.Range
Set sh = ActiveDocument.Shapes.AddShape(1, 0, 0, 72, 72, _
    rng)
For i = 1 To 138
    sh.AutoShapeType = i
    sh.Visible = True
    sh.TextFrame.TextRange = sh.AutoShapeType
    Delay 0.5
Next i

End Sub
```

The program calls the *Delay* subroutine, which is shown in Example B-2.

Example B-2. The Delay Subroutine

```
Sub Delay(rTime As Single)

' Delay rTime seconds (min=.01, max=300)

Dim OldTime As Variant
```

Example B-2. The Delay Subroutine (continued)

```
' Safety net
If rTime < 0.01 Or rTime > 300 Then rTime = 1

OldTime = Timer
Do
    DoEvents
Loop Until Timer - OldTime >= rTime

End Sub
```

The TextFrame Object

Each Shape object has a text frame associated with it that holds any text associated with the object. The TextFrame property returns this TextFrame object. The
TextFrame object in turn has a TextRange property that returns a Range object representing the text in the text frame. Thus, for example, to set the text for a particular shape, you write:

```
sh.TextFrame.TextRange.Text = "Some text"
sh.TextFrame.TextRange.Font.Size = 10
sh.TextFrame.TextRange.Font.Name = "Arial"
sh.TextFrame.TextRange.Font.Bold = True
```

The FillFormat Object

The FillFormat object is used to set various formatting for a Shape object. It is
accessed using the Fill property of the Shape object. Among the properties of the
FillFormat object are BackColor, ForeColor, Pattern, and Visible. To set one of the
color properties, use the RGB color model, as in the following example:

```
sh.Fill.ForeColor.RGB = RGB(230, 230, 230)   ' 10% gray
```

In this line, the three parameters represent the concentration of red, green, and
blue, respectively. The range is from 0 (no color) to 256 (full color). Thus:

```
RGB(0,0,0)
```

is black and:

```
RGB(256,256,256)
```

is white. To get a certain percentage X of gray, just set each color equal to:

```
(100 - X) * 256
```

as in the previous example (10% gray is $(100 - 10) \times 256 = 230$).

Examples

To illustrate the use of AutoShapes, the code in Example B-3 inserts a dampened sine curve of small stars in the drawing layer. The output from this code is shown in Figure B-7.

Example B-3. The DrawSine2 Subroutine

```
Sub DrawSine2()

' Dampened sine wave of small stars

Const pi = 3.1416

Dim i As Integer
Dim x As Single, y As Single
Dim rng As Range       ' For starting point
Dim n As Single        ' Cycle length in inches
Dim k As Integer       ' k stars
Dim ScaleY As Single ' Vertical scaling
Dim sSize As Single  ' Star size
Dim sDamp1 As Single  ' Dampening factor
Dim sDamp2 As Single  ' Dampening factor
Dim cCycles As Integer  ' Number of cycles
Dim sh As Shape

cCycles = 3
sDamp1 = 1
sDamp2 = 0.2
n = 2
k = 20
ScaleY = 0.5
sSize = InchesToPoints(0.1)

' Start at insertion point
Set rng = Selection.Range

' Loop for first curve with phase shift
For i = 1 To cCycles * k
   x = n * i / k
   y = ScaleY * Sin((2 * pi * i) / k + n) * _
      (sDamp1 / (x + sDamp2))
   y = InchesToPoints(y)
   x = InchesToPoints(x)
   Set sh = ActiveDocument.Shapes.AddShape _
      (msoShape5pointStar, x, y, sSize, sSize, rng)
   sh.Fill.ForeColor.RGB = RGB(192, 192, 192)   ' 25% gray
   sh.Fill.Visible = msoTrue
Next i

End Sub
```

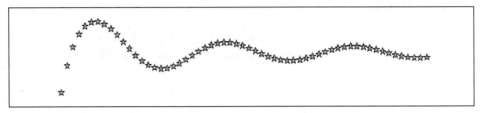

Figure B-7. A dampened sine wave of stars

The code in Example B-4 produces a random series of stars, each containing a single letter that together spells a name. Note that each time the program is run, the pattern is different. One output example from this code is shown in Figure B-8.

Example B-4. The DrawName Procedure

```
Sub DrawName()

' Random placement of large stars with name

Const pi = 3.1416

Dim i As Integer
Dim x As Single, y As Single
Dim z As Single
Dim rng As Range        ' For starting point
Dim n As Single         ' Cycle length in inches
Dim k As Integer        ' k stars
Dim sSize As Single     ' Star size
Dim sh As Shape
Dim sName As String     ' Name to display

sName = "Steven Roman"
n = 5
k = Len(sName)
sSize = InchesToPoints(0.5)

' Start at insertion point
Set rng = Selection.Range
Randomize Timer
z = 0#

' Loop for first curve with phase shift
For i = 1 To k
    If Mid(sName, i, 1) <> " " Then
        x = n * i / k
        x = InchesToPoints(x)

        ' Get random 0 or 1. Go up or down accordingly.
        If Int(2 * Rnd) = 0 Then
            z = z + 0.2
        Else
            z = z - 0.2
```

Example B-4. The DrawName Procedure (continued) (continued)

```
    End If

    y = InchesToPoints(z)
    Set sh = ActiveDocument.Shapes.AddShape _
        (msoShape5pointStar, x, y, sSize, sSize, rng)

    ' Add shading
    sh.Fill.ForeColor.RGB = RGB(230, 230, 230)
    sh.Fill.Visible = msoTrue

    ' Add text
    sh.TextFrame.TextRange.Text = Mid(sName, i, 1)
    sh.TextFrame.TextRange.Font.Size = 10
    sh.TextFrame.TextRange.Font.Name = "Arial"
    sh.TextFrame.TextRange.Font.Bold = True

    End If
Next i

End Sub
```

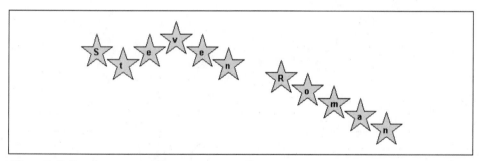

Figure B-8. Random stars spelling a name

Example B-5 prints a rose (either three-petal or four-petal). Figure B-9 shows the output in the four-petal case.

Example B-5. The DrawRose Procedure

```
Sub DrawRose()

' Draw rose of small stars

Const pi = 3.1416
Dim t As Single
Dim i As Integer
Dim x As Single, y As Single
Dim rng As Range       ' For starting point
Dim n As Single        ' Number of stars per cycle
Dim k As Integer       ' Number of cycles
Dim sSize As Single    ' Star size
```

Example B-5. The DrawRose Procedure (continued)

```
Dim r As Integer        ' half the number of petals
Dim sh As Shape

' For a 3-petal rose
r = 3
k = 1
n = 100

' For a 4-petal rose
'r = 2
'k = 2
'n = 150         ' Number of stars

sSize = InchesToPoints(0.03)

' Start curve at insertion point
Set rng = Selection.Range

For i = 1 To n
    t = k * pi * i / n
    x = Sin(r * t) * Sin(t)
    y = Sin(r * t) * Cos(t)
    x = InchesToPoints(x)
    y = InchesToPoints(y)
    Set sh = ActiveDocument.Shapes.AddShape _
        (msoShape5pointStar, x, y, sSize, sSize, rng)
Next i

End Sub
```

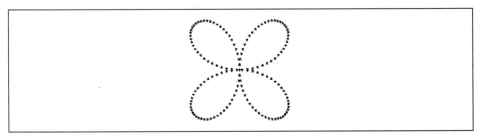

Figure B-9. A four-petal rose

Example B-6 prints a spiral to the drawing layer. The output is shown in Figure B-10.

Example B-6. The DrawSpiral Routine

```
Sub DrawSpiral()

' Draw spiral of small stars

Const pi = 3.1416
```

Example B-6. The DrawSpiral Routine (continued)

```
Dim t As Single
Dim i As Integer
Dim z As Single
Dim x As Single, y As Single
Dim rng As Range        ' For starting point
Dim n As Single         ' Number of stars per cycle
Dim k As Integer        ' Length of spiral
Dim sSize As Single     ' Star size
Dim sh As Shape

n = 80        ' Number of stars
k = 8         ' Length
sSize = InchesToPoints(0.03)

' Start curve at insertion point
Set rng = Selection.Range

For i = 5 To n
   t = k * pi * i / n
   x = 2 * (1 / t) * Sin(t)
   y = 2 * (1 / t) * Cos(t)
   x = InchesToPoints(x)
   y = InchesToPoints(y)

   Set sh = ActiveDocument.Shapes.AddShape _
      (msoShape5pointStar, x, y, sSize, sSize, rng)
   z = 256 * i / n
   sh.Line.ForeColor.RGB = RGB(z, z, z) ' vary line color
   sh.Line.Visible = msoTrue
Next i

End Sub
```

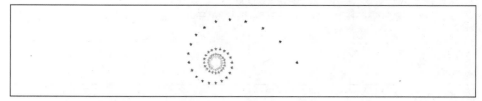

Figure B-10. A spiral of small stars

Example B-7 prints a hypocycloid. (It may take a few minutes to complete.) The results are shown in Figure B-11. (The insertion point in Figure B-11 is included to indicate the relative placement of the shapes.)

Example B-7. The DrawHypocycloid Routine

```
Sub DrawHypocycloid()

' Draw hypocycloid of small stars

Const pi = 3.1416
```

Example B-7. The DrawHypocloid Routine (continued)

```
Dim t As Single
Dim i As Integer
Dim x As Single, y As Single
Dim rng As Range       ' For starting point
Dim n As Single
Dim k As Integer
Dim sSize As Single  ' Star size
Dim r As Integer
Dim r0 As Integer
Dim R1 As Integer
Dim sh As Shape
Dim sc As Single

r = 1
r0 = 3 * r
R1 = 8 * r

n = 400
k = 4
sc = 0.1
sSize = InchesToPoints(0.03)

' Start curve at insertion point
Set rng = Selection.Range

For i = 1 To n
   t = k * pi * i / n
   x = (R1 - r) * Cos(t) + r0 * Cos(t * (R1 - r) / r)
   y = (R1 - r) * Sin(t) - r0 * Sin(t * (R1 - r) / r)
   x = sc * x
   y = sc * y
   x = InchesToPoints(x)
   y = InchesToPoints(y)
   Set sh = ActiveDocument.Shapes.AddShape _
       (msoShape5pointStar, x, y, sSize, sSize, rng)
Next i

End Sub
```

Figure B-11. A hypocycloid

WordArt

A WordArt object is a special type of Shape object. WordArt is accessible from the Drawing toolbar. A WordArt sample is shown Figure B-12.

Figure B-12. Sample WordArt

To create a WordArt object, use the *AddTextEffect* method of the Shapes collection. The syntax is:

```
ShapesCollection.AddTextEffect(PresetTextEffect, Text, _
    FontName, FontSize, FontBold, FontItalic, Left, Top, _
    Anchor)
```

Most of these parameters are self-explanatory. The **Anchor** parameter is the same as for the *AddShapes* method. The **PresetTextEffect** parameter specifies the type of WordArt object and can be any of the **MsoPresetTextEffect** constants **msoTextEffect1** through **msoTextEffect30**. The values of these constants correspond to the formats listed in the WordArt Gallery dialog box (numbered from left to right and from top to bottom).

The code in Example B-8 will display each of the 30 different WordArt text effects. It should be run on an empty document.

Example B-8. The ShowWordArtEffects Procedure

```
Sub ShowWordArtEffects()

Dim sh As Shape
Dim rng As Range
Dim i As Integer

Set rng = Selection.Range
Set sh = ActiveDocument.Shapes.AddTextEffect(msoTextEffect1, _
    "PresetTextEffect xx", "Arial", 24, False, False, _
    0, 0, rng)
For i = msoTextEffect1 To msoTextEffect30
    sh.TextEffect.PresetTextEffect = i
    sh.TextEffect.Text = "PresetTextEffect " & Format(i)
    sh.Visible = True
    Delay 1
Next i

End Sub
```

C

Getting the Installed Printers

As discussed in Chapter 11, *The Application Object*, the ActivePrinter property can be used to set the active printer. This raises the issue of how to determine the installed printers on a given computer. Unfortunately, VBA does not seem to provide a way to do this. (Visual Basic has a Printers collection, but Visual Basic for Applications does not.)

In this appendix, I describe a program for getting this printer information. As mentioned in Chapter 11, this program uses the Windows API. To use this program, just type it into your own code, as described next.

The first step is to declare some special constants in the Declarations section of a standard module:

```
Public Const KEY_ENUMERATE_SUB_KEYS = &H8
Public Const HKEY_LOCAL_MACHINE = &H80000002
Public Const SUCCESS = 0&
```

Next, I need to declare a user-defined type. I have not discussed these data structures in this book, but a user-defined type is essentially just a custom data type. Enter the following code into the Declarations section:

```
Type FILETIME
    dwLowDateTime As Long
    dwHighDateTime As Long
End Type
```

Then I need to declare three API functions. As you can see, these are relatively complicated functions, as VBA functions go, but not as API functions go. Enter the following in the Declarations section:

```
Declare Function RegOpenKeyEx Lib "advapi32.dll" Alias _
    "RegOpenKeyExA" (ByVal hKey As Long, ByVal lpSubKey As _
    String, ByVal ulOptions As Long, ByVal samDesired As _
    Long, phkResult As Long) As Long
```

```
Declare Function RegEnumKeyEx Lib "advapi32.dll" Alias _
    "RegEnumKeyExA" (ByVal hKey As Long, ByVal dwIndex As _
    Long, ByVal lpName As String, lpcbName As Long, ByVal _
    lpReserved As Long, ByVal lpClass As String, lpcbClass _
    As Long, lpftLastWriteTime As FILETIME) As Long

Declare Function RegCloseKey Lib "advapi32.dll" _
    (ByVal hKey As Long) As Long
```

I am now ready for the main procedure, which will extract the names of the installed printers from the Windows Registry. Its code is shown in Example C-1.

Example C-1. Getting the Names of Installed Printers

```
Public Sub GetInstalledPrinters(ByRef sPrinters() As _
   String, ByRef cPrinters As Long)

' Sets cPrinters to the number of installed printers.
' Sizes and fills sPrinters array with the names
' of these printers.

Dim ft As FILETIME
Dim KeyHandle As Long
Dim KeyName As String
Dim KeyLen As Long
Dim Response As Long

On Error GoTo ERR_INSTALLED_PRINTERS

ReDim sPrinters(1 To 5)
cPrinters = 0

' Open Registry key whose subkeys are installed printers
Response = RegOpenKeyEx(HKEY_LOCAL_MACHINE, _
   "SYSTEM\CurrentControlSet\Control\Print\Printers", _
   0, KEY_ENUMERATE_SUB_KEYS, KeyHandle)

' If Error display message and exit
If Response <> SUCCESS Then
   MsgBox "Could not open the registry key."
   Exit Sub
End If

' Loop to get subkeys
Do
   KeyLen = 1000  ' Plenty of room for printer name
   KeyName = String(KeyLen, 0)   ' Fill with 0s

   Response = RegEnumKeyEx(KeyHandle, cPrinters, _
      KeyName, KeyLen, 0&, vbNullString, 0&, ft)

   ' If unsuccessful, then exit
   If Response <> SUCCESS Then Exit Do
```

Example C-1. Getting the Names of Installed Printers (continued)

```
    ' Next free index
    cPrinters = cPrinters + 1

    ' Make room if necessary
    If UBound(sPrinters) < cPrinters Then
        ReDim Preserve sPrinters(1 To cPrinters + 5)
    End If

    ' Add to array
    sPrinters(cPrinters) = Left(KeyName, KeyLen)

Loop

RegCloseKey KeyHandle

Exit Sub
ERR_INSTALLED_PRINTERS:
   MsgBox Err.Description
   Exit Sub
End Sub
```

The *GetInstalledPrinters* procedure has two parameters. The first is a String array named **sPrinters**, and the second is a Long named **cPrinters**. The procedure will set the value of **cPrinters** to the number of installed printers and resize and fill the **sPrinters** array with the names of the printers.

Example C-2 shows how to use the *GetInstalledPrinters* subroutine. It simply gathers the printer names in a single String variable and displays that variable.

Example C-2. Calling the GetInstalledPrinters Subroutine

```
Sub DisplayInstalledPrinters()

Dim sPrinters() As String
Dim cPrinters As Long
Dim i As Integer
Dim msg As String

' Get the installed printers
GetInstalledPrinters sPrinters(), cPrinters

' Create the message and display it
msg = ""
For i = 1 To cPrinters
   msg = msg & sPrinters(i) & vbCrLf
Next i

MsgBox msg, , cPrinters & " Printers"

End Sub
```

The output of this macro on my system is shown in Figure C-1.

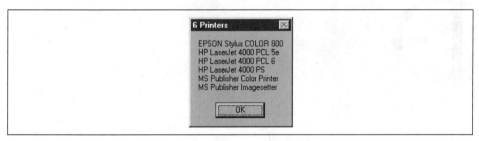

Figure C-1. Installed printers

One word of caution: before executing the *GetInstalledPrinters* subroutine for the *first* time (through the *DisplayInstalledPrinters* macro or any by other means), be sure to save all of your work in all of your open applications. If you have made an error in typing in this program, the result may be a systemwide computer crash, in which case you will lose all unsaved work!

D

High-Level and Low-Level Languages

In this appendix, I examine the position of Visual Basic as a programming language by taking a somewhat closer look at high-level and low-level languages, with some examples for comparison.

A *low-level language* is characterized by its ability to manipulate the computer's operating system and hardware more or less directly. For instance, a programmer using a low-level language may be able to easily turn on the motor of a floppy drive, check the status bits of the printer interface, or look at individual sectors on a disk, whereas these tasks may be difficult, if not impossible, with a high-level language. Another benefit of low-level languages is that they tend to perform tasks more quickly than high-level languages.

On the other hand, the power to manipulate the computer at a low level comes at a price. Low-level languages are generally more cryptic—they tend to be farther removed from ordinary spoken languages and are therefore harder to learn, remember, and use. *High-level languages* (and application-level languages, which many people would refer to simply as high-level languages) tend to be more user-friendly, but the price we pay for that friendliness is less control over the computer and slower running programs.

To illustrate, consider the task of printing some text. A low-level language may only be able to send individual characters to a printer. The process of printing with a low-level language might go something like the following:

1. Check the status of the printer.

2. If the printer is free, initialize the printer.

3. Send a character to the printer.

4. Check to see if this character arrived safely.

5. If not, send the character again.

6. If so, start over with the next character.

The "lowest" level language that programmers use is called *assembly language*. Indeed, assembly language essentially has complete control over the computer's hardware. To illustrate assembly language code, the following program prints the message "Happy printing." Don't worry if these instructions seem meaningless— you can just skim over them to get the feel. In fact, the very point I want to make is that low-level languages are much more cryptic than high-level languages. (Lines that begin with a semicolon are comments. I have left out error checking to save a little space.)

```
; --------------------
; Data for the program
; --------------------
; message to print
Message DB            'Happy printing', 0Dh, 0Ah

; length of message
Msg_Len EQU           $-Message

; --------------------
; Initialize printer 0
; --------------------
mov ah,1
mov dx,0
int 17h

; --------------------
; Printing instructions
; --------------------
; get number of characters to print
mov cx,Msg_Len

; get location of message
mov bx,offset Message

; get printer number (first printer is printer 0)
mov dx,0

Print_Loop:

; send character to printer 0
mov ah,0
mov al,[bx]
int 17h

; do next character
inc bx
loop Print_Loop
```

For comparison, see how this same task would be accomplished in the BASIC programming language:

```
LPRINT "Happy printing"
```

The difference is pretty obvious.

As I have discussed, high-level languages are generally designed for a specific purpose. Generally, this purpose is to write software applications of a specific type. For instance, Visual C++ and Visual Basic are used primarily to write standalone Windows applications. Indeed, Microsoft Word itself is written in Visual C++. As another example, FORTRAN (which is a contraction of *Formula Translation*) is designed to write scientific and computational applications for various platforms (including Windows). COBOL is used to write business-related applications (generally for mainframe computers). For more information on this subject, see Table 2-1.

At the highest level in the programming language hierarchy, we find programs such as Word VBA, whose *primary* purpose is not to manipulate the operating system or hardware, nor to write standalone Windows applications, but rather to manipulate a high-level software application, in this case Microsoft Word.

Just for fun, let us take a brief look at a handful of the more common programming languages.

BASIC

The word BASIC is an acronym for *Beginners All-Purpose Symbolic Instruction Code*, the key word here being *beginners*. BASIC was developed at Dartmouth College in 1963 by two mathematicians: John Kemeny and Thomas Kurtz. The intention was to design a programming language for liberal arts students, who made up the vast majority of the student population at Dartmouth. The goal was to create a language that would be friendly to the user and have a fast turnaround time so it could be used effectively for homework assignments. (In those days, a student would submit a program to a computer operator, who would place the program in a queue, awaiting processing by the computer. The student would simply have to wait for the results—there were no PCs in the 1960s!)

The first version of BASIC was very simple; indeed it was primitive. For example, it had only one data type: floating-point. (VB data types are covered in Chapter 5, *Variables, Data Types, and Constants.*) Since then BASIC has made tremendous strides as a personal computer programming language, due mostly to the embrace of the language by Microsoft.

Even to this day, however, the BASIC language, and its offshoot Visual Basic, do not in general get much respect among computer scientists or academicians. The

BASIC language gets a bad rap on two fronts. First, it is generally considered a weak language in the sense that it does not provide very much control over the computer's hardware (or operating system), at least as compared to other languages such as C. Second, BASIC has a reputation for not "forcing" (or in some cases even allowing) programmers to use good programming style. (I say more about programming style in Chapter 2, *Preliminaries*.)

For comparison with some other languages, here is a BASIC program that asks the user for some numbers and then returns the average of those numbers. Lines beginning with an apostrophe are comment lines that are ignored by the computer:

```
' BASIC program to compute the average
' of a set of at most 100 numbers

' Ask for the number of numbers
INPUT "Enter the number of numbers: ", Num

' If Num is between 1 and 100 then proceed
' IF Num > 0 AND Num <= 100 THEN

    Sum = 0
    ' Loop to collect the numbers to average
    FOR I = 1 TO Num
        ' Ask for next number
        INPUT "Enter next number: ", NextNum
        ' Add the number to the running sum
        Sum = Sum + NextNum
    NEXT I

    ' Compute the average
    Ave = Sum / Num

    ' Display the average
    PRINT "The average is: "; Ave

END IF

END
```

Visual Basic

Microsoft took the BASIC programming language to new heights when it developed Visual Basic. In the early 1990s, Microsoft faced a dilemma. Windows was (and is) a considerably more complex operating system than DOS, so much so that only professional programmers could effectively use Microsoft's main programming tool for creating Windows-based applications—the Microsoft Windows SDK, which is based on the C language. (These days, this tool has given way to a more modern tool, Microsoft Foundation Classes, which is still not for the casual programmer.)

But Microsoft wanted more people to be able to create Windows applications, since it was good for business. So in 1991, the company introduced Visual Basic (VB), which essentially combined the BASIC language with a visual programming environment that allowed users to create graphical components easily, such as windows, command buttons, text boxes, option buttons, and menus that are required by Windows applications. The underlying language for VB is called Visual Basic for Applications, or VBA, although this term was not coined until later in the development of VB.

The first version of Visual Basic was little more than an interesting toy. It did not really have the power to create serious Windows applications. However, it provided a necessary starting point for further development of the product. Each successive version of Visual Basic has taken major steps forward in sophistication, so that now VB is by far the most widely used programming language for PCs. (Microsoft estimates that over 3 million people use some form of Visual Basic, about half of whom program using some form of Office VBA, the rest using the standalone VB product.)

While VB has become a very respectable tool for creating standalone Windows applications, the real popularity of VBA lies in the fact that it is the underlying programming language for the Microsoft Office application suite, which probably has closer to 100 million users, each of whom is a potential VBA programmer. Indeed, presumably the reason that you are reading this book is that you want to join the group of VBA programmers.

VBA is a high-level programming language that underlies several important Windows applications, including Microsoft Word, Excel, Access, and PowerPoint, as well as Microsoft Visual Basic. (By the way, Microsoft Outlook uses VBScript instead of VBA.) In addition, companies other than Microsoft can license VBA and use it as the underlying programming language for their applications.

Each so-called *host application* provides extensions to VBA to accommodate its own needs and idiosyncrasies. For instance, since Word deals with documents, Word VBA needs to understand such things as headers and footers, grammar checking, page numbering, and so on. On the other hand, since Excel deals with spreadsheets, Excel VBA needs to understand such things as cells, formulas, charts, and so on. Finally, since VB is designed for writing standalone Windows applications, it must excel at manipulating Windows controls (text boxes, command buttons, list boxes, and so on).

This is not to say that there is no overlap between the various flavors of VBA—there is. Moreover, Microsoft's ActiveX Automation allows one flavor of VBA to communicate with another and thereby use the other's strengths. For instance, it is possible within a Word VBA program to perform some computations using Excel

VBA. (I discuss how to program Word from within another application in Appendix A, *Programming Word from Another Application.*)

Indeed, it makes far greater sense for VBA to provide a core programming language that can be extended in different ways to accommodate different host applications, rather than trying to make a single programming language that serves all intended applications, for this would bloat the language considerably and reduce its flexibility when it comes to new applications.

C and C++

The C programming language, a descendant of several older languages (including B) was developed by Dennis Ritchie at Bell Laboratories in 1972. C is a simple language in its syntax with relatively few instructions. However, it has been extended considerably by Microsoft (among others) for use in the PC environment.

The strength of C and its descendants (such as C++) lies in the fact that it combines the advantages of a high-level programming language (such as relative readability) with the ability to reach down to the operating system and hardware levels of the computer. Unfortunately, the power of C can sometimes be dangerous in the hands of, shall we say, programmers of only modest capability. Also, the syntax of C allows for what some programmers consider "clever" or "elegant" programming style, but which may be more accurately termed "highly unreadable."

For comparison purposes, here is the C language version of the BASIC program that computes the average of some numbers. I think you will agree that it is not quite as readable as the earlier BASIC version. Lines beginning with // are comment lines that are ignored by the computer:

```c
// C program to compute the average
// of a set of at most 100 numbers

#include <stdio.h>

void main(void)
{
        // Declare some variables
        int Num, i;
        float Sum, NextNum, Ave;

        // Ask for the number of numbers
        printf( "Enter number of numbers: " );
        scanf( "%u", &Num );

        // If Num is between 1 and 100 then proceed
        if( (Num > 0) && (Num <= 100) )
        {
            Sum = 0.0;
```

```
        // Loop to collect the numbers to average
        for( i = 1; i <= Num; i++ )
        {
            // Ask for next number
            printf( "Enter next number: " );
            scanf( "%f", &NextNum );

            // Add the number to the running sum
            Sum += NextNum;
        }

        // Compute the average
        Ave = Sum / Num;

        //Display the average
        printf ("The average is: %f\n", Ave );
    }
}
```

An object-oriented extension to C, known as C++, was developed in the early 1980s by Bjarne Stroustrup (also at Bell Labs). This is not the place to go into a discussion of object-oriented programming. Instead, allow me to refer you to my book *Concepts of Object-Oriented Programming with Visual Basic*, published by Springer-Verlag.

Visual C++

Despite the significant strides that Visual Basic has taken, it is not, in general, the preferred language for creating complex standalone Windows applications. That role belongs to Microsoft's Visual C++.

Actually, this is a good thing. Microsoft must guard against trying to make any single language the solution for too many diverse programming needs. Such an effort can only be counterproductive. By increasing the power of VB (and VBA) in order to handle more diverse and sophisticated application programming, the language becomes more complex and difficult to learn and use. This will result in the language being used by fewer people.

Visual C++ is a marriage between the C++ programming language and the Windows graphical environment. Visual C++ is not nearly as user-friendly as Visual Basic. This is due in part to the nature of the underlying language (C is less friendly than BASIC), in part to the fact that C++ is a fully object-oriented language and therefore naturally more complicated, and in part to the fact that Visual C++ is designed to control the Windows environment at a more fundamental level than Visual Basic. For instance, Visual Basic does not provide ways to create a text box whose text can use more than one color, set the tabs in a list box, or change the color of the caption in a command button, and so on. Simply put, when programming in VB (or VBA), you must sacrifice power in some directions in favor of power in other directions and a simpler programming environment.

Pascal

Pascal was developed by Niklaus Wirth (pronounced "Virt") in the late 1960s and early 1970s. The goal was to produce a language that could be implemented easily on a variety of computers and that would provide students with a model teaching language. That is to say, Pascal is full of features that encourage well-written and well-structured programs. Indeed, many universities teach Pascal to their computer science students as a first language. Pascal has also migrated to the personal computer arena, first with Borland's Turbo Pascal and more recently with Borland's visual programming environment called Delphi.

For contrast, here is how our program to compute the average would look in Pascal. Text contained within curly braces ({}) are comments that are ignored by the computer:

```pascal
{ Pascal program to compute the average
  of a set of at most 100 numbers }

program average (input, output);
        { Declare some variables }
        var
            Num, i : integer;
            Ave, Sum, NextNum : real;
        begin
            { Ask for the number of numbers }
            writeln('Enter the number of numbers');
            readln(Num);
            { If Num is between 1 and 100 then proceed }
            if ((Num > 0 ) and (Num <= 100)) then
                begin
                    Sum := 0;
                    { Loop to collect the numbers to average }
                    for i := 1 to Num do
                        begin
                            { Ask for next number }
                            writeln('Enter next number');
                            readln(NextNum);
                            { Add the number to the running sum }
                            Sum := Sum + NextNum;
                        end

                    { Compute the average }
                    Ave := Sum / Num;

                    { Display the average }
                    writeln('The average is: ', Ave);
                end
        end
```

FORTRAN

FORTRAN is a contraction of *Formula Translation,* the name of which comes from a technical report entitled "The IBM Mathematical FORmula TRANslating system" written by John Backus and his team at IBM in the mid 1950s. FORTRAN is primarily designed for scientific calculations and has the distinction of being the first widely used high-level programming language. Backus made some rather interesting claims about FORTRAN: for instance, that it was not designed for its beauty (a reasonable statement), but that it would eliminate coding errors and the consequent debugging process!

Here is the FORTRAN version of our little averaging program. Lines that begin with a C are comments:

```
C FORTRAN PROGRAM TO COMPUTE THE AVERAGE
C OF A SET OF AT MOST 100 NUMBERS

        Real SUM, AVE, NEXTNUM
        SUM = 0.0

C Ask for the number of numbers
        WRITE(*,*) 'Enter the number of numbers: '
        READ(*,*) NUM

C If Num is between 1 and 100 then proceed
        IF NUM .GT. 0 .AND. NUM .LE. 100 then
            C Loop to collect the numbers to average
            DO 10 I = 1, NUM
                C Ask for next number
                WRITE(*,*) 'Enter next number: '
                READ(*,*) NEXTNUM
                C Add the number to the running sum
                SUM = SUM + NEXTNUM
10          CONTINUE
            C Compute the average
            AVE = SUM/NUM
            C Display the average
            WRITE(*,*) 'The average is: '
            WRITE(*,*) AVE
        ENDIF

        STOP
        END
```

COBOL

COBOL is an acronym for *Common Business Oriented Language* and was developed in the late 1950s by Grace Hopper for the purpose of writing business-related programs, which she felt should be written in English. However, it seems rather that the language was developed with the express purpose of avoiding all mathematical-like notation, with the inevitable consequence that conciseness and readability is also avoided.

At any rate, I could only bring myself to code a COBOL sample program that adds two numbers:

```
* COBOL PROGRAM TO ADD TWO NUMBERS

IDENTIFICATION DIVISION.
PROGRAM-ID.ADD02.
ENVIRONMENT DIVISION.
DATA DIVISION.

WORKING-STORAGE SECTION.
01           FIRST-NUMBERPIC IS 99.
01           SECOND-NUMBERPIC IS 99.
01           SUM             PIC IS 999.

PROCEDURE DIVISION.

PROGRAM-BEGIN.

DISPLAY "ENTER FIRST NUMBER ".
ACCEPT FIRST-NUMBER.

DISPLAY "ENTER SECOND NUMBER ".
ACCEPT SECOND-NUMBER.

COMPUTE SUM = FIRST-NUMBER + SECOND-NUMBER

DISPLAY "THE SUM IS: " SUM.

PROGRAM-DONE.
STOP RUN.
```

In BASIC, the preceding program would be:

```
INPUT "Enter first number: ", n1
INPUT "Enter second number: ", n2
PRINT "The sum is: ", n1 + n2
```

This clearly points out the extreme verbosity of COBOL.

Lisp

BASIC, C, Pascal, and FORTRAN are in many ways quite similar. Also, programs written in these languages can be made quite readable, especially if the programmer intends to make it so. There are other languages that seem not to be readable under any circumstances. For instance, Lisp was developed in the late 1950s by John McCarthy and Marvin Minsky at MIT for the purpose of doing list processing (hence the name) in connection with artificial intelligence applications.

In Lisp, everything is a list. Here is a sample:

```
; LISP sample program to define a predicate
;       that takes two lists and returns the value
; T (for true) if the lists are equal and F otherwise
(DEFINE (
        '(equal (LAMDBA (list1 list2)
                (COND
                ((ATOM list1) (EQ list1 list2))
                ((ATOM list1 NIL)
                ((equal (CAR list1) (CAR list2))
                    (equal (CDR list1) (CDR list2)))
                (T NIL)
            )
        ))
))
```

This sample points out one fact. Whatever else you might think of Microsoft, we can at least thank them for choosing BASIC (VBA) as the underlying language for the Microsoft Office suite!

Index

About the Author

Steven Roman is a Professor of Mathematics at the California State University, Fullerton. He has taught at a number of other universities, including MIT, the University of California at Santa Barbara, and the University of South Florida.

Dr. Roman received his B.A. degree from the University of California at Los Angeles and his Ph.D. from the University of Washington. He has authored 31 books, including a number of books on mathematics, such as *Coding and Information Theory, Advanced Linear Algebra,* and *Field Theory,* published by Springer-Verlag. He has also written a series of 15 small books entitled *Modules in Mathematics,* designed for the general college-level liberal arts student. Dr. Roman has written *Access Database Design and Programming* and *Developing Visual Basic Add-Ins* for O'Reilly & Associates. He has also authored *Concepts of Object-Oriented Programming with Visual Basic* and *Understanding Personal Computer Hardware,* an in-depth look at how PC hardware works, both published by Springer-Verlag. He has just finished a book entitled *Learning Excel Programming,* to be published by O'Reilly. Dr. Roman is interested in combinatorics, algebra, and computer science.

Colophon

The animal appearing on the cover of *Learning Word Programming* is a Beisa oryx (*Oryx gazella beisa*), a brownish-grey subspecies of East African antelope. The oryx is distinctively marked with black and white face and leg patterns; their white underbelly is outlined with a black stripe. The oryx is about the size of a deer (1.5–2.4 meters long), with slightly curved, parallel, ridged horns up to four feet long; these are used for defense in both sexes.

The Beisa oryx is located throughout eastern Africa, particularly Ethiopia, in short-grass steppes, semi-desert, and savannah habitats, feeding upon leaves, grasses, fruits, and other plant materials. They are gregarious, traveling in herds of a few dozen, and eating several times a day. Their enemies include large cats, such as leopards, lions, and cheetahs, as well as hyenas and human hunters. Their territory has dwindled due to excessive hunting. The Beisa oryx once appeared on one of a series of Ethiopian stamps celebrating the nation's wildlife.

Nancy Kotary was the production editor and copyeditor for *Learning Word Programming*; Sheryl Avruch was the production manager. Kristine Simmons was the proofreader. Mary Anne Mayo and Jane Ellin provided quality control. Kimo Carter provided production support. Ruth Rautenberg wrote the index.

Edie Freedman designed the cover of this book, using a 19th-century engraving from the Dover Pictorial Archive. The cover layout was produced with Quark XPress 3.32 using the ITC Garamond font. Whenever possible, our books use RepKover™, a durable and flexible lay-flat binding. If the page count exceeds RepKover's limit, perfect binding is used.

The inside layout was designed by Nancy Priest and implemented in FrameMaker 5,5 by Mike Sierra. The text and heading fonts are ITC Garamond Light and Garamond Book. The illustrations that appear in the book were created in Macromedia FreeHand 7 and Adobe Photoshop 4 by Robert Romano. This colophon was written by Nancy Kotary.

More Titles from O'Reilly

Windows Programming

Access Database Design & Programming

By Steven Roman
1st Edition June 1997
270 pages, ISBN 1-56592-297-2

This book provides experienced Access users who are novice programers with frequently overlooked concepts and techniques necessary to create effective database applications. It focuses on designing effective tables in a multi-table application; using the Access interface or Access SQL to construct queries; and programming using the Data Access Object (DAO) and Microsoft Access object models.

VB & VBA in a Nutshell: The Languages

By Paul Lomax
1st Edition October 1998
656 pages, ISBN 1-56592-358-8

For Visual Basic and VBA programmers, this book boils down the essentials of the VB and VBA languages into a single volume, including undocumented and little documented areas essential to everyday programming. The convenient alphabetical reference to all functions, procedures, statements, and keywords allows VB and VBA programmers to use this book both as a standard reference guide to the language and as a tool for troubleshooting and identifying programming problems.

Learning VBScript

By Paul Lomax
1st Edition July 1997
616 pages, includes CD-ROM
ISBN 1-56592-247-6

This definitive guide shows web developers how to take full advantage of client-side scripting with the VBScript language. In addition to basic language features, it covers the Internet Explorer object model and discusses techniques for client-side scripting, like adding ActiveX controls to a web page or validating data before sending it to the server. Includes CD-ROM with over 170 code samples.

Visual Basic Controls in a Nutshell

By Evan S. Dictor
1st Edition May 1999 (est.)
512 pages (est.), ISBN 1-56592-294-8

This quick reference covers one of the crucial elements of Visual Basic: its controls, and their numerous properties, events, and methods. It provides a step-by-step list of procedures for using each major control and contains a detailed reference to all properties, methods, and events. Written by an experienced Visual Basic programmer, it helps to make painless what can sometimes be an arduous job of programming Visual Basic.

Learning Perl on Win32 Systems

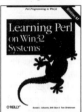

By Randal L. Schwartz,
Erik Olson & Tom Christiansen
1st Edition August 1997
306 pages, ISBN 1-56592-324-3

In this carefully paced course, leading Perl trainers and a Windows NT practitioner teach you to program in the language that promises to emerge as the scripting language of choice on NT. Based on the "llama" book, this book features tips for PC users and new, NT-specific examples, along with a foreword by Larry Wall, the creator of Perl, and Dick Hardt, the creator of Perl for Win32.

Developing Visual Basic Add-Ins

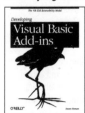

By Steven Roman
1st Edition December 1998
186 pages, ISBN 1-56592-527-0

A tutorial and reference guide in one, this book covers all the basics of creating useful VB add-ins to extend the IDE, allowing developers to work more productively with Visual Basic. Readers with even a modest acquaintance with VB will be developing add-ins in no time. Includes numerous simple code examples.

Windows Programming

Developing Windows Error Messages

By Ben Ezzell
1st Edition March 1998
254 pages, Includes CD-ROM
ISBN 1-56592-356-1

This book teaches C, C++, and Visual Basic programmers how to write effective error messages that notify the user of an error, clearly explain the error, and most important, offer a solution. The book also discusses methods for preventing and trapping errors before they occur and tells how to create flexible input and response routines to keep unnecessary errors from happening.

Inside the Windows 95 File System

By Stan Mitchell
1st Edition May 1997
378 pages, Includes diskette
ISBN 1-56592-200-X

In this book, Stan Mitchell describes the Windows 95 File System, as well as the new opportunities and challenges it brings for developers. Its "hands-on" approach will help developers become better equipped to make design decisions using the new Win95 File System features. Includes a diskette containing MULTIMON, a general-purpose monitor for examining Windows internals.

Win32 Multithreaded Programming

By Aaron Cohen & Mike Woodring
1st Edition December 1997
724 pages, Includes CD-ROM
ISBN 1-56592-296-4

This book clearly explains the concepts of multithreaded programs and shows developers how to construct efficient and complex applications. An important book for any developer, it illustrates all aspects of Win32 multithreaded programming, including what has previously been undocumented or poorly explained.

Windows NT File System Internals

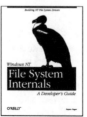

By Rajeev Nagar
1st Edition September 1997
794 pages, Includes diskette
ISBN 1-56592-249-2

Windows NT File System Internals presents the details of the NT I/O Manager, the Cache Manager, and the Memory Manager from the perspective of a software developer writing a file system driver or implementing a kernel-mode filter driver. The book provides numerous code examples included on diskette, as well as the source for a complete, usable filter driver.

Inside the Windows 95 Registry

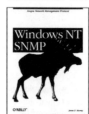

By Ron Petrusha
1st Edition August 1996
594 pages, Includes diskette
ISBN 1-56592-170-4

An in-depth examination of remote registry access, differences between the Win95 and NT registries, registry backup, undocumented registry services, and the role the registry plays in OLE. Shows programmers how to access the Win95 registry from Win32, Win16, and DOS programs in C and Visual Basic. VxD sample code is also included. Includes diskette.

Windows NT SNMP

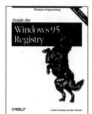

By James D. Murray
1st Edition January 1998
464 pages, Includes CD-ROM
ISBN 1-56592-338-3

This book describes the implementation of SNMP (the Simple Network Management Protocol) on Windows NT 3.51 and 4.0 (with a look ahead to NT 5.0) and Windows 95 systems. It covers SNMP and network basics and detailed information on developing SNMP management applications and extension agents. The book comes with a CD-ROM containing a wealth of additional information: standards documents, sample code from the book, and many third-party, SNMP-related software tools, libraries, and demos.

Eliminating Annoyances

Windows 98 Annoyances

By David A. Karp
1st Edition October 1998
464 pages, ISBN 1-56592-417-7

Based on the author's popular Windows Annoyances Web site (http://www.annoyances.org), this book provides an authoritative collection of techniques for customizing Windows 98. It allows you to quickly identify a particular annoyance and immediately offers one or more solutions, making it the definitive resource for customizing Windows 98. Includes a CD with a trial version of *O'Reilly Utilities: Quick Solutions for Windows 98 Annoyances.*

O'Reilly Utilities: Quick Solutions for Windows 98 Annoyances

Software developed by
Mark Bracewell & David A. Karp
1st Edition October 1998
CD-ROM with full online Help
ISBN 1-56592-549-1

O'Reilly Utilities: Quick Solutions for Windows 98 Annoyances is the stand-alone software companion to David Karp's *Windows 98 Annoyances* book. This software provides immediate, automated solutions for many of the key annoyances described in the book, as well as other important new enhancements to Windows 98. Developed in cooperation with David Karp, *O'Reilly Utilities* allows you to immediately improve your productivity with dozens of Windows extensions that go beyond Tweak UI and make common tasks easier, such as group file renaming, file copying, and customizing the desktop. Even better, we've built programs into this package that solve some of the most aggravating behaviors of Windows and other applications.

Excel 97 Annoyances

By Woody Leonhard, Lee Hudspeth & T.J. Lee
1st Edition September 1997
336 pages, ISBN 1-56592-309-X

This book uncovers Excel 97's hard-to-find features and tells how to eliminate the annoyances of data analysis. It shows how to easily retrieve data from the Web, details step-by-step construction of a perfect toolbar, includes tips for working around the most annoying gotchas of auditing, and shows how to use VBA to control Excel in powerful ways.

Office 97 Annoyances

By Woody Leonhard, Lee Hudspeth & T.J. Lee
1st Edition October 1997
396 pages, ISBN 1-56592-310-3

This book illustrates step-by-step how to get control over the chaotic settings of Office 97 and shows how to turn the vast array of applications into a simplified list of customized tools. It focuses on the major components of Office 97, examines their integration or lack of it, and shows how to use this new Office suite in the most efficient way.

Outlook Annoyances

By Woody Leonhard,
Lee Hudspeth & T. J. Lee
1st Edition June 1998
400 pages, ISBN 1-56592-384-7

Like the other Microsoft Office-related titles in the Annoyances series, this book points out and conquers the annoying features of Microsoft Outlook, the personal information management software included with Office. It is the definitive guide for those who want to take full advantage of Outlook and transform it into the useful tool that it was intended to be.

Eliminating Annoyances

Windows Annoyances

By David A. Karp
1st Edition June 1997
300 pages, ISBN 1-56592-266-2

A comprehensive, detailed resource for all intermediate to advanced users of Windows 95 and NT version 4.0. This book shows step-by-step how to customize the Win95/NT operating systems through an extensive collection of tips, tricks, and workarounds. Covers **Registry**, **Plug and Play**, networking, security, multiple-user settings, and third-party software.

Word 97 Annoyances

By Woody Leonhard, Lee Hudspeth & T.J. Lee
1st Edition August 1997
356 pages, ISBN 1-56592-308-1

Word 97 contains hundreds of annoying idiosyncrasies that can be either eliminated or worked around. This informative book takes an in-depth look at what makes Word 97 tick and shows you how to transform this software into a powerful, customized tool.

Web Programming

CGI Programming on the World Wide Web

By Shishir Gundavaram
1st Edition March 1996
450 pages, ISBN 1-56592-168-2

This book offers a comprehensive explanation of CGI and related techniques for people who hold on to the dream of providing their own information servers on the Web. It starts at the beginning, explaining the value of CGI and how it works, then moves swiftly into the subtle details of programming.

Web Programming

Dynamic HTML: The Definitive Reference

By Danny Goodman
1st Edition July 1998
1088 pages, ISBN 1-56592-494-0

Dynamic HTML: The Definitive Reference is an indispensable compendium for Web content developers. It contains complete reference material for all of the HTML tags, CSS style attributes, browser document objects, and JavaScript objects supported by the various standards and the latest versions of Netscape Navigator and Microsoft Internet Explorer.

JavaScript: The Definitive Guide, 3rd Edition

By David Flanagan & Dan Shafer
3rd Edition June 1998
800 pages, ISBN 1-56592-392-8

This third edition of the definitive reference to JavaScript covers the latest version of the language, JavaScript 1.2, as supported by Netscape Navigator 4.0. JavaScript, which is being standardized under the name ECMAScript, is a scripting language that can be embedded directly in HTML to give web pages programming-language capabilities.

Web Client Programming with Perl

By Clinton Wong
1st Edition March 1997
228 pages, ISBN 1-56592-214-X

Web Client Programming with Perl shows you how to extend scripting skills to the Web. This book teaches you the basics of how browsers communicate with servers and how to write your own customized web clients to automate common tasks. It is intended for those who are motivated to develop software that offers a more flexible and dynamic response than a standard web browser.

Web Programming

Frontier: The Definitive Guide

By Matt Neuburg
1st Edition February 1998
618 pages, 1-56592-383-9

This definitive guide is the first book devoted exclusively to teaching and documenting Userland Frontier, a powerful scripting environment for web site management and system level scripting. Packed with examples, advice, tricks, and tips, *Frontier: The Definitive Guide* teaches you Frontier from the ground up. Learn how to automate repetitive processes, control remote computers across a network, beef up your web site by generating hundreds of related web pages automatically, and more. Covers Frontier 4.2.3 for the Macintosh.

Learning VBScript

By Paul Lomax
1st Edition July 1997
616 pages, includes CD-ROM
ISBN 1-56592-247-6

This definitive guide shows web developers how to take full advantage of client-side scripting with the VBScript language. In addition to basic language features, it covers the Internet Explorer object model and discusses techniques for client-side scripting, like adding ActiveX controls to a web page or validating data before sending to the server. Includes CD-ROM with over 170 code samples.

O'REILLY®

TO ORDER: **800-998-9938** • **order@oreilly.com** • **http://www.oreilly.com/**
OUR PRODUCTS ARE AVAILABLE AT A BOOKSTORE OR SOFTWARE STORE NEAR YOU.
FOR INFORMATION: **800-998-9938** • **707-829-0515** • **info@oreilly.com**

How to stay in touch with O'Reilly

1. Visit Our Award-Winning Web Site

http://www.oreilly.com/

★ "Top 100 Sites on the Web" —*PC Magazine*
★ "Top 5% Web sites" —*Point Communications*
★ "3-Star site" —*The McKinley Group*

Our web site contains a library of comprehensive product information (including book excerpts and tables of contents), downloadable software, background articles, interviews with technology leaders, links to relevant sites, book cover art, and more. File us in your Bookmarks or Hotlist!

2. Join Our Email Mailing Lists

New Product Releases

To receive automatic email with brief descriptions of all new O'Reilly products as they are released, send email to:
listproc@online.oreilly.com
Put the following information in the first line of your message (*not* in the Subject field):
subscribe oreilly-news

O'Reilly Events

If you'd also like us to send information about trade show events, special promotions, and other O'Reilly events, send email to:
listproc@online.oreilly.com
Put the following information in the first line of your message (*not* in the Subject field):
subscribe oreilly-events

3. Get Examples from Our Books via FTP

There are two ways to access an archive of example files from our books:

Regular FTP

- ftp to:
  ftp.oreilly.com
  (login: anonymous
  password: your email address)
- Point your web browser to:
  ftp://ftp.oreilly.com/

FTPMAIL

- Send an email message to:
  ftpmail@online.oreilly.com
  (Write "help" in the message body)

4. Contact Us via Email

order@oreilly.com
To place a book or software order online. Good for North American and international customers.

subscriptions@oreilly.com
To place an order for any of our newsletters or periodicals.

books@oreilly.com
General questions about any of our books.

software@oreilly.com
For general questions and product information about our software. Check out O'Reilly Software Online at **http://software.oreilly.com/** for software and technical support information. Registered O'Reilly software users send your questions to: **website-support@oreilly.com**

cs@oreilly.com
For answers to problems regarding your order or our products.

booktech@oreilly.com
For book content technical questions or corrections.

proposals@oreilly.com
To submit new book or software proposals to our editors and product managers.

international@oreilly.com
For information about our international distributors or translation queries. For a list of our distributors outside of North America check out:
http://www.oreilly.com/www/order/country.html

O'Reilly & Associates, Inc.
101 Morris Street, Sebastopol, CA 95472 USA
TEL 707-829-0515 or 800-998-9938
        (6am to 5pm PST)
FAX 707-829-0104

Titles from O'Reilly

International Distributors

UK, EUROPE, MIDDLE EAST AND AFRICA (EXCEPT FRANCE, GERMANY, AUSTRIA, SWITZERLAND, LUXEMBOURG, LIECHTENSTEIN, AND EASTERN EUROPE)

INQUIRIES

O'Reilly UK Limited
4 Castle Street
Farnham
Surrey, GU9 7HS
United Kingdom
Telephone: 44-1252-711776
Fax: 44-1252-734211
Email: josette@oreilly.com

ORDERS

Wiley Distribution Services Ltd.
1 Oldlands Way
Bognor Regis
West Sussex PO22 9SA
United Kingdom
Telephone: 44-1243-779777
Fax: 44-1243-820250
Email: cs-books@wiley.co.uk

FRANCE

ORDERS

GEODIF
61, Bd Saint-Germain
75240 Paris Cedex 05, France
Tel: 33-1-44-41-46-16 (French books)
Tel: 33-1-44-41-11-87 (English books)
Fax: 33-1-44-41-11-44
Email: distribution@eyrolles.com

INQUIRIES

Éditions O'Reilly
18 rue Séguier
75006 Paris, France
Tel: 33-1-40-51-52-30
Fax: 33-1-40-51-52-31
Email: france@editions-oreilly.fr

GERMANY, SWITZERLAND, AUSTRIA, EASTERN EUROPE, LUXEMBOURG, AND LIECHTENSTEIN

INQUIRIES & ORDERS

O'Reilly Verlag
Balthasarstr. 81
D-50670 Köln
Germany
Telephone: 49-221-973160-91
Fax: 49-221-973160-8
Email: anfragen@oreilly.de (inquiries)
Email: order@oreilly.de (orders)

CANADA (FRENCH LANGUAGE BOOKS)

Les Éditions Flammarion ltée
375, Avenue Laurier Ouest
Montréal (Québec) H2V 2K3
Tel: 00-1-514-277-8807
Fax: 00-1-514-278-2085
Email: info@flammarion.qc.ca

HONG KONG

City Discount Subscription Service, Ltd.
Unit D, 3rd Floor, Yan's Tower
27 Wong Chuk Hang Road
Aberdeen, Hong Kong
Tel: 852-2580-3539
Fax: 852-2580-6463
Email: citydis@ppn.com.hk

KOREA

Hanbit Media, Inc.
Sonyoung Bldg. 202
Yeksam-dong 736-36
Kangnam-ku
Seoul, Korea
Tel: 822-554-9610
Fax: 822-556-0363
Email: hant93@chollian.dacom.co.kr

PHILIPPINES

Mutual Books, Inc.
429-D Shaw Boulevard
Mandaluyong City, Metro
Manila, Philippines
Tel: 632-725-7538
Fax: 632-721-3056
Email: mbikikog@mnl.sequel.net

TAIWAN

O'Reilly Taiwan
No. 3, Lane 131
Hang-Chow South Road
Section 1, Taipei, Taiwan
Tel: 886-2-23968990
Fax: 886-2-23968916
Email: benh@oreilly.com

CHINA

O'Reilly Beijing
Room 2410
160, FuXingMenNeiDaJie
XiCheng District
Beijing, China PR 100031
Tel: 86-10-86631006
Fax: 86-10-86631007
Email: frederic@oreilly.com

INDIA

Computer Bookshop (India) Pvt. Ltd.
190 Dr. D.N. Road, Fort
Bombay 400 001 India
Tel: 91-22-207-0989
Fax: 91-22-262-3551
Email: cbsbom@giasbm01.vsnl.net.in

JAPAN

O'Reilly Japan, Inc.
Kiyoshige Building 2F
12-Bancho, Sanei-cho
Shinjuku-ku
Tokyo 160-0008 Japan
Tel: 81-3-3356-5227
Fax: 81-3-3356-5261
Email: japan@oreilly.com

ALL OTHER ASIAN COUNTRIES

O'Reilly & Associates, Inc.
101 Morris Street
Sebastopol, CA 95472 USA
Tel: 707-829-0515
Fax: 707-829-0104
Email: order@oreilly.com

AUSTRALIA

WoodsLane Pty., Ltd.
7/5 Vuko Place
Warriewood NSW 2102
Australia
Tel: 61-2-9970-5111
Fax: 61-2-9970-5002
Email: info@woodslane.com.au

NEW ZEALAND

Woodslane New Zealand, Ltd.
21 Cooks Street (P.O. Box 575)
Waganui, New Zealand
Tel: 64-6-347-6543
Fax: 64-6-345-4840
Email: info@woodslane.com.au

LATIN AMERICA

McGraw-Hill Interamericana
Editores, S.A. de C.V.
Cedro No. 512
Col. Atlampa
06450, Mexico, D.F.
Tel: 52-5-547-6777
Fax: 52-5-547-3336
Email: mcgraw-hill@infosel.net.mx

O'REILLY®